T0330549

China's New Role in the World Economy

The remarkable rise of China over the past three decades has been unprecedented in both its scale and speed. Analysts around the world have attempted to understand the causes of this unique event and to predict how long it will last.

China's rise has also raised two important questions. The first concerns the stability and the sustainability of China's growth, which has been accompanied by growing internal and external imbalances, rising inequality at home, environmental degradation and an increased risk of catastrophic climate change, and has happened in spite of the continuing, if diminished, role of the state in many sectors of the economy.

The second question concerns trying to guess what the effect of China's rise will be on its relations with the rest of the region, the world and the existing global order. It seems only a matter of time until China becomes the world's largest economy, and history suggests that it is unthinkable that this event would be without geopolitical consequences.

The chapters in this volume draw on papers originally presented to the 34th Pacific Trade and Development Conference held in Beijing in 2010 to discuss these two big questions and China's changing role in the world economy. This book will be welcomed by students and scholars of Chinese economics, business and politics, and those interested in the pervasive impact of China's development on the global economy.

Yiping Huang is Professor of Economics at the China Macroeconomic Center, National School of Development, Peking University, Beijing, and Adjunct Professor at the Crawford School of Public Policy, Australian National University.

Miaojie Yu is Associate Professor at the China Center for Economic Research, National School of Development, Peking University, Beijing.

Pacific Trade and Development Conference Series
Edited by Peter Drysdale
Crawford School of Public Policy
Australian National University

Titles published by Routledge in association with the PAFTAD International Secretariat and the East Asian Bureau of Economic Research, Australian National University include:

Globalization and the Asia Pacific Economy
Edited by Kyung Tae Lee

The New Economy in East Asia and the Pacific
Edited by Peter Drysdale

Competition Policy in East Asia
Edited by Erlinda Medalla

Reshaping the Asia Pacific Economic Order
Edited by Hadi Soesastro and Christopher Findlay

Challenges to the Global Trading System
Adjustment to globalisation in the Asia-Pacific region
Edited by Peter A. Petri and Sumner La Croix

Multinational Corporations and the Emerging Network Economy in Asia and the Pacific
Edited by Juan J. Palacios

International Institutions and Asian Development
Edited by Shiro Armstrong and Vo Tri Thanh

The Politics and the Economics of Integration in Asia and the Pacific
Edited by Shiro Armstrong

China's New Role in the World Economy
Edited by Yiping Huang and Miaojie Yu

China's New Role in the World Economy

Edited by
Yiping Huang and Miaojie Yu

Routledge
Taylor & Francis Group

LONDON AND NEW YORK

First published 2013 by Routledge
2 Park Square, Milton Park, Abingdon, Oxon OX14 4RN

Simultaneously published in the USA and Canada by Routledge
270 Madison Avenue, New York, NY10016

Routledge is an imprint of the Taylor & Francis Group, an informa business

British Library Cataloguing in Publication Data
A catalogue record for this book is available from the British Library

Library of Congress Cataloging in Publication Data
China's new role in the world economy / edited by Yiping Huang and Miaojie Yu.
p. cm. -- (Pacific trade and development conference series)
Drawn from papers presented to the 35th Pacific Trade and Development conference in Vancouver in 2012.
Includes bibliographic references and index.
1. China--Economic policy--2000- 2. China--Economic conditions--2000- 3. China--Commerce. 4. China--Foreign economic relations. I. Huang, Yiping, 1964- II. Yu, Miaojie.
HC427.95C45646 2012
337.51--dc23
2012037992

ISBN 978-0-415-69116-1 (hbk. : alk. paper)
ISBN 978-0-203-07828-0 (ebook)

Typeset in Sabon by Clarus Design, Canberra, Australia

Contents

Figures

Tables

Boxes

Contributors

Bijun Wang is a doctoral candidate in the China Center for Economic Research, Peking University, Beijing.

Cai Fang is Director of the Institute of Population and Labor Economics, Chinese Academy of Social Sciences, Beijing.

Wendy Dobson is Co-director of the Institute for International Business, Rotman School of Management, University of Toronto, Canada.

Patrick Douglass is an international economist at the US Department of the Treasury, Washington, DC.

Du Yang is a Professor at the Institute of Population and Labor Economics, Chinese Academy of Social Sciences, Beijing.

Stephen Howes is Professor of Economics, and Director of the Development Policy Centre and International & Development Economics at the Crawford School of Public Policy, Australian National University, Canberra.

Nicholas Lardy is the Anthony M. Solomon Senior Fellow at the Peterson Institute for International Economics, Washington, DC.

Li Shi is Professor of Economics at the School of Economics and Business, and Director of the Center for Income Distribution and Poverty Studies, Beijing Normal University.

Ligang Song is Associate Professor and Director of the China Economy Program at the Crawford School of Public Policy, Australian National University, Canberra.

Razeen Sally is a Senior Lecturer in International Political Economy and Political Science, and Co-director of the European Centre for International Political Economy, Brussels.

Wang Meiyan is a Professor in the Institute of Population and Labor Economics, Chinese Academy of Social Sciences, Beijing.

Yang Yao is Director of the China Center for Economic Research, Peking University, Beijing.

Yiping Huang is Professor of Economics at the China Macroeconomic Research Center, National School of Development, Peking University, Beijing, and Adjunct Professor at the Crawford School of Public Policy, Australian National University, Canberra.

Xun Wang is a Research Fellow at the China Economic Research Center, Stockholm School of Economics.

Preface

The US subprime crisis was probably the defining moment in the emergence of a new international economic order that features a much more prominent role for the emerging market economies. This was evident in late 2008, when President George W. Bush hosted in Washington DC, not a G7/8 Summit, but the first G20 Summit, in order to collectively fight the global crisis and recession.

For several decades, China has been the largest and most dynamic emerging market economy in the world. In many economic areas such as commodities, consumer goods and foreign exchange, China is already a major player. If current economic trends continue, China will soon become the largest economy in the world.

Historically, transition from one superpower to another has signalled significant changes to the world. Given China's differences from the developed market economies, its rise probably generates anxiety among members of the international economic community, especially China's close economic partners across the Pacific.

In December 2010, the Pacific Trade and Development Conference (PAFTAD) series assembled, on the beautiful campus of Peking University in the north-western suburbs of Beijing, a group of leading thinkers from around the region to explore the theme 'China's new role in the world economy'. Papers presented at the conference are gathered together in this volume.

More than 20 years ago, PAFTAD held its twentieth conference in Beijing to assess Chinese economic reform and its international context. If, in those days, it was the international dimensions of Chinese growth that were an issue, people nowadays feel them in their daily lives, wherever they live. Clearly, the PAFTAD series has been at the forefront of analyses of the Chinese economy and its global and regional implications.

The China Center for Economic Research (CCER) of the National School of Development at the Peking University was the local host of the thirty-fourth conference. CCER Director, Yang Yao, and his assistant, Jiao Wang, were responsible for all the arrangements for the conference.

Peter Drysdale played the usual leadership role, as he has over the past several decades, in defining the theme, identifying paper writers and discussants, and making financial arrangements for the conference. At all stages of the management of this project, Luke Hurst also gave devoted and excellent service through the PAFTAD International Secretariat.

The PAFTAD programme is supported by a consortium of international donors and serviced by the PAFTAD International Secretariat in the Crawford School of Public Policy at the Australian National University.

We are especially grateful to the PAFTAD International Steering Committee and the donors, whose support continues to make this important work possible. They include the Ford Foundation, the Canadian International Development Research Centre, the Korean Institute of International Economic Policy, Toronto University, the National University of Singapore, the Taiwan Institute of Economic Research, Columbia University, Sanaree Holdings, the Australian National University and last, but not least, CCER at Peking University, which mobilized host support for PAFTAD 34.

We also wish to thank Clarus Design for editorial and pre-press production work, and Routledge for publishing this volume. We also benefitted immensely from the support and encouragement of Hugh Patrick and Wendy Dobson during completion of this project.

Yiping Huang and Miaojie Yu
Beijing, May 2012

Abbreviations

ABC	Agricultural Bank of China
AD	anti-dumping
AMRO	ASEAN+3 Macroeconomic Research Office
APEC	Asia Pacific Economic Cooperation forum
ASEAN	Association of Southeast Asian Nations
BOC	Bank of China
BRIC	Brazil Russia India China
BRIIC	Brazil Russia India Indonesia China
CAC	capital account control
CAFTA	China–ASEAN FTA
CBRC	Chinese Banking Regulatory Commission
CCB	China Construction Bank
CCER	China Center for Economic Research
CEPA	Closer Economic Partnership Agreement
CEPII	Centre d'Étude Prospectives et d'Informations Internationales
CGE	computable general equilibrium [modelling]
CMIM	Chiang Mai Initiative multilateralized
CNOOC	China National Offshore Oil Corporation
CPI	consumer price index
CSRC	China Security Regulatory Commission
CULS	China Urban Labor Survey
ECFA	Economic Cooperation and Framework Agreement
ESERD	Energy Saving and Emissions Reduction in Power Generation
EU	European Union
FDI	foreign direct investment
FE	fixed effects
FIE/s	foreign invested enterprise/s
FREP	financial repression index
FSAP	Financial Sector Assessment Program
FSB	Financial Stability Board
FTA/s	free trade agreement/s
FTAAP	Free Trade Area of the Asia–Pacific

G7	The Group of Seven: an informal forum for the Finance Ministers of Canada, France, Germany, Italy, Japan, the UK and the USA
G20	The Group of 20: the Finance Ministers and Central Bank Governors of Argentina, Australia, Brazil, Canada, China, the European Union, France, Germany, India, Indonesia, Italy, Japan, Mexico, Russia, Saudi Arabia, South Africa, the Republic of Korea, Turkey, the United Kingdom and the United States of America
GATS	General Agreement on Trade in Services
GDP	gross domestic product
GEC	global economic crisis
GW	gigawatts
HPAE/s	high performing Asian economy/ies
ICBC	Industrial and Commercial Bank of China
ICT	information and communication technologies
IMF	International Monetary Fund
ISP/s	internet service provider/s
JSF	*Jingi shiyong fang* [price-subsidized housing]
LDC/s	least-developed country/ies
LLC/s	limited liability company/ies
LM	Lagrangian multiplier
LNG	liquefied natural gas
LZF	*Lianzu fang* [rent-subsidized public housing]
MIIT	Ministry of Information Industries and Technology
MLSG	minimum living standard guarantee
MNE/s	multinational enterprise/s
MOFCOM	Ministry of Commerce
NBS	National Bureau of Statistics
NIE/s	newly industrialized economy/ies
NPC	National People's Congress
NPL/s	non-performing loan/s
NRCMI	New Rural Cooperative Medical Insurance
NTB/s	non-tariff barrier/s
OECD	Organisation for Economic Co-operation and Development
OFDI	outbound FDI
PAFTAD	Pacific Trade and Development Conference
PAYG	pay as you go
PBOC	People's Bank of China
PCA	principal component analysis
POLS	pooled ordinary least squares
PPP	purchasing power parity
PTA/s	preferential trade agreement/s
QDII	Qualified Domestic Institutional Investor
QFII	Qualified Foreign Institutional Investor

RAM/s	recently acceded member/s [WTO]
RCA	revealed comparative advantage
RE	random effect
RMB	renminbi
RRR	reserve requirement ratio
RTA/s	regional trade agreement/s
SAFE	State Administration of Foreign Exchange
SDR/s	special drawing right/s
SOCB/s	state-owned commercial bank/s
SOE/s	state-owned enterprise/s
SPS	sanitary and phytosanitary
TBT	technical barriers to trade
TNC	transnational corporation/s
TPP	Trans-Pacific Partnership
TRIMS	Trade-Related Investment Measures agreement
TRIPS	Trade Related Aspects of Intellectual Property Rights agreement
TRQ/s	tariff-rate quota/s
UK	United Kingdom
UN	United Nations
UNCTAD	UN Conference for Trade and Development
UNFCCC	United Nations Framework Convention on Climate Change
URBMI	Urban Residents Basic Medical Insurance
USA	United States of America
VAT	value-added tax
WBMI	Workers Basic Medical Insurance
WTO	World Trade Organization
ZXB	*Zhufang xianjin butie* [housing cash-subsidy]

1 Introduction

Yiping Huang[1]

When Mao Zedong and his comrades arrived in Beijing from the remote northwest town of Yan'an in 1949 to establish the People's Republic, they inherited a war-torn, poor, closed, agrarian economy. With an aim to catch up with the UK and US economies within 10 and 15 years, respectively, the communist government designed a central planning system to mobilize resources for economic development. That programme, however, failed spectacularly in the end. Despite a period of impressive urban industrial growth, the economy was on the verge of collapse by the end of the 1970s. While urban industry churned out large volumes of low-quality and unwanted heavy-industry products, consumer goods were in severe shortage. Farmers often could not even feed themselves in a normal year. And the economy had little interaction with the outside world.

In December 1978, Deng Xiaoping and the other leaders decided to embark on economic reform, which led to what is now widely described as China's 'economic miracle'. GDP growth averaged about 10 per cent a year during the reform period, which lifted at least 400 million people out of poverty. Today, China is already the world's second-largest economy. Its economic influence is felt by people all over the world, from Australian iron ore miners to American consumers, and from European luxury goods producers to African construction workers. Judging from its importance in global markets for labour-intensive goods, commodities and foreign exchanges, China is already a global economic power. In fact, some experts have proposed that China and the USA form the Group of Two (G2) to jointly manage important international affairs (Bergsten *et al.* 2008).

The ascendancy of the Chinese economy will likely be one of the most important global events during the first half of the twenty-first century. Rapid income growth in the world's most populous country should significantly reduce the global challenge of poverty alleviation and substantially raise average living standards. As the largest economy in the world for the past century, the USA has been a key architect of the current international economic system. If China does overtake the US economy in the coming decades, as some expect, then it will probably also play a role in shaping the future of the international economic system. In order to assess the implications of this historical change for global economic and political development, at least three questions need to be addressed:

- Can China's rapid economic growth continue in the coming decade?
- What are the global influences of the Chinese economy?
- How might China want to change the international system?

SUSTAINABILITY OF CHINESE GROWTH

The ascendancy of the Chinese economy within a relatively short period from the late 1970s is, as noted above, widely regarded as an economic miracle. Economists have offered various explanations for this extraordinary performance:

- Justin Lin, Cai Fang and Zhou Li argued in their award-winning book *The China Miracle* that the key was transition from a strategy of heavy-industry-orientated development to a strategy of comparative-advantage-orientated development (Lin *et al.* 1995).
- Barry Naughton suggested the term 'growing out of the plans' as an interpretation of China's rise; that is, allowing incremental growth of the market-orientated, private activities, while maintaining support to the old central-planned activities and state-owned enterprises (SOEs) (Naughton 1995).
- Jeffery Sachs and Wing Thye Woo, however, pointed out that Chinese economic success was explained not by its policy innovation but rather by its convergence to the typical market system of East Asia; the system that previously underpinned the ascendancy of the other Asian economies (Sachs and Woo 2000).

Despite the differences in their angles and perspectives, these and many other economists appear to share a consensus view that the fundamental change leading to the great success of the Chinese economy was its transition from a centrally planned to a market system. This is certainly correct. The central planning system created at least two types of inefficiency problems in the economy: the misallocation of resources among different industries and activities, and productive inefficiency at the micro level. The removal of these problems was indeed able to produce a dramatic expansion of economic activity.

But this is only part of the story. In fact, overemphasis on the role of market liberalization could prevent a proper understanding of China's extraordinary economic performance, especially from the perspective of its implications for other underdeveloped countries. Many low-income countries probably have had freer market systems than China's but, for decades, they have failed to achieve significant economic growth. In September 1993, the World Bank published its famous report, *The East Asian Miracle*, which examined the experience of eight high performing Asian economies (HPAEs). The World Bank summarized the essence of the HPAEs' public policy as involving limited price distortion and careful policy intervention.

In my view, the unique policy that contributed to China's extraordinary economic performance was its asymmetric approach to market liberalization during the reform period – in other words, the almost complete liberalization of product markets but the maintenance of heavily distorted factor markets. Free markets for products ensure that production decisions are based on demand and supply conditions in the economy, and resources are allocated efficiently. Distortions in factor markets are a way of providing incentives for economic entities and, sometimes, for overcoming market failures (Huang 2010).

Factor market distortions, including distortions in markets for labour, land, capital, energy and other resources, also played an important role in promoting strong economic growth during the reform period. One example is China's foreign direct investment (FDI) policy. In the early years of economic reform, the Chinese Government designed a range of preferential policies to attract FDI, including tax holidays, free use of land, subsidized credit, and cheap inputs such as energy and water. Government support for FDI projects also reduced problems related to an undeveloped legal system for property rights protection. In typical economics textbooks, such policies are described as policy distortions. But they have been successful. By 2010, cumulated FDI inflows into China had reached US$923 billion since 1997. Today, foreign-invested firms (FIEs) account for more than half of China's total exports.

How did such cost distortions affect the economy in general?

At the simplest level, the distortions may be viewed as a production subsidy; that is, cost distortions are like producer subsidy equivalents. They boost profits from production. This was essentially why China quickly rose as a global manufacturing centre within a few years following its accession to the World Trade Organization (WTO). There was no better place to produce than in China – labour was cheap, capital was cheap, land was cheap, energy was cheap, producers enjoyed tax exemptions, and there was no real charge for pollution.

Low costs also stimulated investment. Most important was the cheap capital. Capital was by far the most important element in total cost distortions over the past 10 years. This explains why China moved into heavy industries so quickly in the early twenty-first century even though the government still hoped to create more jobs. As the investment share of GDP was close to 50 per cent, it is easy to understand why China consumes such large volumes of raw materials.

Cost distortions make Chinese products very competitive in international markets. This was behind the unusual growth in China's economic openness, with the export share of GDP rising from 8 per cent in 1978 to 35 per cent in 2008, an unusually high level for a large economy. This also explains why China's international influence is disproportionate to its income level and even its economic size. Close to 70 per cent of Chinese GDP is externally oriented (exports plus imports), compared with 20–30 per cent for the USA and Japan. This also explains why China exports so much capital.

Nevertheless, over the years, alongside strong economic growth these distortions also created a series of structural problems:

- Low costs inevitably lead to overuse and inefficiency of production inputs. This problem is most clearly highlighted by China's unusually high energy- and commodity-intensive GDP. That China consumes so many resources at its current income level leads many to worry that the world does not have enough resources to support its future growth.
- Low costs and the associated state interventions also lead to important imbalance problems. While investment and exports are unusually strong, consumption has been weakening relative to the overall economy for the past decade. Massive investment raises the question of potential bubbles in the economy, and large external surpluses invite external disputes with economic partners. The private sector, which is generally discriminated against in state-dominated resource allocation, also faces significant hurdles in development.
- The distortions and interventions may be self-sustaining as, over time, special interest groups are formed to resist further liberalization. For instance, SOEs enjoy policy preferences and monopoly profits. They have become strong opponents of market liberalization. Some analysts worry about state capitalism and interlocking interests between the state and the SOEs.

Premier Wen Jiabao once described Chinese growth as 'unbalanced, inefficient, unstable and unsustainable'. Therefore, important changes have to be made in order for rapid economic growth to continue. A key theme of the last two Five-Year Plans was to transform the growth model, by reducing structural imbalances, increasing resource efficiency and improving income distribution. Liberalization of factor markets needs to be a central element of the policy package facilitating transition of the growth model.

The good news is that positive changes are already taking place. In the labour market, wages have been growing faster than GDP for the past few years. Some economists argue that China has probably reached the so-called Lewis turning point at which the labour market shifts from labour surplus to labour shortage. This is already significantly affecting manufacturing competitiveness and economic structure. The government has also gradually started the process of liberalizing energy prices. Capital market liberalization remains the most important outstanding item on the agenda. It is encouraging that, for the past few years, the currency has been appreciating steadily, and the central bank has been actively promoting its internationalization. We may see major breakthroughs in the coming years on liberalization of interest rates, exchange rates and the capital account. In the meantime, the economy also showed initial signs of rebalancing. The current account surplus fell from 10.8 per cent of GDP in 2007 to 2.8 per cent in 2011. Some analyses even suggest that consumption share of GDP has started to rise.

In any case, the Chinese economy is probably in the middle of a new transition, from economic miracle to normal development. If reforms of factor markets and other areas proceed steadily, as we expect they will, then the Chinese economy may move into a new stage of economic development, with slower growth, higher inflation, more equal income distribution, more balanced economic structure, accelerated industrial upgrading and more dramatic economic cycles.

CHINA'S GROWING GLOBAL INFLUENCES

Although Chinese GDP per capita is still only around US$5,000 at the moment, it is already a major player, sometimes even a dominant one, in global economic affairs. Perhaps this is best seen in international markets for commodities, labour-intensive manufacturing goods and foreign exchange.

Chinese influence in global commodity markets already extends far beyond the iron ore market. Its shares in total global consumption of aluminium, nickel, zinc and copper are generally in the 20–30 per cent range. Its shares in global consumption of iron ore, cement and coal are already above 50 per cent. China's share in the world crude oil market is much lower, given the dominance of coal in the structure of its energy consumption. But before the global financial crisis, China regularly contributed about half of the incremental demand for crude oil. In early 2009, when the world economy was still in deep recession, world copper prices started to lead the recovery of global commodity prices. This was initially triggered by the expectation of increased demand in China, associated with its 4 trillion yuan stimulus package and planned investment in the state power grids.

Chinese demand has been recognized as the most fundamental driver of global commodity markets and prices. More importantly, there is little sign of this ending any time soon. Currently, China's annual housing construction is equivalent to the total housing stock of all Australia. With the expected continuation of massive urbanization in the coming decade, the market expects strong Chinese demand for commodities to continue. This is the basis of the so-called 'super-cycle' of the global commodity markets.

Commodity markets offer only one example of China's global economic influence. China's dominance in the world consumer-goods markets emerged even earlier. From the mid 1980s, China started to export cheap garments, footwear, travel bags and toys, benefiting from FDI from the neighbouring economies of Hong Kong, Korea and Taiwan. In the following decade, the Pearl River Delta and the Yangtze River Delta quickly became production bases for labour-intensive manufactured goods. By the late 1990s, China's share in total in the world's labour-intensive manufactured exports had already reached close to 20 per cent, exceeding that of Japan and the newly industrialized economies combined.

Walmart stores across America, for instance, are full of products made in China. Global brand names such as Louis Vuitton and Apple all set up factories in China to take advantage of cheap production costs. Today, the Chinese manufacturing industry is the largest in the world. It has become a truly global manufacturing centre. In the 1980s and 1990s, Chinese travelling to overseas destinations would bring back some souvenirs for family members and friends. Soon, however, these travellers found it increasingly difficult to buy souvenirs not made in China.

On 1 January 2005, Chicago journalist Sara Bongiorni and her family made a New Year's resolution not to buy made-in-China products for a year. As result, the Bongiorni family had an eventful year shopping for non-Chinese products. It was sometimes difficult to find products that were not made in China, such as birthday candles and sports shoes. And even if they did, the prices were normally at least 20 per cent higher than Chinese products. More importantly, even if they were able to find products made in Korea or Japan, there was no guarantee that these products contained no components made in China (Bongiorni 2007).

China is not only the biggest supplier of consumer goods but is also the biggest consumer of many products, especially luxury products. For instance, China is already the world's largest market for automobiles and Louis Vuitton bags. Chinese demand for luxury goods is much bigger than that reported in the sales data in China. Many rich people travel to Hong Kong, Tokyo, Singapore, New York, Paris and London to buy brand names, taking advantage of lower taxes and higher quality.

Another example of China's global economic influence is the global currency market. Up until now, the Chinese currency, the renminbi, has not been freely convertible, and its exchange rate is still heavily managed by the People's Bank of China. In other words, the renminbi cannot be traded in the international markets. Nevertheless, it is already one of the most important currencies of the world. International forums such as the International Monetary Fund (IMF) annual conferences and the G20 Summit often discuss the subject of renminbi exchange-rate policy. Through statistical analyses, Takatoshi Ito has concluded that many central banks in Asia already target the renminbi exchange rate as a critical reference parameter in their own exchange-rate policy decisions (Ito 2010). He estimated that the renminbi was already as important as the US dollar.

The renminbi exchange rate has also been at the centre of contentious international economic policy debates. American politicians and opinion leaders constantly blamed an undervalued renminbi for causing a high unemployment rate and large current account deficit in the USA. Meanwhile, many other developing countries, including India, Russia and Brazil, voiced their concern about global macro-economic instabilities caused by distortions in the renminbi exchange rate. While some attention to the renminbi should be expected given China's growing importance in global trade and economic growth, the degree and range of these concerns are still somewhat surprising.

In the meantime, more and more individuals and institutions are willing to accept and hold renminbi. In recent years, the Chinese authorities have made serious efforts to internationalize the currency by promoting the use of the renminbi for international economic transactions and establishing an offshore renminbi market in Hong Kong. By the end of the first quarter of 2011, Hong Kong households and institutions already held a total of 400 billion yuan (renminbi). The value of trade settlement using renminbi with some neighbouring economies also reached 900 billion yuan in 2010. More importantly, some central banks also started to hold renminbi in their official reserves, which by then had reached about 830 bilion yuan. The largest holders are the Hong Kong Monetary Authority (200 billion yuan), the Bank of Korea (150 billion yuan), the Monetary Authority of Singapore (130 billion yuan), the Bank of Indonesia (100 billion yuan), Bank Negara Malaysia (80 billion yuan) and the Central Bank of Argentina (70 billion yuan).

Finally, China's overall influence on global economic affairs also increased significantly. During the years preceding the global financial crisis, China regularly contributed about one-third of the growth of global GDP. This share was much bigger than those of the USA, Europe, Japan and any other emerging market economy during the same period. Although China's overall influence is still not comparable to that of the USA, it has already become an important factor for determining the performance of the other countries. According to model simulation applying the Oxford Economic Forecasting model, Asian economic growth would accelerate by 1.1 per cent if the US economy expanded by 1 per cent. Similarly, Asian growth would pick up by 0.5 per cent if the Chinese economy expanded by 1 per cent. During the 2008 global financial crisis, the quick turnaround of Chinese investment and real GDP growth were important factors supporting stabilization and recovery of global commodity markets and growth in many of the neighbouring Asian economies, including Japan.

WHAT DOES CHINA WANT?

China's roles in international economic affairs are likely to grow rapidly as it is set to overtake the US economy in aggregate income terms in the coming decade. While the world welcomes the ascendancy of China, it may also feel nervous about the upcoming transition of global superpowers. For instance, what does it mean for the international economic architecture if China supersedes the USA as the world's largest economy?

The current international economic system, established in the mid 1940s at the end of the Second World War, contains three key features. First, the USA is a dominant leader in designing and enforcing the international economic rules. Second, the US dollar is the cornerstone of the international monetary system, both before and after breakdown of the Breton Woods system. And, finally, three international organizations, the IMF, the World Bank and the WTO, are responsible for maintaining international economic order.

For more than half of a century, this system facilitated steady growth of the global economy. Recently, however, there have been growing calls for reform of the international economic system. Two important events, in particular, have strengthened these demands. The first has been the ascendancy of the emerging market economies, and a natural call for some of them to move from the periphery to centre stage of international economic decision-making. And the second was the subprime crisis in the USA, which has raised serious questions about the future international roles of the USA and the US dollar.

The current international economic system is modelled mainly on the economic systems of the developed countries, especially that of the USA. It promotes free trade, free investment, free markets and strict market discipline. But the subprime crisis revealed problems with the US system. Economists have raised questions about the effectiveness of monetary policy, financial regulation and the international reserve system. While there may not be consensus about what should happen next, there is general consensus that this system needs to be adapted to suit the new global economic and market conditions.

The world economy is indeed very different today from what it was more than 60 years ago when the current system was first set up. Now the emerging market economies are already important players in the world economy. Of the world's 20 largest economies, more than half are emerging market economies. For instance, the five BRICs countries – Brazil, Russia, India, China and South Africa – account for 42 per cent of the world's population and 18 per cent of global GDP. Many emerging market economies have already begun to assert their influence in world economic affairs through the G20 summit process. It is now appropriate for the advanced and emerging market economies to work together in changing some of the international economic rules.

It is not surprising that there are some tensions between China and the established powers in the international economy (Huang *et al.* 2011). The first type of tension relates to potential conflict between existing and rising powers. As China is likely to overtake the USA to become the largest economy in the world in the coming decade or two, suspicions of the other party's intentions are common on both sides. Problems in the transition of world leadership from one national state to another in the past were often resolved through wars. Although such suspicions have not led to real conflict between China and the USA, they could cause difficulties for cooperation in the international economic system.

The second type of tension is ideological. Many in the West still view China as a typical communist country. Such perceptions deepened in the wake of the global financial crisis as the state and SOEs assumed more power over economic activities in responding to the crisis. As a result, many foreign and domestic experts are confused about the future direction of Chinese economic reform and, in particular, whether China will move toward deepening market-orientated reform or revert to state control of the economy. These changes could also reduce the trust between China and the rest of the world.

The third type of tension, which is common between advanced and emerging market economies, relates to conceptions of the ideal economic system. Most advanced market economies believe in a free market system with limited state intervention in economic activities, although clearly to a lesser extent in much of Europe than in the USA. During past decades, most emerging market economies have adopted market-orientated reforms and, consequently, have achieved remarkable economic growth. Many of them, however, remain cautious about completely free markets, including the full liberalization of their capital accounts, especially with regard to short-term capital flows.

These potential tensions require careful management through various arrangements at the bilateral, regional and international levels. Many of them can be eased through enhanced mutual understanding and deepened cooperation. In a globalized world economy, the rise of China does not have to come at the cost of the USA or other major economies in the world: as evidenced in the past 30 years, this is not a zero-sum game. Together with the USA, China has a strong interest in supporting the thrust of the existing system, and any positive suggestions for reforming the existing system initiated by China or other emerging market economies are likely to also be in the interest of the USA.

Moreover, the differences between China and the existing major economic powers may diminish over time as China continues its reform and becomes more globalized, and the world's ruling institutions themselves are transformed into a multipolar system. The IMF's latest decision to permit temporary use of capital control measures is one such example.

China demands changes to the international economic system because it no longer reflects the reality of the world economy. It is also because the system is no longer the most credible or efficient arrangement, given, for instance, the weakening position of the US dollar. Some others in the industrial world now share these views. And, finally, it is because the current system is unfair in some areas, such as the dominance of the USA and some European countries in international economic organizations. Reforms are urgently needed to give a stronger voice to the emerging market economies as a whole in international economic decisions. International economic rules should also better reflect new economic and market conditions, such as the complex array of products in global financial markets. The world also needs a new international reserve system that can support continued stable growth of the global economy.

So, what does China want?

China wants the transformation of the international economic system to reflect the new reality of the world economy, especially the increasing importance of emerging market economies. At the same time, China also wishes to preserve the positive features of the current system that have contributed to the global economic prosperity during recent decades, especially the promotion of free trade, free flows of capital and globalization. China has been a principal beneficiary of the current international system and is keen to help improve it. China is not interested in building a completely new system alongside the existing one. But the new international economic system should give more influence to emerging market economies and should pay more attention to the conditions of developing countries when making economic rules.

China supports the G20 process, which probably represents the best compromise between efficiency and representativeness. The G7 or G8, the so-called the 'rich countries' club', is an institution of the past. China values the partnership with the USA but does not seek to institutionalize the G2 framework for international economic affairs.

International organizations should take on further global responsibilities, such as macro-economic surveillance, financial regulation and global liquidity management. But before that they will also need to introduce reforms in order to become more representative, more efficient, more effective and fairer. The governance structure of international organizations should be changed to better reflect the growing importance of the emerging market economies. And the making of international economic rules should also pay more attention to the actual conditions of the developing countries.

The global reserve system is in urgent need of reform. Chinese officials recently proposed a shadow basket of special drawing rights (SDRs) to include some currencies of the BRICs countries before the next official SDR adjustment in 2015. In the perceivable future, however, a multi-reserve system is more likely. China is interested in seeing the renminbi play a part in the future, alongside the euro and some other currencies. For the time being, it is in the best interest of China, the USA and the rest of the world to ensure a stable dollar.

What can China offer?

As the largest and most dynamic emerging market economy, China can also contribute to the smooth reform of the international economic system. This is consistent with China's goal of working with other countries to build a harmonious world. As China has demonstrated in the past, in negotiations on the sticky issues of climate change and global rebalancing, it prefers to resolve problems through cooperation, not confrontation.

The Sino–US partnership is a necessary but not sufficient condition for international economic cooperation in many areas. The regular Strategic and Economic Dialogue between the two countries is an important platform for the two sides to exchange views on key bilateral and multilateral issues. China can also work with the other BRICs members to develop emerging market policy positions and jointly push these proposals in global platforms like the G20 and the IMF.

China can help support a stable dollar in foreign-exchange markets, such as through smooth management of its large foreign-exchange reserves. But this requires cooperation by the USA in the proper management of its fiscal and monetary policies. China can also assist the rebalancing process by proactively reducing its own current account surplus. It is probably also in China's own interest to contain trade protectionism around the world and to help conclude the Doha Round of trade negotiations.

And, finally, what are China's own responsibilities?

First, as the world's second-largest economy, China needs to abandon its small-country mentality. Economic decisions by any large country should take into account the possible reactions of other countries. Exchange-rate policy serves as a good example. Currency distortions in a small country have no impact on the rest of the world, but in a large country like China they can cause significant changes in global trade and production structures.

Second, nationalistic sentiment is very harmful for China's further opening up to the outside world. In particular, conspiracy theories have been popular in discussions of external economic relations, especially those with the USA. If China cannot effectively minimize the influence of cold-war mentalities on international economic policy decisions, it will not be able to become a credible partner for other countries in reforming the international economic system.

Third, China should further promote liberalization of its own economy and move closer to a market economy, including reforms of its exchange-rate regime, capital account controls and distortions in other factor markets. At the same time, China should also promote private-sector development and contain the influence of the state sector, especially in international economic areas. This is critical for supporting an open and efficient international economic system.

And, finally, it is probably also time for China to learn to work with the USA and other G20 members to provide public-good services for the world economy. China and the other emerging economies, in return for more rights, should be willing share more of the responsibility in maintaining a stable global economic environment, enforcing the international economic rules and assisting countries temporarily struck by unfavourable shocks.

The chapters in this book consider important dimensions of reform and change in the Chinese economy that will determine whether there is success or failure in effecting the domestic and international transitions that the growth of the Chinese economy now requires. An outline of its argument follows.

OUTLINE OF THE BOOK

The chapters of this book are organized around the questions raised above and examine the nature and sustainability of Chinese growth, the effect that this growth has had on the rest of the world and how China, in light of its growing power, can or should relate to the global system.

In Chapter 2, Ligang Song sets the scene for following chapters by cataloguing the most important elements of China's economic development since the 1970s. He puts this development in its historical context, pointing out that China's imminent predominance in the global economy is a return to the situation that prevailed before the industrial revolution in Europe.

In his chapter Song also sketches some of the principal effects of China's growth on the rest of the world. Much of China's growth has been on the back of regional processing trade (of which more in Chapter 3), which has led China to run trade deficits with ASEAN, Taiwan, Japan and Korea, and trade surpluses with developed countries. China's huge demand for commodities has also led to a third resource boom in the postwar period, with dramatically increased commodity exporters' terms of trade.

Accompanying this economic growth has been a huge growth in carbon emissions, a topic discussed in greater detail in Chapter 5. Song points out, however, that reducing carbon emissions cannot be China's burden alone – if China acted unilaterally to reduce emissions, heavily emitting industries would move offshore. Reducing emissions will therefore require a more comprehensive international approach.

In Chapter 3, Yang Yao analyses the effects of China's double transition – huge rural–urban migration and an accelerated demographic transition. The double transition has made Chinese labour very cheap. This, coupled with the relatively high levels of education of the Chinese labour force, has made China the centre of the regional processing trade.

Like Sally (Chapter 8), Yao argues that the processing trade, which accounts for 50 per cent of China's exports and 30 per cent of its imports, is responsible for China's trade surpluses and points out that such trade is carried out mostly by foreign companies seeking to take advantage of the abundance of Chinese labour.

Yao argues that the double transition is also responsible for China's internal imbalances. By keeping wages low even as GDP is growing, Yao points out, households' share of national income will fall, while the shares of firms and government will rise. As firms and government tend to invest their increased income, national savings will rise. Because China's internal and external imbalances are caused by these structural changes, Yao argues they will disappear once the double transition has run its course, which he predicts will be in 15–20 years' time.

Cai Fang, Wang Meiyan and Du Yang address a similar question in their study of the Chinese labour market (Chapter 4). Based on evidence from a number of surveys, they conclude, in contrast to Yao, that China reached the Lewis turning point in 2003 and record that, between 2003 and 2008, migrant workers' wages grew 10.3 per cent annually.

Cai Fang *et al.* argue that this wage growth will be permanent and sustained. They see its principal causes as the demographic transition, which will cause China's labour force to start contracting after 2015, and the development of labour market institutions, particularly more frequent revisions of minimum wages and the growth of trade unions.

The end of surplus labour will lead to a convergence of skilled and unskilled wages in China, and Cai Fang *et al.* provide evidence that this has already started happening. The end of surplus labour should not, however, present a risk to Chinese growth. In agriculture, rising wages have prompted investment in physical capital and technological change. In manufacturing, wage rises have been outweighed by growth in labour productivity, but they have also provided an incentive for manufacturing to move to the less-developed central and western regions. Finally, growing wages will lead to the creation of a new group of Chinese consumers, which will help redress China's internal imbalance.

An oft-proposed solution to China's low savings has been the expansion of the Chinese welfare system, which is reviewed by Li Shi in Chapter 9. He points out that social protection and the provision of public services has lagged behind economic growth in China, and that this has led to a number of growing social problems. Although poverty rates have fallen, income inequality has risen sharply. Labour has also become far more mobile. While this has made it difficult to measure changes in employment, it is clear that unemployment has risen. The rise of these social problems has also precipitated growing social conflict.

Li Shi's survey covers the minimum living standard guarantee, medical care, education, housing affordability and employment insurance. Many of the most pressing problems in these areas relate to the differential provision of services to rural and urban dwellers. This problem has been compounded by the huge rural–urban migration covered by Yao (Chapter 3) and Cai Fang *et al.* (Chapter 4), as most migrants do not qualify for services in the city.

Li Shi also enters into debates on specific components of the social security system. In the area medical care he points to the debate over the extent to which provision of medical services should be privatized and what proportion of costs individuals should bear. In education, he argues that the reform should be directed at improving the quality of primary and secondary education, particularly in rural areas. In housing, he argues that the government should provide more low-rent and cheap housing to counter the dramatic rise in housing prices.

China's growth has been spurred by liberalization of trade in goods, although liberalization in other areas remains incomplete, as the following chapters discuss. In Chapter 6, Yiping Huang and Xun Wang provide a comprehensive review of financial liberalization. They argue that dramatic liberalization of the Chinese financial system began as long ago as 1978, but they recognize that certain essential reforms have yet to be implemented. They argue that this partial liberalization of the financial market was a deliberate policy, designed to make GDP grow as rapidly as possible.

In this context, they set out to evaluate two opposing theoretical propositions: McKinnon's (1973) claim that financial repression suppresses economic growth, and Stiglitz's (1994) rejoinder that, at least for developing countries, financial repression might boost growth. The authors construct an aggregate financial repression index to measure the effectiveness of financial repression in boosting GDP growth. They find that, while financial repression stimulated GDP growth in the 1980s and 1990s, over the past decade it has, in fact, depressed GDP growth.

Yiping Huang and Xun Wang further argue that financial repression is also a source of growing risks to the Chinese economy. In light of these facts, they take the position that it is time to allow markets to determine interest rates, end the role of the government in credit allocation, develop capital markets and float the exchange rate, although they argue with Sally (Chapter 8) and against Lardy and Douglass (Chapter 7) that the currency is not currently substantially undervalued.

In Chapter 7, Nicholas Lardy and Patrick Douglass review the reforms made to make China's capital account fully convertible. Until now, China's capital account liberalization has focused on removing restrictions on FDI inflows. Only since 1999 has China started to remove restrictions on FDI outflows. They argue, contrary to Dobson (Chapter 11), that this has primarily been motivated by a desire to secure better access to primary resources for Chinese companies. The authors express some scepticism about how far internationalization of the currency, which is a goal of the Chinese Government, can proceed, before controls on the current account are removed.

Lardy and Douglass also present what they believe are the preconditions to liberalize the capital account without disrupting the economy. These are the existence of a strong domestic banking system, developed domestic capital markets and a correctly valued currency, to guarantee that capital account liberalization doesn't bring with it sudden large and destabilizing capital out- or inflows.

They argue that, in China's case, these preconditions are only partially met. Central bank controls on interest rates must be removed to strengthen the banking system, corporate debt markets are underdeveloped, and the Chinese currency is, in their view, still undervalued.

In Chapter 10, Yiping Huang and Bijun Wang investigate whether China's outward direct investment (ODI) follows a distinct model, different from the ODI of developed countries. China's ODI has grown rapidly since 2003.

The majority (69.4 per cent) of China's stock of ODI is owned by SOEs, which enjoy certain advantages.

The authors show that China's ODI is concentrated in sectors where China does not enjoy a comparative advantage. This is particularly so for services, which accounted for 76.8 per cent of China's ODI, exceeding the average for either developed or developing countries. The authors then attempt to determine econometrically what are the determinants of Chinese ODI. They find that the determinants of Chinese outward investment are indeed different from those of other economies with large ODI.

The most striking result of the regressions the authors conduct is that comparative advantage in services for OECD countries attracts Chinese ODI to those countries, but does not in the case of non-OECD countries. The authors speculate that one of the motives for Chinese ODI is therefore a desire to learn from the experiences of, and acquire the technologies of, the service sectors of OECD economies.

The remaining chapters cover how China has interacted with the rest of the world and the international system. Stephen Howes, in Chapter 5, tackles the tricky global problem of climate change. He points out that, although Chinese emissions have grown enormously over the past 10 years, making China the world's largest emitter, per-capita emissions remain low. Nevertheless, China has many incentives to act, not only because of the risks from unmitigated climate change, but also to fix domestic environmental problems and related public health issues, deal with China's energy security, and give Chinese firms a technological advantage in low-carbon technology.

There is currently a plethora of emissions-reduction policies promulgated by the Chinese Government, but no price on emissions. Howes concedes a number of benefits from pricing emissions, but argues that that alone would have no effect on Chinese emissions. Focusing on the energy sector, he points out that the role of the central government in setting energy prices and centrally planning the development of generation capacity means that the signal to agents to change their behaviour that a carbon price is meant to send would not be received.

For this reason, Howes recommends reform of the energy sector in China, although cautions that this will not be without its difficulties; partial reform might even make mitigation more difficult. Reforms designed to reduce imbalances, particularly factor market reforms, would also reduce China's emissions intensity by shrinking the role of energy-intensive industries, which benefit disproportionately from these distortions in the Chinese economy. Howes is also fairly positive about China's role in international climate change negotiations.

In Chapter 8, Razeen Sally reviews the history of China's trade liberalization, both before and since joining the WTO in 2001. Before joining the WTO, the impetus for liberalizing reforms in China was domestic and unilateral. This liberalization created the conditions in which China could accede to the WTO; it was not a consequence of accession. As a result, most trade in goods has been liberalized, although trade in services remains much more restricted.

Sally argues that, since joining the WTO, China has for the most part been a productive and active member, as it well aware of the benefits it derives from well-functioning multilateral trade rules. On the other hand, domestic, unilateral liberalization has more or less ceased since accession, and China has instead been very active in negotiating preferential agreements with countries in its region, a point also explored by Dobson (Chapter 11).

Such agreements lead to limited increases in volumes of trade. Sally therefore argues that the way forward for China is for it to finish meeting its WTO commitments and take unilateral action to exceed them. In WTO negotiations, Sally argues that China must start to play a leading role in binding members to the unilateral liberalizing measures they have already taken. Furthering the cause of trade liberalization will also depend on China enjoying good relations with its neighbours and other major trading nations and regions.

In Chapter 11, Wendy Dobson takes up the expectation, borne of China's economic weight, that China be a leader in the continued development of global economic governance. Dobson identifies a cleavage in China between those who tend to favour greater assertiveness on China's part and those who think China should continue to passively comply with the existing international rules for the time being. In its interactions so far, she notes that China's engagement with international government has been governed by pragmatism and self-interest.

Specifically, the author claims China sees the G20 as a way of reforming existing international institutions and preserving international economic stability. Like Sally (Chapter 8), she argues that pursuing preferential agreements is not in China's interest and that it should have played a more important role in bringing the Doha Round to a close.

Certainly, Dobson argues that there is a global consensus on the need for the reform of global economic institutions, but not on the nature of this reform. Some have suggested a larger, more consensual decision-making for these organizations, while others have argued for a more decentralized system with various sub-global groupings. Within this, Dobson notes that China at least accepts the principles that currently govern global economic government. The difficulty lies in pragmatically and cooperatively applying those principles.

NOTE

1   China Macroeconomic Center, National School of Development, Peking University, Beijing, yhuang@ccer.edu.cn.

REFERENCES

Bergsten, C. Fred, Charles Freeman, Nicholas Lardy and Derek J. Mitchell (2008) *China's Rise: Challenges and Opportunities*, Washington, DC: Peterson Institute of International Economics.

Bongiorni, Sara (2007) *A Year Without 'Made in China': One Family's True Life Adventure in the Global Economy*, New York: John Wiley & Sons.

Huang, Yiping (2010) 'Dissecting the China puzzle: asymmetric liberalization and cost distortion', *Asia Economic Policy Review*, 5(2): 281–295.

Huang, Yiping, Weihua Dang and Jiao Wang (2011) 'Reform of the international economic system: what does China want?', in Jane Golley and Ligang Song (eds), *Rising China: Global Challenges and Opportunities*, Canberra: ANU E-Press.

Ito, Takatoshi (2010) 'China as number one: how about the renminbi?', *Asian Economic Policy Review*, 5(2): 249–276.

Lin, Justin Yifu, Cai Fang and Li Zhou (1995) *The China Miracle: Development Strategy and Economic Reform*, Hong Kong: Chinese University of Hong Kong Press.

McKinnon, R.I. (1973) *The Order of Economic Liberalization: Financial Control in the Transition to a Market Economy*, Baltimore, MA: Johns Hopkins University Press.

Naughton, Barry (1995) *Growing Out of the Plan: Chinese Economic Reform, 1978–1993*, Cambridge, UK: Cambridge University Press.

Sachs, Jeffrey D. and Wing Thye Woo (2000) 'Understanding China's economic performance', *Journal of Policy Reform*, 4(1): 1–50.

Stiglitz, J.E. (1994) 'The role of the state in financial markets', in M. Bruno and B. Pleskovic (eds) *Proceedings of the World Bank Annual Conference on Development Economics (1993)*, supplement to the *World Bank Economic Review* and the *World Bank Research Observer*, pp. 19–52, Washington, DC: World Bank.

World Bank (2003) *The East Asian Miracle: Economic Growth and Public Policy*, (World Bank Policy Research Report), New York: Oxford University Press.

2 China's rapid growth and development

A historical and international context

Ligang Song[1]

INTRODUCTION

Openness to international trade and investment is an integral part of the Chinese reform process. Within a relatively short time frame (1978–2009) China has profoundly transformed the way in which it engages with the rest of the world.

The process of domestic marketization, a key element of Chinese reform, has been significantly enhanced by engaging with the outside world through various forms of international exchange, including trade, investment flows, technology transfer, spread of knowledge and human exchange.

China's integration has brought one-fifth of the global population into the world trading system, which has increased market potential and integration to an unprecedented level. This increased scale and depth of international specialization propelled by the enlarged world market has offered new opportunities to boost world production, trade and consumption, with the potential to increase the welfare of all the countries involved.

Chinese integration into the global economy has also forced a worldwide reallocation of economic activities. This has increased various kinds of friction in China's trading and political relations, as well as generating several globally significant (negative) externalities. These externalities include:

- increasing competition from China's low-cost production and the accompanying rising share of Chinese-made products that are provided to the world market;
- China's role in causing global economic imbalances;
- rising commodity prices, including energy and minerals prices, caused largely by China's rapidly increasing demand for the resources to fuel its development; and
- rising greenhouse gas emissions, resulting from the rapid pace of industrialization and rising standard of living in China.

The challenges these situations reveal are of huge global significance and are often further complicated due to the geopolitical considerations of many of China's major trading partners. Confronting these challenges in a cooperative and constructive way is the only sensible way to move forward in order to prevent jeopardizing world economic growth and prosperity. As pointed out by Findlay and O'Rourke (2007: 545):

> [I]n the longer run, the gradual rise of India and China to their natural roles as major economic and political superpowers was not only the best news for global human welfare in a generation, but promised to raise a variety of geopolitical challenges which as yet remain unpredictable.

This chapter discusses, from a historical perspective, the increasing importance of the Chinese economy in the global economy. It examines the emerging changes and issues in the global economic landscape, including fast-growing trade and capital flows among countries and regions; the global imbalances; the increasing demand on global resources and climate change. It assesses how these emerging challenges could affect China's long-term growth and the role that China and its major trading partners can play in addressing various global issues unilaterally and multilaterally, and in global and regional cooperation initiatives. Finally, it discusses how China could better prepare for the new role it is expected to play on the world stage, and the policy implications for deepening the reform and adjusting China's growth strategy.

CHINA'S RISE, FALL AND RISE AGAIN: HISTORICAL PERSPECTIVE

China was the largest economy until the early nineteenth century (Figure 2.1). In fact its industrial and commercial development can be traced back to even earlier. For example, Hartwell (1962, 1966, 1967; cited by Findlay and O'Rourke 2007) demonstrated the remarkable expansion in the production of iron and steel in China during the Northern Sung dynasty (960–1126). The scale of total production, and of the levels of output and employment in individual plants, was far in excess of anything attained by England in the 18th century, at the time of the industrial revolution. Hartwell estimated that iron production in China in 1078 was of the order of 150,000 tons annually. The entire production of iron and steel in Europe in 1700 was not much above this, if at all. Furthermore, the growth rate of Chinese iron and steel production was no less remarkable, increasing twelve-fold in the two centuries from 850 to 1050 (Findlay and O'Rourke 2007).

Figure 2.1 shows that there has been a long-term pattern of rise, fall and rise again in China's position relative to the major economies of Western Europe and North America. This U-shape trend over the past 200 years has been dictated by a period of de-industrialization in China since the mid 19th century, as shown by the precipitate fall of its share of gross domestic product (GDP) in the world economy, and of re-industrialization since the late 1970s, shown by the rapid increase in its share of world GDP. Maddison (2005) has predicted that China's share of world GDP will surpass that of the USA by 2030.

As shown in Table 2.1, China and India had enjoyed per-capita industrialization levels of between 70 and 80 per cent of Britain's in 1750 but, by 1913, a forty- or even fifty-fold gap had opened up. By this time, India's share of world manufacturing output was just 1.4 per cent, and China's 3.6 per cent.

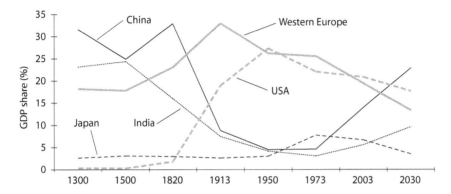

Figure 2.1 Changing GDP shares in the world: China and the major economies, 1300–2030 (%, based on 1990 international dollar). Source: Maddison (2005: Table 5).

Table 2.1 Per-capita levels of industrialization, 1750–1913. UK in 1900 = 100; 1913 boundaries

Country	1750	1800	1860	1913
Austria–Hungary	7	7	11	32
Belgium	9	10	28	88
France	9	9	20	59
Germany	8	8	15	85
Italy	8	8	10	26
Russia	6	6	8	20
Spain	7	7	11	22
Sweden	7	8	15	67
Switzerland	7	10	26	87
United Kingdom	10	16	64	115
Canada	n.a.	5	7	46
USA	4	9	21	126
Japan	7	7	7	20
China	8	6	4	3
India	7	6	3	2
Brazil	n.a.	n.a.	4	7
Mexico	n.a.	n.a.	5	7

Source: Bairoch (1982: 281).
n.a. = not available.

The share of Europe and her British offshoots was a staggering 89.8 per cent (Findlay and O'Rourke 2007).

The trend of re-industrialization taking place in China since the beginning of the last quarter of the twentieth century has been accompanied by an overall trend of de-industrialization in today's developed countries. China's rise as an economic powerhouse occurs amid this historical transformation, consisting of structural adjustment in industrialized countries in relation to emerging economies including China. This trend of de-industrialization in developed countries and re-industrialization in China is clearly illustrated by the rising proportion of industrial workers in the workforce of China as compared with that of most developed countries (Figure 2.2).

The transformation has been enhanced by the process of globalization. Globalization has had a powerful impact on economic integration involving both developed and developing countries in the post-Second World War period. It has broadly affected all aspects of open economies, ranging from production, consumption, trade and technology transfer, to the way that markets function and how the social, economic and political institutions change in response to the requirements of globalization.

This is the historical context in which China embarked on the road of reform and opening up, beginning from the late 1970s. Globalization has not only allowed China to pursue cheaper sources of energy and raw materials, but also has provided access to markets for finished manufactured products that have been produced more cheaply by the seemingly unlimited supply of labour flowing from rural areas into the industrial sector in China

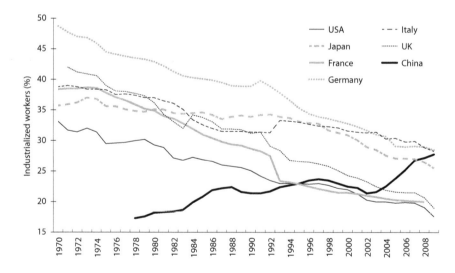

Figure 2.2 Changing shares of industrial workers in the total employment in China and the industrialized countries, 1970–2009. Sources: Data for China are from the China Statistical Yearbook (2010), and those for other countries from Bureau of Labour Statistics at http://www.bls.gov/fls/#tables.

(Figure 2.3). With more than 200 million industrial workers producing manufactured goods in China, along with exports (dominated by manufactured goods) accounting for more than 30 per cent of China's total GDP, it is expected that China's rapid industrialization will have a substantial domestic impact as well as on the global economy.

China has become one of the largest economies and, with an annual average growth rate of 9.8 per cent for over three decades (1978–2009), is on its way to becoming the largest economy. This historical rise of China is well illustrated by comparing it and the USA. According to the national account figures, China's GDP was 30.7 per cent of that of the USA in 2008, about 22 percentage points higher than the corresponding value in 1970. If purchasing power parity (PPP) is used, China is already very close to the USA; for example, in 2008, China's GDP, gross capital formation, total manufacturing output and exports of goods and services were 92, 90, 98 and 89 per cent, respectively, of those of the USA. These figures clearly show that the rate at which China is catching up with the USA has accelerated since 2000 (Figure 2.4).

Several other key economic measures reflect the dynamism of the Chinese economy and the accelerated pace of its approach to the economic status of the USA (Figure 2.5). The incremental change in China's GDP in 2007 relative to 2006 was larger than that of the USA for the first time during the previous 38 years. This trend extended further in 2008. If GDP–PPP is applied, the total incremental value of China was about three times as large as that of the USA over the period 2001–2008. The concept of 'total incremental value' is used to moderate the sizeable fluctuations that occur in some years. For example, China's incremental GDP–PPP in 2008 was 18 times that of the USA (Figure 2.6).

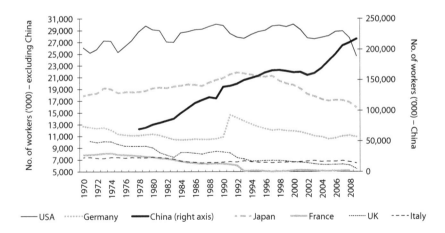

Figure 2.3 Total numbers ('000s) of industrial employment in China and other major industrialized countries, 1970–2009. Sources: Data for China are from the China Statistical Yearbook (2010), and those for other countries from Bureau of Labour Statistics at http://www.bls.gov/fls/#tables.

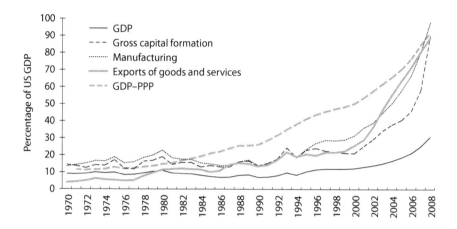

Figure 2.4 Ratios of China to the USA of the key measurements, 1970–2008 (%, taking the USA as 100). Sources: United Nations, http://unstats.un.org/unsd/snaama/dnlList.asp; GDP–PPP are from 'CO$_2$ emissions from fuel combustion', http://www.iea.org/co2highlights/.

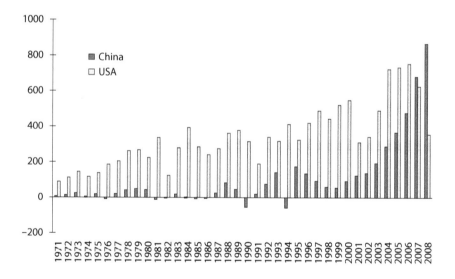

Figure 2.5 The incremental GDP of the USA and China, 1971–2008 (US$ billion, current prices). Source: United Nations, http://unstats.un.org/unsd/snaama/ dnlList.asp.

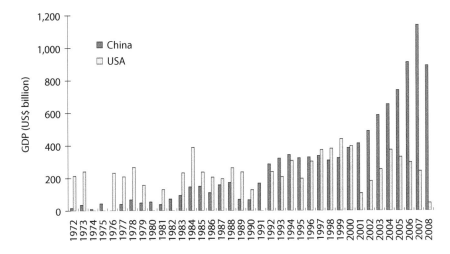

Figure 2.6 The incremental GDP (PPP) of the USA and China (US$ billion (2000), 1972–2008). Source: GDP–PPP data from 'CO$_2$ emissions from fuel combustion', http://www.iea.org/co2highlights/.

IMPACT OF CHINA'S RE-INDUSTRIALIZATION

Market integration and internal transformation

Although the family planning policy adopted by the government in the early 1980s reduced the overall growth rate of population, the massive migration from rural to urban China has supplied the much needed labour force to fuel industrialization. Without internationalization of the economy, there was no way for China to absorb the huge number of migrant rural workers into its industrial sector. Therefore, a key element of China's integration into the global economy has been the assimilation of a large proportion of the migrant rural workers into the country's booming export sector. As such, the international orientation of the economy is intrinsically linked to the process of domestic transformation. This allowed an unprecedented process of urbanization to take place while the urban population increased by about 300 million during the past 30 years, which largely contributed to the productivity gains and rapid economic growth of China.

This pattern of development has enabled China to capitalize on its underlying comparative advantage, which has also demonstrated a pattern of dynamic change (Song 1996). As a result, China's exports have shifted from predominantly primary goods such as oil and agricultural products at the beginning of the reform period; to labour-intensive products such as textile and clothing during the first two decades of reform; to capital-intensive products such as steel, machinery and automobiles in the current phase of reform. Also increasing are exports of technology-intensive products such as information and communications equipment, software and green energy technology.

While a similar economic transformation was taking place in other East Asian economies such as Korea and Singapore, in China (Song 2010: 6):

> What is unprecedented historically is its scale. The size of China's population, market and geography, and the dynamism that flowed from economic reform and transformation are what define its impact on the rest of the world. Despite a still relatively low per capita income, the sheer size of the Chinese economy has made China a significant player in world production, consumption, trade and increasingly international finance and the environment.

The economic transformation and the internationalization of the Chinese economy has delivered rising income per capita in the world's most populous country for a sustained period at a scale and pace previously unobserved in human history. This is a significant factor contributing to global poverty reduction. Without including China and India, both inter- and intranational inequality would have shown a steep rise after 1980 (World Bank 2006).

China's increasing role in the global economy

China's rapid economic growth has increased its standing in the world economy. Figure 2.7 shows that China's shares of GDP, gross capital formation, manufacturing, exports of goods and services, carbon emissions and energy consumption, as well as GDP measured by PPP, have been increasing as global proportions since the early 1990s, and the trends have been accelerating

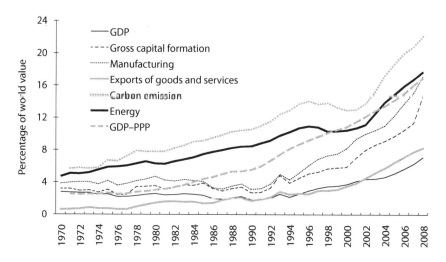

Figure 2.7 China's increasing role in the world, 1970–2008 (%). Sources: United Nations, http://unstats.un.org/unsd/snaama/dnlList.asp); GDP–PPP data from 'CO$_2$ emissions from fuel combustion', http://www.iea.org/co2highlights/.

since 2002. For example, China's manufacturing share increased from about 5 per cent in the mid 1990s to over 16 per cent of world total manufacturing in 2008, while its share of capital formation increased from 5 per cent to 14 per cent of global investment over the same period.

China's impact is particularly felt through the pressure it exerts on trading relations with its key trading partners, the associated global structural transformation and the environment. China's growth is driving rapid changes in the global and regional economic and political landscapes. Its rising economic weight in the global economy is affecting its economic and political relations with the rest of the world. The rapid pace of industrialization in recent years has led to China's shares of both energy consumption and carbon emissions increasing exponentially.

Trade imbalances

With the rapid structural transformation in the world economy, there has not been the same tendency for trade to balance between the emerging economies and the developed countries. This differs from the experience of persistent trade surplus in East Asian trade with developed countries during the periods of rapid growth in Japan, Korea and Taiwan, and Singapore.

China was running trade deficits in the early years (1978–1985) of reform (Table 2.2), mainly because it exported primary products and imported industrial products. Since 1990, except for 1993, China has been running trade surpluses due to its increasing reliance on labour-intensive exports, largely due to the low cost of labour. Processing trade also has played an important role in contributing to China's rising trade surpluses.

Processing trade and attracting foreign direct investment has allowed China to develop a unique pattern of specialization with respect to its relations with other East Asian economies on the one hand and developed countries on the other. China imports large amounts of intermediate goods and materials from other East Asian economies to develop its processing trade, and has thus consistently been running trade deficits with these economies, including Japan, Korea and the ASEAN countries. Among them Taiwan has had the largest trade surplus with mainland China. China then exports the final products to the US, European, and Hong Kong markets, enjoying trade surpluses with these economies. This emerging pattern, which centres on China's relations with both developing and developed countries, is transforming the structure of world trade.

Because of the low cost of producing those final goods in China, the import prices of goods to developed-country markets have remained low. In the US market, for example, import prices have varied by country or region of origin (Figure 2.8). For imports from Canada, the European Union and Latin America, prices increased by about 25 per cent from 2003 to 2010. By contrast, the prices for imports from China have remained low and almost unchanged over the same period.

Table 2.2 China's imports and exports and balance of trade, 1978–2008

Year	(US$ 100 million)			
	Total imports and exports	*Total exports*	*Total imports*	*Balance*
1978	206.4	97.5	108.9	−11.4
1980	381.4	181.2	200.2	−19.0
1985	696.0	273.5	422.5	−149.0
1990	1,154.4	620.9	533.5	87.4
1991	1,357.0	719.1	637.9	81.2
1992	1,655.3	849.4	805.9	43.5
1993	1,957.0	917.4	1,039.6	−122.2
1994	2,366.2	1,210.1	1,156.1	54.0
1995	2,808.6	1,487.8	1,320.8	167.0
1996	2,898.8	1,510.5	1,388.3	122.2
1997	3,251.6	1,827.9	1,423.7	404.2
1998	3,239.5	1,837.1	1,402.4	434.7
1999	3,606.3	1,949.3	1,657.0	292.3
2000	4,742.9	2,492.0	2,250.9	241.1
2001	5,096.5	2,661.0	2,435.5	225.5
2002	6,207.7	3,256.0	2,951.7	304.3
2003	8,509.9	4,382.3	4,127.6	254.7
2004	11,545.5	5,933.2	5,612.3	320.9
2005	14,219.1	7,619.5	6,599.5	1,020.0
2006	17,604.0	9,689.4	7,914.6	1,774.8
2007	21,737.3	12,177.8	9,559.5	2,618.3
2008	25,632.6	14,306.9	11,325.6	2,981.3

Sources: 1978 data from the Ministry of Foreign Trade; data since 1980 from China Customs statistics.

The relatively low prices of Chinese imports have forced other countries to keep their prices low in order to maintain their market shares. For example, the prices of exports from Japan, ASEAN and Asian newly industrialized economies (including Hong Kong, Singapore, South Korea and Taiwan) to the US market were also unchanged over the same period. China and its neighbours have thus kept the general price level low in the USA, through this kind of unique pattern of specialization and trade. This, in turn, has contributed to an increase in consumption in the USA, through the improvement in household real income

However, this beneficial effect on price has been overshadowed by the more contentious issue of trade imbalances between China and the USA, which has led to the current debate on the exchange-rate policy in China. While China is running trade deficits with other East Asian economies, its bilateral trade surplus with the USA has been increasing, especially since China's entry to the World Trade Organization in 2002 (Table 2.3).

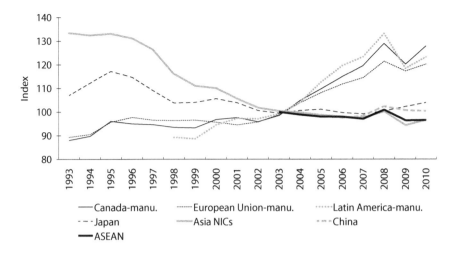

Figure 2.8 US import price indexes by locality of origin, 1993–2010: December 2003 = 100. Source: US Bureau of Labor Statistics, http://www.bls.gov/web/ximpim.supp.toc.htm#long_tables. Note: NIEs are newly industrialized economies, which include Hong Kong, Singapore, South Korea and Taiwan.

China's share of the total US trade deficit has risen rapidly from 21 per cent in 2002 to 43 per cent in 2009. One of the reasons for this is the rapid increase in Chinese imports since the early 2000s. For example, the share of US imports that came from China increased from 11 per cent in 2002 to about 20 per cent in 2009, while the share of US exports to China rose from 3 per cent to 6 per cent over the same period. This ever-increasing trade imbalance between the USA and China has been the main contributing factor to global economic imbalances, which need to be dealt with using a structural approach.

Impact on commodity prices and terms of trade

With its per-capita income increasing by more than five times during the period 1978–2000, China entered the so-called mid-phase of industrialization. This is characterized by an increasing share of manufacturing industry in the total economy. Within manufacturing industry, those capital-intensive and heavy industries such as steel, machinery and chemicals started playing a more important role in the economy. These industries rely more heavily on energy and minerals as inputs to production, contrasting with the early phase of industrialization, which was characterized by labour-intensive production. This is the fundamental cause for the sudden surge in China's demand for energy and resources since 2002.

The enormous demands of China's industries for energy and minerals have led to the third resource boom in the postwar period, characterized by

Table 2.3 The USA's bilateral trade with China, 2002–10 (US$100 million and %)

Year	Imports from China	Import shares	Exports to China	Export shares	Trade deficits	Share of deficits
2002	1,334	11.12	220.5	3.18	–1,114.4	21.97
2004	2,105	13.8	347.2	4.24	–1,758.1	24.87
2006	3,057	15.94	555.2	5.32	–2,505.6	28.48
2008	3,563	16.42	714.6	5.49	–2,848.6	32.8
2009	3,095	19.28	695.8	6.58	–2,399.8	43.75
Jan.–Aug. 2010	2,292	18.48	558.1	6.78	–1,734.0	41.55

Sources: Calculated using data from China Customs at
http://www.customs.gov.cn/default.aspx?tabid=400 and the US Bureau of Economic Analysis
at http://www.bea.gov/internation/bp_web/list.cfm?anon=71&registered=0.

steep rises in commodity prices, including those for energy (Figure 2.9) and raw materials such as iron ore and metals.[2]

Despite its own rich resource endowments, in per-capita terms China is well below the world average for most of the key resources. This has pushed China to rely on overseas supplies of energy and minerals to meet its growing demand for resources.

China's per-capita energy consumption appears close to the world average (Table 2.4). However, if coal is excluded, China's per-capita consumption of all other energy products is far below world averages, this being especially true for both nuclear power and natural gas. This is one of the reasons why China has been rapidly developing its nuclear power capacity, and increasing domestic production and imports of natural gas.

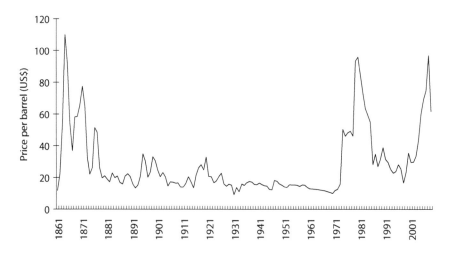

Figure 2.9 Crude oil prices (US$ per barrel, 2009 price), 1861–2009. Source: BP Statistical Review of World Energy (June 2010).

Table 2.5 reports the latest data on China's consumption of key energy and metals and their shares of the world total. They illustrate the immense size of China's rising demand for resources. China became a net importer of oil in 2003 and a net importer for coal in 2009, despite the fact that China has been the largest coal producer in the world. In 2009, China consumed 10 per cent, 47 per cent and 48 per cent of the world's oil, coal and steel, respectively.

With the various constraints on the supply side, China's rising demand for resources has been pushing up world prices for key commodities to levels that surpass those reached during previous resource booms. As a result, the commodity terms of trade are moving in favour of resource exporters such

Table 2.4 International comparison of energy consumption per capita, 2009 (tonnes of oil equivalent)

	Oil	Natural gas	Coal	Nuclear power	Hydro-electric	Total
USA	2.75	1.92	1.62	0.62	0.20	7.11
France	1.36	0.60	0.16	1.44	0.20	3.76
Germany	1.38	0.85	0.86	0.37	0.05	3.52
Japan	1.55	0.62	0.86	0.49	0.13	3.65
United Kingdom	1.20	1.26	0.48	0.25	0.02	3.21
China	0.31	0.06	1.16	0.01	0.11	1.64
World average	0.57	0.39	0.48	0.09	0.11	1.65

Sources: Energy consumption data from BP Statistical Review of World Energy (June 2010); population data are from US Census Bureau, International Data Base, http://www.census.gov/ipc/www/idb/informationGateway.php.

Table 2.5 China's consumption of key energy and metals and their shares in the world

	2009	2009	2009	2008	2008
	Oil (million tonnes)	Coal (million tonnes of oil equivalent)	Steel (million tonnes of finished steel products)	Copper (million tonnes)	Aluminum (million tonnes)
China	405	1,537	542	4.81	12.60
World	3,882	3,278	1,121	18.03	38.17
China's share of world consumption (%)	10.43	46.88	48.34	26.67	33.01

Sources: Oil and coal data from BP Statistical Review of World Energy (June 2010); steel data from World Steel in Figures 2010 by World Steel Association; China data for copper and aluminum from http://www.mlr.gov.cn/zljc/201008/t20100819_742459.htm; global data for copper and aluminum from http://www.smm.cn/information/newsdetail.aspx?newsid=14403.

as Australia and Russia and against importers of resources such as China and Japan (Figure 2.10).

Changes in commodity terms of trade have also affected developed countries, but to a much lesser extent on emerging countries. Like the consequences of the previous resource booms, including the oil shocks in the 1970s, the current trend of changing commodity terms of trade carries with it important implications for global macro-economic change and economic development.

Will the current resource boom last? The answer to this question depends on the future trajectory of Chinese industrialization. McKay *et al.* (2010) estimate the turning point (the peak level in terms of its per-capita steel use) of China's Kuznets curve for steel at US$15,449 GDP per capita – a point that, on its post-1980 trajectory of 7 per cent compound growth, China would reach around 2024. At that time, China's per-capita steel demand is predicted to be between 700 and 800 kg, but closer to the latter. This is higher than the peak level reached in the USA, much higher than those reached by the Commonwealth of Independent States and Europe, but lower than the peaks seen in Japan and Korea.

A simple calculation provides a sense of how much difference this range of peak levels can make with respect to the total demand for steel. With China's total population projected to reach 1.395 billion by 2025 (UN 2010), reaching the peak level of 700 kg would mean that China needs to produce nearly 1 billion tonnes of steel, while a peak level of 800 kg would

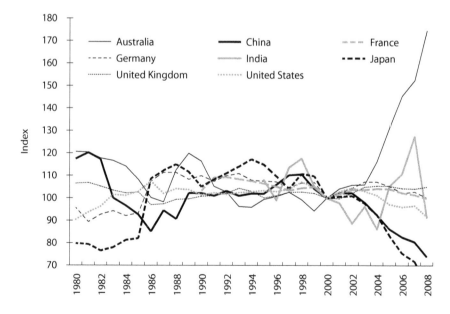

Figure 2.10 Net barter terms of trade index (2000 = 100). Source: http://data. worldbank.org/indicator/TT.PRI.MRCH.XD.WD?page=5.

mean that 1.1 billion tonnes of steel will be needed to meet the demand (the current level of steel production is about 600 million tonnes).

It is possible that China will sustain a relatively high level of intensity for some time after it has reached the peak level of steel intensity, as happened in Japan and Western Europe. If so, it means the current resource boom will last even longer. The projected trajectory will have important implications for both supply of and demand for resources, as well as for long-term global macro-economic development. It also raises environmental impact concerns.

Carbon emissions and international cooperation

The Intergovernmental Panel on Climate Change (IPCC 2007) calls for cutting global greenhouse gas emissions by at least half by 2050, in order to avoid potentially dangerous climate change. China will play a crucial role in achieving this global target on emissions. This is because China's total carbon emissions and its share of total world emissions have been increasing since 1971, and its total carbon emissions have accelerated since 2002 (Figure 2.11). As a result, China's incremental carbon emissions have surged as well. Since 2002, the incremental carbon emissions of China have become very close to or larger than that of the rest of the world (Figure 2.12). In 2007, China surpassed the USA to become the world's largest carbon emitter.

However, in contrast to total emissions and their rising trend, China has a relatively low level of per-capita emissions. China's per-capita emissions were 4.91 tonnes in 2008, only 26.7 per cent those of the USA, and close to the world average. If a 'cumulative carbon emission per capita' indicator is used,

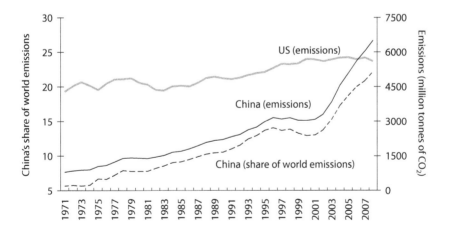

Figure 2.11 China's carbon emissions and share of world emissions, 1971–2008.
Source: from 'CO$_2$ emissions from fuel combustion', http://www.iea. org/co2highlights/.

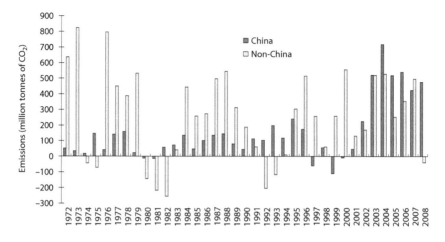

Figure 2.12 Incremental carbon emissions, 1972–2008. Source: from 'CO$_2$ emissions from fuel combustion', http://www.iea.org/co2highlights/.

then China's was just 5.8 per cent of that of the USA and 37 per cent of the world average level in 2002 (Figure 2.13) reflecting the fact that the accelerated phase of industrialization in China has happened only relatively recently.

The low per-capita emissions of China can be linked to the relatively low GDP per capita. China's emissions per unit of GDP, calculated using the current exchange rates, are one of the highest in the world, just below the level of Russia and Iran and more than five times that of the USA in 2008 (Figure 2.14). If GDP–PPP is used, the difference between China and other countries turns out to be much smaller; only 26.4 per cent higher than that of the USA in 2008 (Figure 2.15).

Given the scale, pace and future trajectory of China's industrialization, it is expected that China's total emissions, as well as its emissions per capita (both accumulative and incremental), will continue to grow. An encouraging sign is that China plans to reduce the carbon intensities of production and has adopted various measures to achieve this goal. It is in China's interest to do so as the country is paying a high price for the environmental degradation caused by its drive for industrialization.

China was singled out by Western politicians and media for dragging its feet at the international climate change negotiations at Copenhagen; such accusations have previously always targeted the USA (Zhang 2010). In contrast to this criticism, Garnaut (2010) argues that the Chinese domestic commitment to reduce the emissions intensity of production by 40–45 per cent from 2005 levels by 2020 is the most ambitious, and the most important to the global climate change mitigation effort, that has been accepted by a major economy.

Facing the pressure of structural changes against the rising costs of production including land, labour, energy and minerals, China will be compelled to upgrade its industries to produce more valued-added products. In so doing,

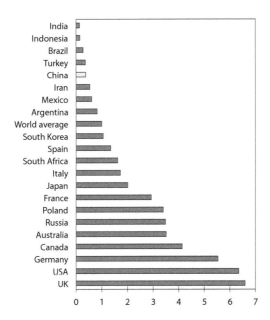

Figure 2.13 Cumulative carbon emissions per capita, from fossil fuels and cement manufacture, 1850–2002 (world average = 1). Sources: Calculated using population data and cumulative emissions data. Population data are for 2002, from US Census Bureau, International Data Base, at http://www.census.gov/ipc/www/idb/informationGateway.php. Cumulative emissions data from Baumert *et al.* (2005).

it will shift its out-of-date industries to relatively backward interior regions or offshore, in a similar fashion to those industries that were transferred to China from Japan, Korea, Taiwan and Hong Kong in the early years of development. This process has started and will accelerate as labour costs rise.

This trend has important implications for the overall reduction of emissions. For example, if the central government, to meet the emissions target, imposes strict environmental standards requiring compliance by all regions, including poor provinces, more industries will be forced to move to other, less-developed countries, including those in South Asia, Central Asia, Latin America and Africa.

Without China imposing environmental standards for those outflowing industries, or those industries facing tough environmental regulation by the recipient countries (both are unlikely to happen), then China's achievement in reducing its total emissions (or their intensity) will not help to reduce total global emissions globally.

By using stricter environmental standards, a government drives capital out of the country. The domestic emissions reduction is accompanied by an increase in foreign emissions. If the capital moves to a pollution haven, the

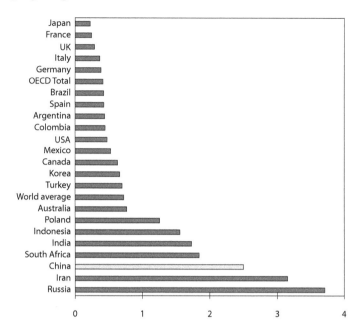

Figure 2.14. Carbon emissions per unit of GDP, using 2008 exchange rates (kg CO_2 per US dollar, 2000 prices). Source: 'CO_2 emissions from fuel combustion' at http://www.iea.org/co2highlights/.

net effect may actually be an increase in emissions and thus the unilateral policy addressing the international environmental problem may even be counterproductive.

(Rauscher 1997: 231)

This suggests that a more comprehensive international approach is needed; for example, an agreement on the environmental regulation imposed on outflowing direct investment.

There is an issue regarding the potential economic impact of climate change on the future pattern of growth in China (McKay and Song 2010). The question here is the extent to which any Chinese commitment to low carbon growth will alter the future structure of the Chinese and global economies. The issue is significant, as the earlier adopters of industrial strategies were not subject to any self-imposed constraint on growth. Further, China's relatively recent engagement with an industrial-led growth path, and its immense backwardness before this engagement, means that the middle phase of industrialization, characterized by rapidly growing energy and emissions intensities, and ongoing increases in global market share, is still ahead of it. This is an uncomfortable reality for both China and the world. The importance of relative price signals, industrial structure, strategic leadership and technology transfer are all emphasized.

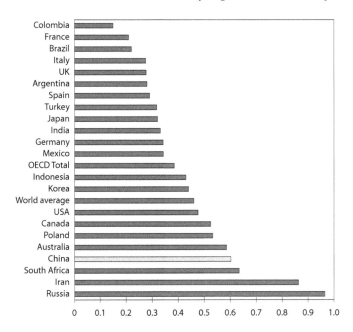

Figure 2.15 Carbon emissions per unit of GDP, using PPP, in 2008 (kg CO_2 per US dollar, 2000 prices). Source: 'CO_2 emissions from fuel combustion' at http://www.iea.org/co2highlights/.

With the prospect that a global framework for emissions mitigation will move forward strongly in the next few years, coupled to the observation that material conflict between industrial-led growth and the biosphere is already starkly evident in China, such constraints may become increasingly binding.

CHINA AND GLOBAL ADJUSTMENTS AND WAYS FORWARD

Confronting the rising China is probably the most challenging task facing the world community in the twenty-first century. The formidable forces of competitiveness still unfolding have been underscoring the rising China as the largest manufacturing powerhouse in the world. 'Changes in competitiveness redistribute profits as well as income and employment between countries, for given aggregate demand conditions' (Blecker 1999: 141). This is the main cause of rising anxiety among the countries involved in trading with China. The solution to this problem lies in structural adjustment in China and its trading partners. However, for this approach to work, it needs time for the adjustment to take place and the presence of the institutional arrangements that accommodate the tasks of adjustment.

For China, this will entail diverging from its current industrialization path, which exhibits a modest but not overwhelming bias towards external demand, to a strategy of domestic market integration and internally driven development (McKay and Song 2010). This reorientation will be shaped by the unique constraints that China faces relative to its predecessors. One of these is that China has moved beyond self-sufficiency across the gamut of resources at a low relative income level, and is thus expected to pressure the global demand–supply balance in a fashion that is essentially without precedent.

There is also an issue as to what extent the current trajectory of industrialization will have to change when China becomes more actively engaged in dealing with structural issues at home and abroad, against the background of the unwinding of global imbalances. This latter issue has profound implications for Chinese economic strategy. Although structural changes will take time, China should now move towards achieving more balanced trade, not by exporting less but by importing more (Table 2.6).

Adjusting its exchange-rate policy is surely a significant part of the strategy of dealing with the imbalance problem, but a more important task for China from the structural point of view is to boost its domestic demand. The way in which China has been integrated with the global economy may be termed as 'asymmetrical', in that the adjustment on the supply side has been much quicker and more thorough than the demand-side adjustment, which is very much lacking. This asymmetrical development between supply and demand has been causing the problems of weak domestic demand and rising income inequality. As a result, China has to rely heavily on exports to prevent its supply capacity worsening trade imbalances as, again due to lack of domestic demand, its imports are unlikely to match the rapid growth of exports. Domestic demand in the short term can be increased through domestic institutional reform; for example, by urbanizing the large numbers of migrant workers in order to change their consumption behaviour (Song *et al.* 2010).

This new strategy will also lead to greater outflow of direct investment from China, so that China can import more goods from other countries that have a comparative advantage in producing those goods. China may lose some employment in the short term, but employment will be boosted by the

Table 2.6 Import shares (%) of consumer products by selected country and region, 2006–09.

Countries	2006	2007	2008	2009
China	1.29	1.48	1.67	2.08
USA	21.38	19.59	17.88	18.54
European Union	13.93	14.05	13.93	15.20
Japan	4.72	4.23	4.23	5.16
Korea	1.01	1.05	1.02	1.07
Hong Kong	2.85	2.76	2.74	3.07
ASEAN	2.09	2.07	2.36	2.36

Source: Calculated using data from the United Nations Comtrade.

enlarged domestic market. The rapid increase in foreign direct investment (FDI) by China in recent years, from a very low base, is only the beginning of the process (Figure 2.16). Again, similar to the way that the world accommodates the rising trade shares by China, discords and frictions will occur in accommodating the rise in China's FDI. This is another aspect of the adjustments that both China and its trading partners need to confront.

The issue of global imbalance is essentially a payment issue caused by structural changes in the world economy. Historically, there were parallel cases of the persistent deficits in the exchange of Western goods with the East caused by exports of porcelain, tea, silk and spices from China and India to Western Europe during the fourteenth and fifteenth centuries. This payment problem (trade deficits) was settled with silver obtained, increasingly, from the Americas. Findlay and O'Rourke (2007: 212) write, '[I]t was the flood of silver released around the globe by the mines of the New World that was the lifeblood of the "circulatory system" of the world economy', and Braudel (1975: 212; cited in Findlay and O'Rourke 2007) writes that:

> a steady flow of gold and silver coins of every description, travelling from west to east, following the rotation of the Earth, carrying along with them a wide range of commodities as a kind of supplementary currency, and loosing in the opposite direction a rich and varied stream of different commodities and precious goods from east to west.

The current problem of the persistent trade deficits of the USA with China is essentially the same kind of payment problem. Unfortunately, the flood of declining dollars (unlike the flood of silver 600 years ago) will

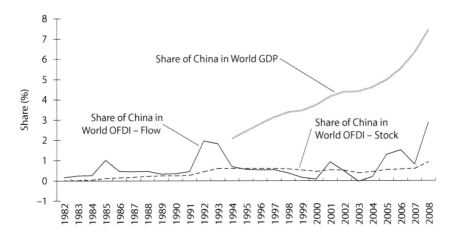

Figure 2.16 Shares of China's overseas direct investment and its GDP in world total overseas investment (flow and stock) and world GDP, 1982–2008.
Source: Calculated using data from the *Statistical Yearbook of China* and UNCTAD.

not help in resolving the balance-of-payments problem. It could make it worse.

The attention on the imbalances is unfortunately focused almost exclusively on the issue of revaluing the currency of the surplus country in order to overcome trade imbalances. This approach tends to sideline the task of dealing with those more fundamental structural issues that have been complicated by the exchange rate volatility and misalignment occurring in the post-Bretton Woods era. History also tells us that strong currencies (with or without the backing of precious metals) are associated with strong and rising economies. China as a rising economic player is far from being ready to play the leading role in reshaping the current global currency system, but there is increasing potential for China to contribute to this effort, because the global financial and currency system needs an anchor for maintaining much needed stability.

For the USA, domestic adjustments are very much needed too for dealing with the global imbalances. Fighting the global financial crisis is essential, but the USA should not lose sight of the need to deal with more fundamental structural issues, including its deficit problems. What China has done in the direction of change proposed will surely help the USA to deal with its problems, and vice versa. The USA and China have common interests in dealing with the global imbalances, for their current benefit and beyond. Both countries also share common interests in maintaining an open trading regime for those structural adjustments to work. Geopolitically, cooperation between the two countries will help in maintaining regional and global security and thereby in reducing the fiscal burden on the USA. In the end, the ultimate aim is to prevent the unpredictability and uncertainties from becoming the real obstacles to achieving the objectives of continuous growth and prosperity in the world economy in the 21st century and beyond.

For those tasks to be successful, the world community needs to respond strategically to the challenges of readjustment by guarding against rising protectionism: and the most effective way of doing so is to improve the global governance system, including the multilateral trading system. A rising power needs to take a leadership role in championing globalization (Garnaut and Song 2006). As warned by Findlay and O'Rourke (2007: 535), 'If anything, history suggests that globalization is a fragile and easily reversible process, with implications not just for international trade, but for the international division of labour and economic growth as well.' They also provided the suggestion (Findlay and O'Rourke 2007: 538):

> As history shows, income distribution matters not just in its own right, but because of the political reactions it can provoke. The implication is that those wishing to maintain an open trading system also need to propose a range of complementary domestic policies, including but not limited to educational, training, and welfare programs, if they are to maintain political support for liberal trade policies.

CONCLUSIONS

This chapter discusses the significance of China's emergence as one of the largest economies in the world and considers ways of reducing unpredictability and uncertainties associated with the task of confronting the challenges of a rising China. The chapter makes the point that what the world community is confronting now and in the foreseeable future, are structural rather than short-term issues, with a pattern of change carrying with it some historical significance. Therefore, what is needed is a structural approach to dealing with those structural issues, and the countries involved need to be aware that there will be substantial adjustment cost associated with this kind of approach. Any attempts to seek quick fixes in resolving these issues, including the call for revaluing the surplus countries' exchange rates (though the realignment of exchange rates is one of the key elements of the structural approaches) in dealing with the global imbalances, are not likely to succeed.

It is also unwise to simply try to maintain the status quo with a hope that solutions will be found down the track one way or another. This is because such an attitude is likely to lead to more-conflicting outcomes, such as economic disintegration resulting possibly from rising protectionism, that would eventually benefit no one. The chapter argues that meeting these concerns and externalities requires an understanding of the ever-increasing degree of economic interdependence between countries, but especially between the surplus and deficit countries. It also stresses the importance of adopting both individual and collective actions in dealing with structural problems.

In practical terms, it also requires that tremendous adjustments take place in many parts of the world. These adjustments are not only required for individual countries, especially China and its major trading partners, but also for the institutions governing the international political and economic system. This is because maintaining a relatively open and multilateral political and trading system in which China is expected, together with other major countries, to play a leadership role is the only effective way in which the behaviour of the rising powers can be framed in, or constrained by, the rules-based system. Maintaining such a system can also make incumbent powers more accommodating and cooperative. This multilateral framework provides an important institutional basis on which expansion of international trade continues to be a positive-sum game rather than a zero-sum one, and the global common goals such as poverty reduction, climate change, and regional and international security can be achieved.

NOTES

1 Crawford School of Public Policy, The Australian National University. I thank Tang Jie for his help with assembling the data and preparing the figures and tables used in the chapter.
2 The first two resource booms were related to the periods of rapid growth of Japan, Korea and other East Asian economies back to the 1970s and 1980s.

REFERENCES

Bairoch, P. (1982) 'International industrialisation levels from 1750 to 1980', *Journal of European Economic History,* 2(11): 269–331.

Baumert, K., T. Herzog, and J. Pershing (2005) *Navigating the Numbers: Greenhouse Gas Data and International Climate Policy,* Washington, DC: World Resources Institute.

Blecker, Robert (1999) 'Kaleckian macro models for open economies', in Johan Deprez and John T. Harvey (eds) *Foundations of International Economics: Post Keynesian Perspectives,* pp. 116–150, London and New York: Routledge.

Braudel, F. (1975) *The Mediterranean and the Mediterranean World in the Age of Philip II,* volume 1, London: Collins.

Findlay, Ronald and Kevin H. O'Rourke (2007) *Power and Plenty: Trade, War, and the World Economy in the Second Millennium,* Princeton, NJ and Oxford: Princeton University Press.

Garnaut, Ross (2010) 'China as a great power: some implications for Australia', an address to the Australia China Business Council, Victoria Division, 13 May 2010, Melbourne, available at http://www.acbc.com.au/deploycontrol/files/upload/acbc_vic_event_RossGarnaut_lunchaddress.pdf.

Garnaut, Ross and Ligang Song (2006) 'Truncated globalisation: the fate of the Asia Pacific economies?', in Hadi Soesastro and Christopher Findlay (eds) *Reshaping the Asia Pacific Economic Order,* pp. 46–58, London: Routledge.

Hartwell R. (1962) 'A revolution in the Chinese iron and coal industries during the Northern Sung, 960–1126 A.D.', *Journal of Asian Studies,* 21(2): 153–162.

—— (1966) 'Markets, technology, and the structure of enterprise in the development of the eleventh-century Chinese iron and steel industry', *Journal of Economic History,* 26(1): 29–58.

—— (1967) 'A cycle of economic change in imperial China: coal and iron in northeast China, 750–1350', *Journal of the Economic and Social History of the Orient,* 10(1): 102–159.

IPCC (Intergovernmental Panel on Climate Change) (2007) *Climate Change 2007: Mitigation of Climate Change,* (Contribution of Working Group III to the Fourth Assessment Report of the IPCC), B. Metz, O.R. Davidson, P.R. Bosch, R. Dave and L.A. Meyer (eds) Cambridge and New York: Cambridge University Press.

McKay, Huw and Ligang Song (2010) 'China as a global manufacturing powerhouse: strategic considerations and structural adjustment', *China and World Economy,* 18(1): 1–32.

McKay, Huw, Yu Sheng and Ligang Song, 2010, 'Chinese metal intensities in comparative perspective', in Ross Garnaut, Jane Golley and Ligang Song (eds) *China: The Next Twenty Years of Reform and Development*, pp. 73–98, Canberra: Australian National University Press and Washington, DC: Brookings Institution Press.

Maddison A. (2005) 'Asia in the world economy 1500–2030 AD', Heinz W. Arndt Memorial Lecture, Canberra, 10 November 2005, available at http://kisi.deu.edu.tr/yesim.ucdogruk/ECN%20232/maddison_Asia.pdf.

Rauscher, Michael (1997) 'Environmental regulation and international capital allocation', in Carlo Carraro and Domenica Siniscalco (eds) *New Directions in the Economic Theory of the Environment*, pp. 193–238, Cambridge and New York: Cambridge University Press.

Song, Ligang (1996) 'Institutional change, trade composition and export supply potential in China', in Manuel Guitian and Robert Mundell (eds) *Inflation and Growth in China*, pp. 190–225, Washington, DC: International Monetary Fund.

—— (2010) 'The scale of China's economic impact', *East Asia Forum Quarterly*, 2(1): 6–8.

Song, Ligang, Jiang Wu and Yongsheng Zhang (2010) 'Urbanisation of migrant workers and expansion of domestic demand', *Social Sciences in China*, 31(3): 194–216.

UN (United Nations) (2010), Population Division of the Department of Economic and Social Affairs of the United Nations Secretariat, *World Population Prospects: The 2010 Revision*, available at http://esa.un.org/unpd/wpp/index.htm.

World Bank (2006) *World Development Report 2006: Equity and Development*, Washington, DC: World Bank.

Zhang, Zhongxiang (2010) 'Copenhagen and beyond: reflections on China's stance and responses', *East–West Center Working Papers, Economics Series*, No. 111, Honolulu, HI: East–West Center.

3 Double transition and China's export-led growth[1]

Yang Yao[2]

INTRODUCTION

China has achieved near double-digit growth rates since it began economic reform and opening its market in 1978. The reform has transformed the Chinese economy from a planned economy to a mixed economy in which the market plays a dominant role in resource allocation. Much of China's remarkable growth between 1978 and 2000 can be explained by the reform. However, the more recent and faster growth in the last decade has been driven mainly by exports. Joining the World Trade Organization (WTO) in 2001 allowed China to fully integrate into the world system and to fully capitalize its large labour supply induced by the 'double transition', namely drastic demographic transition and a fast pace of industrialization. Using the growth trajectory of other East Asian economies as a reference, China can be expected to sustain rapid economic growth for the next 10–15 years, before its growth rate converges to its long-run, steady-state rate.

Export-led growth has also created structural problems that have to be overcome for more balanced growth. The most significant problems are high savings and a persistent current account surplus. Despite China's low income level, it has been exporting its savings to much richer countries. The slow growth of domestic consumption and its declining share in gross domestic product (GDP) are related to this problem. This can be attributed mostly to the slower growth of household income relative to the growth of GDP. The other side of the story is the faster growth of corporate income and government revenue. Enterprises have reinvested most of their profits, and the government has spent a large portion of its revenue on capital formation. As a result, China is still an investment-driven economy.

The fundamental cause of these imbalance problems can be traced to China's double transition. Because of the double transition, wage rates are suppressed and the benefits coming from the growth of trade have mostly accrued to capital returns and government taxes. As a result, the share of labour income has declined and this, in turn, has caused the share of consumption in GDP to decline. This then has led to the increasing share of national savings in GDP. Because of the diminishing marginal return to capital, the growth of investment cannot catch up with the growth of savings, consequently the current account keeps increasing.

This chapter has three strands. First, it provides a review of China's export-led growth and its links with China's double transition. Second, it discusses the sustainability of China's export-led growth in the next 20 years. Third, it analyzes the structural problems created by export-led growth and shows how those problems are linked to China's double transition.

EXPORTS AND ECONOMIC GROWTH IN CHINA

China began its export-led growth in the mid 1980s, inspired by the successes of its East Asian neighbours. In the 1980s, two theories had facilitated the adoption of the export-led growth model. One was the gradient theory (Xia 1982). A version of the 'Flying Geese' model, the gradient theory divides China into three regions – eastern, central, and western – which are assigned different levels of priority of development. According to the theory, the eastern (coastal) region should start economic development first, followed by the central region, then the western region. This theory was written into the government's Seventh Five-Year Plan, for the period 1986–90 (State Council 1986). As a piece of evidence for its impact on government policy, the share of the central government's investment in the coastal region increased from 39.5 per cent in the period 1953–78 to 53.5 per cent in the period 1979–91 (Yao 2008). The other theory was the theory of the 'Great International Circulation' (Wang 1988), which set processing trade as China's long-term strategy of economic development. Processing trade had already started in Guangdong province by the mid 1980s. This theory was dramatic because it elevated processing trade to a national strategy.

Figure 3.1 presents China's volumes of trade between 1978 and 2008. A turning point – 2001 – can be clearly identified in the figure. China joined the WTO in 2001, so it is not surprising to find that it became a watershed for China's foreign trade. From 2001 onward, exports grew 27.3 per cent per annum and imports grew 24.8 per cent per annum. This gap has generated China's current account surplus, especially since 2004. The rapid growth of trade has substantially increased China's trade dependency; total trade volume as a share of GDP has reached 65 per cent, and exports as a share of GDP have grown to 35 per cent. Figure 3.2 presents the share of exports in GDP for the period 1978–2008. The turning point in 2001 seen in Figure 3.1 is also apparent in Figure 3.2.

It is widely recognized that China's exports rely heavily on processing trade. This is evident in Figure 3.3, which presents the shares of processing trade in total trade. The peak was reached at the end of the 1990s, when processing trade accounted for almost 60 per cent of China's total trade. Since then the shares of processing trade in both exports and imports have declined. Now the shares of processing in China's exports and imports are, respectively, about 50 per cent and about 30 per cent. It is noteworthy that processing trade, by definition, creates trade surplus. Indeed, China's trade surplus has been almost entirely created by processing trade since the early 1990s. Figure 3.4 shows China's surplus in processing trade and all trade. In most years before 2007, the processing trade surplus was larger than all trade surpluses, implying that regular trade incurred deficits. In the period between 2001 and 2005, when China's trade surplus surged, the processing trade surplus was much higher than the total trade surplus, more than double the latter in 2003 and 2004. Although China's domestic firms are engaged in processing trade, foreign firms are more significant players. For example, Apple's suppliers (most noticeably the Taiwanese electronics company Foxconn) alone created a US$1.9 billion surplus for China in 2007 (Xing 2010). Labour is the most important input in processing trade production; foreign companies engage in processing trade in China to exploit the low costs offered by China's abundant labour supply.

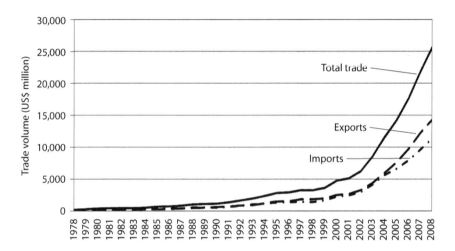

Figure 3.1 China's trade volumes, 1978–2008. Source: NBS (2009a).

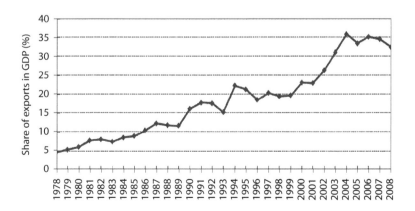

Figure 3.2 The share of exports in China's GDP, 1978–2008. Source: NBS (2009a).

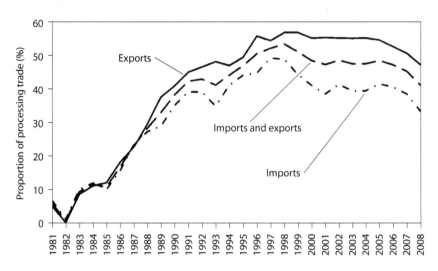

Figure 3.3 The shares of processing trade in China's total trade, 1981–2008. Source: NBS (2009a).

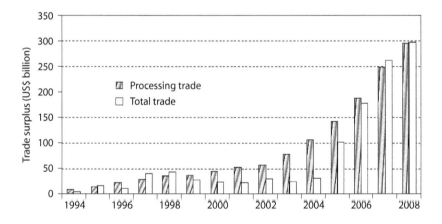

Figure 3.4 Trade surplus in China. Source: Xing (2010).

Consistent with Figure 3.3, the total trade surplus has been catching up with the processing trade surplus in recent years and became larger than it in 2007 and 2008. The declining share of processing trade, however, has not resulted in a declining total trade surplus, because the processing trade surplus has been increasing.

The contribution of exports to China's economic growth is significant. Net exports accounted for 6–12 per cent of China's GDP between 2002 and 2008; the overall contribution of exports to GDP is higher because of backward and forward linkages. Studies have found that the overall contribution of exports to GDP ranges from 11 per cent to 19 per cent depending on the method of measurement used (Lin and Li 2002; Li 2003; Shen and Wu 2003; Lu and Xu 2005; Fan *et al.* 2005).[3] Using the mid-point of these estimates, i.e. 15 per cent, we reach the conclusion that the contribution of exports to China's GDP growth between 2002 and 2008 was 4.1 percentage points (15 per cent × 27.3 per cent). Because China's GDP grew by an average of 10 per cent per annum in that period, the contribution of exports to China's GDP growth was 41 per cent. Exports grew by 42 per cent in the first half of 2010. This means that their contribution to GDP growth would reach 6.3 percentage points if this rate of growth were sustained for the whole year.

THE DOUBLE TRANSITION AND EXPORT-LED GROWTH

The growth of China's trade since joining the WTO can only be described as extraordinary. What are the factors that led to the growth? The prevailing view in the policy circle of the USA, the country with half of its trade deficit coming from China, seems to suggest that the undervalued yuan is the most important cause (PIIE 2010). This view is based on two related premises: the yuan is severely undervalued, and its appreciation will reduce Sino–American trade imbalances. Although some studies (e.g. PIIE 2010) find that the yuan is undervalued by 20 per cent or more, other studies find more moderate figures. For example, Wang and Yao (2008, 2009), whose results will be introduced later in this section, take structural change as a factor weakening the Balassa–Samuelson effect and find that the yuan was undervalued by only about 6 per cent in May 2008. As for the effects of the yuan's appreciation, there are surprisingly few quantitative studies. One recent study by Li *et al.* (2011) calculates, in the framework of a cross-country computable general equilibrium (CGE) model, the effects of the yuan's appreciation by 5, 10 and 20 per cent against the US dollar. They find that a moderate appreciation of 5 or 10 per cent would actually increase China's trade surplus because of the low substitution between American and Chinese exports. A large appreciation of 20 per cent would have significantly negative effects on the Chinese economy – for example, employment would drop by 3.03 per cent and GDP by 3.18 per cent, but would have negligible effects on the American economy – for example, both employment and GDP would increase by only 0.16 per cent.

Although the exchange rate is an important parameter determining international trade, focusing only on the exchange rate prevents us from studying more-fundamental forces that determine the international division of labour. In the case of China, the double transition is one such force.

Key features of the double transition

The double transition refers to two profound transformations happening in China. One is its fast pace of industrialization and the accompanying rural–urban migration; the other is the extraordinary demographic transition since China implemented the one-child policy in 1979.

In the 1980s, industrialization was mostly carried out by the indigenous township and village enterprises scattered in the coastal region and urban peripherals in inland provinces. In later years, industrialization has been driven mostly by exports. The coast has intrinsic locational advantages over the inland, resulting in 90 per cent of China's exports coming from the nine coastal provinces and cities (Tong 2008). The export industries on the coast draw large labour migration from the inland provinces. Figure 3.5 shows the number of migrant workers between 1993 and 2009. The number of migrant workers increased in the early 1990s until the Asian financial crisis brought a large setback in 1997. The growth of migration has been phenomenal since 1997. By 2008, the number reached 130 million. Despite this large-scale migration, however, the countryside still has a labour force of 468 million, 45 per cent of the national total. As agriculture accounts for only 11 per cent of the national GDP, the low agricultural wage inevitably restrains the wage rates of migrant workers from rising.

The one-child policy is estimated by the Chinese authorities to have avoided 400 million births in the past 40 years (NBS 2009b). Although the figure can be debated, it is evident that population growth has slowed in China. One of the consequences has been the drastic increase of the working-age ratio in China. Figure 3.6, from Bloom *et al.* (2007), compares the working-age (or dependency) ratios in different regions in the world. In the figure, the line of East Asia reflects the trend of China because the Chinese population accounts for nearly 90 per cent of the East Asian total. Compared with other regions, especially South Asia, which is the second-most populous region in the world, China's demographic transition has two distinctive

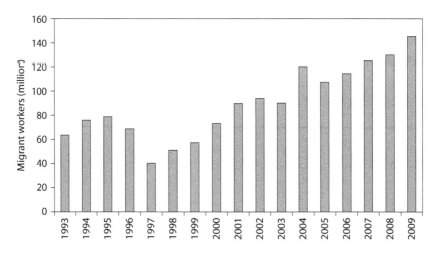

Figure 3.5 Rural–urban migration, 1993–2009. Source: MHRSS (2009). Note: The figures are for the number of migrant workers at the year end.

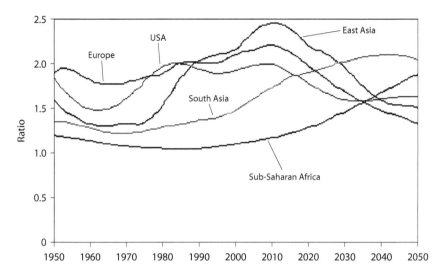

Figure 3.6 Working-age ratios in the world. Source: Bloom *et al.* (2007).

features: one is that it is very abrupt, and the other is that the working-age ratio reaches very high levels. Both features are results of China's one-child policy. Because the birth rate has declined sharply, the young-age dependency ratio has dropped quickly. On the other hand, the old-age dependency ratio is not immediately increasing. Thus, the result is a fast increase of the working-age ratio. However, this is for only a short period because the old-age dependency ratio increases quickly as people born in the 1940s and 1950s age. In fact, 2010 is the turning point beyond which China's working-age ratio will decline, and come back to the 1980 level by 2040. Compared with South Asia, this is a compressed demographic transition.

The double transition and China's export-led growth

The double transition has determined China's extraordinary growth model, especially since China joined the WTO. The double transition has given China vast comparative advantage in labour resources, and the accession to the WTO has allowed China to fully utilize this advantage. Figure 3.7, from Schrader (2010), compares China's manufacturing wage rates with other East Asian economies. Clearly, China has the cheapest labour force among the economies shown in the figure. However, the Chinese labour force is relatively well trained. China is catching up with the world average in terms of educational attainment although its per-capita income is ranked 110th in the world (UNDP 2009). In response, East Asia manufacturing has gone through a reconfiguration led by China. China has become the assembly centre and the surrounding countries the suppliers of materials and intermediate goods.

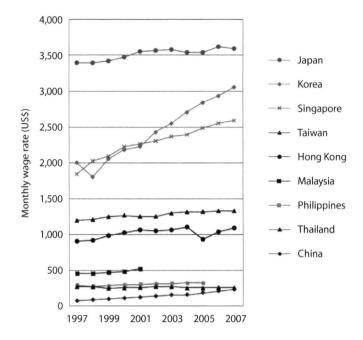

Figure 3.7 Monthly manufacturing wage rates in East Asian economies (2007 US$).
       Source: Schrader (2010).

Trade-flow data clearly show that China has become the engine of exports in East Asia, replacing the United States and Japan. Table 3.1, from Li and Song (2006), compares the shares of ASEAN exports going to China, the United States and Japan in the 1990–2003 period. Although China lagged behind the United States for the whole period, there was a clear trend that China was replacing the United States and becoming the most significant destination for ASEAN exports. Between 1990 and 1995, China's demand accounted for only 8.27 per cent of ASEAN's total exports; between 2000 and 2003, the figure grew to one-third.

Figure 3.8 presents the integration of the Chinese economy with its two most important regional trade partners, Japan and Korea. Japan's exports

Table 3.1 Demand shares (%) of China, USA and Japan for ASEAN exports

	China	*US*	*Japan*
1990–2003	16.15	19.15	4.60
1990–1995	8.27	14.48	7.36
1996–2000	15.92	33.17	4.22
2001–2003	32.85	5.01	0.44

Source: Li and Song (2006).

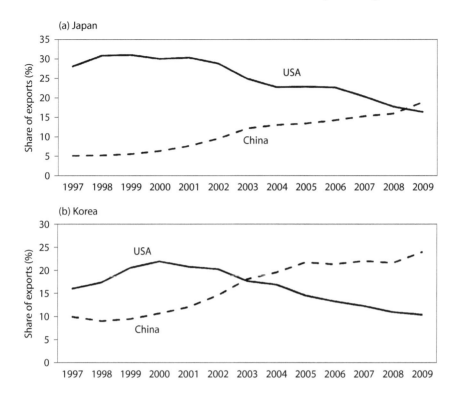

Figure 3.8 Shares of (a) Japan and (b) Korea's exports to China and the USA (%).
Source: Author's calculation based on COMTRADE data.

to the United States declined from more than 30 per cent of its total exports at the end of the 1990s to 17 per cent in 2009. In the meantime, its exports to China increased from just 5 per cent in 1997 to 19 per cent in 2009. The change seen with Korea's exports has been no less dramatic. In the mid 1990s, no more than 10 per cent of its exports went to China; in 2009, the figure was close to 25 per cent. In contrast, its share of exports to the United States declined from 22 per cent (the highest since 1997) in 2000 to 10 per cent in 2009. Both countries run a surplus with China. In fact, China runs trade deficits with most economies in East and Southeast Asia (Xing 2010), and its largest surplus comes from North America and Europe.

One recent study allows us to gauge the contribution of demographic dividends to China's exports. Using panel data of world trade flows for 192 countries, Tian *et al.* (2010) incorporate the working-age ratio in the traditional gravity equation and find for the period 1962–98 that the working-age ratio has strong predictive power for bilateral trade. Applying the most conservative estimate to China, it is found that demographic transition contributed to 12.6 per cent of the country's growth of exports between 1976 and 2006. In addition, China's exports today would have been about 30 per cent lower if China had followed India's path of demographic transition during the past 30 years. This shows the effect of family planning in China.

The role of the Balassa–Samuelson effect

China's extraordinary growth of exports and accumulation of official foreign reserves, standing at US$2.5 trillion by the end of October 2010, would have led to the real appreciation of the yuan and eroded China's export advantages created by the double transition. One of the driving forces is the Balassa–Samuelson effect (the B–S effect), which states that a country's currency will experience real appreciation if its tradable sector has higher rates of technological progress than its non-tradable sector, relative to other countries. In China, the labour productivity of the manufacturing sector (which produces tradable goods) has increased 12-fold since the early 1990s, whereas the labour productivity of the service sector (which produces non-tradable goods) has increased only four-fold in the same period (Lu and Liu 2007). This shows that China's growth has been largely driven by the tradable sector. In addition, the differential of productivity growth between the tradable and non-tradable sectors is much larger than in other countries, so one naturally expects that the yuan would experience real appreciation. Figure 3.9 presents two series of data. One is China's per-capita GDP relative to that of the United States, and the other is the real exchange rate between the Chinese yuan and the US dollar, both for the period 1994–2009 and taking 1994 as 100. The year 1994 is chosen as the starting year because China unified the dual exchange rates in that year. Per-capita GDP is highly correlated with a country's labour productivity in the tradable sector, so the series of per-capita GDP indicates the catch-up of

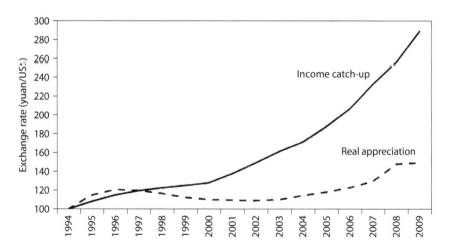

Figure 3.9 Income catch-up and the yuan's real appreciation. Source: Author's calculation based on data from the EIU database.

the labour productivity of China's tradable sector relative to the labour productivity of the US tradable sector. The B–S effect then predicts this series should be positively correlated with the series of real exchange rates. This is indeed what is shown in the figure, although the correlation coefficient is small: if China's relative per-capita income increased by 1 per cent, the yuan would have a real appreciation of 0.26 per cent. Indeed, there was real devaluation in the period 1996–2002, although income catch-up was robust in that period.

The weak evidence of the B–S effect deserves an explanation. One explanation is that the yuan was grossly overvalued in the planning period and there was a period of devaluation in the 1980s and early 1990s (Lu 2010). Wang and Yao (2009) provide an explanation based on structural change. There are two channels for the B–S effect to happen. One is nominal appreciation, and the other is the increase of prices of non-tradable goods. For most of the time since 1994, China has adopted a crawling peg to the dollar, so the role of the first channel has been limited. The function of the second channel is through the wage rate. Productivity growth in the tradable sector requires that labour be paid more in that sector. This will put upward pressures on the wage rate in the non-tradable sector because of free movement of labour. Although the prices of tradable goods will not change because they are determined in the international market, the prices of non-tradable goods will increase in response to higher wages. Structural change brings labour out of agriculture and suppresses wage growth, however, so it weakens price growth in the non-tradable sector.

Wang and Yao (2009) study China in a panel dataset of 185 countries and regions for the period 1960–2004. The share of rural population is used as the proxy for the stage of structural change. A higher share of the rural population indicates that a country is in an earlier stage of structural change, and the wage rate increases more slowly when the productivity of the tradable sector increases relative to other countries. Then the following equation is estimated:

$$\ln rer_{i,t} = \alpha_1 + \beta_1 \ln ry_{i,t} + \beta_2(rural_{i,t} \times \ln ry_{i,t}) + \lambda Z_{i,t} + \gamma Year + u_{i,t} \tag{1}$$

where $rer_{i,t}$ is the real exchange rate of country i's currency with respect to the US dollar in year t, $ry_{i,t}$ is the ratio between country i's per-capita income and the US per-capita income in year t, $rural_{i,t}$ is the percentage share of rural population of country i in year t, $Z_{i,t}$ is a set of control variables, $Year$ is a set of year dummies, $u_{i,t}$ is an error term, and the Greek letters are parameters to be estimated. Following the literature, the relative income $ry_{i,t}$ capture a country's relative labour productivity in the tradable sector. We then expect β_1 to be positive. The parameter of interest is β_2, which measures the dampening effect of structural change on the B–S effect and thus is expected to be negative. Table 3.2 presents the key results for the full sample of 185 economies and for four income groups. It is shown that β_1 is positive in all samples and statistically significant in all but the high-income group. In the full sample, β_1 is estimated to be 0.7477, meaning that a one per cent income catch-up would induce a real appreciation of about 0.75 per cent. This is much larger than the elasticity found for China in Figure 3.9.

China's low elasticity can be explained by its early stage of structural change. Table 3.2 shows that β_2 is negative and statistically significant in all but the high-income group. In the high-income group, β_2 is significantly positive. In high-income countries, urbanization has finished and there is a process of suburbanization. This may explain the unusual results found for this group of countries. The results for the other income groups indicate that the strength of the B–S effect is related to the stage of structural change. China is a lower middle-income country and its average share of rural population between 1994 and 2009 was 62.5 per cent. According to the results for lower middle-income countries, therefore, the B–S effect for China in the period 1994–2009 is 0.27, almost exactly the elasticity obtained from Figure 3.9.

Long-term perspectives of export-led growth in China

As the sustainability of China's export-led growth depends on the pace of China's double transition, two questions are relevant: (1) When will China deplete its demographic dividend? and (2) Has China already passed the so-called Lewis turning point?

There is not much disagreement on the first issue because demographic transition can be almost perfectly predicted with current data on birth and death rates. It is clear in Figure 3.6 that the working-age ratio in East Asia as a whole will decline from 2010, but until 2025 it will not be below 2, the cut-off point for demographic dividends. China should do better

Table 3.2 Structural change and the Balassa–Samuelson effect

	Full sample	High-income countries	Higher middle-income countries	Lower middle-income countries	Low-income countries
ln $ry_{i,t}$	0.7477	0.0249	0.5204	0.5217	0.9773
	(0.0341)	(0.0670)	(0.0585)	(0.0767)	(0.0590)
$rural_{i,t} \times$ ln $ry_{i,t}$	−0.0090	0.0105	−0.0046	−0.0040	−0.0122
	(0.0006)	(0.0025)	(0.0009)	(0.0012)	(0.0010)
No. Countries	185	36	33	55	61
No. Obs.	4,104	884	715	1,160	1,345
Adjusted R^2	0.75	0.73	0.61	0.61	0.58

Source: Wang and Yao (2009).

Note: Standard errors are reported in parentheses.

than this because Japan is already on the fast track of ageing. Figure 3.10 presents a prediction for China by Cai and Wang (2005). Although ageing will be a serious problem by 2040 (the share of people over 60 years old will reach one fourth of the total population) and old-age dependency will rise fast in the coming decades, the overall dependency ratio will increase to above 0.5 (or the working-age ratio will decline below 2) only after 2030. Therefore, it is safe to conclude that China would enjoy demographic dividends for another 15 to 20 years even if the one-child policy is not changed soon.

There have been vigorous debates on the second issue related to the Lewis turning point, however. In his seminal paper, Lewis (1954) proposed the notion of 'surplus labour', namely labour that does not contribute marginally to agricultural production. When a country has surplus labour in agriculture, its industry can expand at a constant and low wage rate. The Lewis turning point refers to the point beyond which a developing country has depleted its surplus labour, and its industry has to face rising wage rates. Some scholars believe that China has passed (or is close to passing) the Lewis turning point because the wage rates of migrant workers have been increasing rapidly in recent years (Garnaut and Huang 2006; Cai 2008). This view, however, has been challenged by several other studies.

Knight *et al.* (2010) find in their multiple-year surveys that migrant wage rates did not rise fast until 2009. Table 3.3 presents their data. Between 2004 and 2008, migrant workers' monthly wages increased by an average annual rate of only 4.6 per cent, which was not only lower than the growth rate of urban wages, but also lower than the growth rate of rural income (Figure 3.11). Migrant workers' wages only increased drastically in 2009.

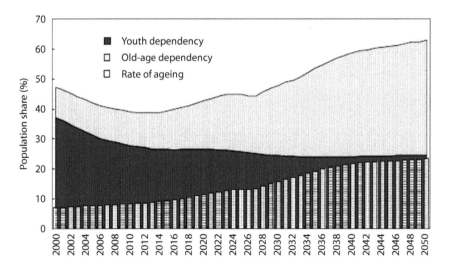

Figure 3.10 Prediction of dependency and ageing in China. Source: Cai and Wang (2005).

Table 3.3 Monthly wages of migrant workers, 2003–09

	Nominal wage (yuan)	Nominal wage growth (%)	Real wage growth (%)
2003	781		
2004	802	2.8	–1.1
2005	855	6.5	4.7
2006	933	11.5	10.0
2007	1,060	11.2	6.4
2008	1,156	9.1	3.2
2009	1,348	16.6	17.3

Source: Knight *et al.* (2010).

This trend seems to have continued in the first half of 2010, symbolized by a 30 per cent wage increase at Foxconn after a series of suicides in the company's Shenzhen factory, and a 20 per cent wage increase at a Honda parts supplier after a workers strike against the company. However, even if the wage increases were real and sustainable, they may not be taken as decisive evidence that China has passed the Lewis turning point. The reason is that wage increases may be a result of the increase in migrant workers' reservation wages (or in Lewis' words, the institutional wage), rather than a result of permanent outward shifts of industrial demand.

Migrant workers' reservation wages are determined by their income in the countryside. As Figure 3.11 shows, rural net income has been rising fast since 2004. This growth has been driven by two factors. The first factor is the changes in government policies. Agricultural taxes were abolished in 2006,

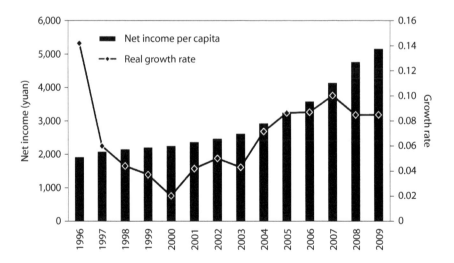

Figure 3.11 Rural monthly net income and its real growth, 1996–2009.
Source: NBS website at http://www.stats.gov.cn.

Table 3.4 CPI and growth of food prices, 2004–09 (%)

	CPI	Growth of food prices	Food prices growth > CPI
2004	3.9	9.9	6.0
2005	1.8	2.9	1.1
2006	1.5	2.3	0.8
2007	4.8	12.3	7.5
2008	5.9	14.3	8.4
2009	−0.7	0.7	1.4

Source: NBS website at http://www.stats.gov.cn.

returning about 100 yuan per annum to each rural resident. In addition, the central government provides direct subsidies for grain production, whereby an average farm household can get 700 yuan per annum. These two policies have raised the level of farm income, but have only a one-time growth effect.

The second factor is related to unbalanced inflation and is more important in raising the growth rate of rural income. Since the early 1990s, China's inflation has been led by the growth of food prices. Table 3.4 compares the consumer price index (CPI) and the growth of food prices between 2004 and 2009. The last column presents the gap between the CPI and the growth of food prices. It is evident that food prices have increased much faster than the overall CPI in most of the years. It is reasonable to believe that this gap has contributed significantly to the real growth of rural income, although not all of it goes to farmers.

My identification of the rise of migrant workers' reservation wages as the cause for the rise in migrant wages has been confirmed by a study by Yao and Zhang (2010). They use province-level data to estimate the demand and supply curves for migrant workers for each year between 1998 and 2007. Their demand curve is of the conventional form:

$$\ln L^1_i = c + \gamma_1 w_1 + \gamma_2 GDP_i + \gamma_3 P_i + e_i \qquad (2)$$

where L^1_i is the number of migrant workers in province i, GDP_i is the per-capita GDP in province i, P_i is its population, e_i is an error term, and the Greek letters and c are parameters to be estimated. Per-capita GDP is added to control the level of income, which could raise the industrial wage; the size of population is meant to control the market size in a province, that may raise the demand for industrial labour. The supply curve contains a portion of completely elastic supply, as suggested by Lewis's theory of surplus labour. Specifically, let A_i be the per-capita net income in the countryside of province i, then the institutional wage, w_i^*, sustaining the unlimited supply of labour, is estimated by the following equation:

$$w_i^* = \alpha_1 + \beta_1 A_i + u_{1i} \qquad (3)$$

where α_1 and β_1 are parameters to be estimated and u_{1i} is the error term. Let w_i be the wage rate of migrant workers. Their labour supply curve then consists of two parts:

$$w_i = w_i^*, \text{ if } w_i < w_i^* \tag{4}$$

and

$$w_i = \alpha_2 + \beta_2 \ln L^1_i + \beta_3 \ln PR_i + u_{2i}, \text{ if } w_i \geq w_i^* \tag{5}$$

In equation (5), PR_i is the rural population in province i, α_1, β_2 and β_3 are parameters to be estimated, and u_{2i} is the error term.

Equation (2) can be estimated with ordinary least squares. Equations (3)–(5) constitute an endogenous switching regression model and can be estimated by the maximum likelihood method. Figure 3.12 presents the demand and supply curves for 1998, 2002, 2005 and 2007. The demand curve is shifting out through the years, consistent with China's industrial expansion. The supply curve moves upward, suggesting that migrant workers' reservation wages are increasing. The key message from the figure is that the cross of the demand and supply curves has always been at the flat portion of the supply curve – indicating that China has never passed the turning point. In fact, there are larger labour surpluses in more-recent years. This seemingly puzzling result is consistent with the trend of

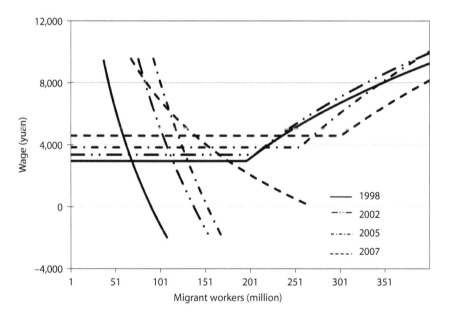

Figure 3.12 Demand and supply of migrant workers, 1998, 2002, 2005 and 2007.
Source: Yao and Zhang (2010).

technological change in Chinese agriculture, which substitutes machinery for manpower.

Yao and Zhang's (2010) study does not tell us when surplus labour will be depleted in China. The study by Knight *et al.* (2010) allows us to gauge an answer for this question. Based on a probit estimation for migration using individual data, Knight *et al.* (2010) find that there were 80 million potential migrant workers who had not migrated in 2007. In the period 1998–2009, the number of migrant workers increased, on average, by 8.7 million each year. This means that it would take 9.2 years to absorb these potential migrant workers if that speed were maintained. It should be noted, however, that urbanization will not be finished in China even if the surplus labour is depleted. In the past 30 years, China's urbanization rate has been increasing by an average of one percentage point each year. As the current urbanization rate is only 46 per cent, it will therefore take a long time for urbanization to reach a steady state in China.

In summary, the double transition will likely last for another 15–20 years in China. During this period, China will continue its export-led growth and will likely sustain high economic growth rates. This will allow China to become, by the early 2030s, the largest economy in the world at today's prices. At nominal prices, the date will be much earlier, possibly in the early 2020s.[4]

STRUCTURAL PROBLEMS OF CHINA'S EXPORT-LED GROWTH

Export-led growth has brought serious structural imbalance problems to China. The two most noticeable problems are (1) the share of consumption has declined sharply in the last decade, and (2) there are persistently underutilized savings. Figure 3.13 presents the expenditure components of Chinese GDP from 1978 to 2008, and it shows that the share of consumption has been in overall decline since 1978. Much of the early decline can be explained by faster income growth. However, the sharp decline after 2000 cannot be easily explained by income growth. In the past several years, consumption dropped to less than 50 per cent of GDP. The other side of the story is that savings increased to more than 50 per cent of GDP. The trouble is China cannot absorb this huge savings by domestic investment. Standing at more than 40 per cent of GDP, domestic investment still falls short of savings, leaving about 10 per cent of GDP as net savings in the form of the current account surplus, most of which is net exports.

Why is China saving so much? One explanation is that Chinese people save because of a saving culture, the lack of social security, and uncertainty about the future. Although those factors do contribute to a high residential savings rate, it is crucial to realize that the share of household savings in national savings declined dramatically from 56 per cent to 43 per cent between 1992 and 2007 (Figure 3.14). In contrast, the share of corporate savings increased from

29 per cent to 36 per cent, and the share of government savings increased from 15 per cent to 21 per cent in the same period.[5] It is a research challenge to find an explanation for those two opposite trends.

Although other factors, especially distortionary government policies, have contributed to the imbalance problem.[6] My opinion is that China's double transition has been the fundamental force driving the declining share of consumption in GDP, and the declining share of household savings in national savings. It is also the fundamental force for increasing shares of net savings. I now provide a narrative model and some evidence for these claims.

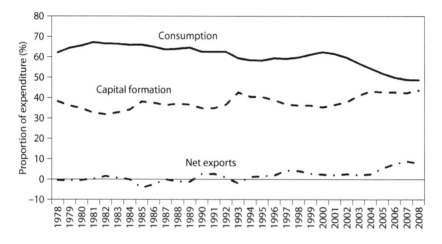

Figure 3.13 GDP expenditures, 1978–2008. Source: NBS website at http://www.stats. gov.cn.

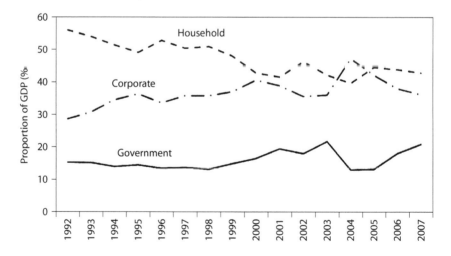

Figure 3.14 Components of national savings as shares of GDP, 1992–2007. Source: NBS (2009b).

The double transition generates China's low wage rates (Figure 3.7) and gives China comparative advantage in exporting labour-intensive products. In particular, China becomes a major site for processing trade production in which labour is the single most significant domestic input. Facing slowly growing wage rates, income generated by the expansion of exports accrues disproportionately to corporations. Capital becomes cheaper, and corporations invest more. As a result, labour productivity increases. Because wage rates do not increase at the same pace, the share of labour income in GDP declines. And because labour income is the major component of household income, and corporations reinvest most of their profits, the share of consumption in GDP declines. The other side of the coin is the increasing share of savings in GDP. However, because household income as a share of GDP has declined, and the average propensity of household savings does not change very much, the share of household savings in national savings has declined. Lastly, because of the diminishing marginal return to capital, the rate of growth of corporate and government investment cannot keep up with the rate of growth of the national savings. As a result, the current account surplus increases.[7]

Between 1991 and 2009, labour productivity in the manufacturing sector grew by 12.3 per cent per annum (Lu 2010), but the wage rate grew by only 7.1 per cent per annum (Schrader 2010). The cumulative effect of this large gap cannot be underestimated. Indeed, it has led to a sharp decline of household income and drastic increases of corporate income and government revenue as shares of national income (Figure 3.15). Household income accounted for 67 per cent of national income in 1997, but for only 50 per cent in 2007.

A recent study by Xu and Yao (2010) links China's demographic transition to its current account surplus. They use panel data of OECD countries

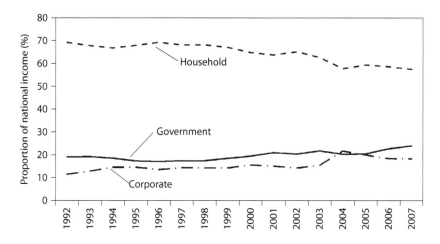

Figure 3.15 Distribution of national income. Source: Bai and Qian (2009).

to find that the age dependency ratio is a significant factor contributing to a country's current account surplus. When the age dependency ratio declines by 1 percentage point, the share of current account surplus in GDP increases 0.2 percentage points. Applying this result to a comparison between China and India, one finds that demographic dividends enable China to have a ratio of current account surplus in GDP 4.4 percentage points higher than India's.

In summary, China's imbalance problems have their roots in the double transition. Taking this view, one realizes that the imbalance problems will be eased gradually as China moves to finish the double transition in the next 15–20 years. This is a relatively long period, however. In between, the imbalance problems may lead to serious social and political unrest, disrupting China's growth trajectory.

CONCLUSION

Export-led growth has sustained high growth rates in China. The fast growth of exports is a result of the combination of China's double transition and its full integration into the world market system. Export-led growth will continue for another 10–15 years before China completes the double transition in demography and industrialization. Along the way, export-led growth has also created serious imbalance problems, especially a large quantity of savings with a large part of it being underutilized. The evidence reviewed in this chapter shows that, like export-led growth itself, the imbalance problems are rooted in China's double transition.

This last conclusion has a strong implication for the current debates on global imbalances. Although other factors (such as the exchange rate, distortion of factor prices, a weak financial sector and an investment-orientated government) also contribute to China's imbalance problems, the double transition is more fundamental than those factors. Because the double transition is an inevitable process, new thinking is required to deal with China's – and for that matter, the world's – imbalance problems. Two points are particularly worth mentioning here. First, focusing on nominal parameters such as the exchange rate will not solve the imbalance problems. Second, the purpose of structural adjustment should not be directed to eliminating imbalances, but should be geared towards how to utilize the savings created by the surplus countries. Furthermore, we will soon see other emerging countries, notably India, start exporting their savings when savings from China start drying up as it finishes its double transition.

NOTES

1 The author thanks the 2009 National Philosophy and Social Science major project 'Economic imbalances and medium-term solutions' for financial support. This chapter is based on the paper 'The relationship between China's export-led growth and its double transition of demographic change and industrialization', published in *Asian Economic Papers*, 10(2): 52–76 (2011).

2 China Center for Economic Research (CCER) and National School of Development (NSD), Peking University, No. 5, Yiheyuan Road, Beijing, 100871, China, yyao@ccer.pku.edu.cn

3 Methods based on the input–output table generally produce lower figures, and methods based on regressions generally produce higher figures.

4 The exact years of real and nominal income catch-up are 2032 and 2022, respectively. The estimation assumes that China grows by 7 per cent and the United States grows by 2 per cent in real terms, respectively. The estimation for nominal income catch-up also assumes that the inflation rates in the United States and China keep to their averages of the period 1981–2008, 3.5 per cent and 5.9 per cent, respectively, and the yuan appreciates by 2 per cent per annum against the dollar.

5 There was a redefinition of government income in 2004. This caused a sudden drop of government savings and a sudden increase of corporate savings in that year. Before that year, income coming from firms with government controlling shares was counted as wholly owned by the government; after that year, income has been counted as the shares held by the government.

6 For example, Woo (2008) attributed the failure of China's financial system to intermediate all of the growing savings into investments to the fear of the state monopoly banking system of future non-performing loans and its discrimination against domestic private enterprises.

7 Notice that our discussion does not rely on the life-cycle theory to make the linkage between the double transition and high savings rates in China. Although empirical evidence for the life-cycle theory is weak, here we emphasize the channel of abundant labour supply. That is, the double transition increases labour supply, so wage growth is suppressed, and the benefits of the expansion of trade accrue disproportionately to corporations and the government.

REFERENCES

Bai, Chong-En and Zhenjie Qian (2009) 'Who is squeezing out household income?' ['Shui Zai Jiya Jumin Shouru'], *Social Sciences in China* [*Zhongguo Shehui Kexue*], 30(5): 99–115.

Bloom, David, David Canning, Richard Mansfield and Michael Moore (2007) 'Demographic change, social security systems, and savings', *Journal of Monetary Economics*, 54(1): 92–114.

Cai, Fang (2008) *Lewis Turning Point: a Coming New Stage of China's Economic Development* [*Liuyisi Zhuanzhedian: Zhongguo Jingji Fazhan Xin Jieduan*], Beijing: Social Science Academic Press.

Cai, Fang and Dewen Wang (2005) 'Demographic transition: implications for growth', *Working Paper*, No. 47, Beijing: Institute of Population and Labor, CASS.

Fan, Bonai, Xiaotai Mao and ShuangWang (2005) 'On the contribution of export to economic growth: 1952–2003' ['Zhongguo Chukou Maoyi Dui Jingji Zengzhang Gongxianlu De Shizheng Yanjiu: 1952–2003'], *International Trade Journal [Guoji MaoyiWenti]*, 2005(8): 5–9.

Garnaut, Ross and Yiping Huang (2006) 'The turning point in China's economic development', in Ross Garnaut and Ligang Song (eds) *The Turning Point in China's Economic Development*, pp. 1–11, Canberra: Asia Pacific Press.

Knight, John, Quheng Deng and Shi Li (2010) 'The puzzle of migrant labour shortage and the rural labour surplus in China', *Department of Economics Working Paper Series*, No. 494, Oxford: University of Oxford.

Lewis, Arthur (1954) 'Economic development with unlimited supplies of labour', *The Manchester School of Economics and Statistics*, 22(2): 139–191.

Li, Jie (2003) 'An empirical study on export's contribution to GDP growth' ['Chukou Dui GDP Zengzhang De Shizheng Yanjiu'], *World Economy [Shijie Jingji]*, 2003(4): 31–34.

Li, Kunwang and Ligang Song (2006) 'China's trade expansion and its impact on the Asian Pacific economies', *China Economic Quarterly [Jingjixue Jikan]*, 5(2): 591–608.

Li, Xin, Zhi Wang and Dianqing Xu (2011) 'Impacts of RMB appreciation on China and the Unites States: a multi-country comparative general equilibrium model', *China & World Economy*, 19(2), 19–39.

Lin, Justin and Yongjun Li (2002) 'Export and economic growth in China: a demand-side analysis', *CCER Working Paper*, No. C2002008, Beijing: China Center for Economic Research, Peking University.

Lu, Feng (2010) 'Labor productivity and macroeconomic cycles in China', *China Economic Observer,* Beijing: National School of Development, Peking University.

Lu, Feng and Liu Liu (2007) 'Growth of the labor productivity in China's two sectors and an international comparison', *China Economic Quarterly*, 6(2): 357–380.

Lu, Huijuan and Xiaoping Xu (2005) 'Reexamining the impact of export on China's economic growth' ['Chukou Dui Zhongguo Jingji Zengzhang Yingxiang De Zaikaocha'], *Quantitative Economic Methods and Econometric Research [Shuliang Jingji Yu Jiliang Jingji]*, 2005(2): 136–142.

MHRSS (Ministry of Human Resources and Social Security) (2009) *Chinese Labor Statistical Yearbook*, Beijing: Statistical Press.

NBS (National Bureau of Statistics) (2009a) 'The financial flows table', in *China Statistical Yearbook*, Beijing: China Statistical Press.

— (2009b) *New China 60th Anniversary Report Series*, No. 5 [*Xin Zhongguo Chengli 60 Zhounian Xilie Baogao Zhiwu*], available at http://www.stats.gov.cn/tjfx/ ztfx/qzxzgcl60zn/t20090911_402586311.htm.

PIIE (Peterson Institute of International Economics) (2010) 'Renminbi undervaluation, China's surplus, and the US trade deficit', *Policy Brief*, Washington, DC: PIIE.

Schrader, Anke (2010) *Long-term Wage Trends in China*, New York: Conference Board.

Shen, Lisheng and Zhenyu Wu (2003) 'The contribution to economic growth from export in China: an empirical analysis based on the I–O table' ['Chukou Dui Zhongguo Jingji Zengzhang D Gongxian: Jiyu Touru-Chanchu Biao De Shizheng Fenxi'], *Economic Research [Jingji Yanjiu]*, 2003(11): 33–41.

State Council (1986) *The Seventh Five-year Plan for Economic and Social Development, The People's Republic of China* [*Zhonghua Renmin Gongheguo Jingji He Shehui Fazhan DiqigeWunian Jihua*], Beijing: Remin Press.

Tian, Wei, Yang Yao, Miaojie Yu and Yi Zhou (2010) 'Demography and export', *CCER Working Paper*, Beijing: China Center for Economic Research, Peking University.

Tong, Jiadong (2008) 'Foreign trade in China and its prospects', paper presented at 30 Years of Economic Development in China conference, 16–17 October, Ninbo, China.

United Nations Development Program (UNDP) (2009) *Human Development Report*, New York: UNDP.

Wang, Jian (1988) 'Choose the right long-term development strategy – a framework for "The Great International Circulation" economic development strategy', *Economic Daily*, 5 January 1988.

Wang, Zetian and Yang Yao (2008) 'An estimation of the equilibrium exchange rate of RMB' ['Renminbi Junheng Huilu Yanjiu'], *Journal of Financial Research* [*Jingrong Yanjiu*], 2008(12): 22–36.

—— (2009) 'Structural change and the Balassa–Samuelson effect' ['Jiegou Bianqian Yu Balassa–Samuelson Xiaoying'], *The Journal of World Economy* [*Shijie Jingji*], 2009(4): 38–49.

Woo, Wing Thye (2008) 'Understanding the sources of friction in US–China trade relations: the exchange rate debate diverts attention away from optimum adjustment', *Asian Economic Papers*, 7(3): 65–99.

Xia, Yulong (1982) 'The gradient theory and regional development' ['Tidu Lilun He Quyu Fazhan'], *Research and Advices* [*Yanjiu Yu Jianyi*], 1982(3): 3–5.

Xing, Yuqing (2010) 'Processing trade, exchange rates, and China's bilateral trade surpluses', paper presented at the Beijing Forum, 6 November, Beijing.

Xu, Jianwei and Yang Yao (2010) 'The new international division of labor, financial integration, and global imbalances' ['Guoji Fengong Xin Xingtai, Jinrong Shichang Fazhan Yu Quanqiu Shiheng'], *The Journal of World Economy* [*Shijie Jingji*], 2010(3): 1–30.

Yao, Yang (2008) 'The political economy of government policies toward regional inequality in China', in Yukon Huang and Alessandro Magnoli Bocchi (eds) *Reshaping Economic Geography in East Asia*, pp. 218–240. Washington, DC: World Bank.

Yao, Yang and Ke Zhang (2010) 'Has China passed the Lewis turning point?', *China Economic Journal*, 3(2): 155–162.

4 Understanding changing trends in Chinese wages

Cai Fang, Wang Meiyan and Du Yang[1]

INTRODUCTION

In 2010, Foxconn, the world biggest manufacturer of electronic products, took a lead in putting up wages. This was a one-off increase in remuneration by over 30 per cent, in part to offset social opprobrium arising from 12 cases of suicide among its employees. If this rate of wage growth was typical of the Chinese economy overall, then it would suggest that 2010 was a year of significant wage rises. But closely following the dynamics of migrant workers' wages, it is clear that this event is just a continuation of the trend in wage increases since 2003 – the year that witnessed the first labour shortage and thus a year of great significance in Chinese economic development.

In classical economic theory about the determinants of wage prices in developing economies, Arthur Lewis described a dual economy in which there is a large pool of surplus labour in agriculture (Lewis 1954). In this framework, the industrial sector can grow only by absorbing this surplus labour force. However, when the growth in labour demand in the urban industrial sector exceeds the growth in labour supply drawn from agriculture, the economy reaches its turning point – *the Lewis turning point*. At this point, firms can find suitable workers only by raising wages, despite the fact that a surplus in the *rural* labour force continues to exist.

The debate over whether China has arrived at its Lewis turning point is thus examined in the context of the broader implications of the changing trends of Chinese wages. This chapter discusses in-depth issues related to wage increases for ordinary workers, their root causes and their implications for decision-making for public policy and private business.

WAGE INCREASES AS A GENERAL TREND

Wages in China have long been trending upwards, especially since the late 1990s when there were mass redundancies and productivity was enhanced as a result. As shown in Figure 4.1, average and selected sectoral wages have been growing at above 8 per cent since the turn of the century, the fastest in the world by any measure. However, the data on wages in China are complicated. The values in Figure 4.1 reflect mainly the wage rates for formal employees and must therefore be treated with caution. Given that migrant workers, who mainly take informal jobs in non-agricultural sectors, make up one-third of urban employment, the increase in their wages deserves special examination.

Shortage of migrant workers

Even as urban local workers' wages began to rise sharply after 2003, the wage stagnation suffered by their migrant counterparts turned the corner only in 2004, when a migrant labour shortage appeared for the first time (Cai Fang *et al.* 2009). During 2003–08, the annual growth rate of migrant workers' wages was 10.3 per cent, a significant surge in comparison with the previous stagnation, and a phenomenon never before seen in the country's history. Although several studies argue that there has not yet been any meaningful increase in migrants' wages, the figures cited by the National Bureau of Statistics (NBS) are more authoritative and show a notable rise. Most importantly, disputing the actual increase in ordinary workers' wages cannot be justified when there is an obvious reaction to it by both domestic and international investors.

Many Chinese scholars and policy-makers find it difficult to accept that there is a widespread labour shortage in China, because the longstanding existence of surplus labour in agriculture has made itself not only a legacy but also conventional wisdom. But many major newspapers in China and abroad have reported a shortage of migrant workers; and the most recent source available dealing with the issue in detail is a survey conducted by the Chinese Manufacturers' Association of Hong Kong (CMA 2010). According

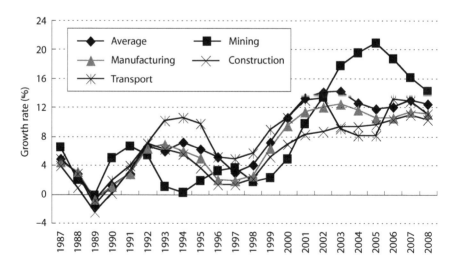

Figure 4.1 Growth rates (3-year smoothed) of wages in selected sectors. Source: National Bureau of Statistics and Ministry of Labour and Social Security, *China Labour Statistical Yearbook* (various years), China Statistics Press.

to this survey, which involved 222 enterprises in the Pearl River Delta region of southern China, 90 per cent of enterprises claimed they have had difficulty in recruiting adequate numbers of workers and that, on average, 21 per cent of jobs are vacant.

Taking a look at how enterprises, governments and workers respond to the labour shortage is informative. China is known for its developmental state model; that is, the local governments' duties are closely tied to firm performance (Oi 1999). When local firms have operational problems they complain to the local government. In response to wide complaints of labour shortages, the local governments react in various ways, such as establishing job agencies or signing contracts of labour dispatch with agencies in labour-supply regions.

Migrant workers (especially the new generation) also tend to change jobs frequently. In some enterprises the annual employee turnover rate is over 80 per cent. In one interview, a young migrant worker told a journalist he had changed jobs 40 times within the previous 4 years.

If the law of supply and demand applies to labour markets, then the logical result of the labour shortage is an increase in wages. In addition, as a more fundamental response to the wage increase in the Chinese coastal regions, there has been a tendency for industries and investments to shift to the Chinese central and western provinces and neighbouring countries (see Ruan Jianqing and Zhang Xiaobo 2010).

Increase in migrant workers' wages

When discussing the turning point of economic development characterized by wage rises, Lewis (1954) emphasized that it is only the increase in wages for *unskilled* workers that matters, since there is always scarcity of skilled workers at all stages of economic development. However, wages data for urban formal employees in China's statistics are so aggregated they are unable to reflect the status of unskilled workers; therefore, it is best to take migrant workers' wages as a proxy for those of unskilled workers.

Before 2001, there were no statistics distinguishing migrant workers' wages from urban workers' wages. When announcing a survey of migrant workers conducted in 2004, the commissioner of the NBS asserted that the migrant workers in the Pearl River Delta regions earned essentially the same wages as their predecessors had earned 20 years before. This was incorrect. In fact, at the time he made this comment to the media, the data showed that migrants' wages had already started to rise and that a migrant labour shortage was appearing in China for the first time. Figure 4.2 shows that not only have the wages in manufacturing and construction increased constantly – which reflects mainly the general trend of wages, since they do not specifically represent migrant workers' wages – but also that migrant workers' wages have been catching up.

Apart from the NBS source presented in Figure 4.2, there are other individual surveys and news reports that assert even higher levels of, and more

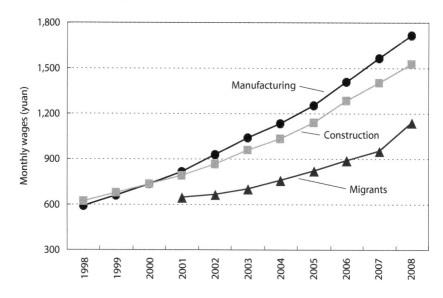

Figure 4.2 Migrant workers' wages are catching up with those of workers in the manufacturing and construction sectors. Sources: Wages of workers in manufacturing and construction are calculated according to data from National Bureau of Statistics and Ministry of Human Resources and Social Security, *China Labour Statistical Yearbook* (various years), China Statistics Press; wages of migrants are calculated according to data from National Bureau of Statistics, *China Yearbook of Rural Households Survey* (various years), China Statistics Press.

rapid increases in migrants' wages. For example, a survey conducted in early 2010 by the People's Bank of China, the central bank, shows that the average monthly wage of migrant workers was 1783.2 yuan in 2009 – a 17.8 per cent increase in real terms over the previous year (PBC–DSS 2010).

Comparing local and migrant workers' wages requires aligning of wage rates with working hours, because the two groups work in different ways. According to a survey conducted in 2010 (the China Urban Labor Survey or CULS),[2] migrant workers work 27 per cent more hours per week than urban local workers. Migrants have to work longer in order to get higher monthly wages. The same survey also shows that, while migrants earned only 88.2 per cent of the wages of local urban workers, their monthly wages were slightly higher (by 5.6 per cent) than those of urban workers, after adjusting for the difference between them in weekly working hours.

As the migrants' demographic characteristics change, the new-generation migrant workers tend to work fewer hours than their predecessors. CULS's results show that migrant workers worked nearly 12.4 hours less than their predecessors in 2005. That is, the growth of migrants' wages, and their convergence with urban locals' wages, implies a larger surge in actual wage rate (if measured by hourly wage rate).

FORCES SUPPORTING THE WAGE INCREASE

The rise in China's wages is not a regional and temporary phenomenon, but countrywide and persistent. The following factors explain how the increase in wages of ordinary workers, particularly migrants, will be sustained in the long run.

Demographic factors

As a result of demographic transition, change in the population's age structure has been reducing the growth of the labour force. Before China reaches its population peak of just over 1.4 billion around 2025, the growth of the working-age population is predicted to fall at an annual rate of 13.6 per cent in the period 2004–11 and to become zero around 2015 and negative afterwards (see Figure 4.3). After a short break during the 2009 financial crisis, the labour shortage, which first appeared in 2003, resurged in September 2009 and became widespread after the 2010 lunar new year. Given that the root cause of the labour shortage is demographic, wage increase will continue and is likely to accelerate.

Demographic characteristics also shape changes in wage trends. The rural-labour exodus that began in the 1980s with Chinese reform has evolved into a high tide of migration since the mid 1990s. Now a new generation of migrant workers has emerged. According to a NBS survey, migrant workers aged between 16 and 30 numbered nearly 90 million in 2009, accounting for 61.6 per cent of the total migrant workforce (NBS–DRS 2010). The

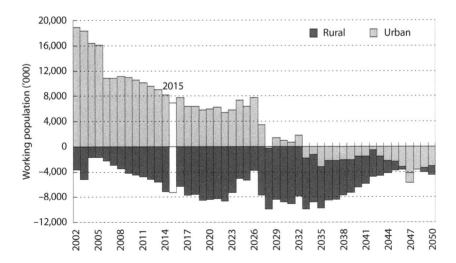

Figure 4.3 Predicted change in China's working-age population, 2002–50. Source: Based on Ying Hu (2009).

CULS results also show a dramatic alteration in the demography of migrant workers. Compared with their older counterparts, the younger generation of migrants has the following characteristics. First, they are better educated, with 42.3 per cent of 16–30-year-olds having graduated from senior high school or higher (college), compared with 25.3 per cent for those aged between 31 and 40, and 20.1 per cent for those between 41 and 50. Second, 13.1 per cent of 16–30-year-old migrant workers are single children – a product of the nationally implemented family-planning programme – whereas the proportion of those aged 31–40 is 3.3 per cent, and 2 per cent for those aged 41–50. Third, 32.8 per cent of the young migrants had actually lived in cities and towns before they reached the age of 16, whereas the percentage for the two older groups is 24.9 per cent and 25.3 per cent, respectively.

Such demographic factors may influence the regional pattern of migrants' wages. As previous studies indicate, rural labourers with more-advantageous demographic characteristics – that is, better educated and younger – are more likely to migrate, and tend to migrate farther from home for longer periods (Du Yang and Wang Meiyan 2010). In the near future, with the trends that witnessed labour-intensive industries transferring to inland provinces, and industrial upgrading taking place in the coastal provinces, the younger generation of migrants will work and live in the eastern regions while the older generation will be more likely to work near their home towns in the central and western regions. The spatial difference in migrant workers' wages will therefore remain, but be more a reflection of differentials in individual characteristics than of regional segmentation of the labour market.

Labour market institutions

Labour market institution building is accelerating, providing legitimate and institutional support for reasonable increases in wages (Cai Fang 2010). One example is the change in size and frequency of minimum wage adjustment (Du Yang and Wang Meiyan 2008). Municipal authorities have been increasing local wage levels more often since 2004. Helping drive this is the pressure from growing labour shortages and, for that matter, the central government's requirement that minimum wages be adjusted every second year. The number of cities adjusting their local minimum wage standards has increased, as has the size of each adjustment. During the 2009 financial crisis, no Chinese cities increased minimum wages, since the policy priority at the time was to stabilize employment. From 2010, when the Chinese economy had clearly recovered from the recession, a wide range of cities began to raise minimum wages again.

Moreover, the government began to strengthen the role of trade unions in protecting workers' rights and to introduce collective bargaining on working conditions and compensation. In response to workers' growing demands for higher pay and better protection in the labour market, the development of labour-market institutions will create a framework for a well-balanced growth of wages. As the Lewis turning point arrives, more job opportunities imply that ordinary workers have gained their right to vote with their feet. Borrowing Albert Hirschman's (1970) explanation of how, and under what conditions, people express their dissatisfaction in modern society, the case of China's labour market is like this: assured by obtaining rights to exit, workers increasingly tend to voice their dissatisfaction about pay, working conditions and other benefits in the workplace.

CHANGES IN WAGE DIFFERENTIALS

It is commonly agreed among economists that wage differentials are caused by differences between workers in their inherent human capital – education, health and skills – and by discrimination in the labour market. As in other developing countries and in the early stages of development of industrialized economies, the features of wage differentials in China have been driven by massive surplus labour in rural areas. There was no scarcity of unskilled labour before the Lewis turning point but, in contrast, there has been a shortage of skills everywhere and at all times, resulting in an ever-widening gap between the wages of unskilled and skilled workers as returns on human capital increase. On the other hand, the household registration (or *hukou*) system, by institutionally segmenting the labour market between rural and urban sectors, has effectively legitimized wage discrimination against migrant workers who work in cities without legal residency.

Since the Chinese economy reached its Lewis turning point in 2003, however, the demand for unskilled workers has become higher. This contrasts with demand for skilled workers, which remains unchanged. Widespread shortage of labour, particularly for migrant workers, has created disincentives for managers to continue discriminating against migrant workers in wages paid. Both circumstances tended to induce wages convergence between unskilled and skilled workers. This section provides evidence of wages convergence and draws implications for the wider Chinese economy.

Three major participants of the urban labour market

In coping with the shock brought about by the global financial crisis in 2008–09, the Chinese Government designated migrant workers, college graduates and urban workers as vulnerable groups needing special assistance. In 2009, 4.7 million new migrant workers entered the urban labour market, while there were 5.2 million college graduates and 3.8 million resident urban workers.

These three major participants represent differences in both human capital and in *hukou* status of the urban workforce, and those differences result in wage differentials between and within groups. While there are within-group wage differentials – for example, those between unskilled and skilled wages among migrant workers and resident urban workers, there are also differentials between groups – for example, those between migrant workers and resident workers and between ordinary workers and college graduates.

Since migrant workers are typically used as a proxy for relatively less-educated and less-protected workers in the urban labour market, changes in their wages can be compared with those of the other groups in order to see the trend in wages convergence. Within-group differentials of wages also deserve examination.

Regional differences in migrant workers' wages

There are three factors that influence the regional pattern of migrant workers' wages. First, the differences in economic development levels, employment opportunities and consumption price levels determine that the eastern provinces have higher wage rates for migrant workers. Second, labour-market integration, namely increasing labour mobility as institutional barriers are eliminated, tends to create conditions for wage convergence. Third, regional development policies influence regional disparities in migrants' wages. The centrally implemented strategy of 'going to the west' has allocated huge investments to the western regions that stimulate infrastructure construction and capital-intensive industries, and the transfer of manufacturing creates more jobs in the central regions. All those factors generate a convergence of wages.

These regional patterns and dynamics are reflected in Table 4.1. First, while the wages in the eastern regions have been the highest, the wage rates of the three regions have been converging. Second, by receiving the transferred investments from coastal regions, the central regions have gained more employment opportunities and thus had a faster rate of growth in wages than the eastern regions. Third, due to the faster and more capital-intensive growth in the western regions, the wage rates for migrant workers there have increased faster than in the eastern and central regions.

Table 4.1 Migrant workers' wages (yuan per month) by region

Year	East	Central	West
2003	760	570	560
2005	912	760	788
2006	981	821	869
2008	1,150	1,085	1,083
2009	1,221	1,159	1,183
Average annual growth rate (%) (2003–09)	8.22	12.55	13.27

Sources: Migrant workers' wages by year are from 'Monitoring survey reports on migrant workers', from the website of National Bureau of Statistics at http://www.stats.gov.cn/; the annual growth rate in migrant workers' wages was calculated by the authors.

Changes in wage differentials between migrants and others

Wages convergence between migrant and resident urban workers will first be considered. Comparing migrants' wages with average wages in manufacturing and construction (both sectors are absorbers of unskilled workers), the ratios of average wages of the two sectors to wages of migrant workers changed little in the period 2003–08. This does not show strong evidence of wages convergence, because the two sectors are also characterized by employment of unskilled workers. By utilising CULS data collected in five large Chinese cities, a clear-cut distinction between migrant and resident urban workers can be seen. The survey data show that the ratio of average wages of urban workers to wages of migrant workers dropped from 1.17 in 2005 to 1.08 in 2010.

A slightly more sophisticated statistical approach involves running a regression of wage determination in urban labour markets with mixed samples containing both migrant and resident urban workers to see how the factors determining wages have changed in recent years. The results of this show that, controlling for other factors, the effect of *hukou* status on wage differentials between migrants and urban residents reduced significantly. By simply holding non-urban *hukou* status, the average wage rate of migrant workers was 11 per cent lower than that of their resident urban counterparts in 2001, but the effect was reduced to 9 per cent in 2005 and 5 per cent in 2010 (Cai Fang and Du Yang 2011).

A more striking fact is the wages convergence between migrant workers and first-employed college graduates. In the period 2003–09, the annual growth rate in migrants' wage rates was 9.9 per cent and that of first-employed graduates 4.3 per cent, causing the wages of those two groups to converge: the ratio of graduates' to migrants' wages fell from 2.25 in 2003 to 1.65 in 2009 (Figure 4.4). Among the 145 million migrant workers outside their home townships in 2009, 89.6 per cent were graduates with senior high or lower levels of schooling. Therefore, the narrowing gap between their wages and those of college graduates indicates that, after the Lewis turning point, the effect of labour shortage on wage rates was greater than that of education.

Wages convergence within migrant worker groups

Migrant workers hold different educational attainments and thus their earnings differ in accordance with differential returns on schooling. Among them, 11.7 per cent are educated to elementary school level or are illiterate, 64.8 per cent are educated to junior high school level, 13.1 per cent are educated to senior high school level and 10.4 per cent have received higher education. The returns on those levels of education fell between 2001 and 2010. An econometric estimate based on surveys of migrant workers in five Chinese cities (CULS) showed that the wage differentials among workers caused by different education attainments contracted. Taking the return to

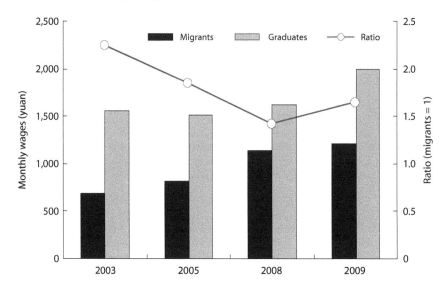

Figure 4.4 Wages convergence between migrants and graduates. Source: Migrants'
wages are from National Bureau of Statistics, *China Yearbook of Rural
Households Survey* (various years), China Statistics Press; graduates'
wages are from 'Surveys on employment situation of graduates', from
the website of Institute of Economics of Education, Peking University, at
http://iee.gse.pku.edu.cn/.

junior high school education as the reference, the relative return on higher
education (the extra return over that of junior high) fell from 80.4 per cent
in 2001 to 75.3 per cent in 2005 and 57.1 per cent in 2010, and the relative
return on senior high reduced from 25.9 per cent in 2001 to 17.3 per cent
in 2005 and 16.9 per cent in 2010.[3]

Thus, migrants' wages have converged since the Lewis turning point was
reached in 2003. Taking the Gini coefficient as a measurement of wage
differentials, the CULS data show that the Gini coefficient of migrants'
wages fell from 0.396 in 2001 to 0.334 in 2005 and 0.319 in 2010. Figure
4.5 shows that lower-paid migrants in earlier years (2001 or 2005) gained
faster growth in wage rates in the period 2001–05 to 2010, while those at
the higher end gained a relatively slower growth in wages.

THE RISE OF LABOUR COSTS AND FALL OF LABOUR
INPUTS IN AGRICULTURE

There are two concerns about the increase in ordinary workers' wages in
China. The first is whether the rise in wages is part of a long-term trend. If
it is caused by a changing labour supply and demand relationship following
the Lewis turning point, rather than by institutional barriers deterring labour

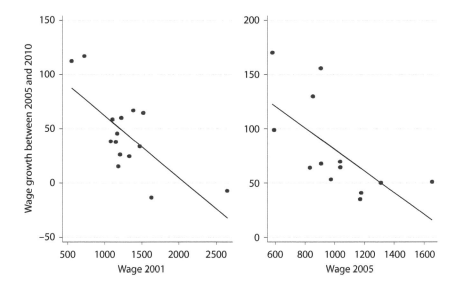

Figure 4.5 Wages of lower-end migrants grew faster. Source: calculated according to CULS (see Note 2).

mobility (or labour disputes), then wage rises will continue until the wages gap between the modern and traditional sectors vanishes. This is a process that may take some time. The second concern is whether such a wage rise will cause inflation. This is partially related to the first concern. If the labour shortage is a result of the Lewis turning point but labour productivity in agriculture can be enhanced, inflation will not occur. However, if the growth in the labour productivity of agriculture cannot offset the effect of the reduction of labour brought on by rising wages, there may be insufficient food production. The next sections examine those issues.

Rise of labour costs in agriculture

There are various arguments about the major causes of this labour shortage. It is hypothesized by some observers that, in addition to the Lewis turning point's arrival, some of the following factors may also be important in creating the labour shortage:

- the mismatch between skills demanded by enterprises and skills supplied by labourers;
- the existing institutional obstacles, such as the *hukou* system and spatial segmentation of the labour market; and
- government-implemented policies favourable towards agriculture that raise rural labourers' reservation wages and which drive a reluctance to work in non-agricultural sectors at the current wage rate.

While detailed empirical studies are required to respond to those arguments, in general they can be ruled out as being decisive factors if labour costs are increasing (and labour inputs are being reduced) in agriculture, which is where the surplus labour originates from.

First of all, the speed at which the wage rates of hired workers have grown in agriculture since 2003 should be considered. Before the late 1990s, when the labour force was usually in surplus, hired labour was rarely seen in the agricultural sectors. But as rural labourers migrated in mass to urban jobs, it became common to hire paid workers in agriculture. Therefore, the wages of hired agricultural workers can be considered an indicator of the degree of labour surplus. As is shown in Figure 4.6, the wage levels and dynamics of wages are clear-cut before and after 2003, the year of the Lewis turning point. Whereas there had been stagnation of wage rates in all farming sectors in the period 1998–2003, in the period 2003–08, their annual growth rates have gone up substantially – 15.1 per cent in grain production, 11.3 per cent in oilseed production, 21.4 per cent in pig farming with 50 pigs or more, 9.4 per cent in vegetable production and 11.7 per cent in cotton production (Figure 4.6). They have thus, in essence, kept pace with, if not exceeded, the increase in migrant workers' wages.

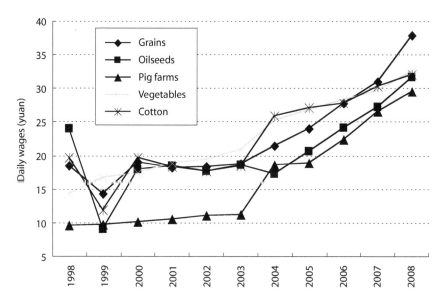

Figure 4.6 Hired workers' wage rates in agriculture subsectors. Source: Calculated according to data from National Development and Reform Commission, *Compilation of National Farm Product Cost–Benefit Data*, China Statistics Press; and National Bureau of Statistics, *China Statistical Yearbook*, China Statistics Press. Note: Grain refers to the average of rice, maize and wheat; oilseeds refers to the average of peanut and rapeseed; vegetables refers to the average of vegetables in medium- and large-size cities.

Second, the daily wages of a typical farm household labourer should be considered. This is a kind of shadow wage rate for the household labourer, as it takes into account the costs of living, labour market wage rates and the opportunity costs of household labourers engaged in farming. The growth of such a wage indicator has closely followed the path of that for hired workers' wages. After stagnation in the period 1998–2003, wages increased dramatically, with an annual growth rate of 9.5 per cent (Wang Meiyan 2010).

The basic idea of the Lewis turning point is that labour surplus falls as a result of mass labour migration from the rural to urban sectors, and the wages of ordinary workers increase constantly. As rational producers, farmers would respond to the changes by altering their input strategy.

Reduction of labour input in agriculture

As labour costs increase, farmers respond in two ways, both of which reduce labour input in agriculture. First, in agricultural production, labour and physical capital (machinery and equipment) can, to some extent, be substituted for each other. That is, if the labour cost increases faster than capital costs, farmers tend to reduce the input of labour by using more labour-saving technologies (like power tools, tractors, planters and towing machinery). Second, if the increase in labour costs causes disincentive to farmers planting agricultural crops, farmers will reduce labour input by either reducing the area they cultivate or by planting more extensively. However, before looking at the ways farmers actually react in the face of the labour-cost increases, the real reduction of labour input should be examined.

Rice, maize and wheat are major crops in China, accounting for 77 per cent of grain production and 53 per cent of total agricultural crops in 2008. These crops can be taken as an example to see how much and how fast labour input has fallen since the Lewis turning point. As shown in Figure 4.7, while the labour input in grain production has been steadily shrinking in the period examined, the year 2003 does indicate a turning point. After 2003 the labour input to the three crops declined more rapidly and simultaneously. In the period 2003–08, the work days per mu (equivalent to 0.165 acres) in the production of rice, maize and wheat fell by 30.8 per cent, 30.1 per cent and 32.2 per cent, respectively.

Technological change in agriculture

Statistically, employment in the agriculture sector was not determined by how many workers it needed but was a residual of the country's total employment. That is, while the agriculture sector's portion of the whole workforce declined over time, the actual numbers of labourers engaged in agriculture rose and fell in proportion to the rises and falls in the numbers

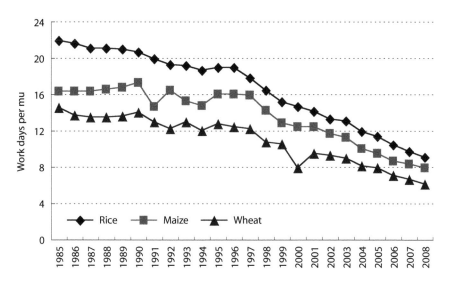

Figure 4.7 Changes in labour inputs of grain production. Source: National Development and Reform Commission, *Compilation of National Farm Product Cost–Benefit Data*, China Statistics Press.

of labourers needed in non-agricultural sectors. Once labour became a scarce factor of production, use of technology in agriculture changed as a natural response to the change in the endowment of production factors.

The level of technological advancement in agriculture is, in general, directed by the relative prices of production factors. The process of agricultural mechanization can also be understood with reference to the Lewis turning point. In the period 1978–98, when there was a surplus of labour in agriculture, the annual growth rate in the capacity of large- and medium-size tractors was 2 per cent, while that of small-size tractors was 11.3 per cent. In the period 1998–2008, as the labour force shifted from agricultural to non-agricultural sectors and there emerged stronger demand for labour-saving technology, the capacity of large- and medium-size tractors increased by 12.2 per cent annually and that of small-size tractors fell by 5.2 per cent. Changes in the growth rates of different sizes of tractor-towing machinery show a similar trend, with the annual growth rate of large- and medium-size tractor-towing machinery increasing from zero growth in the period 1978–98 to 13.7 per cent in 1998–2008, whereas the annual growth rate of small tractor-towing machinery declined from 12.1 per cent to 6.9 per cent in the same period.[4]

In the meantime, the inputs of physical capital in agriculture, as a substitute for the input of labour, have risen dramatically. During the period 2003–08, for example, the capital inputs per unit area of rice, maize and wheat increased in real terms by 51.1 per cent, 32.0 per cent and 41.0 per cent, respectively.[5] It is clear that, for all these grain crops, inputs of physical capital are increasing even faster than the labour input is declining. As a result of falling labour input and faster rising physical input in production, Chinese agriculture's capital–labour ratio, which is denoted by the ratio of physical input to labour input, has risen rapidly since 2003. According to the theory of induced technological changes coined by Hayami and Ruttan (1980), this labour-saving tendency during the rapid progress of agricultural mechanization is the natural result of the end of the surplus labour force in agriculture. It is hardly surprising that the total factor productivity of the agriculture sector has also witnessed a rapid rise during the same period, increasing by 38 per cent between 1995 and 2008, with a sudden rise after 2003 (Wen Zhao 2010). The fact that a potential negative effect due to the decline in labour input in agricultural capacity has been offset by an actual positive effect generated by the enhancement of labour productivity in agriculture has helped to reduce the pressure on the economy from food price inflation.

Will wage inflation weaken economic growth?

Investors fear that wage increases may weaken the comparative advantage of China's labour-intensive industries. There are three reasons why this fear is misplaced. First, the more-rapid growth of labour productivity ensures that wage inflation will not harm the comparative advantage of manufacturing. Based on nationwide data from manufacturing firms, in the period 2000–07, while workers' compensation in real terms increased by 91.8 per cent, the marginal product of labour increased by 178.7 per cent (Figure 4.8). It is clear that the wage-to-labour productivity ratio deter-

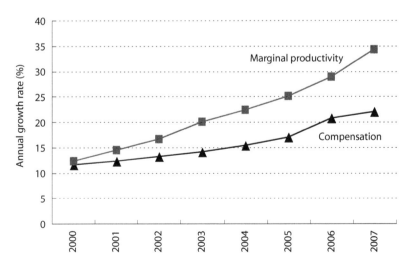

Figure 4.8 Compensation and labour productivity in China's manufacturing sector.
Source: Cai Fang *et al.* (2008).

mines a firm's, sector's or country's competitiveness. Regardless of whether it is based on marginal productivity of labour or average productivity of labour, the calculated unit labour costs – the ratio of work-compensation to labour-productivity – declined by more than 30 per cent in total or over 5 per cent annually in the period concerned.

Second, China's sheer geographic size and regional diversity creates opportunity for the central and western provinces to inherit labour-intensive industries that become outdated in the coastal regions. In the conventional flying geese paradigm, when one country encounters labour-cost increases, labour-intensive industries are usually transmitted to its less-advanced counterpart countries, because the latter hold comparative advantage in those industries. That is what happened among East Asian economies from the 1960s when Japan became the first country in the region to enter its Lewis turning point (see, e.g., Akamatsu 1962; Vernon 1966; Okita 1985; Kojima 2000). Such a paradigm can be revised into a domestic version in China's case. This means the labour-intensive industries can continue growing in the less-developed regions.

During the first years of this century, the capacity of industrial development in the central and western regions has substantially improved, as the result of the central government's implementation of the going-to-the-west strategy aimed to invest in infrastructure in favour of those regions. That has created conditions for those regions to catch up with the coastal regions and carry on the transferred industries. For example, immediately after the 30 per cent increase in wages, Foxconn moved its main factories to Zhengzhou, the capital city of Henan (the most populous province in central China), where it plans to recruit 200,000 local workers.

Third, continuing wage increases will create a new group of consumers in China, in turn generating a rebalance in the Chinese economy (as well as in the world economy) and sustain its growth. In 2009, there were 145 million Chinese migrant workers, accounting for more than one-third of urban employment. By adding those rural non-agricultural workers who work within their home townships, the number of rural-origin non-agricultural workers (15 years old and above) is as large as that of the working-age population of the United States.

Three things should be borne in mind about this population size. First, although the migrant workers' wage rate is below the average of the urban labour market, the huge number of migrant workers makes their total earnings a significant income and potential consumption expenditure. Second, since migrants workers are at the bottom of the income distribution, increases in their income imply a reduction in societal inequality. Third, as is generally expected, the low-income group of people have a higher marginal propensity to consume; that is, the relationship between income and consumption in this group is highly elastic. They are thus more likely to become the next mass consumers in China, supporting its transformation from export-led to domestic-demand-driven growth.

CONCLUSION AND POLICY IMPLICATIONS

This chapter has discussed the nature of wage convergence in China, and some of its implications. It has shown that wages have been growing in China for a number of years already. The rise of wages was shown to be due to a shortage of unskilled labour and migrant workers consequent on various factors including demographics, labour mobility and differentiation, and the legal structure of the Chinese labour market. These forces have driven a real convergence in the wages of Chinese workers as China's industrial complex becomes more technologically sophisticated.

Wage convergence between unskilled and skilled workers is often seen as evidence that an economy has arrived at its Lewis turning point (Minami 2010), but the implications of rising wages are not unambiguously good. Several policy steps need to be taken, most importantly with regard to inequality, if China is to best take advantage of the changing wage structure. In the Chinese economy, there is an opportunity for the Lewis turning point to intersect with the Kuznets turning point (Kuznets 1955) i.e. for income inequality to reach its peak and begin to drop. If that happens in China, income distribution can be expected to improve, which not only moderates the existing social tensions caused by income inequality but also sustains economic growth by creating domestic mass consumption. However, whether the meeting of the Lewis turning point with the Kuznets turning point can be translated into a stimulus for improving income distribution and economic growth depends on related policy adjustments.

First, labour market reforms are a necessary condition for a rational movement in wages of ordinary workers. But wage increases are, in fact, a double-edged sword. On the one hand, an improvement of household income potentially strengthens social cohesion and sustains economic growth. On the other hand, rising wages increase production costs for enterprises and can cause inflation. The lessons from the past, in advanced countries and those trapped in the middle-income bracket, suggest that labour-market institutions, including industrial relations legislation, minimum wage regulations, collective bargaining and social protection, serve as a platform to coordinate the demands by different interest groups and reach compromises.

Second, as the Chinese population ages, labour shortage will become the norm in the labour market. As this scarcity of labour is factored in by market participants, the inputs of physical capital will face steeper diminishing returns. Under these circumstances, economic growth can hardly be sustained if a noticeable improvement in total factor productivity does not occur. Hayashi and Prescott (2002) found that the lost decade of Japanese economic growth can largely be attributed to poor total factor productivity, which was in turn caused by protecting inefficient firms and old industries. The large share of state-owned enterprises in the whole economy also increases the risk that the Chinese economy will follow in Japan's footsteps.

Finally, the increase and convergence of wages indicates that a change in comparative advantage is occurring, although that does not necessarily imply an immediate disappearance of comparative advantage in labour-intensive industries for the Chinese economy as a whole. Workers (both present and future) are urgently required to upgrade their education attainments and skills to meet the demand of a technologically upgraded industrial structure. Even in a developed country like the USA, the 'left-behind' workforce whose members did not upgrade their skills is experiencing the pain of joblessness. One problem for China in this regard is that wage convergence tends to generate a disincentive to complete schooling. To avert this potential trap requires coordination between the education system and the labour market.

NOTES

1 Institute of Population and Labor Economics, Chinese Academy of Social Sciences.
2 The China Urban Labor Survey, or CULS, is a series of surveys conducted by the Institute of Population and Labor Economics, Chinese Academy of Social Sciences in 2001, 2005 and 2010. It representatively sampled labourers in urban households and migrant households, and surveyed both individual labourers and households in Shanghai, Wuhan, Shenyang, Fuzhou and Xi'an.
3 Calculated from CULS. The China Urban Labor Survey, or CULS, is a series of surveys conducted by the Institute of Population and Labor Economics, Chinese Academy of Social Sciences in 2001, 2005 and 2010.
4 Calculated according to data from the National Bureau of Statistics (various years) *China Statistical Yearbook*, Beijing: China Statistics Press.
5 Calculated according to data from the National Development and Reform Commission (various years) *Compilation of National Farm Product Cost–Benefit Data*, Beijing: China Statistics Press.

REFERENCES

Akamatsu, Kaname (1962) 'A historical pattern of economic growth in developing countries', *Developing Economies*, 1(1): 3–25.
Cai Fang (2010) 'China's farmers-turned workers in global spotlight: on deepening of urbanization with Chinese characteristics', *International Economic Review*, 2: 40–53.
Cai Fang, Dewen Wang and Qu Yue (2008) 'Flying geese within borders: how China sustains its labor-intensive industries?', *Economic Research Journal*, 9, 4–14.
Cai Fang and Du Yang (2011) 'Wages increase, wages convergence, and Lewis turning point in China', *China Economic Review*, in press.
Cai Fang, Du Yang and Wang Meiyan (2009) 'Migration and labor mobility in China', *Human Development Research Paper*, No. 9, New York: United Nations Development Programme.
CMA (Chinese Manufacturers' Association of Hong Kong) (2010) *Business Prospect Survey Report on Members in Pearl River Delta Regions, 2010*, available at at http://cma.org.hk/files/uploads/201005251724112010Report_Finalize.pdf.

Du Yang and Wang Meiyan (2008) 'The implementation of minimum wage system and its effects in China', *Journal of Graduate School of Chinese Academy of Social Sciences*, 6: 56–62.

—— (2010) 'New estimate of surplus rural labor force and its implications', *Journal of Guangzhou University (Social Science Edition)*, 9(4): 17–24.

Hayami, Yujiro and Vernon Ruttan (1980) *Agricultural Development: An International Perspective*, Baltimore, MD and London: The Johns Hopkins University Press.

Hayashi, Fumio and Edward C. Prescott (2002) 'The 1990s in Japan: a lost decade', *Review of Economic Dynamics*, 5(1): 206–235.

Hirschman, Albert O. (1970) *Exit, Voice, and Loyalty: Responses to Decline in Firms, Organizations, and State*, Cambridge, MA: Harvard University Press.

Kojima, Kiyoshi (2000) 'The "flying geese" model of Asian economic development: origin, theoretical extensions, and regional policy implications', *Journal of Asian Economics*, 11(4): 375–401.

Kuznets, Simon (1955) 'Economic growth and income inequality', *American Economic Review*, 45(1): 1–28.

Lewis, W. Arthur (1954) 'Economic development with unlimited supplies of labor', *The Manchester School of Economic and Social Studies*, 22(2), 139–191. [Reprinted in A.N. Agarwala and S.P. Singh (eds.) (1958) *The Economics of Underdevelopment*, Bombay: Oxford University Press.]

Minami, Ryoshin (2010) 'Turning point in the Japanese economy', presented at the Institute of Asian Cultures Toyo University project workshop, 'Discussion on the changes in East Asia labor market based on Lewisian turning point theory', Tokyo, 18–19 July.

NBS–DRS (National Bureau of Statistics, Department of Rural Surveys) (2010) 'A monitoring survey report on migrant workers in 2009', in Cai Fang (ed.) *Report on China's Population and Labor (No. 11): Labor Market Challenges in the Post-Crisis Era*, Beijing: Social Sciences Academic Press.

Oi, Jean C. (1999) 'Local state corporatism', in Jean C. Oi (ed.) *Rural China Takes Off: Institutional Foundations of Economic Reform*, Berkeley, CA: University of California Press.

Okita, Sabro (1985) 'Special presentation: prospect of Pacific economies', in Korea Development Institute (ed), *Pacific Cooperation: Issues and Opportunities,* Report of the Fourth Pacific Economic Cooperation Conference, Seoul, Korea, 29 April–1 May, pp. 18–29.

PBC–DSS (Department of Survey and Statistics, People's Bank of China) (2010) 'The 5th monitoring report on migrant workers', in Cai Fang (ed.) *Report on China's Population and Labor (No. 11): Labor Market Challenges in the Post-Crisis Era*, Beijing: Social Sciences Academic Press.

Ruan Jianqing and Zhang Xiaobo (2010) 'Do geese migrate domestically?: evidence from the Chinese textile and apparel industry', *IFPRI Discussion Paper* 1040, Washington, DC: International Food Policy Research Institute (IFPRI), available at http://www.ifpri.org/sites/default/files/publications/ifpridp01040.pdf.

Vernon, R. (1966) 'International investment and international trade in the product cycle', *Quarterly Journal of Economics*, 80(2): 190–207.

Wang Meiyan (2010) 'The rise of labor cost and the fall of labor input: has China reached Lewis turning point?', *China Economic Journal*, 3(2): 139–155.

Wen Zhao (2010) 'Analysis on potentials of China's agricultural growth after Lewis turning point', unpublished working paper.

Ying Hu (2009) 'Estimation of China's urban and rural economically active population size in the years 2000–2008', *Chinese Population Science*, 6: 14–22.

5 Climate change mitigation
A defining challenge for China

Stephen Howes[1]

INTRODUCTION

Reducing greenhouse gas emissions is a defining challenge for China in two senses. First, it is required to avert dangerous and potentially catastrophic climate change. And, second, an effective response to climate change requires fundamental economic reforms and poses critical questions for China's emergence on the international stage as a superpower. Success on the mitigation front will be a good indicator of overall domestic reform progress and of China's peaceful and responsible global rise.

The next section presents a summary of China's historical and projected emissions trajectory, an assessment of its mitigation target, and an analysis of its objectives in relation to energy and the environment. The third section examines the desirability and feasibility of carbon pricing as an instrument to achieve these objectives, while the fourth section analyzes the importance of energy-sector and broader economic reform for mitigation. The fifth section of the chapter, which considers the very difficult international environment for mitigation, and proposes some strategies for China, is followed by a concluding section.

The analysis is in terms of carbon dioxide (CO_2) from fossil fuels, with a particular focus on the electricity sector. This is partly for tractability, partly because of the growing importance of CO_2 emissions from fossil fuels and partly because they are separately targeted by China. The next three sections draw on World Bank (2010a), which I co-authored with Leo Dobes. This report was written for the Asia Pacific Economic Cooperation (APEC) forum economies, and so has an Asia–Pacific focus which is a natural lens through which to analyze China's efforts and challenges.

CHINA'S CLIMATE CHANGE MITIGATION CHALLENGE AND OBJECTIVES

China's emissions trajectory

China's rise to industrial superpower status – illustrated by comparative steel production volumes in Figure 5.1 – has accelerated global emissions growth. China is now the largest emitter of CO_2 (from fossil fuels), with 25 per cent of the global total in 2009, considerably ahead of the second-largest annual emitter, the United States with 17 per cent (PBL 2010). China has been responsible for 72 per cent of the world's growth in CO_2 emissions (from fossil fuels) between 2000 and 2009, a period during which China's emissions grew at an annual average rate of 9.4 per cent, and the rest of the world's at 0.8 per cent (PBL 2010).

Of course, in per-capita or accumulated terms, China's emissions still greatly lag behind those of the United States. However, one can safely say that there can be no satisfactory global response to climate change without the active participation of China.

China's historical emissions trajectory is unique. Emissions growth in any country is a function of GDP growth, as well as changes in energy intensity (the ratio of energy consumption to GDP) and the carbon intensity of energy. As Figure 5.2 shows, using the APEC economies to illustrate, in most developing economies emissions closely track output, whereas in most developed economies emissions lag output. With output growing faster in (successful) developing economies, not surprisingly emissions grow much faster in many developing than in most developed economies.

The close link between emissions and output in developing economies reflects two features. First, the carbon intensity of energy among developing economies has been on a slight upward trend, reflecting the move away from biomass, and an increasing dominance of coal-fired generation. Burke (2010)

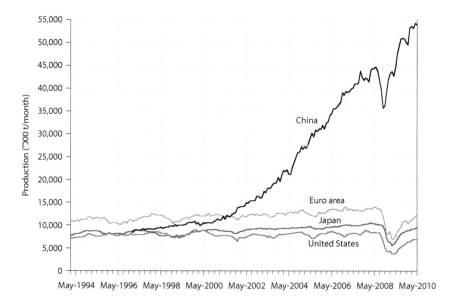

Figure 5.1 China: rise of a steel giant; production of steel in China, Europe, Japan and the United States, 1994–2010. Note: Steel production in thousands of tonnes per month, seasonally adjusted. Source: OECD Main Economic Indicators, World Steel Institute; compiled by Outlook Economics (2010).

demonstrates that the carbon intensity of energy of a developing economy increases as the economy develops, before it starts to decline. Second, energy intensity is remarkably flat among most developing economies (Sheehan 2008); that is, energy grows at roughly the same rate as output.

As Figure 5.2 shows, China's experience is consistent with the generalization that the carbon intensity of energy will increase over time in developing economies. China in fact has the fifth-highest carbon intensity of energy of the world's large economies (with populations above 20 million). This unfortunate environmental reality reflects China's relatively strong endowment of coal.

However, China's experience is a clear exception to the otherwise well-supported generalization that the energy intensity of developing economies remains constant over time. China's energy intensity fell over the 1980s and 1990s, as a result of market liberalization, the relative decline of heavy industry and perhaps power shortages, but has flattened out since 2000. As a result, as Figure 5.2 shows, emissions in China before 2000 grew more slowly than GDP, but have since roughly tracked GDP.

Perhaps the biggest analytical question relating to mitigation in China is whether the 2000–05 experience represents a new norm, and how hard it will be to revert to the decline in energy intensity seen in previous decades. It is too early to answer this question definitively and, as discussed below, recent data are unclear. However, Figure 5.3 suggests that whereas China entered its reform era with an extraordinarily high energy intensity, it has now become much more like a 'normal' developing country in terms of both the level and trend of its energy intensity.[2] This itself would suggest that, in the absence of deliberate policy action, China's energy use and thus its emissions will continue to track GDP closely.

Alarmed by the sharp growth in energy use over the Tenth Five-Year Plan (2000–05), China has sought to reduce energy intensity over the Eleventh Five-Year Plan, with a target of a 20 per cent reduction between 2005 and 2010. As Zhou *et al.* (2010) explain, China has pursued this target by cascading it downwards into a series of targets for provinces and large enterprises. Thus, each province has been given its own energy intensity reduction target (above, below or equal to 20 per cent). Similarly, each province has translated its goal into targets for its cities and counties. The top 1,000 enterprises have also been required to show energy savings, and have each been given their own, tailored targets. Each provincial leader has been required to sign a contract taking responsibility for its energy intensity target with the central government. City and country leaders have likewise been required to sign contracts with their provincial government. Contracts have also been signed with enterprise managers. Progress of both provinces and enterprises is reported annually at the highest political level, and is taken into account during the performance evaluation of provincial, local and enterprise managers. China has also set detailed quantitative targets for closing down old and inefficient plants and factories in major industrial sectors. It has also established ten new projects to introduce more efficient coal-fired power plants,

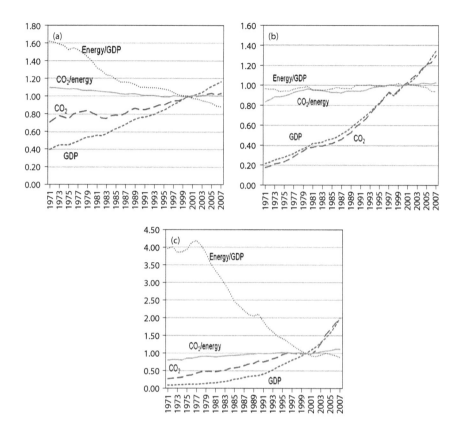

Figure 5.2 CO_2, GDP, emissions intensity of energy, and energy intensity of GDP for three groups of APEC economies, 1971–2007 (2000 = 1): (a) mature developed economies, (b) developing and newly developed economies excluding China and Russia, and (c) China. In most developing economies, but not in China (until recently), CO_2 emissions track GDP. Notes: Mature developed economies are Australia, Canada, Japan, New Zealand and USA. Developing and newly developed are all others apart from China and Russia. Data for Papua New Guinea are missing. GDP is measured in billions of constant year (2000) US dollars, using purchasing power parities (PPPs) to convert from local currency. Energy is measured in Mtoe (million tonnes of oil equivalent), and CO_2 is measured in millions of tonnes. Source: IEA (2009a).

and to promote energy-efficient lighting and more efficient buildings, and so on. These projects have been backed by high levels of government spending, expected to exceed US$10 billion by the central government alone in the last year. Several fiscal policies have also been used. Energy-intensive industries have been subjected to higher electricity prices and reduced export rebates.

The success which China has had in achieving its objective of a 20 per cent reduction in energy intensity is unclear. Official statistics suggested an ini-

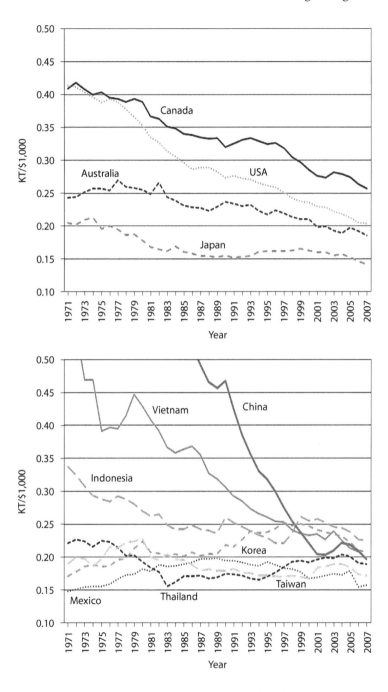

Figure 5.3 The ratio of energy consumption to GDP for selected APEC economies, 1971–2007. China's energy intensity used to be extraordinarily high, but now looks average. Note: See notes to Figure 5.2. Source: IEA (2009a).

tial decline in energy intensity, accelerating as the global financial crisis hit (because energy-intensive exporters were hit hard), but then a reversal during the infrastructure-intensive stimulus period. In May 2010, Chinese authorities announced that energy intensity had increased by 3.2 per cent in the first quarter of 2010 relative to the first quarter of 2009, and also announced an 'iron hand' crackdown, with new measures to ensure the 20 per cent target is met. Media reports indicate that factories have been shut down and, in some cases, electricity generators stood down in order to achieve the target. Latest announcements indicate a 15.6 per cent reduction in the first 4 years, and then a further 3 per cent reduction in the first 9 months of 2010, which would put the 20 per cent target well within reach by the end of the Eleventh Five-Year Plan period.

However, China's published statistical data suggest a reduction in energy intensity of only 10 per cent up to 2009 (updated from Howes (2010)). Measurement changes introduced as a result of the 2009 Economic Census make published 2005 and 2009 energy figures non-comparable. A consistent series of energy statistics has yet to be released, neither has any justification for the large revision in energy figures been provided. It is not clear that official announcements should be accepted at face value without further scrutiny.

Given the uncertainty around recent trends in energy intensity, an alternative is to look at proxies for and drivers of energy demand and intensity. Figure 5.4 shows that most relevant intensities have increased, with only oil intensity declining. Between the first half of 2005 and the first half of 2010, China's steel production increased by 94 per cent, cement by 86 per cent and electricity by 75 per cent (first-quarter comparison), all above the extraordinarily rapid rate of GDP growth of 71 per cent (an annual average growth in GDP of 11.3 per cent). Given these figures, the only way a reduction in energy intensity could have occurred (beyond oil) is by improvement within these sectors, leading to more efficient steel, cement and electricity production. No doubt this has occurred, but whether the improvement in efficiency has been enough to offset these adverse trends is unclear.

While further analysis is needed, these figures cast doubt on whether the 20 per cent target has been achieved, and show that whatever improvements China has made with respect to energy efficiency have come not because of but despite the underlying structural trends in the economy.

It is also important to put the energy intensity figures in perspective. What matters for environmental outcomes is not ultimately reductions in energy, or even emissions intensity, but emissions themselves. Even if energy intensity targets have been met, China's emissions growth continues to be supercharged because of the country's extraordinarily high GDP growth. China's reported 8.4 per cent annual average growth in CO_2 emissions (from fossil fuels) between 2005 and 2009 (PBL 2010) is well above most 'business as usual' or 'reference case' scenarios for that country. The 2008 *World Energy Outlook* (IEA 2008) has CO_2 emissions in China growing at an annual average of 5.1 per cent between 2006 and 2015 under its

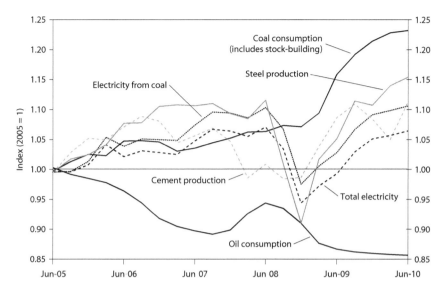

Figure 5.4 Steel, cement, electricity and electricity from coal production, as well as coal consumption, have all risen relative to GDP since 2005 in China. Notes: Series show production series divided by GDP at constant prices and indexed to 2005 = 1. Series are seasonally adjusted. Coal production and import and export data are updated from the NBS and Chinese customs websites before seasonal adjustment. (June quarter 2010 data are a forecast based on data to May.) Note that coal consumption as derived implicitly includes stock-building which would probably have been positive in the last quarter of 2008 as the global financial crisis hit. Also the NBS coal production source data, used to calculated coal consumption, have probably not been adjusted for changes in the number of coal mines in the economic census between 2005 and 2009. Sources: OECD Main Economic Indicators Database, China NBS website, ADB database, Chinese Customs, Outlook Economics CHN-TRYM database; compiled by Outlook Economics (2010).

reference case. In projections from the World Bank (2010b), annual average emissions growth between 2010 and 2015 is 4.6 per cent. Even Garnaut *et al.* (2009), who assume continued rapid growth in developing economy emissions under business as usual, project 7.1 per cent annual average emissions growth for China between 2005 and 2015. It is remarkable that China is exceeding these projections in a period that encompasses a global downturn.

China's mitigation objectives

In 2009, for the first time, China announced that it would subject itself to an emissions constraint. It would aim to reduce CO_2 emissions intensity in 2020 by 40–45 per cent compared with 2005. China has also adopted a renewable energy target of 15 per cent by 2020, up from 8 per cent in 2006.

The Chinese emissions target is an ambitious one which will not be met without considerable policy effort. Figure 5.5 illustrates this point by comparing national targets relative to estimates for 'business as usual' derived largely from Garnaut *et al.* (2009) for a range of APEC economies. China's target comes in as at least as ambitious as those of several other much richer economies, including Korea, Canada and the United States. Achieving it would require 30 per cent lower emissions than China would experience under business as usual. If China's target is achieved, its absolute and per-capita emissions would still increase, but by much less than would otherwise be the case. Its per-capita emissions at the end of the decade would be 7 rather than 10 tonnes, still up from almost 5 tonnes today, but representing a total savings in emissions of about 4 billion tonnes of CO_2 (more than 10 per cent of current annual global emissions of CO_2 from fossil fuels).

Why has China adopted both an emissions target and a renewables target? There are four objectives driving action in the energy–environment space.

First, the risks of unmitigated climate change are clearly a factor, as is China's perceived need to be seen to be contributing to solving this global problem.

Second, China is seeking to tackle national environmental problems. China has 13 of the world's 20 most polluted cities, 30 per cent of its land is damaged by acid rain as a result of sulphur emitted from coal, and health damages from air pollution are expected to reach 13 per cent of GDP in 2020 (see, for example, Zissis and Bajoria (2008)). Millions face serious indoor as

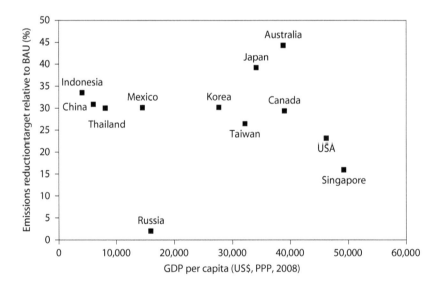

Figure 5.5 2020 APEC emission control targets expressed as a reduction relative to business as usual (BAU). China's emissions reduction target is ambitious. Notes: National targets as recorded in the Copenhagen Accord or other statements. Where a target range has been committed to, the mid-point of that range is selected. Source: World Bank (2010a).

well as outdoor air pollution problems. A meta-analysis of epidemiological studies concluded that 'indoor air pollution from solid fuel use in China is responsible for approximately 420,000 premature deaths annually, more than the approximately 300,000 attributed to urban outdoor air pollution in the country' (Zhang and Smith 2007: 848).

Third, energy security is a growing concern. China has long been reliant on oil imports, and has just recently become a significant coal importer (Figure 5.6). At present production rates, China's currently proven coal reserves will last only another 41 years (World Bank 2010a). That said, energy security concerns will continue to revolve around oil more than coal. China already imports almost 60 per cent of its oil needs, but in 2010 will import less than 10 per cent of its coal. Worldwide, there is a lot of coal left. Garnaut (2008: Table 3.3) reports that, at 2007 production rates, the world has 139 years of coal left in its reserve base, as against only 60 years of gas and 40 years of oil. Also, unlike oil, much of that coal is in secure locations, such as Australia. The volatility and overall upward trend in world energy prices over the last decade (Figure 5.7) have also heightened energy security concerns.

Fourth, China is seeking technological advantage. China, like a number of economies around the world, increasingly views clean energy and, more broadly, low-carbon technology as a future major source of innovation, the 'next big thing'. China seeks to become a leading global supplier and eventually developer of these new technologies. Dechezleprêtre *et al.* (2008) measure technological innovation in respect of climate change mitigation using patent filings. Japan alone is responsible for 37 per cent of the world's climate change mitigation inventions (Table 5.1). The United States is in second position with 11 per cent, and China is in fourth with 8 per cent. China's 2007 Medium and Long-term Development Plan for Renewable Energy explicitly identifies the deployment of Chinese intellectual property domestically as a policy objective.

All four of these objectives are important for China's policy-makers. Together, they make up what is now called the 'green growth' agenda, most famously embraced by Korea. There are of course synergies between the four objectives. By pushing down global energy prices, global action on climate change would improve the terms of trade for economies such as China, and thus improve energy security. But there are also trade-offs. An emissions reduction target on its own might undermine energy security goals. Carbon capture and storage (CCS) is an example. CCS will help reduce emissions, but will also worsen local air pollution and weaken energy security, since it will significantly reduce the efficiency of coal plants. Likewise, some measures to improve energy security can increase emissions. Coal-to-liquid conversion (currently under consideration and/or development in several Asia Pacific economies, including China) will reduce reliance on oil imports, but will increase emissions.

This mix of objectives, and the possibility of trade-offs between them, demands a mix of instruments. This is certainly what we see in China, where a whole raft of instruments, from the command and control and regulatory approaches discussed earlier, to a range of feed-in tariffs and special tax and

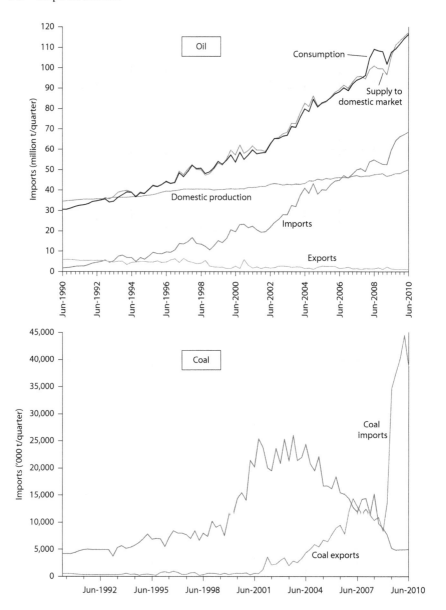

Figure 5.6 Oil and coal imports and exports, and oil consumption and production, China, 1990–2010. China, long and increasingly dependent on oil
imports, is now also a net coal importer. Notes: Series are seasonally
adjusted. Updated trade data taken directly from the customs website
and cross-checked against data from the World Trade Atlas. June quarter
is a forecast based on data up to May. Data source: CEIC Database,
Chinese National Bureau of Statistics, Chinese customs, OECD Main
Economic Indicators Database, World Trade Atlas, Outlook Economics
CHN-TRYM database; compiled by Outlook Economics (2010).

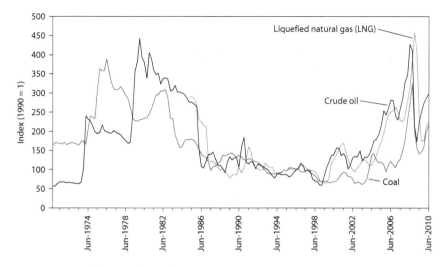

Figure 5.7 World prices for crude oil, LNG and coal, adjusted for inflation (1990 = 1).
World energy prices have been volatile and rising over the last decade. Notes:
Data are quarterly. Series are converted from US dollars to more currency
neutral IMF special drawing rights divided by the G7 CPI to convert them to
constant price terms and then indexed to 1990s levels (average of the decade)
for the purpose of comparison. Oil prices are the IMF indicator series (which
is an average across a number of types of crude). LNG prices are the price of
Russian LNG in Europe. Coal prices are based on Australian thermal coal
export prices. Sources: IMF International Financial Statistics, OECD Main
Economic Indicators; compiled by Outlook Economics (2010).

tariff concessions to promote renewable energy (as summarized, for example, in World Bank 2010a), have been used to date. UNDP (2010: 82) notes
that '[t]here are few, if any, developing economies that have promulgated
as many laws, policies and other measures to support low carbon development as China'. This is probably true not only in relation to developing
economies. What we have not seen so far in China is the introduction of
a carbon price. However, there are several media reports suggesting that
the introduction of a carbon price is now on the agenda. Some of them
suggest that China is contemplating the introduction of a carbon tax. Rates
mentioned are 20 yuan per tonne of CO_2 (about US$3) rising to 50 yuan
by 2020.[3] Other media reports suggest that China will in fact introduce
emissions trading. The next section considers the desirability and feasibility
of the introduction of carbon pricing into China.

CARBON PRICING: DESIRABILITY AND FEASIBILITY

For many economists, the introduction of carbon pricing is a litmus test for
the seriousness of governments in mitigating climate change. For example,

Table 5.1 Top 12 inventors in climate change mitigation technologies, with average percentage of total global inventions across different mitigation technologies

Country	Rank	Average % of world's inventions
Japan	1	37.1
USA	2	11.8
Germany	3	10.9
China	4	8.1
South Korea	5	6.4
Russia	6	2.8
Australia	7	2.5
France	8	2.5
UK	9	2.0
Canada	10	1.7
Brazil	11	1.2
Netherlands	12	1.1
Total		87.2

Source: Dechezleprêtre *et al.* (2008).

Notes: Inventions are measured based on patent count data. The percentages shown average over 13 different climate change mitigation technology areas. These include not only renewable energies, but also relevant inventions in the areas of building, lighting, carbon capture and storage, and cement.

Nordhaus (2008: 22) writes: 'Whether someone is serious about tackling the global-warming problem can be readily gauged by listening to what he or she says about the carbon price.' In Nordhaus's view '[t]o a first approximation, raising the price of carbon is a necessary and sufficient step for tackling global warming'. This section considers whether carbon pricing would be desirable for China, and whether it would be feasible.

Carbon pricing would not suffice as a policy to promote climate change mitigation for China (or other developing economies). Complementary policies would be needed in three areas. First, so-called technology policies, such as research and development subsidies and feed-in tariffs, would be needed to promote technological leadership. Views on the wisdom both of an activist industrial policy objective and of individual instruments to achieve them are mixed, but, taking the objective as given, a more targeted approach to technological innovation and dissemination is needed than is provided by carbon pricing. Second, there is a risk that carbon pricing on its own would lead to substitution from emissions-intensive coal to less-emissions-intensive oil, thus reducing emissions but worsening energy security. This would need to be avoided by complementary policies to tax oil, or again promote renewables, so that the substitution is not from coal to oil but away from fossil fuels altogether (gas is already being promoted but is supply-constrained). Third, there are still several hundred million households reliant on biomass for cooking and heating in China, with serious negative health consequences. A carbon price, as a tax on modern energy, could conceivably make it harder for these households to escape the traditional energy sector. However, the empirical evidence (summarized in Wadhwa *et al.* (2003)) suggests, in fact, that exit from traditional energy is not price sensitive, and that what is more important are complementary policies either to reduce the health costs of using traditional energy sources, or to extend access to the modern sector.

Although not sufficient on its own, carbon pricing would seem to be an essential part of an effective policy response to the mitigation challenge. There is no doubt that if China wants to achieve an ambitious emissions objective, such as the one that it has just adopted, it will have to increase the price of energy. Figure 5.8 summarizes the challenge facing China. It compares China (and Taiwan and Korea) to two sets of developed economies: the USA and Canada on the one hand, and the European Union (EU) and Japan on the other. The USA and Canada have cheap energy (low electricity and petroleum prices) and a high energy/GDP ratio. By comparison, the EU and Japan have expensive energy and a low energy/GDP ratio. China, with relatively low energy prices and high energy intensity, currently looks much more similar to the USA and Canada than it does to Europe and Japan. But China's mitigation objective requires that it ends up looking more like

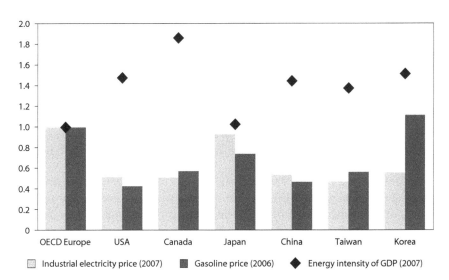

Figure 5.8 Electricity prices, gasoline prices and energy intensity (ratio of energy use to GDP) for USA, Canada and Japan relative to the OECD member economies of Europe. China's future: low energy prices or high energy efficiency? Notes: Energy prices measured in current US$, using market exchange rates; energy intensities measured using PPPs. For energy intensity definitions, see Figure 5.2. Energy efficiency is defined as the inverse of energy intensity. All OECD Europe values are normalized to one. Sources: IEA (2009a, 2010).

Europe and Japan in terms of its energy to GDP ratio. But this in turn must mean much higher energy prices.

Higher energy prices would not only help China reduce emissions, but also have a number of side benefits. First, energy taxes could be a substantial source of revenue. A US$20 carbon price applied across fossil fuels could fetch China more than 2.5 per cent of GDP by 2020 (World Bank 2010a). In general, analysis by the OECD finds that increasing broad-based commodity taxation and reducing personal and corporate taxes enhance efficiency (Arnold 2008; Johansson *et al.* 2008).

Second, energy taxes would be a progressive source of revenue in China. This is very different to the situation in developed countries, where energy is an inferior good (that is, the share of energy in the consumption bundle declines in proportional terms with income). In developing economies, the share of (modern) energy in the consumption bundle typically increases with income (Bacon *et al.* 2010). Therefore, whereas an energy tax is regressive in developed economies, in developing economies it is progressive.

These side benefits are important because mitigation, even if efficient, will not be cheap in China, at least not without revenue recycling. As Figure 5.9 shows, most model estimates show mitigation costs as a percentage of GDP to be much higher in developing countries than developed ones (for a given global carbon price). Even though some developing countries, including China, will benefit from the positive terms of trade impacts of higher domestic energy prices, the fact that they have much higher emissions intensity to begin with drives up their costs of emissions reduction (see Howes 2009b; Lee 2010; Stern and Lambie 2010). However, such costings ignore the revenue impacts of carbon pricing (since they assume the lump-sum recycling of revenues) and also ignore distributional benefits.

Overall, the introduction of a carbon price, as part of a broader policy mix, would be desirable given China's mitigation and related policy objectives. But would it be feasible? This is a question that has yet to receive the attention it deserves.

Feasibility has two dimensions, one that could be considered broadly political (influencing the likelihood of introduction and level of any carbon price), and one broadly economic (influencing the impact of any carbon price once introduced). Increasing energy prices is politically difficult anywhere, but especially in a developing economy such as China. The fact that, as discussed earlier, modern energy is a luxury good in developing economies might improve the welfare consequences of energy price increases, but it might also raise the political costs, since it means that any energy price increase will disproportionately hit the rich who are also likely to be the politically powerful. Moreover, China, again like many developing countries, has limited availability of compensation instruments, which will also make the politics more difficult.

The other political barrier to carbon pricing is international. The tardiness of developed economies outside of the EU to introduce carbon pricing will

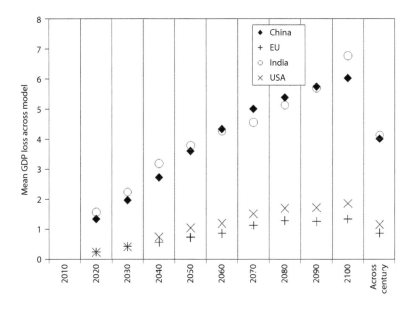

Figure 5.9 Cost of a global carbon price for different economies according to a
number of different economic models. Most models show that, without
revenue recycling, carbon pricing will be relatively expensive for China.
Notes: The models are those used in the EMF-22 modelling exercise to
estimate the cost to GDP of a global carbon price set at a price high
enough, with universal participation, to stabilize the concentration of
greenhouse gases at different target levels. All models are shown for
which cost to GDP results are available (about 10). No international
transfers are assumed. Sources: Lee (2010) and EMF (2009).

inevitably bound the ambition of developing economies. If carbon prices are
introduced, they will be at a low level: current proposals in Indonesia and
China suggest a US$5–10 range. Clearly, the lower the price, the lower the
impact. Europe's carbon price under its emissions trading scheme has been
volatile. At the time of writing, prices are about 14 euros (about US$20).
Prices are expected to rise in the coming years, but neither historical nor
projected prices have been sufficient to deter Germany from engaging in a
'rush to coal': Germany currently has some 20–29 GW of coal and lignite
generation plants under planning or construction (about 30–40 per cent of
current peak demand), and only 3–6 GW of gas (Pahle 2010). Pahle shows
that, at current fuel prices, a carbon price of 40 euros is needed to favour
gas over coal, and argues that investors either don't believe that carbon
prices will reach this level, or are worried that gas prices will continue to
rise relative to coal, and so require an even higher carbon price.

That said, it is important to take a long-term perspective. Given the science, climate change is unlikely to go away as an issue. Over time, as climate
change becomes more evident, more developed economies will introduce

carbon prices, and this political constraint to carbon pricing for developing economies will weaken.

Whatever the level at which it is set, would a carbon price have an impact? We now turn to this question of the economic feasibility of carbon pricing. Clearly, a carbon price on coal would send a strong signal to commercial consumers of coal, such as steel manufacturers. But much of the energy sector in China is regulated, and here matters are more complex. For concreteness, we focus below mainly on the impact of a carbon price in the electricity sector.

A carbon price will, in an otherwise well-functioning market, push up the relative price of emissions-intensive goods, and thereby reduce emissions in four ways. First, it will push consumer demand in the direction of goods which are less emissions intensive (for example, to wear extra clothing and turn down the heating). Second, it will induce suppliers to make their goods less emissions intensive (for example, to make electricity with gas instead of coal). Third, it will lead investors to invest in projects that are less emissions intensive (for example, to build an aluminium smelter that runs on hydro rather than thermal power).[4] And, fourth, carbon pricing will give a financial incentive for innovators to develop new products which are less emissions intensive (for example, to invent a hydrogen or electric car).

The effectiveness of the fourth channel of induced innovation will depend on the extent to which the other three channels are effective. In the case of the electricity sector in China, as I show below, each of the first three channels might in fact be blocked.

Impact of carbon pricing on demand

For a carbon price to have an impact on demand, it clearly needs to be passed on to final consumers. But recent experience suggests that there is no guarantee this will happen. Coal is the dominant fuel for electricity in China. In recent years, the price of coal in China has risen sharply, as illustrated by Figure 5.10, which plots the spot or market price for coal.[5] A lot of coal (about 70 per cent) is sold under long-term contract but, in 2007, price controls for long-term contracts were removed (Rosen and Houser 2007). Contract prices are significantly lower than market prices, but should over time follow the latter upwards. Market coal prices spiked in the middle of 2008, with some prices exceeding 1,000 yuan per tonne. At this point, the Chinese Government capped the market price at 800 yuan.

Through a series of electricity tariff increases, China greatly reduced electricity subsidies over the 1990s. However, China has found it difficult to pass on the increase in coal costs it has recently experienced. China has a formula in place for adjusting the electricity price every 6 months if the coal price changes by more than 5 per cent. However, since the end of 2004, when the formula was introduced, although this condition has been met 10 out of 12 times (in relation to coal market prices), the price of electricity

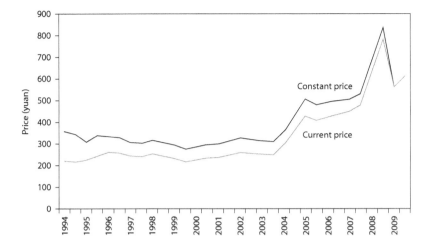

Figure 5.10 Current and constant spot market prices of coal, 1994–2010. The era
of cheap coal in China is over. Notes: 6-month average FOB prices
per tonne (1,000 kg) of coal at the Qinghaungdo Port for three types
of coal (where available): Datong Premium Mix 6k, Shanxi Premium
Mix 5.5k, and Shanxi and Datong Mix 5k. The CPI deflator is used to
obtain the constant price series, using 2009 as the base. Sources: NBS
(2010) and national Chinese coal data.

has been changed only thrice, and by much less than the formula mandated.
In nominal terms, coal prices rose 40 per cent between the first half of 2006
and 2010, but electricity prices by only about 15 per cent. In fact, over the
past few years, electricity selling prices have not even kept pace with inflation, as Figure 5.11 shows.

The result has been a squeeze on margins in the electricity sector, as
seen in Figure 5.12. In 2003, coal costs were less than half of the price
at which grid companies purchased power from generators. In 2008, they
were over 100 per cent and, despite some relief from falling coal prices,
at the end of 2009 coal costs still consumed over 70 per cent of coal-fired
generator revenue. How is the sector managing to survive? Much coal is
still sold under contract, and contract prices would lag spot prices, given
the doubling of the latter since middle of the last decade. Generator profits
are also being squeezed, and the margin between the final selling price and
the wholesale power purchase (generation) price has also fallen. Morse *et
al.* (2009) report that Chinese power companies lost an estimated 70 billion yuan in 2008.

Similar problems with cost pass-through have occurred in the petroleum
sector, as Figure 5.13 illustrates. China announced it was moving to market-
based pricing for petrol in December 2008 but, in May 2009, the government announced that it would set prices to protect consumers when world
oil prices exceeded US$80 a barrel (Kojima 2009).

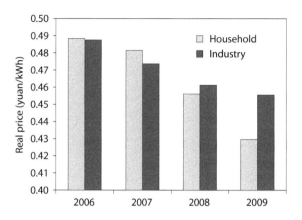

Figure 5.11 Average electricity selling price for industry and households, all of China, 2006–10. Despite rapidly rising coal prices, electricity prices for industry and households in China have not kept pace with inflation in recent years. Notes and sources: National prices are calculated by taking weighted averages for provinces from SERC (2006–09) using total consumption in the province as the weight. Data for Tibet are missing. Average prices (revenue per kWh) are calculated in this way for all consumers and for households. The industry price is then calculated as the average for all categories other than households and agriculture (assumed to pay household prices) using 2007 national electricity consumption data by sector from NBS (2010) for 2007.

Impact of carbon pricing on dispatch

In the electricity sector, the second channel by which a carbon price would reduce emissions is by changing the fuel mix, or the dispatch order. Here again, pre-existing distortions or constraints might limit the impact of carbon pricing. While China has not yet introduced a carbon price, it has tried to introduce a reform to its electricity dispatch system that mimics a carbon price.[6] Under the Energy Saving and Emissions Reduction in Power Generation (ESERD) pilot introduced into five provinces, provinces have been instructed to dispatch generators, not on an across-the-board basis as in the past, but rather according to a mix of economic and environmental criteria. To simplify, the dispatch order is: renewable, nuclear, gas, then coal, with coal plants ordered by their thermal efficiency, from highest to lowest. Note that this is roughly the order that one would expect with a high enough carbon price and, indeed, simulations show implementing ESERD would cut emissions by 10 per cent. However, the pilot provinces have been able to only partially implement this reform, because of the negative financial implications full implementation would have for less efficient coal-fired units. These units are still valuable as reserve capacity but, under the Chinese on-grid tariff system, plants receive a payment only if they are dispatched, and so have no incentive to provide stand-by capacity. Instead, if not regularly dispatched,

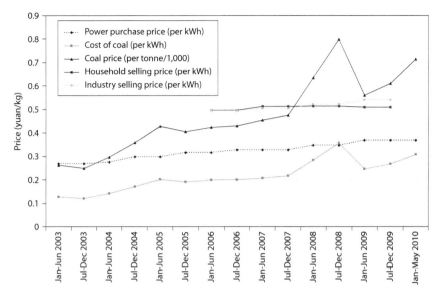

Figure 5.12 Average coal price (yuan/tonne divided by 1,000), estimated coal fuel cost, average generation price and electricity selling price for industry and households (all yuan/kWh), all of China, 2003–10. Coal fuel costs are squeezing margins in the electricity sector. Notes and sources: Current prices used. For household and industry prices, see Figure 5.11. For coal prices, see Figure 5.10. For assumptions on coal efficiency, see Zhao (2008) and China Electricity Council (2010). Values for 2008 and 2009 are interpolated. For the (wholesale or generation) power purchase price, information is used from SERC (2006–09) and public information on tariff increases, averaged across provinces.

they would simply shut down, thereby depriving the system of valuable spare capacity in case of an emergency or a spike in demand. Or, put differently, the policy-induced lack of flexibility in dispatch has undermined the impact of the introduction of a carbon price (or, in this case, a carbon price equivalent).

Impact of carbon pricing on investment

The potential for carbon pricing to influence investment decisions in the electricity sector in China is limited by the continued prevalence of central planning. As Wu *et al.* (2004: 4) write: 'Although the generation sector has already been separated from the utilities in China, investment and construction of new power plants are still under strict control of the government.' Private investment is allowed, but under expansion plans laid down by the central and provincial governments. Zhang and Heller (2004: 35) note:

Although Beijing no longer aims to control how many restaurants will emerge in the next five years, it does see a need to continue to plan and decide how many power plants to build, where to site them, what fuel they should tap and what prices they will charge. As a result, instead of partially withdrawing from business, the government merely switched its role from directly controlling the power industry via repatriation of all revenues and direction by ministerial fiat to indirectly controlling utility state-owned enterprises' (SOEs') access to financial markets and project approval. SOEs in the power sector are not substantially more independent than they were before the reform in terms of power project development.

Price signals are crucial for getting decentralized agents to adjust their actions to meet national targets. However, central planners can directly incorporate national targets into their decision-making, without any price signal at all. The Chinese Government already has capacity targets for all major generation types. Figures that are both official and up-to-date are hard to come by, but form part of the Twelfth Five-Year Plan approved in April 2011. Figure 5.14 presents estimates of what China's 2020 expansion targets are or will be, both for total generation capacity, and for different fuel types. They imply not only a rapid aggregate expansion, but significant continued diversification away from coal to gas, nuclear and wind.

Would planners move further away from coal if they were told to use a carbon price? A precise answer to this would depend on the calculation of the implicit carbon price that would give the outcome shown in Figure 5.14.

Figure 5.13 Actual retail prices for petrol in China, and what they would need to be to cover costs given world prices for crude. Petrol prices in China follow world prices except when world prices are very high. Notes: Cost-covering retail prices are based on the world price for crude and include margins for refining and distribution. In January 2009, China increased the fuel tax from 0.2 yuan/litre to 1.0 yuan/litre. The cost-covering retail price does not include taxes. The price is for Beijing, and for 93-octane gasoline. Source: Li (2010), updated.

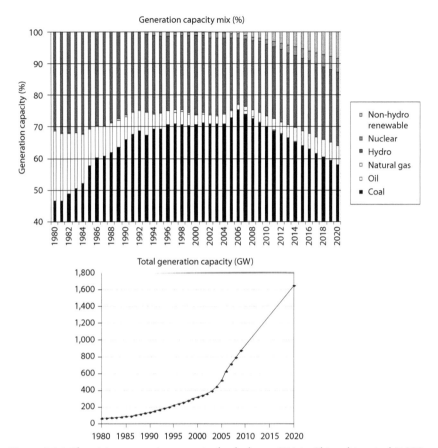

Figure 5.14 Electricity generation capacity by fuel type (%) in China, historical (1980–2009) and projected (2020). China's 2020 generation targets aim to reduce the dominance of coal-fired generation, while doubling total capacity. Notes and sources: Target year is 2020; last year of historical data is 2009; for intermediate years, linear interpolation used. Historical capacity data come from EIA (2010). However, this source doesn't distinguish between coal, oil and gas capacity. The subdivision of thermal capacity into these three types is done using electricity generation data from IEA (2009b) up to 2006 and own sources for 2009 (2007 and 2008 are interpolated). Note vertical axis truncated from below at 40% to magnify the changes envisaged. At the time of writing, there was no public, up-to-date and comprehensive generation expansion plan. Targets were therefore compiled from various public sources. (The Twelfth Five-Year Plan, approved by the Chinese Government in April 2011, contains an updated generation expansion plan.)

However, since China's expansion plans already embody a significant move away from coal, there can certainly be no presumption that the introduction of a carbon price would influence the generation mix, unless the carbon price was itself very high.

BEYOND CARBON PRICING: ENERGY SECTOR AND BROADER ECONOMIC REFORMS

Energy sector reforms

The discussion of the previous section should make it clear that, while carbon pricing might be desirable for China if feasible, it may not be feasible in the electricity sector, and perhaps also in the petroleum sector, in the sense that pre-existing institutional conditions would limit or nullify its effect. In the unregulated segments of the fossil-fuel market, a carbon price would be expected to influence behaviour, but not, as we have seen, in the regulated segments.

This finding points to the importance of energy sector reform to heighten the impact of carbon pricing. This is not necessarily a call for a move away from central planning. Central planning may or may not be efficient, but, as we have seen, it can provide a framework within which environmental considerations can be weighted, even without carbon pricing.

The most important energy sector reform from an environmental perspective would in fact be the strengthening of mechanisms to allow for cost pass-through. This is not only critical to influence patterns of demand. If costs are not passed through, then it is also possible that investment plans that promote more expensive but less-polluting generation sources will not be implemented due to financial constraints.

Strengthening cost pass-through can in theory be done in either of two ways: by liberalization, or by the use of formulae or established procedures that aim to mimic the behaviour of liberalized markets. In practice, these are far from perfect substitutes since, as long as the government retains control of whatever approach is agreed on, it can continue to exercise discretion. China's own experience testifies to this. As noted earlier, China introduced a formula in 2005 to allow for automatic coal cost pass-through in electricity prices, but it has not been implemented. Full liberalization would be possible with respect to petroleum prices, and in relation to generation pricing. Transmission and distribution costs will always need to be regulated, but China could promote cost pass-through by establishing independent regulation.

The conclusion that energy sector reform is needed for an effective mitigation response is therefore well-founded, but potentially misleading unless qualified in two important ways. For concreteness, I again focus on the power sector.

First, it is important to recognize that power sector reforms in developing economies are difficult, and often make slow progress. While there are some success stories, a World Bank (Besant-Jones 2006) review of power sector reforms concludes that overall 'political forces are difficult to align for reform' (Besant-Jones 2006: 14), that interest groups 'constitute a major impediment to reform' (ibid: 16), and that 'successful reform requires sustained political commitment' (ibid: 2). Not surprisingly therefore, 'Power market reforms in developing economies are generally tentative and incomplete, and are still works in progress' (ibid: 4). Power sector privatization is particularly challenging. 'Most privatization-focused power sector reforms in developing economies have stalled, and some have been abandoned in all but name' (Rosenzweig *et al.* 2004: 16).

China is no exception to this generalization. It has made slow progress with electricity reform. In 2002, China split its single, vertically integrated, utility into two grid companies (a large one covering most of the country, and a small one in the south) and a number of generation companies (including five large ones). It experimented with wholesale electricity markets in 2002, but that was short-lived, and generators no longer bid for dispatch but sell at centrally fixed prices. China also established in 2002 a State Electricity Regulatory Commission (SERC), but it focuses on technical rather than economic regulation. Prices are still set by government (although the SERC can offer its advice) and, as noted earlier, mechanisms for cost pass-through have been established but are not used. Central planning is still used to guide generation expansion. The conclusion of the International Energy Agency that in the energy sector 'China is caught between the old planning mechanisms and a new approach' (IEA 2006: 16) is probably as relevant today as when it was written.

Second, partial reforms might actually make it more difficult to introduce mitigation measures. The difficulty of introducing a merit-based dispatch system in China, discussed above, is a good example of this. If electricity in China were provided today by vertically integrated utilities, it would be easy to introduce merit-based dispatch. It would also be easy if generation and transmission (strictly, power-purchase) were split, and generators were compensated using a two-part tariff, separating capacity from actual generation. But what actually happened was that generation and transmission were split, but a two-part tariff was not introduced. It was this partial reform that has made it difficult to introduce merit-based dispatch.

Of course, there are many reasons to undertake energy sector reforms. The main driver is economic. From a climate change perspective, the main reason for introducing energy or power reforms would be to enhance the impact of carbon pricing. The motivations are compelling, but it is important to recognize that if power sector reforms are difficult, then partial reforms are likely, and if partial reforms may have an ambiguous effect, then one cannot be confident that a power sector reform programme will in fact help rather than hinder mitigation, at least in the short term.

Broader economic reforms

It is not cheap energy that is driving China's massive expansion of energy-intensive goods, such as steel (Figure 5.1). Energy prices are low in China compared with Europe and Japan but not compared with the USA (Figure 5.8).

The search for what Rosen and Houser call 'the root causes of (China's) structural over-allocation into energy-intensive industry' (Rosen and Houser 2007: 37) must extend beyond the energy sector. As they argue: 'the pervasive revealed comparative advantage of heavy industry manufactured goods from China is generally rooted in distortions other than energy inputs' (ibid: 38).

China is characterized by both an exceptionally high investment rate and by a high share of industry in value-added, as Figure 5.15, from He and Kuijs (2007), shows. The reasons for this are complex, but include, as argued by Huang, Y. (2010), limited liberalization of China's factor markets. Low interest rates, high reinvestment rates by state-owned enterprises and low land prices in particular have all encouraged capital-intensive industrial production.

Whatever the causes, one of China's main economic policy objectives is rebalancing of the economy. This rebalancing has multiple dimensions: from savings to consumption, from production for foreign markets to production for domestic markets, and from the industrial to the service sector. Rebalancing the economy should not only be good for short-term economic welfare, but should also reduce emissions. Table 5.2 illustrates this point by comparing the share of GDP for China's different sectors with their share of energy use. Industry (the secondary sector) is responsible for 49 per cent of China's GDP, but 84 per cent of China's energy use. A 10 percentage point switch in GDP composition away from industry towards services (the tertiary sector) would, everything else being equal, result in a 14 per cent reduction in energy intensity.

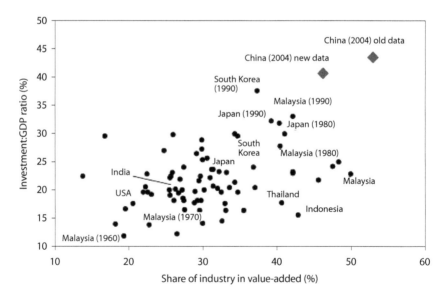

Figure 5.15 China has exceptionally high investment rate and industry/GDP share.
Source: He and Kuijs (2007).

Table 5.2 A switch away from industry to services would help reduce China's energy intensity. Notes: The year is 2007. Construction is included with industry in the secondary sector. Household energy use (about 11% of the total) is included in the secondary share of energy use. Source: NBS (2010).

Sector	Share of GDP (%)	Share of energy (%)	Energy intensity index
Primary (agriculture)	11	3	0.3
Secondary (industry and construction)	49	83	1.5
Tertiary (services)	40	14	0.3
Total	100	100	1

Slower economic growth would also of course help reduce the growth in China's emissions. If China grows at 10 per cent in 2010, as its initial estimates suggest, then its average GDP growth according to the latest figures, between 2005 and 2010 will be just over 11 per cent. This is not only well above the 7.5 per cent target embodied in the 2006–10 Eleventh Five-Year Plan. It will also be China's highest 5-year average growth since the reforms began, which is a remarkable result considering that the period encompasses the global financial crisis. It seems heretical to suggest that China would do better by growing more slowly, but it is possible that slower growth would actually improve welfare. For example, a switch in government spending from infrastructure to health could reduce growth but still be welfare-enhancing as well as emissions-reducing.

As with energy reform, rebalancing will not be undertaken to reduce emissions. But emissions reductions efforts will not succeed unless rebalancing occurs. It is this link between mitigation and rebalancing which, more than any other domestic issue, makes climate change a defining challenge for China. The international challenges China faces in relation to climate change, to which we now turn, are no less daunting.

INTERNATIONAL DIMENSIONS

Recent developments

In 2009, I wrote a chapter in the annual Australian National University 'China update' (Howes 2009a) answering in the affirmative the question of whether China could save the Copenhagen negotiations and deliver a global deal. While some accused the Chinese of wrecking the negotiations, Copenhagen, with Chinese support, in fact delivered all three of the ingredients I argued would be critical for obtaining a global deal.

First, in the run-up to Copenhagen, the Chinese Government announced its domestic emissions target, the 40–45 per cent target discussed above.

Other developing economies followed suit and, by the end of Copenhagen, countries responsible for 80 per cent of the world's emissions had announced economy-wide emissions targets.

Second, the developed countries – which already had emissions targets in place or announced – responded with a financing package, promising 'USD 30 billion for the period 2010–2012 with balanced allocation between adaptation and mitigation' and a 'goal of mobilizing jointly USD 100 billion dollars a year by 2020 to address the needs of developing countries from a wide variety of sources: public and private, bilateral and multilateral' (UNFCCC 2010: 3).

Third, a compromise was reached on the issue of verification or transparency. Developing countries ('Non-Annex I Parties' in UNFCCC parlance) would not be subject to the same requirements as developed countries, but would not get off without commitment either. Rather (UNFCCC 2010: 2):

> Mitigation actions taken by Non-Annex I Parties will be subject to their domestic measurement, reporting and verification the result of which will be reported through their national communications every two years. Non-Annex I Parties will communicate information on the implementation of their actions through National Communications, with provisions for international consultations and analysis under clearly defined guidelines that will ensure that national sovereignty is respected.

Why, with these critical components in place, was Copenhagen nevertheless a failure? It was not because it didn't deliver a legal text. No one expected it to deliver more than a political agreement. The reason is that the political agreement that Copenhagen delivered, the Copenhagen Accord, contained no reference as to how and by when it would be converted into a legal text. Although, one year later, at Cancun, the Copenhagen Accord was subsumed into an official agreement of the Parties to the United Nations Framework Convention on Climate Change (as against being merely 'noted' at Copenhagen itself), there is still no sign of how these agreements (decisions of the Parties) will be converted into a legal agreement which countries can sign.

Why has no agreement been possible on how to convert the Copenhagen agreement into a legal document? The answer to that is there was a fourth issue to which most analysts, including myself, failed to give due consideration, and which has defied attempts at reconciliation, namely the issue of legal form. Essentially, China and other developing countries want developed countries to sign up to a second (post-2012) commitment period for the Kyoto Protocol. They might be willing to negotiate a second agreement covering their own commitments, but only if there is a guarantee of a second Kyoto commitment period. Their view is that Kyoto is the main achievement to date of all the international climate change negotiations (stretching back to the early 1990s) and that the developed countries shouldn't be able to walk away from it. The USA, on the other hand, which has never ratified Kyoto, will have nothing to do with a second commitment period. Japan and Russia have also now indicated their opposition to a second Kyoto commitment period.

There is no obvious resolution to this disagreement. In my view, the divergence of views on this issue makes an international agreement (i.e. a treaty, something that can be signed, as against decisions of the Parties) highly unlikely any year soon.

The deadlock on an international treaty is a blow to international efforts, but not a knockout one. A less formal approach could be used, in which countries make individual efforts, apply peer-group pressure to each other, and develop bilateral and regional trading and other cooperative links. This so-called bottom-up approach would still be guided by decisions of the UNFCCC Parties, although not in as binding or tight a way as it would be under a treaty.

Although the bottom-up approach emerged at Copenhagen as a possible way forward, its development is threatened by a lack of leadership from the USA. The most worrying climate change development since Copenhagen has been the failure of the US Congress to commit the USA either to an emissions target or to a carbon price. Inaction by the USA inevitably has a huge discouragement effect on other countries. There is no doubt that if the USA had put a carbon price in place, then Canada would have one, and Australia. And then Japan and Korea. China would also do more. It would be a circuit breaker. Unfortunately, legislation from the USA is not going to happen in the near future, with the Republicans, dominated by climate-change sceptics, taking control of the House. The USA is not inactive on climate change. Many states are taking action. The US federal government is supporting important technological initiatives, and the President has some powers under the Environmental Protection Act to regulate carbon dioxide emissions. Nevertheless, the USA is not doing enough and, importantly, is not perceived to be leading.[7]

China's response

Climate change poses a geopolitical dilemma for China. It cannot free-ride on the USA, because the USA is not leading. What then should it do? Should it allow the USA to provide an upper bound on global ambition, and thereby ensure an inadequate global effort, or should China itself exercise global leadership on this issue, and thereby let the USA off the hook? More generally, where the dominant superpower is not providing leadership on a key issue, how should the emerging superpower respond?

It is important to recognize the important contributions China has already made. China has already gone far beyond the expectations of many analysts in announcing a target that is both ambitious and unconditional. Before Copenhagen, many distinguished analysts assumed that China and other developing countries would have to be paid for any reduction in their emissions below business as usual. Jeffrey Frankel was a prominent proponent of the view that China and other major developing countries should take on business as usual targets, so that it could make a profit (via the sale of excess emissions permits) from any mitigation effort (Frankel 2007). Such a view is supported by a literal interpretation of the United Nations Framework Convention on Climate Change, Article 4.3 of which famously guarantees developing countries that the 'incremental costs' of their mitigation efforts will be covered by others.

China's commitment is not only unconditional on funding support from other countries. It is also unconditional on the commitments made by other countries. Several developed countries or regions, such as Japan and the EU, have put forward targets that are conditional on the efforts of others. Others, such as the USA and Australia have yet to put forward definitive targets. China's target by contrast is already firm and operational.

What else might be expected from China?

Three additional steps can be considered. First, the biggest contribution China could make would be to make clear progress to its 2020 target. This would not only make a significant contribution to the task of global mitigation, but would also have a significant encouragement effect on other countries. Since the USA cannot be persuaded to lead, perhaps our only chance is that it can be forced to follow. The onus for putting such a strategy in place must fall on other developed countries, but cannot be successfully executed by them alone. China has a critical role to play, as its stance, more than that of any other country, will influence Washington.

The second area where more could be expected from China is in the area of transparency. It is not clear to the outside observer why, even if in a regime honouring the central UNFCCC tenet of 'common but differentiated responsibilities', different reporting standards should apply to different countries. China could be given a grace period to give it time to do the technical work needed to meet global reporting standards. But it is hard to see why, once this period is over, the world's biggest emitter should not be required to meet the world's best standards for reporting and verification. China's low per-capita income and relatively low per-capita emissions require strong differentiation of its target from those of developed countries (for example, China should be allowed to grow its emissions in the immediate future, albeit at a slower rate than in the past), but it is hard to see how these factors should lead to the country being made subject to different verification standards. As discussed earlier, it is not possible to verify from published data China's claim to be on-track to achieving its target of a 20 per cent reduction in energy intensity by 2010 relative to 2005. This undermines the credibility of China's mitigation effort, and inevitably leads to suspicion that China is exaggerating its progress. China can and must do better in terms of international reporting and transparency.

Third, should China adopt a more flexible position in the international negotiations, and drop its insistence on a second Kyoto Protocol commitment period? This would certainly be helpful for overcoming the current stalemate, but may be too much to ask. Geopolitical realities demand that China would need to get something in return for this concession. One could imagine a grand bargain in which China dropped its insistence on a second commitment period for Kyoto in return for the US Senate adopting legislation on climate change. Unfortunately, due to US Senate intransigence, such a bargain is not on the table.

CONCLUSION

Climate change mitigation poses important domestic and international challenges for China. On the domestic front, China has put forward an ambitious emissions reduction target. Achieving it will not be easy. The chapter has highlighted three critical challenges that will need to be addressed if this target is to be achieved.

First, successful mitigation will require that energy prices rise significantly, whether through the introduction of a carbon price or other means. This is not an easy task for any country, and particularly not for one such as China, which still faces significant development challenges. But it is critical not only for reducing emissions, but also for other important policy goals, in particular energy security.

Second, if carbon prices are to fulfil their potential as a mitigation instrument, reform of the energy sector will be required to allow cost pass-through. Reforms to allow a merit-order for generation dispatch, so that environmental as well as economic considerations can be taken into account, will also be important.

Third, to slow energy growth, mitigation will also require a rebalancing of the Chinese economy, away from industry towards services.

Other measures will of course be needed (such as support for research and development, and other regulatory measures), but the three highlighted above will be the most difficult and have the most far-reaching consequences.

On the international front, the failure of the USA to provide leadership on the climate change issue makes for a bleak outlook. The fundamental international question facing China in relation to climate change mitigation is: is it willing to provide leadership on an issue on which the world's superpower is inadequately engaged? Looking forward, as China becomes more and more powerful, increasingly the world will look to it for leadership on important global issues. Climate change will be an important test case of whether China is prepared to rise to the challenge, even when the USA is lagging.

It is unrealistic to think that an international agreement can be reached without greater effort by the USA. But China also needs to do more to show global leadership. The most important contribution it can provide is to make serious progress towards its 2020 target. It also needs to improve the transparency around its official energy and emissions figures, with a view to eventually adhering to the same reporting rules as other major global powers.

Whether China is up to the climate change challenge remains to be seen. Climate change scepticism appears to be a powerful force in China, as it is in many other countries (see, for example, Allan (2010) and Huang W. (2010)). Lack of leadership by the USA reinforces a view in China that climate change is a conspiracy perpetrated by the West designed to keep it in its place (Gou 2010; Liuxiazaihui 2010). Beyond climate change, it remains to be seen whether China is able to complete the reform path it embarked on some 40 years ago, and how it completes its transition to superpower status. However, the point of this chapter is not to make predictions of the likelihood of success. Rather it is to make and elaborate on the point that successful mitigation is a defining challenge for China not only because it is needed to avert dangerous and potentially catastrophic climate change, but also because it will indicate that China is successfully dealing with its other major domestic and international challenges.

NOTES

1 Professor of Economics, and Director, Development Policy Centre and International & Development Economics, Crawford School of Public Policy, Australian National University; Stephen.howes@anu.edu.au. I thank Chung Seungwon and Feng Shenghao for excellent research assistance, and, without implication, Leo Dobes and Frank Jotzo for discussions and collaboration.
2 Note, however, that more recent PPPs give a lower GDP for China and thus would give it a higher energy intensity.
3 See http://www.businessgreen.com/business-green/news/2262857/reports-china-impose-carbon-tax.
4 In a world of partial mitigation, suppliers and investors may also respond by moving emissions-intensive production offshore. This is the problem of carbon leakage.
5 Mao *et al.* (2008) conclude that the price of coal would be 15 per cent higher if all government subsidies in its production and distribution were removed.
6 This paragraph draws on Mercados EMI (2010).
7 The simplest way to see this is to note that the United States' Copenhagen commitment is for a 17 per cent cut in emissions relative to 2005 'in conformity with anticipated U.S. energy and climate legislation, recognizing that the final target will be reported to the Secretariat in light of enacted legislation' (World Bank 2010a: 6). Absent this legislation, the USA is unable even to commit itself to a firm target.

REFERENCES

Arnold, J. (2008) 'Do tax structures affect aggregate economic growth? Empirical evidence from a panel of OECD countries', *OECD Economics Department Working Paper*, No. 643, Paris: Organisation for Economic Co-operation and Development.
Allan, N. (2010) 'China's climate change skepticism', *The Atlantic*, 10 March, available at http://www.theatlantic.com/technology/archive/2010/03/chinas-climate-change-skepticism/37282/.

Bacon, R., Bhattacharya, S. and Kojima, M. (2010) 'Expenditure of low-income households on energy: evidence from Africa and Asia', *Extractive Industries and Development Series*, No. 16, Washington, DC: World Bank.

Besant-Jones, J.E. (2006) 'Reforming power markets in developing countries: what have we learned?', *Energy Mining Sector Board Discussion Paper*, No.19, Washington, DC: World Bank.

Burke, P. (2010) 'The energy supply ladder and its carbon implications', Canberra: Australian National University (mimeo).

China Electricity Council (2010) *2015 年中国煤电装机将达 9.33 亿千瓦* [*China's coal-power generation capacity will reach 933GW in 2015*], available at http://www.cec.org.cn/news/showc.asp?id=132468.

Dechezleprêtre, A., Glachant, M., Hascic, I., Johnstone, N. and Ménière, Y. (2008) 'Invention and transfer of climate change mitigation technologies on a global scale: a study drawing on patent data', *CERNA Working Series,* available at http://ssrn.com/abstract=1414227.

EIA (Energy Information Administration) (2010) *International Energy Statistics,* US Energy Information Administration, available at http://tonto.eia.doe.gov/cfapps/ipdbproject/IEDIndex3.cfm?tid=2&pid=2&aid=7.

EMF (Energy Modelling Forum) (2009) International database available at http://emf.stanford.edu/events/emf_briefing_on_climate_policy_scenarios_us_domestic_and_international_policy_architectures.

Frankel, J. (2007) 'Formulas for quantitative emissions targets', in J.E. Aldy and R.N. Stavins (eds) *Architectures for Agreement: Addressing Global Climate Change in the Post-Kyoto World*, pp. 31–57, Cambridge: Cambridge University Press.

Garnaut, R. (2008) *The Garnaut Climate Change Review*, Cambridge: Cambridge University Press.

Garnaut, R., Howes, S., Jotzo, F. and Sheehan, P. (2009) 'The implications of rapid development for emissions and climate-change mitigation', in D. Helm and C. Hepburn (eds) *The Economics and Politics of Climate Change*, pp. 81–106, Oxford: Oxford University Press.

Gou, H. (2010) *Low-carbon Conspiracy*, Taiyuan: Shanxi Economy Press.

He, J. and Kuijs, L. (2007) 'Rebalancing China's economy – modelling a policy package', *World Bank China Research Paper*, No. 7, Washington, DC: World Bank.

Howes, S. (2009a) 'Can China rescue the global climate change negotiations?,' in R. Garnaut, L. Song and W. Thye Woo (eds) *China's New Place in a World in Crisis*, pp. 409–430, Canberra: Australian National University E Press.

—— (2009b) 'Sustaining growth and mitigating climate change: are the costs of mitigation underestimated?', paper presented to the July East–West Center Conference on Climate Change and Green Growth: Korea's National Growth Strategy.

—— (2010) 'China's energy intensity target: on-track or off?', *East Asia Forum*, 31 March, available at http://www.eastasiaforum.org/2010/03/31/chinas-energy-intensity-target-on-track-or-off/.

Huang, W. (2010) *'Hockey Stick' Scandal, Climate Bubble and the Future of Climate Politics*, Peking University, Beijing: Center for Chinese and Global Affairs.

Huang, Y. (2010) 'China's great ascendancy and structural risks: consequences of asymmetric market liberalization', *Asian–Pacific Economic Literature*, 24(1): 65–85.

IEA (International Energy Agency) (2006) *China's Power Sector Reforms: Where to Next?*, Paris: IEA.
—— (2008) *World Energy Outlook 2008*, Paris: IEA.
—— (2009a) CO_2 *Emissions from Fuel Combustion*, 2009 edition, release 01, available at http://oberon.sourceoecd.org/vl=15178979/cl=15/nw=1/rpsv/statistic/s26_about.htm?jnlissn=16834291.
—— (2009b) *Energy Balances of Non-OECD Member Countries – Extended Balances*, 2009 edition, release 01, Paris: IEA.
—— 2010, *Energy Prices and Taxes – Energy End-use Prices, (US/toe, PPP/unit)*, vol. 2010, release 02, available at http://puck.sourceoecd.org/vl=16663138/cl=15/nw=1/rpsv/statistic/s29_about.htm?jnlissn=1683626x.
Johansson, A., Heady, C., Arnold, J., Brys, B. and Vartia, L. (2008) 'Tax and economic growth', *OECD Economics Department Working Paper*, No. 620, Paris: Organisation for Economic Co-operation and Development, available at http://www.oecd.org/officialdocuments/displaydocumentpdf/?cote=ECO/WKP(2008)28&doclanguage=en.
Kojima, M. (2009) 'Government response to oil price volatility', *Extractive Industries for Development Series*, No. 10, Washington, DC: World Bank.
Lee, H. (2010) 'Regional mitigation costs from EMF22 models', Canberra: Australian National University (mimeo).
Li, J. (2010) 'The economic effect of raising petrol product prices – application of SIC-GE', paper presented to the International Conference on the SIC-GE Model and Policy Simulation, 15–16 April, Beijing.
Liuxiahzaihui (2010) *In the Name of Carbon: The Global Game behind the Scene of Low-carbon Conspiracy*, Beijing: China Development Press.
Mao, Y., Sheng H. and Yang, F. (2008) *The True Cost of Coal*, Greenpeace, the Energy Foundation and WWF, available at http://www.eu-china.net/web/cms/upload/pdf/materialien/TCOC-Final-EN-08_10-28.pdf.
Mercados EMI (Mercados Energy Markets International) (2010) *China Power Dispatch Efficiency Improvement: Final Technical Report*, prepared for Energy Sector Management Assistance Program, Washington, DC: World Bank.
Morse, R.K., Rai, V. and He, G. (2009) 'Real drivers of carbon capture and storage in China and implications for climate policy', *Program on Energy and Sustainable Development, Working Paper*, No. 88, Stanford, CA: Stanford University.
NBS (National Bureau of Statistics of China) (2010) *2009 China Statistical Yearbook*, Beijing: China Statistics Press.
Nordhaus, W. (2008) *A Question of Balance: Weighing the Options on Global Warming Policies*, New Haven, CT: Yale University Press.
Outlook Economics (2010) *China Energy Graphs*, Canberra: Outlook Economics.
Pahle, M. (2010) 'Germany's dash for coal: exploring drivers and factors', *Energy Policy*, 38(7): 3431–3442.
PBL (Netherlands Environmental Assessment Agency) (2010) Database associated with J. Olivier and J. Peters 'No growth in total global CO_2 emissions in 2009', Bithoven, The Netherlands: Netherlands Environmental Assessment Agency, available at http://www.pbl.nl/en/publications/2010/No-growth-in-total-global-CO_2-emissions-in-2009.html.
Rosen, D.H. and Houser, T. (2007) *China Energy: A Guide for the Perplexed*, Washington, DC: Center for Strategic and International Studies, and Peterson Institute for International Economics.

Rosenzweig, M.B., Voll, S.P. and Pabon-Agudelo, C. (2004) 'Power sector reform: experiences from the road', *The Electricity Journal*, 16–18, available at doi:/10.1016/j.tej.2004.10.002.

SERC (State Electricity Regulatory Commission) (2006) *Electricity Regulation Report 2006* [*Dianli jianguan baogao (2006)*], Beijing: SERC.

—— (2007) *Electricity Regulation Report 2007* [*Dianli jianguan baogao (2007)*], Beijing: SERC.

—— (2008) *Electricity Regulation Report 2008* [*Dianli jianguan baogao (2008)*], Beijing: SERC.

—— (2009) *Electricity Regulation Report 2009* [*Dianli jianguan baogao (2009)*], Beijing: SERC.

Sheehan, P. (2008) 'The new global growth path: implications for climate change analysis and policy', *Climatic Change*, 91(3–4): 211–231.

Stern, D. and Lambie, R. (2010) 'Where is it cheapest to cut carbon emissions?', *Environmental Economics Research Hub Research Reports*, No. 1063, Canberra: Crawford School, Australian National University.

UNDP (United Nations Development Programme) (2010) *China and a Sustainable Future: Towards a Low Carbon Economy and Society*, China Human Development Report 2009/10, Beijing: China Publishing Group Corporation.

UNFCCC (United Nations Framework Convention for Climate Change) (2010) *Copenhagen Accord*, FCCC/CP/2009/L.7, 18 December.

Wadhwa, W., Gangopadhyay, S., Bacon, R., Kumar, P., Kojima, M., Lvovsky, K. and Ramaswamy, B. (2003) *India: Access of the Poor to Clean Household Fuels*, UNDP and World Bank Energy Sector Management Assistance Programme, available at http://vle.worldbank.org/bnpp/en/publications/energy-water/india-access-poor-clean-household-fuels.

World Bank (2010a) *Climate Change and Fiscal Policy: A Report for APEC*, Washington, DC: World Bank.

—— (2010b) *Winds of Change: East Asia's Sustainable Energy Future*, Washington, DC: World Bank East Asia and Pacific Region, East Asia Infrastructure Unit.

Wu, F.F., Wen, F. and Duan, G. (2004) 'Generation planning and investment under deregulated environment: comparison of USA and China', *IEEE Power & Energy Society General Meeting*, 2004, 2: 1324–1328.

Zhang, C. and Heller, T.C. (2004) 'Reform of the Chinese electric power market: economics and institutions', *Program on Energy and Sustainable Development, Working Paper*, No. 3, Stanford, CA: Stanford University.

Zhang, J. and Smith, K.R. (2007) 'Household air pollution from coal and biomass fuels in China: measurements, health impacts, and interventions', *Environmental Health Perspectives*, 115(6): 848–855.

Zhao, L. (2008) 'Research on issue of electrovalent composing in China', Masters' dissertation (in Chinese), Dongbei University of Finance and Economics.

Zhou, N., Levine, M. and Price, L. (2010) 'Overview of current energy efficiency policies in China', *Energy Policy*, 38(11): 6439–6452.

Zissis, C. and Bajoria, J. (2008) 'China's environmental crisis', Council on Foreign Relations, available at http://www.cfr.org/publication/12608/chinas_environmental_crisis.html.

6 Financial reform and economic development in China

Yiping Huang[1] and Xun Wang[2]

INTRODUCTION

Chinese economic reform delivered as many puzzles as miracles during the past three decades (Lin *et al.* 1995; Huang 2010b). Its financial reform was no exception, and it created at least two unique combinations:

- a combination of rapid financial development and widespread financial repression; and
- a combination of widespread repressive financial policies and sound macro-economic performance.

When economic reform began in the late 1970s, China had only a mono-bank financial system. Over the years, it built a comprehensive financial system with all types of financial institutions, financial intermediation and financial assets. The proportion of broad money supply (M2) to GDP, which is a good indicator of financial deepening, was about 180 per cent in 2010. In fact, China's M2 was already greater than that in the USA, although the Chinese economy was only about one-third the size of the US economy.

Meanwhile, China possesses almost all features typical of financial repression. The People's Bank of China (PBOC) still heavily regulates key interest rates, i.e. the commercial banks' deposit and lending rates. Real deposit rates are frequently in negative territory. PBOC also regularly adjusts the reserve requirement ratio. The authorities intervene in capital allocation decisions, strongly favouring state-owned enterprises (SOEs). And the government still limits market competition and restricts certain types of cross-border capital flows.

Contrary to the predictions by conventional theory (McKinnon 1973; Shaw 1973), repressive financial policies did not prevent strong macro-economic performance in China. During the reform period, real GDP growth in China averaged about 10 per cent. Except in 1985, 1988, 1994 and 2004, inflation was largely low and stable. Within a short period of 30 years, China emerged from a poor, closed, agrarian economy to an open economy, the second-largest in the world.

The above two combinations naturally raise a number of research questions. Why did the Chinese policy-makers push for quantitative financial development but, at the same time, retain repressive financial policies? And since the Chinese economy still achieved strong performance despite financial repression, is financial liberalization really desirable?

The purpose of this chapter is to provide a comprehensive review of financial liberalization during the reform period – its progress, logic, impact, challenges and options. Specifically, the following questions are explored:

(1) What were the main features of financial liberalization and financial development during the reform period?
(2) Why did the policy-makers choose those financial policies?
(3) How did financial liberalization or financial repression affect China's macro-economic performance?
(4) What are potential costs of the remaining repressive financial policies?
(5) Should China push to complete financial liberalization and, if yes, when and how?

In general, Chinese financial reform was relatively strong on building frameworks and expanding sizes of the financial system but relatively weak on improving quality and liberalizing the markets. This special feature was primarily driven by the government's intent to achieve the fastest GDP growth possible. Repressive financial policies, including negative real interest rates and intervention in capital allocation, were adopted as means of promoting economic growth. This is consistent with China's overall policy strategy of asymmetric liberalization of product and factor markets (Huang 2010a, b). Repressive financial policies are one of the most important elements of factor market distortion.

The financial repression index, which was originally constructed by Huang and Wang (2011), indicates that China's financial liberalization is probably halfway through. Empirical analyses also confirmed that the impact of financial repression on economic growth turned from positive in the 1980s and the 1990s to negative during the first decade of the twenty-first century. More importantly, while financial repression helped China maintain financial stability in the past, it has now become a source of financial risk and instability. It is time for China to seriously contemplate options for completing the 'unfinished revolution' in the financial area.

The chapter is organized as follows. The next section reviews the literature by highlighting the two opposing effects of financial repression on economic performance – the McKinnon effect and the Stiglitz effect. The third section assesses the progress of financial reform in four main areas – constructing the framework, growing the industry, improving governance and liberalizing the market – then tries to explain the logic behind the policy-makers' choice of the reform path. Then follows a quantitative examination of the evolution of China's financial policies and their impact on economic growth. The fifth section discusses the risks facing the economy and options for progressing it. Some concluding remarks follow.

LITERATURE REVIEW: THE McKINNON EFFECT VERSUS THE STIGLITZ EFFECT

That financial intermediation affects economic development has long been recognized in the economic literature, dating back to Schumpeter (1911). Levine (2005) summarized five main functions of the financial system: producing information ex ante about possible investment and capital allocation; monitoring investment and exerting corporate governance; facilitating trade, diversification and management of risk; mobilizing and pooling savings; and easing exchange of goods and services.

If financial development is such a positive factor for economic development, why is financial repression so common in developing countries? Roubini and Sala-i-Martin (1995), for instance, argued that a government might want to repress the financial sector because it would be an 'easy' source for financing the public budget. In order to increase the revenue from money creation, governments subject to large income-tax evasion might choose to increase seigniorage by repressing the financial sector and increasing inflation rates.

More relevant to the current study is the question about the impact of financial liberalization or financial repression in developing or transition economies. McKinnon (1973) was the first to coin the term 'financial repression', by which he meant policies regulating interest rates, setting high reserve requirements and allocating resources. McKinnon argued that such policies would impede financial deepening, hinder efficiency of the financial system and retard economic growth. We refer this negative impact of financial repression as the *McKinnon effect* in this chapter.

According to McKinnon and his supporters, interest rate repression had two primary negative effects. First, it reduced the incentive for economic agents to hold surplus in forms of financial assets. Thus, the quantity of financial savings forthcoming would be restricted, with negative implications for rates of investment and economic growth. Second, if interest rates were fixed at below market levels, there would be excess demand for credit and a need for administrative rationing. As a result, low-return investments might gain funding at the expense of high-return investments (Shaw 1973).

Similarly, Pagano (1993) showed that financial policies such as interest rate controls and reserve requirements reduced the financial resources available for financial intermediation activities. Similarly, King and Levine (1993) discovered that financial sector distortions reduce the rate of economic growth by lowering the rate of innovation.

Long and Sagari (1991) argued that mobilizing savings for investment, exerting effective corporate governance for state-owned enterprises (SOEs) and selecting non-state firms to finance are all important elements of a successful transition to a market economy. Financial reform in transitional economies is more comprehensive than in most developing countries because it involves not only liberalization, but also building the structure and framework of the financial system.

Experience of both transition and developing economies highlights the difficulties in establishing successful commercial banking systems that could allocate financial resources efficiently (Bonin and Szekely 1994; Haggard and Lee 1995; Nissanke and Aryeetey 1998). Policy on lending, barriers to inter-regional financing, distorted pricing, poor managerial incentives and lack of prudential financial regulation can often undermine financial performance.

However, some economists have also raised questions about the universal validity of the McKinnon effect. For instance, Stiglitz (1994) argued that it might be easier for many developing countries to deal with problems of market failure and financial risk under financial repression. If the government can mobilize and allocate savings effectively, then such state intervention could be positive for economic development. In this chapter, we refer this positive impact of financial repression as the *Stiglitz effect*.

Fry (1997) argued that there are important prerequisite conditions for successful financial liberalization. Such conditions normally include adequate prudential regulation and supervision of financial institutions and markets; a reasonable degree of price stability; fiscal discipline, taking the form of sustainable government borrowing; avoidance of inflationary expansion of reserve money by the central bank; profit maximizing, competitive behaviour by financial institutions; and a tax system that does not impose discriminatory taxes on financial intermediation.

Unfortunately, these prerequisite conditions or assumptions do not always hold in many developing and transition economies (Diaz-Alejandro 1985). Some economists have argued that well-designed government intervention could be preferable to a fully liberalized financial system in terms of promoting economic development (Stiglitz 1994; Hellman *et al.* 1997). Stiglitz (2000) further pointed out that the recently increased frequency of financial crises was closely associated with financial market liberalization in developing countries.

Fry (1997) argued that perverse reaction to higher interest rates by insolvent and/or non-profit-motivated firms was the primary reason for failure of financial liberalization in some countries. The insolvent firms simply continued, if they could, to borrow whatever they needed to finance the losses. Such firms bid up the interest rate until normally solvent, profit-motivated firms could no longer gain access to credit or became insolvent due to the high cost of borrowing.

Existing empirical studies produced mixed results, with some supporting the McKinnon effect while others validate the Stiglitz effect. For instance, Roubini and Sala-i-Martin (1992) demonstrated that a fraction of the weak growth experience in Latin American countries could be explained by financially repressive policies. Using time-series data for Malaysia, Ang and McKibbin (2007) discovered that financial liberalization, through removal of repressive policies, had a favourable effect on stimulating financial development. Arestis and Demetriades (1997) and Demetriades and Luintel (2001) found, on the other hand, that financial repression in South Korea actually had positive effects on its financial development.

Similarly, economists were also divided on of the effects of financial liberalization in China. Liu and Li (2001) confirmed positive contributions of financial liberalization to economic growth during China's reform period. Lardy (2008) estimated that financial repression, mainly negative real interest rates, cost Chinese households about 255 billion yuan (US$36 billion) or 4 per cent of GDP, in addition to lowering overall economic efficiency. According to Lardy (2008), the corporates, the banks and the government, respectively, captured a quarter, a quarter and a half of the implicit net tax imposed on households by financial repression.

However, Maswana (2011: 15) suggested that although repressive financial policies were bad for allocative efficiency, they probably created what he described as 'adaptive efficiency', the ability of the government to quickly adapt to the changing environment. Li (2004) also argued that mild financial repression helped China maintain the financial stability needed for reform. But, over time, financial repression inflicted increasing costs in terms of lowering economic efficiency. Moreover, it tended to be self-propelling and self-sustaining, creating a low-efficiency trap that prevented financial sector liberalization.

LOGIC OF CHINESE FINANCIAL REFORM

China's financial reform has come a long way since the beginning of economic reform. In the pre-reform period, China had a mono-bank system. The PBOC served as both the central bank and the commercial bank. The central planning system had little need for financial intermediation as almost all funds were allocated by government plans. When the leaders decided to start economic reforms in the cold winter of 1978, they immediately began the task of creating banks and many other financial institutions. Today, China already has a very comprehensive financial system.

In retrospect, we may group China's financial reform measures during the reform period into four broad areas. The first area was construction of a financial framework. In 1978, the authorities established the Bank of China (BOC), the China Construction Bank (CCB) and the Agricultural Bank of China (ABC). In 1984, the government set up a separate central bank, still called the PBOC, by transferring all the commercial activities to the newly created Industrial and Commercial Bank of China (ICBC). In 1995, the National People's Congress (NPC) passed the Law of PBOC, which explicitly defined the policy objectives and responsibilities of the central bank. In 1990 and 1991, the government set up the Shanghai and Shenzhen stock exchanges, respectively, and created the China Security Regulatory Commission (CSRC), a national regulatory body, in 1992.

The second area was promotion of quantitative financial development. In addition to creating the 'big four' banks (ABC, BOC, CCB and ICBC), the authorities also approved the creation of about a dozen joint-stock banks, more than 100 city commercial banks and numerous foreign-owned banks, foreign bank branches and representative offices. The number of listed companies in the domestic A-share market increased from 10 in 1990 to 1,781 in 2009. The total stock market capitalization grew from less than 500 billion yuan in 1993 to 32.7 trillion yuan at its peak in 2007. However, while China's financial deepening, indicated by a rising proportion of broad money supply (M2) to GDP, is already well ahead of most developing and advanced economies, its financial intermediation still relies disproportionately on the banking sector.

The third area is reform of financial institutions. Many of the financial institutions were originally created as SOEs. They were often subject to heavy state intervention and created huge financial risks. At the time of the Asian financial crisis, the average non-performing loan (NPL) proportion was estimated at between 25 and 40 per cent. Most banks were technically insolvent. Since then, the authorities have made serious efforts to transform these state-owned commercial banks (SOCBs) into true financial entities, including writing off of NPLs, injecting public capital, introducing foreign strategic investors, and public listing. Many banks also adopted international standard accounting, loan classification, information disclosure and risk-control systems. Unfortunately, most banks still behave more like SOCBs than listed commercial entities. Extraordinary loan growth in China during the global financial crisis provided a useful reference about banks' risk management.

The fourth, and final, area is liberalization of financial markets. This included allowing market competition and letting demand and supply determine asset prices. The proportion of the SOCBs in the banking sector, for instance, declined from 90 per cent to close to 50 per cent during the reform period. The authorities also liberalized most asset prices such as interest rates, bond yields and stock prices. However, the PBOC still controls the base deposit and lending rates for the commercial banks, and intervenes heavily in the foreign-exchange market. Over the years, the government lifted controls over many types of cross-border capital flows, although it retained relatively tight restrictions on debt financing, outward foreign direct investment (FDI) and portfolio investment in stocks, bonds, money market derivatives and mutual funds.

Comparatively speaking, China has made remarkable progress in putting into place the basic framework of the financial system and in expanding financial assets. The Chinese financial system already resembles a modern financial sector in advanced economies, although important quality differences remain; for example, China still lags significantly in freeing up key financial market prices, especially interest and exchange rates. Also, while there has been significant improvement in both the behaviour of financial institutions and the allocation of financial resources, the commercial banks are still subject to heavy state intervention. It is probably fair to conclude that the Chinese Government has made serious efforts to build a modern financial sector but is not willing to give up all control over it.

So why did the financial reform show such a unique pattern of being strong on framework and quantity but weak on market and quality? We try to explain the logic of China's financial reform applying the framework identified by Huang in a series of recent studies on asymmetric liberalization of the product and factor markets (Huang 2010a, b). Huang noted that, during China's reform period, the product markets were almost completely liberalized, with prices freely determined by demand and supply. But factor market distortions, such as in energy prices and exchange rates, remained widespread and serious. Some of these distortions were legacies of the central planning system, while others were newly introduced during the reform period.

Such distortions had a common feature: they repressed factor prices and lowered production costs. They were like subsidies to producers, exporters and investors, artificially raising profits of production, increasing returns to investment and improving competitiveness of Chinese exports. They helped promote economic growth, but also caused serious internal and external imbalances (Huang and Tao 2010; Huang and B. Wang 2010).

Huang and his co-authors argued that the main rationale behind the asymmetric liberalization approach was the government's objective of achieving the fastest possible economic growth. GDP growth was the single most important economic indicator determining local officials' chances of promotion (Li and Zhou 2005). Therefore, asymmetric liberalization was an intentional choice by the government. Free markets for products helped overcome the inefficiency problem of the central planning system. Meanwhile, the government retained distortions in factor markets to subsidize certain economic activities and to allocate resources according to policy priorities (Huang 2010a, b).

The same logic is applicable to China's financial liberalization. From the very beginning of economic reform, Chinese policy-makers recognized the importance of finance for growth, as well articulated by Gurley and Shaw (1955), Levine (2005) and many others. Therefore, the government immediately got on with the task of building a modern financial system from scratch. It resulted in rapid growth of financial infrastructure, including banking sector and capital markets, and financial assets, including loans, stocks, bonds and other financial products. Rapid financial development is consistent with the general style of the market-orientated reform (Lin *et al.* 1995; Sachs and Woo 2000). Empirical examinations have confirmed the positive impact of financial development on economic growth during China's reform period (Wang 2011).

The policy-makers probably also understood the McKinnon-effect benefits of financial liberalization. The government continuously expanded the roles of market mechanisms in the financial system. It introduced joint-stock and foreign banks to promote competition. It also gradually allowed market-determined interbank market rates and treasury bond yields, and increased flexibility in the exchange rates. It even slowly reduced restrictions on certain types of cross-border capital flows, especially inward FDI.

But liberalization was not the entire story of Chinese financial reform. The government continued to play an important part in operation of the financial system, such as controls of interest rates and exchange rates, interventions in capital allocation, and restrictions on cross-border capital flows.

Why did the government choose financial repression instead of full liberalization during the reform period? Perhaps the government also understood that there were Stiglitz-effect benefits of financial repression for some countries.

First, repressive financial policies were consistent with the general asymmetric liberalization approach – supporting growth through repressed factor costs (Huang 2010a, b). Specifically, depressed interest and exchange rates were like subsidies to investors and exporters. An undervalued currency, for instance, promoted exports and discouraged imports. This was particularly true during the years following the Asian financial crisis as the government pursued both strong economic growth and a large current account surplus. Similarly, very low real interest rates encouraged investment, which at least in part contributed to the rising share of investment in GDP during the reform period.

Second, repressive financial policies ensured sufficient resources for economic activities and, particularly, priority areas identified by policy-makers. Due to excess demand for funds, mandatory capital allocation became necessary when interest rates were kept below market levels. More importantly, however, the government often used the financial sector as an important means supporting economic policy. During the global financial crisis, for instance, the government pushed the banks to lend massively, alongside the stimulus package, to boost growth. Similarly, the government also called upon the banks to support its 'go west' policy in the late 1990s.

Third, repressive financial policies were necessary for the gradual and 'dual-track' reform approach (Naughton 1995). A key feature of the Chinese reform was to let economic activities grow outside the planning system, without initially hurting the planned economy (Fan 1994). This implied that the government needed to continuously support the SOEs, even if they were not profitable. During the 1990s, many banks provided the so-called 'stability loans' or policy loans to failing SOEs. The government eventually had to abandon this practice due to the increasing financial burden on the banking system. But the initial support, which was made possible under repressive policy, was critical for ensuring the smooth progress of economic reforms.

And, finally, repressive financial policies might be critical for maintaining financial stability during the early stages of economic development (Hellman *et al.* 1997; Stiglitz 1994, 2000). Since China did not have the necessary conditions for successful financial liberalization earlier, it was probably easier for the government to deal with problems of market failure and financial instability. China's own experiences provided some evidence for this argument. Without majority state ownership of the SOCBs and a relatively tightly controlled capital account, China would probably have suffered a major banking crisis during the Asian financial crisis and a recession during the global financial crisis.

QUANTITATIVE ASSESSMENT OF FINANCIAL REPRESSION

We take two steps to assess the impact of financial repression in China. First, we try to construct an aggregate financial repression index (FREP). This should provide a picture of how repressive financial policies evolved during the reform period. Second, we analyze the exact impact of FREP on economic growth using a provincial panel dataset for China. We are particularly interested in knowing if this impact varies over time.

The aggregate measure of financial repression, by definition, covers a list of policy variables. In empirical studies, economists often use different approaches to measure financial repression. The easiest indicator is negative real interest rates (see, for instance, Roubini and Sala-i-Martin (1992) and Lardy (2008)). Others sometimes use simple or weighted averages of the policy variables. In this exercise, we follow Ang and McKibbin (2007) by applying the principal component analysis (PCA) approach, which was originally developed by Demetriades and Luintel (1997, 2001).

We adopt a relatively broad definition of financial repression, which includes indicators in six areas:

1. negative real interest rates;
2. interest rate controls;
3. capital account regulations;
4. reserve requirement ratio (RRR);
5. lending by SOCBs; and
6. SOEs' share in outstanding loans.

We calculate the real interest rate by subtracting CPI from the one-year base deposit rate and, following Agarwala (1983) and Roubini and Sala-i-Martin (1992), we set it to 0 if it is positive, to 0.5 if it is negative but higher than minus 5 per cent and to 1 if it is lower than minus 5 per cent. Therefore, a higher index indicates a greater degree of repression.

Interest rate control is the proportion of types of interest rates subject to government controls. At the start of the reform, there were 63 types of interest rates under controls, including 14 types of deposit rates, 14 types of lending rates, 19 types of preferred lending rates, 10 types of foreign-currency deposit rates and 6 types of foreign-currency lending rates.

Capital-account control (CAC) is a *de jure* indicator. Applying classifica-tions of the Organisation for Economic Co-operation and Development (OECD) and China's State Administration of Foreign Exchange (SAFE), we estimate degrees of restrictions for all 11 categories of capital-account transactions. We first set each category to 1.00, meaning strict control, for the years before 1978. Likewise, an index of 0.75 indicates strong control, 0.50 moderate control, 0.25 weak control and zero a liberalized system. CAC is the average score for all categories. A higher score represents stricter capital-account control.

The RRR is the ratio set by the PBOC. However, there was no reserve requirement policy before 1984. For those years, we set RRR to the ratio of the deposits that PBOC as the commercial bank could not dispense, such as fiscal deposits, basic construction deposits and deposits of non-profit institutions.

The shares of the SOCBs, including both the 'big four' and the three policy banks in total outstanding loans, and of the SOEs in total outstand-ing loans, reveal the importance of the state sector in loan allocation from lenders' and borrowers' sides, respectively.

The purpose of the PCA approach is to derive common statistical compo-nents from all the above six variables to compute an aggregate index. This method avoids the usual issues of multicolinearity among different variables and double counting of the key components. It often involves three steps. First, we apply various statistical tests to determine the appropriateness of PCA for the sample. Second, by examining the total variance explained by principal components, we decide on the number of principal components that should be extracted. Finally, to compute the aggregate FREP, we then set the formula according to the results of the examination of total variance. The technical procedures and results are explained in detail in Huang and Wang (2011).

To make it easier to read, we normalize the FREP series by first setting the reading for a completely liberalized financial system to 0 and the reading at the start of the sample period (year 1978) to 1 (Figure 6.1).[3] FREP fell from 1.00 in 1978 to 0.59 in 2008, which indicates a steady trend of financial lib-eralization during the reform period. In fact, the lowest reading was 0.52 in 2006. The index rebounded in the following years, probably as a result of responses to the global financial crisis.

To examine the exact impact of financial repression on economic growth during China's reform period, we run several regressions of real GDP growth on FREP and a group of control variables:

$$RGDP_t = \alpha + \beta\, FREP_t + \sum_i \gamma_i\, X_{it} + \varepsilon_t$$

where $RGDP_t$ is real GDP growth rate, $FREP_t$ is the financial repression index and X_{it} is a set of control variables including investment share of GDP (inv_t), share of college students in total population (edu_t), trade openness ($trade_t$), government expenditure as share of GDP (gov_t) and share of SOEs

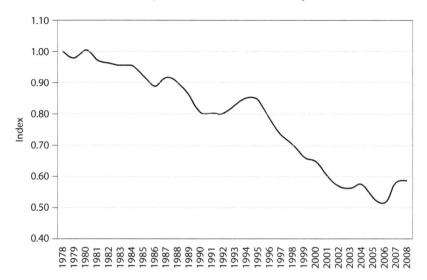

Figure 6.1 Financial repression index for China, 1978–2008 (1978 = 1.00). Sources: Huang and Wang (2011), Wang (2011).

in GDP (*state$_t$*). We use a provincial panel dataset for the years between 1978 and 2008 (for details of data and estimation methods, see Huang and Wang (2011)).

For the purpose of discussion here, we report the results of only four regressions applying the fixed-effect estimation method: one for the entire period 1978–2008, and one each for the three sub-periods, 1978–88, 1989–98 and 1999–2008 (Table 6.1). Also, we focus only on coefficient estimates for *FREP* in the first row, all of which are statistically significant at the 1 per cent significance level. Since the dependent variable is real GDP growth rate and FREP is an index between 0 and 1, the results for the full sample suggest that, were FREP to fall from 1 to 0 (full liberalization), real GDP growth would be *reduced* by 0.17 percentage points.

Surprisingly, the estimated FREP coefficient is positive in the regression covering the entire period. This result implies that financial repression was a positive factor contributing to economic growth during the reform period. It provides an important piece of evidence supporting the Stiglitz effect.

The government's effective mobilization of resources for economic growth is best illustrated by the rising share of investment in China's GDP, from about 30 per cent in 1978 to 48 per cent in 2010. Huang and his co-authors have explained that factor market distortions, especially distortions in the financial system, were key contributors to both rapid economic growth and the growing national investment ratio during China's reform period (Huang and Tao 2010; Huang and B. Wang 2010).

The estimated results for the three sub-periods are even more interesting. While financial repression was found to have a positive effect on growth

Table 6.1 Estimated results of the impact of financial repression on economic growth

	Full sample	1978–88	1989–98	1999–2008
FREP	0.167***	0.787***	0.313***	−0.132***
	(0.041)	(0.132)	(0.073)	(0.037)
INV	0.133***	0.068	0.191***	0.100***
	(0.022)	(0.069)	(0.047)	(0.021)
TRADE	0.010	0.025	0.010	0.007
	(0.008)	(0.034)	(0.014)	(0.012)
EDU	2.361	1.934	0.561	0.438
	(0.539)	(6.445)	(0.627)	(0.745)
GOV	−0.189***	−0.225	−0.518***	−0.169**
	(0.055)	(0.141)	(0.191)	(0.083)
SOE	−0.039*	−0.048***	−0.119***	−0.039*
	(0.020)	(0.011)	(0.031)	(0.023)
Time trend	0.002***	0.008***	0.003***	0.002
	(0.0008)	(0.002)	(0.002)	(0.014)
Year-specific effect	YES	YES	YES	YES
Province-specific effect	YES	YES	YES	YES
Observations	750	275	250	225
R^2	0.179	0.138	0.326	0.187

Sources: Huang and Wang (2010), Wang (2011). Notes: Year-specific effect refers to certain years when there were special events such as the Asian financial crisis and the global financial crisis. Numbers in the parentheses beneath the coefficient estimates are related standard errors, and *, ** and *** indicate statistically significant at 10, 5 and 1 per cent significance levels, respectively.

in the 1980s and the 1990s, this turned negative during the first decade of the twenty-first century, suggesting that, despite the declining trend of state intervention in the financial sector, repressive policies now *reduce* economic growth. This result for the latest period is consistent with the McKinnon effect. State intervention in capital allocation, for instance, might prevent funds from flowing to the most-efficient uses. Repressive financial policies would eventually slow financial development, increase financial risks, depress investment efficiency and reduce economic growth.

The Chinese experience of financial reform provides a bridge between the McKinnon effect and the Stiglitz effect. Repressive financial policies could have both positive and negative effects on macro-economic performance. The net impact depends on the relative importance of these two effects. In the early stages of economic development, when the financial market is underdeveloped, financial repression might help mobilize resources, support financial stability and, therefore, promote economic growth. When the financial system matures, financial repression would more likely reduce capital efficiency, increase financial risks and, therefore, slow economic growth.

While these results provide an interesting perspective for understanding the roles of repressive financial policies in the process of economic development, we must not generalize them too quickly. For instance, we should not take the Chinese experience as evidence that financial repression definitely *raises* economic growth. Financial repression had a positive impact on economic growth during the early stage of Chinese reform, probably because of the government's effective allocation of capital and its ability to control financial risks. Otherwise, financial repression might still be a negative factor for growth.

COMPLETING THE 'UNFINISHED REVOLUTION'

The finding that the growth impact of financial repression in China was dominated by the (positive) Stiglitz effect in the 1980s and 1990s but is now dominated by the (negative) McKinnon effect has important policy implications. Clearly, repressive financial policies have become burdens for macro-economic performance. However, the effect on growth seems small. We should therefore not anticipate sharp acceleration of economic growth following further liberalization.

But maintaining the status quo is no longer an option. Several problems are already growing rapidly in China, which could potentially destabilize the economy and financial markets.

The first problem relates to the behaviour of the financial institutions. For instance, despite adoption of modern corporate structure, the SOCBs remain tightly controlled by the state. The Party appoints the top executives of the banks, including their chairmen and presidents. Important business and personnel decisions are still made by Party committees, not by boards of directors. This was why, when financial risks increased in the wake of global financial crisis, the banks expanded their loan portfolio dramatically. This points to significant financial risks in the near future.

The second problem is state intervention in capital allocation. SOEs now account for less than 30 per cent of industrial output, but they still take away more than half of the total loans. If we include borrowing by local-government entities, the proportion might even be higher. The dynamic small and medium enterprises had to borrow from informal markets, with annual interest rates of above 20 per cent, compared with the commercial banks' one-year base lending rate of 6.25 percent. This implies inefficiency of capital allocation.

The third problem concerns the significantly distorted interest and exchange rates. The underestimated costs of capital caused serious economic imbalances such as overinvestment, underconsumption and large external account surpluses. Investment's share of GDP is already 48.5 per cent, while the current account surplus stayed at above 5 per cent of GDP in 2010. The real negative deposit rates were behind speculative activities in asset markets, and even products. The undervalued currency has been the main cause of massive 'hot money' inflows. All these factors risk the stability of macro-economic conditions and the sustainability of economic growth.

Finally, a fourth problem is declining effectiveness of capital account controls. According to the Mundell Trilemma, a country can achieve two of the following three international economic policy objectives: free flow of capital, a stable exchange rate and an independent monetary policy. Weakening capital restrictions reduce the PBOC's ability to control domestic liquidity conditions and interest rates. In a normal year, the PBOC sterilizes only about 80 per cent of the injected RMB liquidity for foreign exchange market intervention. This contributes to escalating inflation pressure.

While repressive financial policies probably protected the Chinese economy from external shocks in the past, due to lack of market discipline they have now become factors encouraging excessive risk-taking by domestic entities. For instance, during the global financial crisis, banks were assertive in their lending to support growth, while local government borrowed aggressively. According to PBOC's latest data, local government entities hold about one-third of outstanding loans. Assuming one-quarter of such debt is problematic, the banks' non-performing loan ratio could easily rise by 8 percentage points.

And repressive policies are developing a self-sustaining pattern. The only way to prevent the immediate surfacing and worsening of the risks mentioned above is to continue aggressive lending and borrowing to support growth and maintain cash flow. In the worst case outcome, this will be like a Ponzi scheme – dancing will continue until the music stops.

More than a decade ago, Lardy (1998) described Chinese banking reform as an 'unfinished revolution'. Today, the task of financial reform remains unfinished. The negative growth effect discovered for recent years and the growing risks discussed above imply that it is time to seriously consider completing China's financial liberalization. To achieve that goal, the government is faced with wide-ranging reform tasks, including, for instance, establishing an independent central bank, introducing market-based interest rates, giving up intervention in capital allocation, improving governance of financial institutions, developing capital market institutions, increasing exchange-rate flexibility and liberalizing the capital account.

During the past 30 years, China's macro-economic and financial conditions improved significantly, as evidenced by unusual macro-economic stability, healthy fiscal positions, good financial asset quality, a large current account surplus, huge foreign reserves and improved financial regulations. These imply that China already possesses the important prerequisite conditions for a more comprehensive liberalization of the financial system, including achieving capital account convertibility (Huang *et al.* 2011; Huang and Xie 2011).

So what key steps should China take to achieve the ultimate goal of capital account liberalization? McKinnon (1994) proposed the following order of reform for developing countries: (1) fiscal reform; (2) financial and trade liberalization; (3) exchange rate reform; and (4) capital account liberalization. This is a useful sequencing for China to follow, although some steps could take place simultaneously.

China's overall fiscal position is strong. But there is room for significant improvement in several ways. One is to shift the focus of budget expenditure from investment projects to public goods service. The government should also reduce its intervention in commercial banks' lending decisions in order to minimize future fiscal responsibilities. Another area is the operation of the state sector. The government still intervenes in prices of key inputs such as energy, resulting in the need to subsidize companies for operating losses. And, finally, it is important to discipline the spending of local governments and limit their deficits. Local-government borrowing has gone out of control recently, which could lead to serious fiscal consequences in the coming years.

Further substantial reforms are still needed in the financial sector. First, China needs an independent central bank. PBOC has always been an integral part of the State Council, which is the ultimate decision-maker for monetary policies. This is increasingly becoming an issue as the product markets have been almost completely liberalized and the private sector has already contributed more than two-thirds of the economy. The government, obsessed with economic growth, undermines price and financial stability from time to time. An independent PBOC, ideally reporting to the NPC, is critical for improving quality of monetary policy and gaining the confidence of international investors.

Second, it is now critical to introduce market-based interest rates. Currently, the government's key interest rate tools are still the officially determined base lending and deposit rates, which do not necessarily reflect market conditions. Negative real interest rates, for instance, contributed to a persistent overinvestment problem and price bubbles. If capital is not properly priced, then its efficient use is not possible. China already has the other two types of interest rates: interbank rates and risk-free bond yield. But these markets need to be developed further in order to serve as benchmarks for the pricing of capital. This would allow the PBOC to eventually shift to directly target Shibor (the Shanghai interbank offered rate) through various indirect policy tools.

Third, the government must completely give up its intervention in credit allocation, and promote competition in the financial industry. The banks should make their lending decisions based entirely on commercial considerations. And policy-related lending should be the responsibility of the policy banks. In any case, it is illogical for the state sector to continue to take away a disproportionate amount of capital. The government should redefine its role as a majority owner, but not direct operator, of most large financial institutions. Competition should also be increased in the financial industry, through lifting of existing restrictions and the introduction of other financial institutions, such as small banks and foreign security companies.

Fourth, the government should make more efforts to develop the capital markets, especially the corporate bond market. While banks are useful for economic development, direct financing plays different roles in returns and risk-sharing between borrowers and investors. In the meantime, capital market institutions need to be improved significantly. The stock markets, in particular, still exhibit strong symptoms of immature markets. Investors remain highly speculative and show very strong herding behaviour. Incorrect information, insider trading, rumours and market manipulation are still common. Market movements are often influenced more by government policies than by macro-economic circumstances. And stock prices are excessively volatile. The regulators made important efforts to diversify investor groups. The qualified foreign institutional investor (QFII) scheme, however, due to its size and restrictions, plays very limited roles in improving market mechanisms.

One of the most important tasks is to achieve conditional free float of the exchange rate. China adopted the managed float for the renminbi exchange rate in early 1994. After disruptions during the East Asian and global financial crises, the government reintroduced the managed float system in June 2010. The exchange rate, however, remains rigid. The strategy of letting the currency appreciate gradually caused some serious consequences, such as encouraging expectation of further appreciation, hot money inflows, a large current account surplus, massive liquidity, high inflation pressures and rapid accumulation of foreign-exchange reserves.

It is therefore advisable that the authorities achieve free float of the exchange rate by quickly reducing the central bank's intervention in the foreign-exchange market. Two-way fluctuation of the exchange rate, based on changing demand and supply relations, may be possible after a period of rapid currency appreciation. The government may wish to intervene in the market to avoid excessive volatility, such as through a stabilization fund. But such intervention should be two-directional and different from PBOC's current intervention to hold down the value of the renminbi. Capital account liberalization could then take place alongside floating of the exchange rate. Capital account convertibility, however, does not necessarily mean absolutely no restriction on capital flows. Given China's current financial situation and regulatory capability, it is probably better for the country to first aim at basic convertibility. In particular, China should probably retain restrictions on certain types of volatile short-term capital flows, at least initially. This should help avoid excessive shocks to the financial system. It is also consistent with the recent decision of the International Monetary Fund (IMF) to allow temporary use of restriction measures on cross-border short-term capital flows.

Our capital account control index suggests that China has been liberalizing the capital account, especially since the East Asian financial crisis. The State Administration of Foreign Exchange (SAFE) also estimates that about 75 per cent of the 40 items of the control measures monitored by the IMF have been partially, basically or completely liberalized. Current restrictions exist mainly in the following areas: portfolio investment in bond markets, stock markets, derivatives and money markets, mutual fund investments, real estate transactions, debt financing and outward direct investment (ODI).

It should be relative easy to lift restrictions on debt financing and ODI. Cross-border bond issuance can be monitored through debt/equity ratios of individual institutions and short-term debt proportions. ODI projects currently need to acquire approvals from SAFE, the National Development and Reform Commission, and the Ministry of Commerce. The approval procedures have become simpler lately as the government encourages capital outflows through direct investment. Therefore, liberalization in these two areas can be implemented quickly.

Should China also remove restrictions on cross-border portfolio investment immediately? The experience of India, Indonesia and Korea during the global financial crisis suggest that volatile portfolio flows could become an important source of financial market instability. It might therefore be useful to retain some restrictions to avoid excessive volatility. Fortunately, China has already introduced the QFII and qualified domestic institutional investor (QDII) schemes to allow cross-border portfolio flows. One option is to significantly increase the quotas under these two schemes and at the same time substantially weaken the terms, such as the number of days required for fund repatriation. This approach opens cross-border investment channels but at the same time minimizes volatility. The government may eventually abandon the QFII and QDII systems when it feels confident about capital flows.

CONCLUDING REMARKS

The Chinese financial reform during the past three decades is different from that in many other developing countries. It has involved not only liberalization but also development of the financial system, since China had almost no financial intermediation in the pre-reform period. Its financial reform efforts can be classified into four areas: (1) building the framework; (2) growing the scale; (3) reforming the institutions; and (4) liberalizing the markets.

In general, the Chinese reform has been strong on (1) and (2) but weak on (3) and (4). This is reflected in the interesting combination of rapid financial development and serious financial repression. Today, China already has a large and comprehensive financial system, comparable in size with those in many other market economies, but it still exhibits all the features typical of repressive financial policies; from controls of interest and exchange rates to restrictions on capital flows and capital allocation.

We argue that this interesting pattern can be explained by government pursuit of strong GDP growth – a large financial sector enables mobilization of financial resources to support growth, while repressive policies ensure subsidized capital for priority areas of the real economy. These gave rise to another combination of widespread financial repression and strong economic growth during China's reform period.

Empirical analyses of financial repression yield a number of interesting findings. First, the degree of financial repression actually declined steadily during the past three decades. China is probably halfway through financial liberalization. Second, while repressive financial policies had a positive impact on economic growth in the 1980s and 1990s their effect was negative during the first decade of the twenty-first century. The positive impact, which is consistent with the Stiglitz effect, captures the benefit of repressive policies in terms of allocating capital and dealing with problems of financial risk and market failure during early-stage economic development. The negative impact, which is consistent with the McKinnon effect, highlights inefficiency and risks caused by distortion in the price of capital and intervention in capital allocation.

These imply that, while repressive financial policies probably helped economic development in the past, they are now a net burden. More importantly, financial risks are rising as a result of these policies, highlighted by reckless borrowing by local governments and excessive lending by SOCBs. These policies have shown a tendency to be self-sustaining and, if they are not stopped, could cause exponential growth in the risk of financial crises occurring.

It is advisable that the authorities now seriously consider completing the task of financial liberalization in China. The measures implemented should include introduction of market-based interest rates, establishment of an independent central bank, growth of the corporate bond market, improvement of capital market institutions, adoption of a free-floating exchange rate and, finally, realization of capital account convertibility. It is probably best to organize these reform measures around capital account liberalization, following proper sequencing. If the government makes decisive moves, it is possible to complete the remaining tasks during the period of the Twelfth Five-Year Plan (2011–15).

But it is important to recognize that financial liberalization has to take into account the reality of the Chinese economy and financial system. We suggest three areas of policy caution in order to support financial stability after the reform. The first is that while a free-floating exchange rate is desirable, it is possible for the government to install certain buffering mechanisms, such as a government-sponsored stabilization fund, to prevent excessive volatility of the exchange rate. The second is that China should probably aim at achieving basic capital-account convertibility, not full convertibility. This was the reason behind our suggestion of maintaining the QFII and QDII systems for the time being, since portfolio flows are often more dramatic and can be reversed very easily. And the third is to maintain a certain degree of state ownership of large financial institutions to support investor confidence.

NOTES

1 China Macroeconomic Research Center, National School of Development, Peking University, yhuang@ccer.edu.cn.
2 China Economic Research Center, Stockholm School of Economics, xun.wang@hhs.se.
3 According to the derived raw data series of FREP, the number –7.4 represents the state of no financial repression.

REFERENCES

Agarwala, R. (1983) *Price Distortions and Growth in Developing Countries*, Washington, DC: World Bank,

Ang, J.B. and W.J. McKibbin (2007) 'Financial liberalization, financial sector development and growth: evidence from Malaysia', *Journal of Development Economics*, 84(1): 215–233.

Arestis, P. and P.O. Demetriades (1997) 'Financial development and economic growth: assessing the evidence', *Economic Journal*, 107(442): 783–799.

Bonin, John and I. Szekely (eds) (1994) *The Development and Reform of Financial Systems in Central and Eastern Europe*, Cheltenham: Edward Elgar.

Demetriades, P.O. and K.B. Luintel (1997) 'The direct costs of financial repression: evidence from India', *Review of Economics and Statistics*, 79(2): 311–320.

—— (2001) 'Financial restraints in the South Korean miracle', *Journal of Development Economics*, 64(2): 459–479.

Diaz-Alejandro, C. (1985) 'Good-bye financial repression, hello financial crash', *Journal of Development Economics*, 19(1–2): 1–24.

Fan, Gang (1994) 'Incremental changes and dual track transition: understanding the case of China', *Economic Policy*, 19 (supplement December): 99–122.

Fry, M. (1997) 'In favour of financial liberalisation', *Economic Journal*, 107(442): 754–770.

Gurley, J. and E. Shaw (1955) 'Financial aspects of economic development', *American Economic Review*, 45(4): 515–538.

Haggard, Stephan and Chung H. Lee (1995) *Financial Systems and Economic Policy in Developing Countries*, Ithaca, NY: Cornell University Press.

Hellmann, T., K. Murdock and J. Stiglitz, (1997) 'Financial restraint: toward a new paradigm', in M. Aoki, H.-K. Kim and M. Okuno-Fujuwara (eds) *The Role of Government in East Asian Economic Development: Comparative Institutional Analysis*, pp. 163–207, Oxford: Clarendon Press.

Huang, Yiping (2010a) 'China's great ascendancy and structural risks: consequences of asymmetric liberalization', *Asian–Pacific Economic Literature*, 24(1): 65–85.

—— (2010b) 'Dissecting the China puzzle: asymmetric liberalization and cost distortion', *Asian Economic Policy Review*, 5(2): 281–295.

Huang, Yiping and Kunyu Tao (2010) 'Factor market distortion and current account surplus in China', *Asian Economic Papers*, 3(9): 1–36.

Huang, Yiping and Bijun Wang (2010) 'Cost distortion and structural imbalances in China', *China & World Economy*, 18(4): 1–17.

Huang, Yiping and Xun Wang (2011) 'Does financial repression inhibit or facilitate economic growth? A case study of Chinese reform experience', *Oxford Bulletin of Economics and Statistics*, 73(6): 833–855.

Huang, Yiping, Xun Wang, Qin Gou and Daili Wang (2011) 'Liberalization of China's capital account', paper prepared for NYU Conference on China's capital markets, 31 May, New York University.

Huang, Yiping and Peichu Xie (2011) 'Conditions, timing and progress of the capital account liberalization in China', *China Finance*, Issue 14, 2011. (In Chinese)

King, R.G. and R. Levine (1993) 'Finance and growth: Schumpeter might be right', *Quarterly Journal of Economics*, 108: 717–737.

Lardy, Nicholas (1998) *China's Unfinished Economic Revolution*, Washington, DC: Brookings Institution Press.

—— (2008) 'Financial repression in China', *Policy Briefs for International Economics*, No. PB08–8, Washington, DC: Peterson Institute for International Economics.

Levine, R. (2005) 'Finance and growth: theory, mechanisms and evidence', in P. Aghion and S.N. Durlauf (eds) *Handbook of Economic Growth*, Chapter 12, New York: Elsevier.

Li, Hongbin and Li-an Zhou (2005) 'Political turnover and economic performance: the incentive role of personnel control in China', *Journal of Public Economics*, 89(9–10): 1743–1762.

Li, R. (2004) 'Deepening reform and opening wider to ensure sustainable economic growth', speech at the 42nd Annual Meeting of Business Executives, 23 October, Trujillo, Peru.

Lin, Justin Yifu, F. Cai and Z. Li (1995) *The China Miracle: Development Strategy and Economic Reform*, Hong Kong: The Chinese University of Hong Kong Press. [A 2003 revised edition is in print.]

Liu, T. and K.W. Li (2001) 'Impact of liberalization of financial resources in China's economic growth: evidence from provinces', *Journal of Asian Economics*, 12: 245–262.

Long, M. and S. Sagari (1991) 'Financial reform in European economies in transition', in P. Marer and S. Zecchini (eds) *The Transition to a Market Economy*, Vol. 2, pp. 430–442, Paris: OECD.

McKinnon, R.I. (1973) *The Order of Economic Liberalization: Financial Control in the Transition to a Market Economy*, Baltimore, MA: Johns Hopkins University Press.

—— (1994) 'Financial growth and macroeconomic stability in China, 1978–1992: implications for Russia and other transitional economies', *Journal of Comparative Economics*, 18: 438–469.

Maswana, J. (2011) 'China's financial development and economic growth: exploring the contradictions', *Journal of Chinese Economics and Finance*, Issue 3 (2011): 15–27.

Naughton, B. (1995) *Growing Out of the Plan: Chinese Economic Reform, 1978–1993*, New York: Cambridge University Press.

Nissanke, Machiko and Ernest Aryeetey (1998) *Financial Integration and Development – Liberalization and Reform in Sub-Saharan Africa*, London and New York: Routledge.

Pagano, M. (1993) 'Financial markets and growth: an overview', *European Economic Review*, 37: 613–622.

Roubini, N. and X. Sala-i-Martin (1992) 'Financial repression and economic growth', *Journal of Development Economics*, 39: 5–30.

—— (1995) 'A growth model of inflation, tax evasion, and financial repression', *Journal of Monetary Economics*, 35(2): 275–301.

Sachs, J. and W.T. Woo (2000) 'Understanding the Asian financial crisis', in J.D. Sachs and K. Schwab (eds) *The Asian Financial Crisis: Lessons for a Resilient Asia*, pp. 13–43, Cambridge, MA: MIT Press.

Schumpeter, Joseph A. (1911) *A Theory of Economic Development*, Cambridge, MA: Harvard University Press.

Shaw, A.S. (1973) *Financial Deepening in Economic Development*, New York: Oxford University Press.

Stiglitz, J.E. (1994) 'The role of the state in financial markets', in M. Bruno and B. Pleskovic (eds) *Proceedings of the World Bank Annual Conference on Development Economics (1993)*, supplement to the *World Bank Economic Review* and the *World Bank Research Observer*, pp. 19–52, Washington, DC: World Bank.

—— (2000) 'Capital market liberalization, economic growth and instability', *World Development*, 28(6): 1075–1086.

Wang, Xun (2011) 'Financial repression, financial development and economic growth in China, 1978–2008', unpublished PhD dissertation, National School of Development, Peking University, Beijing.

7 Capital account liberalization and the role of the renminbi

Nicholas Lardy and Patrick Douglass[1]

INTRODUCTION

The conventional wisdom among economists for many years was that capital account convertibility provides countries with unambiguous economic benefits via both improved capital allocation and increased opportunities to smooth consumption though international borrowing. This wisdom, it turned out, was based primarily on an a priori argument rather than strong empirical support. Attempts to demonstrate a linkage between international financial integration via capital account convertibility on the one hand, and economic growth on the other, have been disappointing at best (Eichengreen 2001; Prasad and Rajan 2008). Moreover, substantial evidence has accumulated that the introduction of capital account convertibility can, under a variety of circumstances, precipitate financial crises. Finally, in some cases, such as during the Asian financial crisis of the late 1990s, countries that had retained strong capital controls came through crises better than those that had liberalized earlier. More generally, across a large number of individual crises, countries with capital controls in place before the event suffered significantly lower drops in real economic output than countries without such controls.

Despite the erosion of the consensus on its economic benefits, capital account convertibility remains a long-term goal for China. The goal of 'gradually realizing convertibility of the capital account' is explicit in the Twelfth Five-Year Plan, which was approved by the Central Committee of the Chinese Communist Party on 18 October 2010.[2] Earlier, the goal of capital account convertibility was implicit in the State Council's objective of making Shanghai an international financial centre by 2020,[3] and is consistent with the objective of increasing the international use of the Chinese currency, discussed further below. Moreover, high government officials have endorsed capital account convertibility. Yi Gang, Vice-Governor of the People's Bank of China and concurrently the director of the State Administration of Foreign Exchange, in an interview with *Caixin* in the summer of 2010, stated that 'a convertible yuan remains the ultimate goal for the nation's currency exchange rate reform'.[4] Vice-Governor Yi noted that most countries achieve capital account convertibility within 7–10 years after making their currencies convertible for current account transactions. China achieved the latter in December 1996, but Yi explained that China's longer than usual transition was due to its size and unbalanced development.

PRECONDITIONS FOR CAPITAL ACCOUNT CONVERTIBILITY

Broadly speaking there are three important preconditions for moving to capital account liberalization: a strong domestic banking system, relatively well-developed domestic financial markets and an equilibrium exchange rate. We examine each of these in turn.

Strength of the domestic banking system

The first precondition for capital account convertibility is a strong domestic banking system. When capital controls are relaxed, domestic residents (or financial institutions holding funds on behalf of domestic residents) typically diversify the currency composition of their assets, leading to an outflow of funds from the domestic banking system. When a country's banking system is perceived as weak, opening the capital account can accelerate these outflows as depositors move funds to the presumed relative safety of foreign banks. These outflows can lead, in turn, to a sharp decline in the value of the domestic currency. If there are currency mismatches under these conditions, firms and individuals with foreign-currency denominated debts but income denominated totally or largely in domestic currency will experience a sharp increase in the burden of servicing their loans, potentially leading to a broad financial crisis. This concern is particularly salient in China where bank deposits by the end of 2009 reached 61.2 trillion renminbi (RMB) (US$8.96 trillion), an extraordinary 183 per cent of GDP (PBC 2010).[5] Households and non-financial corporations controlled more than 90 per cent of these deposits.

China's banks now appear to be enormously stronger than they were in the mid 1990s when the largest financial institutions were insolvent, which led ultimately to massive government injections of capital and a write-off of the non-performing loans that had accumulated in the banking system over many years (Lardy 1998; Ma Guonan 2006). Following these write-offs, the authorities engineered reforms in the governance of China's largest banks, further injections of capital by foreign strategic investors and public listings of bank shares on the Hong Kong and Shanghai stock markets.

The financial transformation of the banking system that resulted is reflected in three key indicators. First, total non-performing loans of China's major commercial banks came down sharply from RMB2,104 billion (US$254 billion) and 18 per cent of loans outstanding at the end of 2003 to only RMB426 billion (US$62 billion) and 1.6 per cent of loans outstanding by the end of 2009. Second, in 2003, only eight domestic banks accounting for a mere 0.6 per cent of total banking assets met China's minimum capital adequacy requirement, which then was 8 per cent. This rose to 239 banks accounting for 100 per cent of total banking assets by the end of 2009, when the risk-weighted average capital adequacy ratio of China's banking industry stood at 11.4 per cent. Third, after-tax profits of the banking industry as a whole were RMB670 billion (US$98 billion) in 2009, with the return on average equity at 16.2 per cent and return on average total assets at 0.9 per cent (CBRC 2010). These numbers on returns compare extremely favourably with well-regarded international banks such as HSBC and Standard Chartered.[6]

A number of questions could be raised as to whether these data truly reflect strong Chinese bank performance. Are bank capital adequacy ratios overstated by allowing dubious assets to be included in bank capital or by dubious risk weighting? Probably not significantly. On the matter of bank capital, for example, the regulator, the Chinese Banking Regulatory Commission (CBRC), allowed banks to issue subordinated debt and count it as part of their tier-two capital starting in 2004. During the global financial and economic crisis, when bank lending in China soared, the banks maintained their capital adequacy ratios by sharply stepping up their issuance of subordinated debt. It eventuated, however, that the banks were merely selling much of this debt to each other.[7] The regulator, recognizing that these cross-holdings of subordinated debt did nothing to increase capital in the banking system as a whole, ruled in a matter of months that subordinated debt held by other banks could not be counted as part of a bank's capital.[8] Instead, in 2010, the CBRC compelled China's four major banks to raise RMB264.4 billion (US$39.1 billion) in new capital via rights issues and the sale of convertible bonds.[9] With regard to risk weighting of assets, the CBRC eliminated more than a decade ago such questionable procedures as allowing banks to hold little or no capital against loans made to state-owned companies.

Are profits overstated because of lax loan classification standards and weak provisioning requirements? Again, probably not significantly. The CBRC modelled China's loan classification scheme on international standards and has imposed tough provisioning requirements. Loan-loss provisions set aside by commercial banks stood at RMB663 billion (US$97 billion) at the end of 2009, putting the provisioning ratio at 155 per cent, up dramatically from only 20 per cent in 2003 (CBRC 2010).

The more relevant question is to what extent is bank income inflated by the central bank's control of interest rates? The People's Bank of China has controlled the interest rate structure for both deposits and loans of commercial banks for many years. Partial liberalization, which took the form of allowing increasing upward flexibility from benchmark lending rates, began as early as 1997 when banks were allowed to raise lending rates above benchmark rates by as much as 20 per cent. This process culminated in the fall of 2004, when the central bank eliminated the ceiling on lending rates.[10] However, the authorities have not subsequently increased the flexibility around the benchmark lending and deposit rates. Notably, benchmark deposit rates set by the central bank remain a hard constraint on the up side. This protracted stall in interest rate reform seems somewhat surprising given Premier Wen Jiabao's statement at the National People's Congress in the spring of 2009 that China 'will carry forward market-based reform of interest rates'.[11]

The potential flattening effect of central bank control of the interest rate structure on bank earnings arises because the central bank sets a floor on bank lending rates but a ceiling on bank deposit rates. Thus, the central bank directly controls the spreads that banks earn on their deposit-taking and lending activities. Measuring the effect of the central bank's control of interest rates has been a key issue in the assessment of Chinese bank performance by outside analysts for many years. The magnitude of the impact of central bank control of interest rates on bank earnings was recently acknowledged by Xiao Gang, the Chairman of the Bank of China (China's fourth-largest bank by assets). In a posting on the bank's website, he acknowledged that, because of the central bank's control of interest rates, the net interest margins Chinese banks earn on their RMB loans are almost double what they would earn in a liberalized interest rate environment.[12]

If Xiao Gang's estimate that interest rate liberalization would cut the net interest margins of Chinese banks by as much as half is correct, what would this mean for Chinese bank earnings? Clearly, net interest income would fall by almost half. Since net interest income accounted for 63 per cent of the profits of banking institutions in 2009, central bank control of the interest rate structure could be said to result in an inflation of bank profits by as much as 45 per cent (CBRC 2010). Similarly, interest rate liberalization would reduce reported returns on equity and assets by the same proportion. In short, interest rate liberalization would reduce bank earnings substantially and Chinese bank performance would look much weaker in comparison with international peers.

The central bank's control of the structure of interest rates results in financial repression that imposes a heavy implicit tax, particularly on the household sector (Lardy 2008). In China's banking system at the end of 2009 the non-financial corporate sector was a slightly larger source of deposits than were households. But the non-financial corporate sector was actually a net borrower. Households supplied slightly less deposits than corporates, but were a large net depositor since total household borrowing at the time was less than a third of household deposits. In 2009–10 banks paid only 0.36 per cent on demand deposits, and rates ranging from 1.71 per cent on 3-month term deposits to as much as 3.60 per cent on 5-year term deposits.[13] In 2009, the average cost of household deposits at the Industrial and Commercial Bank of China, the China Construction Bank and the China Merchants Bank was, respectively, 1.94 per cent, 1.78 per cent and 1.52 per cent. However, as reflected in Table 7.1, at the same banks the average yield on loans to households was 4.93 per cent, 5.37 per cent and 5.07 per cent, respectively.

Table 7.1 Net interest rate spreads in major banks in China

	Total[a]	Households[b]
Industrial and Commercial Bank of China	2.16	2.99
China Construction Bank	2.30	3.20
China Merchants Bank	2.15	3.55

Sources: Industrial and Commercial Bank of China Ltd, *2009 Annual Results Announcement*, pp. 4, 14, 16; China Construction Bank Corporation, *Annual Report 2009*, pp. 23, 25–26; China Merchants Bank Co. Ltd, *Annual Report 2009*, pp. 26–28.

Notes
a The yield on the average annual balance of interest-generating assets less the cost of the average annual balance of interest-bearing liabilities.
b The average percentage yield on personal loans less the average cost of household deposits.

These numbers mean that these banks achieved spreads on lending to households that exceeded the net interest spread they enjoyed on their entire range of assets and liabilities by approximately two-fifths to two-thirds. This differential arose for two reasons. First, these banks held other assets that earned much less than their returns from lending to households. For example, they earned only 1.6 per cent on required reserves placed at the central bank, and only slightly more on their large holdings of bonds issued by the central bank to sterilize increases in the domestic money supply resulting from its intervention in foreign exchange markets.[14] And second, banks had to pay substantially higher interest rates on some of their liabilities than they paid on household deposits. For example, in 2009, the China Construction Bank paid 3.81 per cent interest on the bonds that it issued, more than twice what it paid on household deposits.

In short, Chinese banks are, for two reasons, highly dependent on their business with households. First, the net interest spreads on this business are much higher than the average net spreads that banks achieve. And second, households are the dominant source of bank funding. Capital account liberalization under these conditions might well compel banks to raise deposit rates to prevent large outflows of deposits, particularly from the household sector. This could have a highly adverse effect on bank earnings. An increase in average deposit rates of only 110 basis points in 2009 would have eliminated all bank profits.

Thus, interest rate liberalization is, for two reasons, an important precondition for capital account liberalization. First, as the above analysis suggests, it is essential to gradually reduce and finally eliminate financial repression before liberalizing the capital account. Otherwise depositors, particularly households, may shift their funds out of the domestic banking system, potentially creating a banking crisis.

Second, interest rate liberalization is essential to the strengthening of China's banking system in the long run. As long as banks operate in a highly cosseted interest rate environment, competition in the banking system will remain limited and banks will have insufficient ability and incentive to price risk appropriately and operate on a commercial basis. Thus, the allocation of funds by the banking system would remain less efficient than would be the case if banks operated in a liberalized interest rate environment.

Level of development of the financial system

A second prerequisite for the liberalization of the capital account is a well-developed capital market. There are at least two reasons for this. First, capital markets can provide an additional source of funding for the corporate sector, thus providing more competition for domestic banks, hastening their transition to operation on a fully commercial basis. Second, deeper local debt markets make it easier for a country to ease restrictions on capital flows because these deeper local debt markets make it easier to absorb large capital inflows without creating asset bubbles in local markets. Finally, if local capital markets are underdeveloped when capital restrictions are eased, domestic firms may borrow funds abroad, creating the possibility of currency and maturity mismatches.

While China has a significant market for government bonds, the local market in corporate debt is not well developed. The magnitude of funds raised through the corporate debt market is small, especially when measured against the funding provided to the corporate sector through the banking system. Moreover, issuance is dominated by a handful of large state-owned institutions, notably the Ministry of Railroads and the major banks. At the end of 2007 the total value of non-financial corporate bonds outstanding was only RMB768.3 billion (US$105.2 billion) (Chinese Securities Regulatory Commission 2008).[15] That was less than 3 per cent of the RMB27.77 trillion (US$3.80 trillion) outstanding in loans from the banking system and also less than 3 per cent of 2007 GDP. By year-end 2009, non-financial corporate bonds outstanding grew by about 40 per cent to reach RMB1,097 billion (US$161 billion) (ADB 2010). However, bank loans outstanding and GDP had expanded almost as rapidly, reaching RMB33.6 trillion (US$4.9 trillion) and RMB34.1 trillion (US$5.0 trillion), respectively, so the ratio of non-financial corporate bonds outstanding to bank loans outstanding and to GDP was only a few tenths of a percentage point higher than in 2007.

In contrast with the corporate bond market, the foreign-exchange forward and swap transactions markets have developed rapidly in recent years. An over-the-counter forward market emerged as early as 1997 but, with a fixed exchange rate against the dollar and the vast majority of foreign trade transactions denominated and settled in dollars, the volume of transactions was modest. With the de-pegging of the RMB to the dollar in mid 2005, however, China launched an interbank foreign-exchange forward market and, in the following year, formally introduced foreign-exchange swap transactions. These markets allowed Chinese exporters and importers to hedge the foreign-exchange risk inherent in an environment in which volatility in the value of the RMB had increased. The combined volume of transactions in these two markets grew rapidly, reaching US$460 billion by 2008 and almost doubled in 2009, reaching US$810 billion (PBC 2010).

Flexibility of the exchange rate

A third precondition for a successful transition to capital account convertibility is an exchange rate that is reasonably close to its underlying equilibrium level. A move to capital account convertibility when an exchange rate is substantially under- or overvalued will precipitate, respectively, capital in- or outflows that can be destabilizing. The preponderance of evidence suggests that the RMB was significantly undervalued in the middle of the last decade. All but one of 18 studies of the Chinese exchange rate surveyed concluded that the RMB was undervalued. The average estimate of the appreciation needed in the real effective exchange rate was 19 per cent, and the appreciation needed was higher for those studies based on data from the period 2005–07 than for studies based on data from the period 2000–04 (Cline and Williamson 2008). More recently, Cline and Williamson pegged the RMB undervaluation at 21 per cent and 14 per cent (both on a real effective basis) in 2009 and 2010, respectively (Cline and Williamson 2009, 2010).

In addition to these direct estimates of the degree of undervaluation, Chinese government intervention in the foreign exchange market to prevent the RMB from appreciating also clearly suggests that the currency is undervalued. This intervention has led to a build-up of official foreign-exchange reserves – from US$412 billion at the end of 2003 to US$2,847 billion at the end of 2010 – that is unprecedented in global history. The vast bulk of this build-up is attributable to China's surpluses on current account, rather than to surpluses on the capital and financial account as a result of net inflows of foreign direct investment, portfolio capital and so forth.[16] The magnitude of the official intervention in the foreign exchange market is so large that it strongly suggests that the government has made little progress in making the value of the exchange rate based more on 'market supply and demand', a goal enunciated in July 2005.[17] Equally unprecedented in the history of the international monetary system is the large-scale open market operations that the central bank has undertaken to partially sterilize the domestic monetary expansion caused by foreign exchange intervention (Cappiello and Ferrucci 2008). This has, in turn, prevented real appreciation of the RMB via the price mechanism.

PROGRESS TO DATE ON CAPITAL ACCOUNT LIBERALIZATION

While China achieved full current account convertibility in late 1996, its progress on capital account convertibility has proceeded slowly and in stages. In December 1993, China's authorities publicly stated that, 'The long-term goal of China's foreign exchange reforms is to realize the convertibility of the RMB. In order to reach this goal, we must move gradually and in the proper sequence of events' (Hu Xiaolian 2009: 449). In effect this has meant achieving convertibility on current account transactions before capital account transactions, and loosening restrictions on capital inflows before loosening restrictions on capital outflows.

In the decade following China's reform and opening, the government showed a new willingness to use foreign capital to fund domestic investment. The majority of this capital came in the form of foreign loans from international financial institutions such as the IMF and the World Bank, and from foreign governments. China's objective was to attract long-term stable forms of investment and take advantage of favourable lending rates abroad. While these loan inflows marked a major policy shift, they remained modest, reaching a peak of just 1.68 per cent of GDP in 1990.

China took more significant steps toward liberalization when it loosened constraints on foreign direct investment (FDI) beginning in the early 1990s. These liberalization policies included:

- shifting decision-making power on the screening and approval of FDI from the central government toward local governments;
- relaxing ownership restrictions away from joint-venture requirements and allowing a greater proportion of FDI to come from wholly owned foreign enterprises;
- increasing managerial autonomy relating to pricing and financial decisions;
- offering concessions on customs duties, income taxes and taxes on profit remittances; and
- relaxing sectoral controls and opening up the services sector, including the banking, retailing and telecommunications industries.

Inward FDI in manufacturing is now almost completely liberalized in China, with the exception of restrictions in some 'strategic' sectors and, in some cases, limits on the extent and form of foreign ownership. There are more restrictions on FDI in China's service sector, particularly telecommunications and financial services including banking, insurance and securities. Foreign companies are permitted to make withdrawals from their foreign exchange accounts and convert local currency to make external current account payments of profits and dividends, so long as the payments are consistent with their business scope and, in the case of joint-venture companies, approved by the firm's board of directors. China's relatively accommodative stance has made it the world's second-largest destination for FDI.

China's recent measures to further liberalize FDI in response to the global economic crisis reflect the major role that FDI has played in driving economic growth over the past 30 years. When FDI inflows reached their peak in 2008, foreign-invested enterprises made up just 3 per cent of total enterprises, yet contributed to 30 per cent of China's total industrial output value, 21 per cent of total tax revenues and 55 per cent of total exports.[18] This trend reversed due to the global financial crisis, when FDI growth fell from 20 per cent in 2008 to minus 13 per cent in 2009, the first time that FDI growth had turned negative in a decade.

To stabilize and expand FDI inflows, in July 2009 the Ministry of Commerce submitted a 42-point proposal to the State Council containing a number of policy recommendations, including measures to further delegate FDI examination and approval rights, and to relax the examination and approval process for individual foreign investments. Of particular significance was a proposal to simplify and moderately relax the foreign-exchange registrations procedures imposed on foreign investors who invest in Chinese real estate enterprises, thereby easing the so-called 'foreign capital restraining order'.[19] There were also proposals to adjust the catalogue of permitted uses for foreign investment and to give local governments more latitude to use preferential policies to attract foreign capital.

The Chinese Government initially focused on designing policies to attract inbound foreign investment and gave little attention to promoting outbound FDI (OFDI). More recently, however, the authorities have begun to view OFDI as a valuable way to secure commodities needed for growth and to further integrate China into the global trading system. The demand for foreign exchange associated with OFDI could slow the pace of accumulation of official holdings of foreign exchange and also provide a way for China to diversify its foreign investments away from US Treasuries.

This more favourable stance toward OFDI emerged clearly in 1999 when the government announced the breakthrough 'Go global' policy with the primary goal making it easier for domestic firms to secure commodities abroad. Over the past decade, government agencies relaxed restrictions on OFDI and, through subsidies, tax breaks, and improved access to financing, actively supported firms going abroad. For example, the Ministry of Commerce (MOFCOM) gradually eased approval procedures over time by delegating greater responsibility to local agencies. In May 2009, it introduced new project approval rules to reduce approval time, lift value thresholds and increase the authority of local MOFCOM branches. Similarly, the CBRC issued guidelines in December 2008 allowing commercial banks to provide loans to firms for use in cross-border mergers and acquisitions.

In addition, the State Administration of Foreign Exchange (SAFE) has provided domestic firms with easier access to foreign exchange by progressively relaxing capital controls and has provided firms investing with more opportunities to raise capital. SAFE draft regulations, published in May 2009, allow domestic firms to register the source of their foreign-exchange financing after their investment overseas rather than requiring approval in advance.[20] These new rules also permit firms to raise capital from more sources, including domestic foreign-exchange loans, foreign exchange purchased with RMB, foreign currency funds already possessed by the firm and retained profits from overseas.

Yet, China's investment outflows are dwarfed by FDI inflows, and its OFDI remains low by most measures.[21] In 2009, China's share of global OFDI flows was 4 per cent and by year-end its share of the stock was 1.2 per cent, a significant increase compared with previous years but still small considering China is now the world's second-largest economy.[22] Overseas FDI assets as a share of GDP were less than 5 per cent in China in 2009, compared with 6 per cent in India, 10 per cent in Brazil and 26 per cent in Russia.

While China opened itself up to FDI inflows from a relatively early stage and liberalized OFDI starting in the late 1990s, measures to liberalize portfolio inflows have remained quite limited. China's Qualified Foreign Institutional Investor (QFII) programme, adopted in 2002, allows a limited number of foreign institutional investors to invest in a specified range of Chinese domestic financial assets. The programme sets quotas on inbound portfolio investment for each participating foreign institution, as well as a quota on the overall size of the QFII programme. To encourage long-term investments in the capital markets and discourage sudden capital outflows, SAFE initially permitted QFIIs to offer only closed-end funds, and subjected their investments to a 3-year lock-up period before the full amount placed could be withdrawn and repatriated. Since then, SAFE has permitted QFIIs to offer open-end funds and has significantly relaxed restrictions on repatriation. Nevertheless, the authorities continue to attempt to influence the composition of capital flows by imposing higher minimum capital requirements on banks and securities companies than on mutual funds and insurance companies.

The QFII scheme was small at its inception and has been allowed to expand only marginally. As of June 2010, the authorities had licensed 89 foreign institutions to participate in the programme. The authorities raised the global ceiling from US$10 billion when the programme began to US$30 billion at the end of 2007 and, in August 2008, increased the maximum initial investment amount for each new institutional investor from US$800 million to US$1 billion. The programme is still small-scale, however. Approved investment funds accumulated stood at US$17.72 billion in the first half of 2010, just 0.6 per cent of China's A-share market capitalization. By keeping fund quotas low, the authorities have limited the ability of foreign financial institutions to play a significant role in the domestic markets and have hindered capital market development.

China's Qualified Domestic Institutional Investor (QDII) programme, introduced in 2006, allows domestic financial institutions to invest abroad using a structure similar to that of QFIIs. While the authorities initially limited QDII investments to fixed-income instruments, they added equities to the permitted mix in 2007, allowing the QDII programme to expand rapidly in size and scope. Early quota demand was driven by the desire of domestic investors to diversify away from domestic markets and take advantage of expected high returns abroad. Most QDII investments are concentrated in instruments traded on the Hong Kong exchange, but agreements between Chinese financial supervisory authorities and counterparts in other countries suggest that the authorities may allow investments in other markets in the future.

After nearly 2 years of steady quota expansion, retail investor interest in QDII funds declined dramatically in response to the global economic crisis. During the 17 months to the end of September 2009, the number of QDII licensed institutions remained fixed at 56 and total approved investment funds accumulated at US$50.7 billion.[23] Demand for quotas was so weak during this period that, by the end of August 2009, domestic investors had invested only half their total approved funds abroad, prompting SAFE to warn that it would reduce quotas for QDII investors that did not make full use of them.[24] However, once global markets recovered and fears of capital outflows subsided, SAFE quickly resumed its quota approvals. Improved foreign market expectations and growing concerns over domestic overheating and Shanghai A-share market volatility have led to renewed interest in QDII quotas. By June 2010, the number of QDII licensed institutions had increased to 81 and total approved investment funds grew to US$64 billion.

Nevertheless, the relatively small size of the QDII programme means that it cannot provide households with a significant means to diversify their savings and enjoy portfolio income greater than what they earn from low-yielding domestic bank deposits. The total approved QDII investment quota as a share of total Chinese household savings deposits has never risen above its 2007 peak of 2.1 per cent. This share was only 1.5 per cent at the end of the first half of 2010. Furthermore, as discussed earlier, QDIIs do not always exhaust their approved investment quotas.

Other channels for outbound capital flows include cross-border lending by China's banks and sovereign wealth fund investments. Policy banks do the bulk of China's external lending, often to secure commodities abroad or to support the outward investments of state-owned enterprises. However, these banks have engaged in a wider variety of international lending recently, including concessionary multi-billion dollar loan agreements with developing countries for local energy and infrastructure projects. The China Investment Corporation has continued to increase its outward investment despite the losses it incurred as a result of the financial crisis. According to one estimate, it invested US$58 billion abroad in 2009, increasing its total overseas holdings to about US$100 billion.[25]

Finally, the internationalization of the RMB could ultimately facilitate the transition to capital account convertibility. China launched this initiative in 2004 when it allowed Hong Kong residents to open RMB deposit accounts in Hong Kong banks. The effort to internationalize the use of the RMB was further boosted in July 2009 when China introduced cross-border trade settlement in RMB. This programme initially ran as a pilot. It was restricted to trade between five Chinese cities and Hong Kong, Macao and ASEAN countries, and was open to all Chinese importers but only a small number of exporting firms. In 2010, the programme was widened in two steps. First, in June 2010, the programme was expanded to include trade transactions between Chinese firms in 20 provinces and cities and the rest of the world. Second, in December, the authorities substantially expanded the number of Chinese exporting companies able to participate in cross-border trade settlement in RMB.[26] As a result, the volume of RMB trade settlement expanded from RMB3.6 billion (US$0.5 billion) in the second half of 2009 to RMB66.7 billion (US$9.8 billion) in the first half of 2010, then RMB126.5 billion (US$18.7 billion) in the third quarter. However, even in the third quarter, only about 2 per cent of China's international trade transactions were settled in RMB. The vast majority of transactions are still settled in US dollars.

Because the cross-border RMB trade settlement continues to be pre-dominantly settlement of Chinese import transactions, the programme has led to a substantial build up of RMB deposits in Hong Kong. By July 2010, RMB deposits in Hong Kong banks totalled RMB103.7 billion or 1.8 per cent of total bank deposits (Subacchi 2010). Deposits continued to build rapidly and, by the end of October 2010, stood at RMB217 billion or twice the mid-year amount.

This build-up has been possible only because of reforms in the ways that RMB deposits can be utilized. Hong Kong banks accepting RMB deposits initially had little alternative to depositing the funds with the Bank of China (Hong Kong), which serves as the clearing bank, but pays only 0.865 per cent on these RMB deposits. Thus, Hong Kong banks were not able to offer attractive interest rates to individuals and firms depositing RMB funds.

To make the holding of RMB deposits more attractive, the Chinese authorities have taken several important steps. First, since 2007, the mainland authorities have gradually approved an expanded issuance of RMB-denominated bonds in Hong Kong. Issuance was initially limited to the Ministry of Finance and domestic Chinese financial institutions but, in 2010, foreign companies were authorized to issue RMB-denominated bonds in Hong Kong. Increasing the availability of higher yielding RMB-denominated financial assets is critical to the increased international use of the RMB.

Second, since August 2010, Hong Kong banks involved in RMB cross-border trade settlement have had access to the onshore interbank bond market. In short, they can now invest their RMB funds in bonds issued in China and traded on the interbank bond market. This allows these banks to purchase higher yielding RMB-denominated financial assets rather than holding low-yielding deposits with the clearing bank. It also permits them to offer higher rates on RMB deposits, making Hong Kong exporters more willing to settle their transactions with their mainland Chinese clients in RMB.

It is not clear whether China, in the short term, is gaining in pure economic terms from this increased internationalization of the RMB. As already noted, RMB settlement has been dominated by Chinese importers rather than exporters. This means that there has been an increase in offshore holdings of RMB which, at the margin, increases rather than decreases the pressure for RMB appreciation in the onshore foreign exchange market. It is sometimes argued that denominating and settling trade contracts in RMB allows Chinese firms to escape foreign exchange risk without assuming any hedging costs. This seems unlikely because, in a competitive market, if foreign firms were required to assume these costs they would adjust their prices appropriately rather than accepting reduced profits.

The more uncertain question is whether internationalization will ultimately help pave the way for capital account convertibility. Since historically substantial capital account convertibility has preceded the international use of currencies, we are to some extent in uncharted territory. To date, the source of all offshore RMB deposits in Hong Kong derives from current account transactions; for example, RMB earnings from exporting to China or from Chinese tourism. Whether or not foreign investors will be happy to hold increasingly significant amounts of RMB deposits offshore while China's capital account remains largely closed will determine the success of the internationalization strategy as currently pursued by the Chinese authorities.

POLICY RECOMMENDATIONS

China has made some progress in relaxing capital controls over the past three decades. The authorities aggressively liberalized inbound FDI from the outset of the reform process, and have substantially liberalized OFDI over the past decade. Nonetheless, most studies measuring the degree to which China's capital account has been liberalized find that China's controls remain highly restrictive, even compared with other emerging markets such as Brazil and Russia (Chinn and Ito 2008; Ito and Chinn 2010). Moreover, substantial obstacles still impede significant further capital account liberalization, particularly the freeing-up of cross-border flows of portfolio capital.

China faces significant obstacles to complete capital account liberalization. The first is the state of the domestic banking system. The banking system has been strengthened substantially over the past decade, but its strong recent financial performance may owe as much to the central bank's interest rate controls as to the improved ability of banks to price risk appropriately. As Xiao Gang has acknowledged: [27]

> Growing big is the best way for Chinese banks to make more money under the current financial environment. This model of growth, however, neither assures the long-term sustainable development of the banking sector nor satisfies the need of a balanced economic and social structure.

Gradual relaxation of remaining interest rate controls, particularly the ceilings on rates for deposits of various maturities, is an essential precondition to the emergence of a robust, fully commercially orientated banking system. This goal was embraced by China's premier in early 2009 and reiterated by the Central Committee in its Twelfth Five-Year Plan approved in October 2010. The hope is that progress will soon be visible on this front.

Second, parts of China's financial system are woefully underdeveloped. While the authorities have made substantial progress in the development of the foreign-exchange forward and swap transactions markets, China's local market for non-financial corporate debt remains tiny at only around 3 per cent of GDP.

Third, China's exchange rate remains somewhat undervalued. Consequently, substantially liberalizing the capital account before the value of the RMB is closer to an underlying equilibrium level could generate large-scale speculative capital inflows based on the expectation of further RMB appreciation. These inflows could undermine the ability of the central bank to maintain price stability. Thus, allowing gradual appreciation of the currency and greater exchange-rate flexibility is also an essential precondition to moving toward further liberalization of the capital account.

NOTES

1 Nicholas Lardy is the Anthony M. Solomon Senior Fellow at the Peterson Institute for International Economics, Washington, DC. Patrick Douglass is an international economist at the US Department of Treasury and a former research analyst at the Peterson Institute. The views expressed herein are the personal views of the authors and do not represent the views of the US Department of the Treasury or of the United States.
2 Chinese Communist Party Central Committee, 'Guiding proposal for formulating the Twelfth Five-Year Plan for National Economic and Social Development', 27 October 2010, available at http://news.xinhuanet.com/politics/2010-10/27, accessed 1 November 2010.
3 State Council, 'Opinion on promoting the rapid development of modern service industries and advanced manufacturing to build an international financial center and an international transportation center in Shanghai', 14 April 2009, available at http://www.gov.cn, accessed 22 November 2010.
4 Hu Shuli and Sun Huixia, 'Central bank unwavering on yuan reform', 31 July 2010, available at http://caing.com, accessed 10 December 2010.
5 The ratio of deposits to GDP in China in 2005 was 155 per cent. That was substantially higher than any other relevant country. For countries in emerging Asia the ratio averaged 60 per cent, in Latin America 25 per cent and in Eastern Europe 45 per cent (Cappiello and Ferrucci 2008). China appears to have become even more of an outlier by 2009.
6 In 2009 the return on average total assets at HSBC and Standard Chartered was 0.3 per cent and 0.8 per cent, respectively; return on equity was 5.1 and 14.3 per cent, respectively. Sources: HSBC, *Annual Report and Accounts 2009*, 1 March 2010, available at http://www.hsbc.com, accessed 8 November

2010; Standard Chartered, *Annual Report 2009*, 26 March 2010, available at http://www.standardchartered.com, accessed 8 November 2010.

7 Fang Huilei, Zhang Man, Chen Huiying and Feng Zhe, 'New draft rules on subordinated bonds will lower banks' capital adequacy ratios and reduce the systemic risk of cross-holding', *Caijing*, 24 August 2009, available at http://english.caijing.com.cn, accessed 24 August 2009.

8 Liu Mingkang, 'Chinese bankers carry hopes for future balanced development', speech to the Asian Financial Forum in Hong Kong, 20 January 2010, available at http://www.cbrc.gov.cn, accessed 18 February 2010.

9 Feng Zhe, 'Bank of China raises 100 Bln yuan in 2010', 14 December 2010, available at http://english.caing.com, *Caixin* online, accessed 14 December 2010.

10 The lower bound on lending rates remained at 0.9 times the benchmark rate, a limit that had been in effect for many years.

11 Wen Jiabao, 'Report on the work of the government', delivered at the second session of the Eleventh National People's Congress, 5 March 2009.

12 Net interest margin is net interest income divided by the average balance of total interest-earning assets. Xiao Gang, 'Don't blame it on the government', Bank of China, 26 August 2010, available at http://www.boc.cn, accessed 27 August 2010.

13 The central bank adjusted interest rates effective 20 October 2010. The People's Bank of China left the benchmark rate on demand deposits unchanged at 0.36%, raised the 1-year deposit rate by 0.25%, and raised the rates on longer term deposits by somewhat larger amounts. The 5-year deposit rate, for example, was raised 0.6%.

14 These bonds are frequently referred to as central bank bills.

15 Data in this paragraph on non-financial corporate bonds outstanding are exclusive of short-term commercial paper.

16 From 2004 through the first half of 2010 China's cumulative current account surplus was three times the cumulative capital and financial account surplus (SAFE 2010: 13).

17 'Public announcement of the People's Bank of China on reforming the RMB exchange rate regime', 21 July 2005, available at http://www.pbc.gov.cn, accessed 21 July 2005.

18 'Continuous drop of FDI leads to promulgation of new FDI policies', *China Economic News*, No. 25, 6 July 2009.

19 The 'foreign capital restraining order' refers to the system in which several government departments actively manage the foreign debts and foreign exchange registration and settlement of foreign investors investing in China's real estate sector.

20 'China to encourage overseas investment with easier procedures', *Xinhua*, 19 May 2009, available at http://english.people.com.cn, accessed 19 May 2009.

21 China's stock of outward investment in 2009 was US$229.6 billion, less than a quarter of the size of the US$997.4 billion China received from inbound foreign investment, according to a SAFE statement on China's international investment position, released 5 May 2010, available at http://www.chinadaily.com/business/2010-05/04/content_9808404.htm, accessed 4 November 2010.

22 Between 2000 and 2006 China accounted an average of about 0.8 per cent of global OFDI flows, more than India and Brazil, which had 0.4 and 0.7 per cent, respectively, but less than Russia which accounted for 1.1 per cent despite its much smaller economy. World Bank, 'Robust recovery, rising risks', *East Asia and Pacific Economic Update*, 2: 26 (October 2010).

23 Many suffered sharp losses during this period, including one fund that had to be liquidated in April 2008 after losing half its principal.

24 Jamil Anderlini, 'QDII scheme back after 17-month break', *Financial Times*, 2 November 2009.
25 World Bank, 'Robust recovery, rising risks', *East Asia and Pacific Economic Update*, 2: 26 (October 2010).
26 Initially only 365 Chinese firms (referred to as mainland designated enterprises) were authorized to settle their export transactions in RMB. In December 2010 this number increased to 67,359.
27 'Don't blame it on the government', *China Daily*, 25 August 2010.

REFERENCES

ADB (Asian Development Bank) (2010) *Asia Bond Monitor* (October), Manila: ADB.
Cappiello, Lorenzo and Gianluigi Ferrucci (2008) 'The sustainability of China's exchange rate policy and capital account liberalization', *Occasional Paper* No. 82, Frankfurt: European Central Bank.
CBRC (China Banking Regulatory Commission) (2010) *Annual Report 2009*, Beijing: China Banking Regulatory Commission.
Chinese Securities Regulatory Commission (2008) *China Securities and Futures Statistical Yearbook 2008*, Beijing: Chinese Securities Regulatory Commission.
Chinn, Menzie D. and Hiro Ito (2008) 'A new measure of financial openness', *Journal of Comparative Policy Analysis*, 10(3): 309–322.
Cline, William R. and John Williamson (2008) 'Estimates of the equilibrium exchange rate of the renminbi: is there a consensus and if not, why not?', in Morris Goldstein and Nicholas R. Lardy (eds) *Debating China's Exchange Rate Policy*, pp. 131–154, Washington, DC: Peterson Institute for International Economics.
—— (2009) '2009 estimates of fundamental equilibrium exchange rates', *Policy Briefs in International Economics*, No. 09–10 (June), Washington, DC: Peterson Institute for International Economics.
—— (2010) 'Estimates of fundamental equilibrium exchange rates, May 2010', *Policy Briefs in International Economics*, No. 10–15 (June), Washington, DC: Peterson Institute for International Economics.
Eichengreen, Barry (2001) 'Capital account liberalization: what do cross-country studies tell us?', *World Bank Economic Review*, 15(3): 341–365.
Hu Xiaolian (2009) 'Convertibility of RMB-denominated capital accounts: process and experience', in Zhu Min, Cai Jingqing and Martha Avery (eds) *China's Emerging Financial Markets: Challenges and Global Impact*, pp. 449–458, Singapore: John Wiley & Sons (Asia).
Ito, Hiro and Menzie Chinn (2010) 'Notes on the Chinn–Ito financial openness index', unpublished manuscript.
Lardy, Nicholas R. (1998) *China's Unfinished Economic Revolution*, Washington, DC: Brookings Institution Press.
—— (2008) 'Financial repression in China', *Policy Briefs for International Economics*, No. PB08–8, Washington, DC: Peterson Institute for International Economics.
Ma Guonan (2006) 'Who pays China's bank restructuring bill?', *CEPII Working Paper*, No. 2006–4, Paris: Centre d'Etudes Prospectives et d'Informations Internationales.

PBC (People's Bank of China) (2010) 'Report on implementation of monetary policy, fourth quarter 2009' [11 February], Beijing: PBC Monetary Policy Analysis Small Group, available at http://www.pbc.gov.cn, accessed 11 February 2010.

Prasad, Eswar S. and Raghuram G. Rajan (2008) 'A pragmatic approach to capital account liberalization', *Journal of Economic Perspectives*, 22(3): 149–172.

SAFE (State Administration of Foreign Exchange) (2010) 'Report on China's international balance of payments in the first half of 2010' (October 12), Beijing: SAFE International Balance of Payments Analysis Small Group, available at http://www.safe.gov.cn, accessed 12 October 2010.

Subacchi, Paola (2010) '"One currency, two systems": China's renminbi strategy', *Chatham House Briefing Paper* 2010/1 (October), available at http://www.chathamhouse.org.uk, accessed 2 November 2010.

8 Chinese trade policy after ten years in the World Trade Organization

A post-crisis stocktake

Razeen Sally[1]

INTRODUCTION

So much has changed since China joined the World Trade Organization (WTO) in late 2001. China has powered through the global economic crisis (GEC) with a turbo-charged fiscal and monetary stimulus equivalent to almost 45 per cent of gross domestic product (GDP) in 2009. It is the leading contributor to post-crisis global growth. Other countries around the world export raw materials and capital goods to power China's continuing industrial revolution. That is also true of other East Asian economies, which, in addition, export parts and components to China for assembly and export elsewhere. Increasingly, they are also gearing up to export finished goods to a booming Chinese consumer market. More than ever, the rest of Asia revolves around China.[2] Gradually, China is asserting itself in international organizations. Its footprint is ever more visible elsewhere in the non-Western world – in its East Asian backyard, and in South Asia, Central Asia, Africa and South America. In the past decade, China has become the leading regional power in Asia, and is on its way to becoming a 'great power' in the wider world, alongside the USA. These trends have clearly accelerated in the wake of the global economic crisis.

China is now one of the 'big three' in the global economy. Until recently, it imported 'global order': it absorbed policies, rules and institutions that materialized from decisions made elsewhere. China still imports global order; but, given its market size, and like the USA and European Union (EU), it now exports global order as well. Decisions made in China reverberate around the world. And they do so to a much greater extent than decisions made in Brazil, Russia and India, the other BRIC countries. China accounts for about 60 per cent of BRIC[3] countries' output, two-thirds of its foreign-exchange reserves and exports, and one-third of its inward investment. China plays in its own league among emerging markets. The other BRICs play in an inferior league; they are still much bigger net importers of global order.[4]

This transformation, within a decade, represents a shift in what could be called China's 'policy terms of trade'. Trade economists from Robert Torrens and John Stuart Mill to Harry Johnson would not be surprised. When China joined the WTO, it regarded itself as a 'price-taker' in the world trading system; it acted rather like a small or medium-size open economy that could only adapt to the international terms of trade. Unilateral liberalization, reinforced by strong WTO commitments, was the policy prescription. Now, Chinese policy-makers think of China as a member of a club of three: like the USA and EU, it can influence international terms of trade and world prices – or so they believe. That shifts the policy inference away from unilateral liberalization to reciprocity. But, given the speed and scale of this transformation, China has evident difficulty in acting like a rule-setter and system-shaper – in other words, like a leader (or co-leader) of the world trade order. That causes problems for China and its trading partners – it creates uncertainty and instability and increases the risk that China might become a 'spoiler' in trade policy.

That is the broad context for assessing Chinese trade policy almost a decade after it acceded to the WTO. The next section of this chapter briefly summarizes policy trends leading up to WTO accession, as well as recent trade and foreign direct investment (FDI) patterns. The third section looks at China in the WTO – its record of implementing WTO commitments and its participation in the Doha Round and dispute settlement. This is followed by a section that considers China's trade-related reforms outside the WTO, especially unilateral measures and preferential trade agreements (PTAs). The fifth section highlights challenges for China's trade policy in several contexts – the WTO, PTAs, key bilateral relationships and global macro-economic tensions. The penultimate section puts Chinese trade policy in a bigger domestic political-economy and geopolitical context. The seventh section sums up the chapter.

TRENDS UP TO WTO ACCESSION; TRADE AND FDI PATTERNS[5]

China's 'reform' and 'opening' started in 1978. But its decisive external opening, and the sweeping industrial and agricultural restructuring that came with it, belong more to the post-Tiananmen phase, especially since 1994. China undertook enormous trade and FDI liberalization during the 1990s – before its WTO accession in 2001 – followed by another big dose of liberalization in line with its WTO commitments. Its WTO commitments are very strong and exceed those of most other developing countries by a wide margin. This holds for disciplines on border and non-border restrictions in goods and services. In addition, there are detailed commitments on transparency procedures to make sure trade-related laws and regulations are implemented, supported by administrative and judicial-review procedures to which individuals and firms are supposed to have recourse.

It is important to note that the primary liberalization thrust, especially in the 1990s, was *domestic* and *unilateral*, coming from the Beijing leadership, which used WTO-accession negotiations as a strategic lever to consolidate and accelerate national reforms. China's WTO commitments, and its participation in the WTO after accession, can be read as more the consequence than the cause of its sweeping unilateral reforms. Furthermore, Chinese unilateral liberalization followed in the footsteps of unilateral liberalization, first by the Northeast, then by the Southeast Asian Tigers, from the 1960s to the 1980s. This is how China inserted itself into regional and global manufacturing supply chains (e.g. in electronics, sports footwear, televisions and radio receivers, office equipment, electrical machinery, power and machine tools, cameras and watches, and printing and publishing). That said, the momentum of further liberalization has stalled in recent years (of which more later).

The simple average tariff has come down from about 40 per cent in 1985 to under 10 per cent today. Tariffs accounted for just 2.5 per cent of total tax revenue in 2009. All China's tariffs are bound in the WTO at very close to applied rates, with an overall bound tariff of 10 per cent. The maximum applied most-favoured nation tariff is 65 per cent. China's weighted average tariff is just over 4 per cent – lowish by developing-country standards and the lowest among large developing countries such as Brazil, Russia, India, Indonesia and South Africa (Table 8.1). This is partly due to numerous duty exemptions and other measures to encourage exports. Trade liberalization also whittled down the impact of border non-tariff barriers (NTBs) to about 5 per cent on the eve of WTO accession. Trading rights have been fully liberalized, most quotas, licences, specific tendering arrangements and price controls have been removed, and there are strong disciplines on state trading enterprises, remaining subsidies and other NTBs. Import quotas were eliminated by 2005, and China agreed to abolish all export subsidies, including those in agriculture, as part of its WTO commitments. Overall, border barriers on goods trade have come down to Southeast Asian levels, and have been locked in by much stronger WTO commitments.

China's commitments to the General Agreement on Trade in Services (GATS) are very strong. On paper, the impact of WTO accession should be to cut services protection by half. In practice, China remains more protected in services than it is in goods trade. It is also generally more restrictive towards FDI. In terms of the Organisation for Economic Co-operation and Development (OECD) FDI Regulatory Restrictiveness Index, it is on a par with India and more restrictive than Russia and Brazil. Above-average levels of restrictiveness appear in key services sectors such as fixed telecoms, banking, air and maritime transport, and electricity (Figure 8.1).

China ranks 79th overall in the World Bank's Ease of Doing Business Index for 2011 – a low score, but clearly ahead of Russia, India, Brazil and Indonesia (Table 8.2). For 'trading across borders' it is far ahead of South Africa, Russia and India. It scores much better than the other BRIIC countries[6] on the cost of importing and exporting. China also occupies 48th position in the World Economic Forum's Enabling Trade Index, which combines indicators on market access, border administration, transport and

Table 8.1 Bound and applied most-favoured nation (MFN) tariffs

Country/economy	Year	Tariff binding coverage (%)	Simple average final bound (all goods)	Simple average applied tariff (manufacturing)	Simple average applied tariff (agriculture)	Simple average applied tariff (all goods)	Trade weighted average (all goods)	Maximum MFN applied duties
European Union	2008–09	100.0	5.2	3.9	13.5	5.3	2.9	166
USA	2008–09	100.0	3.5	3.3	4.7	3.5	2.0	350
Japan	2008–09	99.7	5.1	2.5	21.0	4.9	2.0	641
Brazil	2008–09	100.0	31.4	14.1	10.2	13.6	8.8	97
Russia	2008–09	–	–	10.1	13.2	10.5	10.3	357
India	2008–09	73.8	48.5	10.1	31.8	12.9	6.0	246
Indonesia	2008–09	95.8	37.1	6.6	8.4	6.8	4.1	150
China	2008–09	100.0	10.0	8.7	15.6	9.6	4.3	65
South Africa	2008–09	96.4	19.0	7.5	8.9	7.7	5.0	878

Source: WTO World Tariff Profiles (2010), at http://stat.wto.org/TariffProfile/WSDBTariffPFHome.aspx?Language=E.

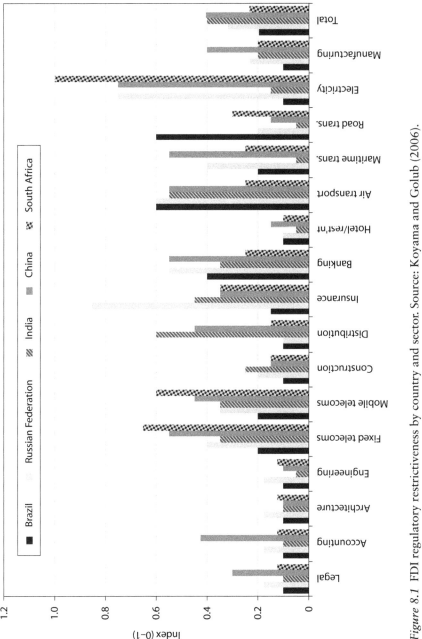

Figure 8.1 FDI regulatory restrictiveness by country and sector. Source: Koyama and Golub (2006).

Table 8.2 World rankings for ease of doing business, 2011

	Ease of doing business	Starting a business	Dealing with construction permits	Registering property	Getting credit	Protecting investors	Paying taxes	Trading across borders	Enforcing contracts	Closing a business
Singapore	1	4	2	15	6	2	4	1	13	2
Hong Kong	2	6	1	56	2	3	3	2	2	15
USA	5	9	27	12	6	5	62	20	8	14
Denmark	6	27	10	30	15	28	13	5	30	5
Korea	16	60	22	74	15	74	49	8	5	13
Japan	18	98	44	59	15	16	112	24	19	1
Thailand	19	95	12	19	72	12	91	12	25	46
Malaysia	21	113	108	60	1	4	23	37	59	55
Vietnam	78	100	62	43	15	173	124	63	31	124
China	79	151	181	38	65	93	114	50	15	68
Indonesia	121	155	60	98	116	44	130	47	154	142
Russia	123	108	182	51	89	93	105	162	18	103
Brazil	127	128	112	122	89	74	152	114	98	132
India	134	165	177	94	32	44	164	100	182	134

Source: World Bank Ease of Doing Business 2011, at http://www.doingbusiness.org/rankings.

commercial infrastructure, and the business environment into an overall index that ranks 118 countries. It scores better than Indonesia (68th), South Africa (72nd), India (84th), Brazil (87th) and Russia (114th). Ahead of China are OECD countries and more advanced emerging markets in Eastern Europe, Latin America, East Asia and the Middle East (the non-OECD group being nearly all small, open economies) (Table 8.3).

China has climbed up the world rankings for trade and FDI with lightning speed (Figures 8.2 and 8.3). It first displaced Japan as the world's second-largest trading nation (third-largest if the EU is counted as one), and then Germany as the world's leading exporter of merchandise goods, with almost 12 per cent of world merchandise exports by 2009 (Figures 8.4 and 8.5). This is far ahead of the other BRICs; and even ahead of India in world services trade (see Figure 8.10). China's trade-to-GDP ratio was 56 per cent in 2009, down dramatically from 74 per cent in 2007, as a result of the GEC (Figure 8.6). This was still higher than for Brazil and India, and still rather high for such a populous country. Nevertheless, *net* exports are much lower – about one sixth of GDP before the crisis. That is because they are mostly produced by labour-intensive assembly of imported components, and generate modest local value-added.

China had a 3 per cent share of global inward FDI stock in 2009, again ahead of the other BRICs (Figure 8.7). It has been the second-largest recipient of FDI in the world since 2000. Inward FDI was US$110 billion in 2008, a massive increase from 2007, although it came down to about US$95 billion in 2009 (see Figure 8.3). Investment is still mainly in manufacturing, but it has increased rapidly in services, accounting for over 40 per cent of total FDI. The government estimates that over 90,000 foreign-invested enterprises (FIEs) have established in services sectors in China, with investments of over US$160 billion.

China's outward FDI has also been increasing rapidly. It reached almost US$50 billion in 2009 (Figure 8.8). The government's 'Go Out' or 'Go Global' policy has spurred the foreign expansion of Chinese firms, mainly state-owned enterprises (SOEs). This outward reach is very recent, so China's stock of outward FDI remains minuscule, especially compared with that of the EU and the USA (Figure 8.9).

Exports and imports shrank when the GEC hit, battered by the collapse in global demand for consumer goods. In 2009, exports fell by 16 per cent and imports by 11 per cent, and the current account surplus almost halved to 5.8 per cent.

China, unlike India, has successfully exploited comparative advantage in labour-intensive manufactures; and it has done so with a tight interlock between trade and FDI. China now accounts for about 40 per cent of manufacturing exports from developing countries. About half of China's trade is 'processing trade': raw materials and components are imported and assembled for the export of final goods all over the world. Multinational enterprises (MNEs) account for 84 per cent of exports and imports involved

Table 8.3 The Enabling Trade Index, 2010

Country/ economy	Overall rank		Market access		Border administration		Transport and communications infrastructure		Business environment	
	Rank	Score	Rank	Score	Rank	Score	Rank	Score	Rank	Score
Singapore	1	6.06	1	5.97	1	6.56	7	5.74	2	6.00
Hong Kong	2	5.70	16	5.12	6	5.96	5	5.79	5	5.94
Denmark	3	5.41	95	3.76	3	6.22	8	5.71	3	5.96
Sweden	4	5.41	96	3.75	2	6.34	9	5.70	10	5.84
Switzerland	5	5.37	58	4.23	10	5.76	10	5.63	8	5.87
USA	19	5.03	62	4.17	19	5.60	11	5.49	37	4.86
Japan	25	4.80	121	3.20	16	5.65	14	5.45	34	4.91
China	48	4.32	79	3.87	48	4.53	43	4.13	41	4.74
Indonesia	68	3.97	60	4.21	67	3.99	85	3.28	60	4.42
South Africa	72	3.95	87	3.78	53	4.25	65	3.64	79	4.11
India	84	3.81	115	3.42	68	3.98	81	3.34	58	4.48
Brazil	87	3.76	104	3.72	80	3.70	66	3.64	83	4.00
Russia	114	3.37	125	2.68	109	2.99	48	4.00	92	3.79

Source: The Global Enabling Trade Report 2010, pp. 10–11, at http://www3.weforum.org/docs/WEF_GlobalEnablingTrade_Report_2010.pdf.

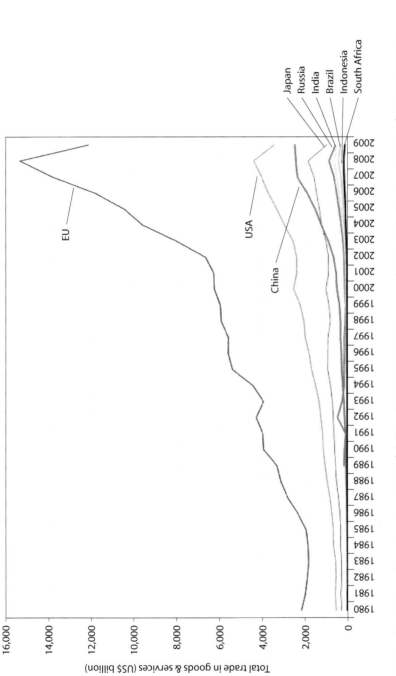

Figure 8.2 Total trade (goods and services) in US$ billion for BRIICs, EU, Japan and USA, including intra-EU trade, 1980–2009. Sources: World Bank, World Development Indicators; UNCTAD Statistical Handbook (2009); WTO International Trade Statistics (2010).

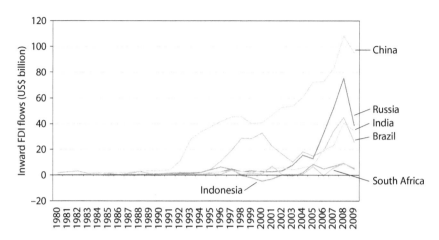

Figure 8.3 Inward FDI flows (US$ billion) for BRIICs, 1980–2008. Source:
UNCTAD World Investment Report 2010 (WIR 2010), at
http://www.unctad.org/templates/WebFlyer.asp?intItemID=5535&lang=1.

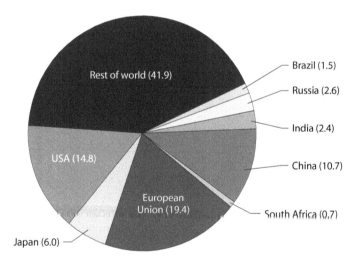

Figure 8.4 BRIICs, EU (excluding intra-EU trade), Japanese and US shares of
world goods and services trade in 2009. Sources: WTO, International
Trade Statistics (2010), at http://www.wto.org/english/news_e/pres10_e/
pr598_e.htm; Eurostat and own calculations.

in China's processing trade. Until the GEC hit, the fastest rates of export
growth were in finished consumer goods such as garments and toys, and in
information and communication technology (ICT) products. In the latter
category, as well as in assorted transport-and-machinery products, China
has become the final-assembly point in East Asian trade and FDI networks
in parts and components, linked in turn to final export markets in the West.

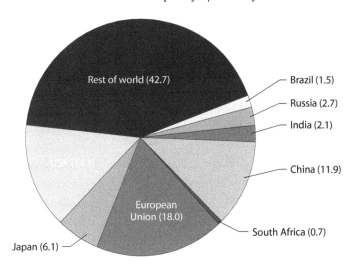

Figure 8.5 BRIICs, EU (excluding intra-EU trade), Japanese and US shares in global exports in goods in 2009. Sources: WTO, International Trade Statistics (2010), at http://www.wto.org/english/news_e/pres10_e/pr598_e.htm; Eurostat and own calculations.

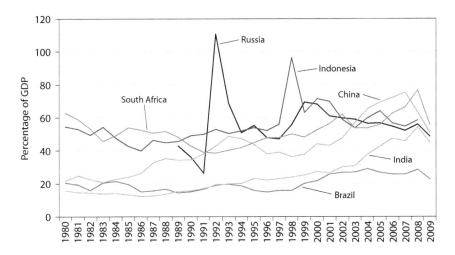

Figure 8.6 Trade in goods and services as a percentage of GDP for BRIICs countries, 1980–2009. Sources: World Bank, World Development Indicators; WTO International Trade Statistics (2010).

In contrast, China's share of world trade in services is still well below its share of world trade in goods (Figure 8.10).

In sum, China has done better than most developing countries, including the other BRICs: first in generating very high rates of growth; and second in translating the latter into employment, poverty reduction and human-welfare

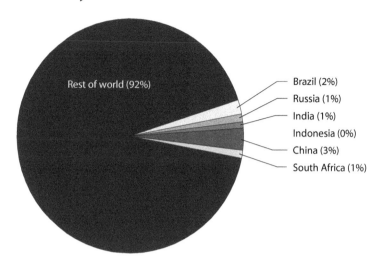

Figure 8.7 Share of world IFDI, BRIICs, 2009. Source: UNCTAD, FDI/TNC database, at http://www.unctad.org/fdistatistics.

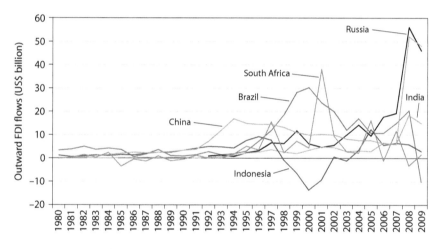

Figure 8.8 Outward FDI flows (US$ billion) from BRIICs, 2000–09. Source: UNCTAD, FDI/TNC database, at http://www.unctad.org/fdistatistics.

improvement for a broad section of the population. High rates of saving and investment have driven this process, but imports and inward investment have also been important, especially in ramping up labour-intensive manufactured exports. That distinguishes China from Japan and South Korea in their earlier postwar take-off phases: they relied much less on imports and inward investment. China still has high regulatory barriers that waste resources, restrict internal trade and generally stifle domestic sources of growth. Tackling these barriers is the next big political and economic challenge.

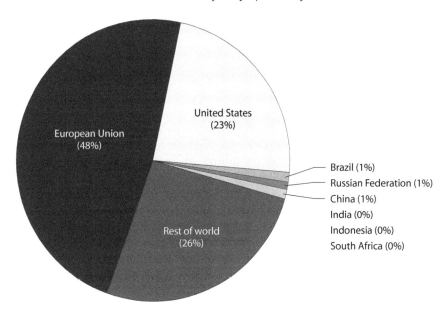

Figure 8.9 BRIICs OFDI stocks, 2009. Source: UNCTAD, FDI/TNC database, at http://www.unctad.org/fdistatistics.

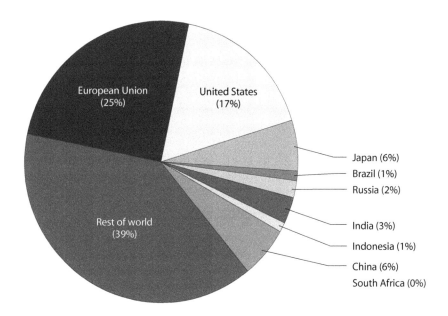

Figure 8.10 BRIICs, EU, Japanese and US shares of world services trade, 2009 (excludes intra-EU trade). Source: WTO International Trade Statistics 2010, at http://www.wto.org/english/res_e/statis_e/its2010_e/its10_toc_e. htm.

CHINA IN THE WTO

In the end-phase of China's accession negotiations, many players and observers feared China might play a spoiler role once inside the WTO. Would it use the WTO as a foreign-policy football? Would it indulge in power plays and provocative rhetoric? Would it undermine multilateral rules?

On balance, the answer to these questions is 'No'. The strength of China's unilateral reforms and WTO commitments, and its integration into the world economy, have made it keenly aware of its stake in well-functioning multilateral rules – more so compared with most other developing countries. China is a textbook example of how WTO accession works in tandem with national market-based reforms. It has become a strong WTO stakeholder, active in multilateral rule-enforcement and dispute settlement – much more so than Japan, for example. It has been very active in the WTO's regular committees, particularly on core rules issues. Arguably, the embedding of China in the WTO has defused manifold international trade tensions that might otherwise have got out of hand; and it has smoothed China's rapid integration into the world economy. In short, China's accession is the WTO's biggest success by far, and the world trading system's most important milestone since the end of the Uruguay Round. It contrasts very favourably with continued deadlock in the Doha Round.

Nevertheless, China's record in the WTO has not been without controversy – not surprising given such a huge and complicated accession. Implementation of WTO commitments has been mixed. A raft of sensitive cases against China, mostly prosecuted by the USA, has been working its way through dispute settlement. China has stayed conspicuously on the sidelines of the Doha Round. At the WTO mini-ministerial meeting in July 2008, it was partly responsible for blocking an overall deal. These are all manifestations of China's difficulty in making a quick transition from a rule-taker to a rule-setter in the WTO. These individual elements are examined in more detail below.

Implementation of WTO commitments[7]

On balance, China has been serious about implementing the bulk of its WTO commitments in timely fashion. That is true of phased tariff reductions, including the elimination of tariffs on goods covered by the Information Technology Agreement; phasing out import quotas, licenses and other border NTBs; and expanding trading rights. The revised Foreign Trade Law, issued in April 2004, provides for trading rights to be granted automatically through a registration process for all domestic and foreign enterprises and individuals. This became effective 6 months before scheduled full liberalization required by China's Protocol of Accession to the WTO. After pressure from the USA, tariff-rate quotas (TRQs) on protected agricultural products were expanded in line with WTO obligations. China has undertaken a huge programme of aligning national technical standards with international standards. In 2005 it reported that 1,416 national standards had been abolished as a result. It has also revised its laws to better protect intellectual property rights in line with the WTO's Trade-Related Intellectual Property Rights (TRIPS) agreement.

On the other hand, the USA, and to a lesser extent the EU, have led loud and vociferous complaints about China's implementation record. Indeed, US complaints have increased and broadened in scope. To quote the US Trade Representative's National Estimate on China's trade barriers in 2008:

> In 2007, US industry began to focus less on the implementation of specific commitments that China made upon entering the WTO and more on China's shortcomings in observing basic obligations of WTO membership, as well as on Chinese policies and practices that undermine previously implemented commitments. At the root of many of these problems is China's continued pursuit of problematic industrial policies that rely on excessive government intervention in the market through an array of trade-distorting measures.[8]

To list some major complaints made by the USA and other WTO members:

- Many WTO commitments are not uniformly applied in China. One example is uneven application of the WTO Customs Valuation agreement by customs officials at Chinese ports.
- Application of technical regulations, conformity-assessment procedures and sanitary and phytosanitary (SPS) measures is arbitrary and inconsistent, with inadequate notification of new or revised measures under the terms of the WTO's Technical Barriers to Trade (TBT) and SPS agreements.
- WTO notification of Chinese government subsidies was overdue and remains incomplete, as it does not cover subsidies from state-owned banks and local governments.
- Intellectual property rights (IPR) laws remain weakly enforced, particularly on copyright protection of a range of goods and services.
- There are substantial infringements of the Agreement on Trade-Related Investment Measures (TRIMS). China agreed not to make import and investment approval conditional on export-performance, local content, foreign-exchange balancing and technology-transfer requirements. But officials continue to 'encourage' such measures without formally requiring them. This can amount to de-facto requirements, especially as officials have substantial discretion in investment-approval procedures.
- It is also alleged that China is not living up to its WTO transparency obligations. Ministries and agencies responsible for drafting new or revised laws and regulations often do not circulate them for public

comment – which is supposed to include foreign enterprises – and do not provide enough time for public comment before enactment.

- Finally, USTR reports note that foreign enterprises remain sceptical about the adjudication of trade-related commercial disputes in designated Chinese forums, such as the China International Economic and Trade Arbitration Commission.

Dispute settlement

An indication of China's serious commitment to the WTO has been its assiduous tracking of dispute settlement. Since its accession it has been a third party to 69 cases, in addition to being a complainant in 7 cases and a respondent in 11. There has been a dramatic increase in cases since 2006–07.[9]

However, for the first 5 years of its WTO membership, China and other major players exercised mutual restraint in taking China-related cases to court. China viewed dispute settlement as a political–diplomatic mechanism to resolve differences through compromise and conciliation, before adversarial legal procedures kicked in. The USA, EU and others also generally refrained from testing China in court. In three cases – VAT-Integrated Circuits, EU-Coke Exports and Anti-Dumping Kraft Linerboards[10] – China made major concessions and settled during the consultation phase, i.e. out of court (Gao 2005, 2007a,b).

Mutual restraint seemed to end in about 2006, when the USA launched a raft of cases against China. The first, on automotive parts, struck at China's automotive industrial policy, which dates back to 2006. The latter includes provisions to encourage domestic production of auto parts. One measure stipulated that, if the number or value of imported parts in an assembled vehicle exceeded specified thresholds, tariffs charged on imported parts should be equal to the tariff on completed automobiles (typically 25 per cent) rather than the tariff applicable to auto parts (typically 10 per cent). The complainants, the USA, EU and Canada, argued that this violated WTO national treatment provisions and constituted a prohibited local-content measure. Significantly, China chose not to settle the matter in consultations but to allow it to proceed to a formal adjudicatory panel (USSTR 2008). The latter ruled against China, a decision confirmed by the WTO's Appellate Body in late 2008. China repealed the measure in 2009.

The USA followed up with more cases. One case concerned Chinese subsidy programmes, e.g. income-tax exemptions and refunds, benefiting a wide range of locally manufactured goods. The USA argued that these measures discriminated against imports and imposed export-performance requirements, thus violating the WTO's Subsidies and Countervailing Measures and TRIMS agreements. During consultations, the USA and China reached agreement on removing the alleged prohibited subsidies.

In 2007 and 2008, the USA filed a case relating to copyright infringement in China; another, also IPR-related, on trading-rights restrictions on copyright-intensive publications and audiovisual products such as films, DVDs, music, books and journals (for which trading rights were restricted to Chinese state-trading enterprises); and one (filed jointly with the EU) on restrictions on financial-information services providers from dealing directly with Chinese clients (rather having to deal exclusively with *Xinhua*, the state news agency). The USA won the two IPR-related cases, while the last case was settled in consultations in late 2008. In all three cases, China agreed to repeal the offending measures.

In 2009, the USA, EU and Mexico took China to dispute settlement over export restrictions on several raw materials used as inputs for downstream production in the USA and EU, especially in steel, aluminium and chemicals. They argued that these measures artificially raised export prices while lowering prices in China, thereby favouring domestic downstream production and exports. The panel ruled against China, and this was upheld by the appellate body in 2011.

These recent cases illustrate that China and its major trading partners have become more forceful in their use of dispute settlement. The USA has initiated cases that go to the heart of Chinese industrial policies and related domestic regulation. And China has become less wary of letting cases proceed to legal contest. On balance, this is healthy. China should be challenged in situations when it might well be in breach of its WTO obligations. Conversely, China should test the legal mechanics of WTO dispute settlement, in order to develop its trade-related legal capacity, defend its rights, and indeed to initiate cases when faced with infractions from its trading partners.

Negotiations and participation in the Doha Round

In stark contrast to its activism in implementing WTO obligations and in dispute settlement, China has been passive and a marginal player in the Doha Round – conspicuously so for the world's leading developing country and second-largest trading nation. It seems to have made a decision to sit out this Round. Many motives have been ascribed to China's quietism. The official rhetoric is that it needs time to digest new WTO obligations and generally acclimatize itself to WTO membership, but this is disingenuous after almost a decade in the club. More to the point, non-activism means that it has not stepped on developed and developing-country toes, and avoided extra pressure to further open its own markets through even stronger WTO commitments. This has come, however, at the cost of not forcefully pursuing its 'offensive' interests, particularly to open other markets for its manufactured exports, and secure stronger disciplines on anti-dumping duties and other 'trade remedies'. To cynics who believe the Doha Round has always been a lost cause, Chinese wisdom and foresight might seem particularly acute.

In terms of style, China, for much of the Round, differed markedly from most other developing countries, including India and Brazil, the two other developing-country 'big beasts'. Unlike them, and indeed unlike the USA and EU, it eschewed polarizing rhetoric and confrontational posturing. It was especially careful not to antagonize the USA, and was also sensitive to other developing countries' fear of the Chinese export juggernaut.

China's overall negotiating position, in common with other Recently Acceded Members (RAMs), is that it is willing to contribute little or nothing beyond its WTO-accession commitments.[11] There is a large gap between the RAMs' strong WTO commitments and the weak commitments of most other developing countries. That is why the Doha mandate and subsequent negotiating texts have accorded special flexibility to the RAMs.

China's negotiating positions on specific issues have been mixed: offensive here, defensive there, and in-between here-and-there, reflecting a big, complicated country with a broad spectrum of internal interests and preferences.

In the *non-agricultural market access* negotiations, China's interests are manifestly offensive: it wants greater access for its manufactured exports in both developed and developing countries. On *agriculture*, it has mixed positions. Domestic sensitivities make it loath to commit to extra liberalization. On the offensive side, it needs lower developed- and developing-country barriers to its growing labour-intensive agricultural exports. It has an interest in banning developed countries' export subsidies and in significantly reducing their trade-distorting domestic subsidies. Hence it joined the G20, led by India and Brazil. Its G20 participation, however, has been low key and non-belligerent. China is defensive in *services*. It has few export interests; and domestic sensitivities make it reluctant to concede stronger GATS commitments. However, as in goods, China is exceptional: in some cases its GATS commitments even exceed those of developed countries.

One of China's biggest priorities concerns *anti-dumping* (AD) and other trade remedies. It has been active in the AD component of the rules negotiations and tabled proposals, mainly with a view to removing, or at least diluting, its 'non-market-economy' status with some WTO members, notably the USA and EU. China has been flexible on Special and Differential Treatment for developing countries, and on the 'Singapore issues' (investment, competition, transparency in government procurement, and trade facilitation).

That said, China's overall position seems to have hardened in the past few years. It has been impervious to US and EU demands to be more flexible with its defensive positions. Finally, during the WTO mini-ministerial in Geneva in July 2008, China emerged from the shadows. Led by its trade minister, Chen Denming, it formed part of the core group of six countries that tried to unblock deals in agriculture and industrial goods. Never before in the Round had it played such a role. But, within this core, it joined forces with India to defend a very generous 'special safeguard mechanism' to protect against agricultural imports, and resisted US pressure to lower its cotton tariffs (Beattie and Williams 2008).

While China belatedly played an up-front role in WTO negotiations, it proved to be defensive, rather than pragmatic and middle of the road. Overall, China's trading partners now expect it to be proactive – to assume co-leadership in the WTO; and China is no longer comfortable as a willing, almost unquestioning taker of rules made by others. But its default position is still to be reactive in WTO negotiations, leaving other big players to take initiatives. This pattern dovetails with a slowdown of liberalization at home and other defensive measures in China's trade policy, especially since 2006. That is the subject of the next section.

CHINA'S TRADE-RELATED REFORMS: UNILATERAL MEASURES AND PREFERENTIAL TRADE AGREEMENTS

China's mixed record in the WTO should be seen, above all, in the context of market reforms at home post-WTO accession. The overriding advantage of WTO accession is that it has locked in the sweeping unilateral reforms of the 1990s and earlier, made China's trade-and-investment regulations more transparent and predictable, and given China a long-term stake in multilateral rules. But faraway Geneva cannot drive reforms in Beijing. The national reform engine has stalled, and industrial-policy interventions have correspondingly increased. China's response to the GEC has reinforced this trend. At the same time, China has been very active with PTAs, especially in its East Asian neighbourhood. I now consider these two aspects of China's trade policy in more detail.

Unilateral measures

There has been paltry unilateral liberalization going beyond China's WTO commitments. One example is the marginal opening of the highly pro-tected securities sector, as a result of US pressure in the US–China Strategic Economic Dialogue. More foreign fund managers have been allowed in as Qualified Financial Institutional Investors. Foreign-equity limits in joint ventures with Chinese securities firms have been increased, and these firms have been allowed to operate in a wider range of products. The govern-ment has also done a U-turn and welcomed foreign private-equity firms to participate in the local market. And it has allowed foreign participation in issuing renminbi (RMB)-denominated bonds and equities as part of its plan to internationalize the use of the renminbi. But these are baby steps, restricted by severe and entrenched controls on capital flows, the exchange rate and domestic interest rates.

These measures are small beer when compared with the huge external opening through the 1990s and up to 2006. But, to a large extent, liberali-zation slowdown is predictable. The Beijing leadership is more concerned with social stability in the wake of the massive social convulsions that have accompanied market reforms. Decision-making is much more collegiate, cautious and incremental; it is less visionary and certainly less committed to strong liberalization. This characterizes the leadership of Hu Jintao and Wen Jiabao, which is strikingly different from the bold, decisive strokes of Jiang Zemin and Zhu Rongji, and of Deng Xiaoping before them.

On trade policy, national reforms and WTO-accession negotiations were highly centralized in the Ministry of Foreign Trade and Economic Cooperation (later the Ministry of Commerce), reporting directly to the State Council. After WTO accession, other regulatory agencies have become more involved. The government faces more lobbying – and resistance to further liberalization – from national regulatory agencies, SOEs and other 'national champions' in the private sector (or with hybrid forms of ownership), state-sponsored trade associations, as well as provincial and municipal governments. The Ministry of Commerce has lost influence relative to other regulatory and interest-group fiefdoms such as the National Development and Reform Commission, the Ministry of Information Industries and Technology (MIIT), and supersized SOEs. Decision-making tends to take place in regulatory silos; it is that much more complex and difficult to coordinate. Economic nationalism in government and the Communist Party is more influential than it was in the 1990s, although it has not quite supplanted pragmatic pro-market reformers. Finally, as China's global economic clout has grown so quickly, so has the temptation to resort to more assertive mercantilism. That translates into unwillingness to open markets unilaterally, haggling hard over reciprocal concessions (especially with the USA) and stepping-up industrial-policy interventions to promote favoured domestic sectors. This reflects the shift in China's policy terms of trade – from systemic price- and rule-taker to leveraging its much greater bargaining power. But it is still far from being an active, constructive rule-setter and system-shaper.

None of the above is cause for wild alarm and panic: China is, to some degree, acquiring the 'normal' economic features and political pressures of a very large, complex market economy. And its already deep integration into the world economy – much deeper than that of Japan, South Korea and Taiwan at an equivalent stage of development – constrains protectionist pressures and their distortive effects on international trade and investment. Still, these pressures need to be contained, especially with a turbulent global economic environment and more protectionist pressures as a result of the recent crisis.

Some major signs of industrial-policy intervention, as well as 'unfinished business' in external liberalization and related structural reforms, are listed below.[12]

First, China's already complex export regime has become considerably more restrictive. Export taxes, reduced VAT rebates on exports, export bans, licensing and quotas are used to restrict exports of a growing number of goods, mainly raw materials and agricultural commodities. The objectives are various: defusing tensions with trade partners (e.g. over garments exports), reducing energy consumption, combating food-price inflation and promoting downstream industries through cheaper inputs. But these measures distort international competition by lowering domestic prices and raising world prices (in products in which China is a major supplier and can shift international terms of trade). China's recent decision to cut export quotas on rare-earth metals by 40 per cent is a classic example. Over two-thirds of world production of these materials is in China.[13]

Second, tax incentives, subsidies and price controls, as well as administrative 'guidance' on investment decisions, are used to favour domestic sectors over imports, especially where SOEs and assorted 'national champions' operate. This approach is evident in iron and steel, petrochemicals, automobiles and auto parts, forestry and paper, non-ferrous metals, telecommunications equipment, semiconductors and other science-and-technology sectors.

Third, China has promoted unique national technical standards, some would say as a regulatory-protectionist device to compensate for falling border barriers. China-specific standards, at variance with international standards, can create high compliance costs for foreign enterprises. Notable examples are encryption for wireless local area networks (WLANs) and standards for 3G mobile phones. Foreign enterprises complain of lack of transparency in Chinese standard-setting bodies due to restricted membership, voting rights and information dissemination. This is exacerbated by standards set by different agencies at national and provincial levels. Foreign enterprises have similar complaints about Chinese conformity-assessment bodies. They also complain about requirements to share commercially sensitive information and intellectual property when submitting samples and information for mandatory testing.

Fourth, services barriers have come down more slowly than goods barriers, and perhaps more slowly than expected after WTO accession. High and discriminatory capital requirements discourage entry for foreign services providers in, for example, telecommunications, insurance and construction (although capital thresholds have been reduced in banking). Licensing procedures have become more transparent and regular, but problems remain, especially in financial services, telecommunications and express-delivery services. Equity and operating restrictions are prevalent in insurance, securities and telecoms, though not (at least formally) in banking. Basic telecommunication services are dominated by four SOEs, all with close links to MIIT, and foreign entry is restricted to joint ventures. But no joint venture involving a foreign-invested enterprise has been licensed since WTO accession. MIIT is reluctant to allow new competition to incumbents in value-added telecom services such as modems, mobile WiFi and voice-over-internet protocol. It has issued 3G licences only to local incumbents.

Equity and severe operating restrictions apply to foreign internet services providers (ISPs). They are hemmed in by the world's most comprehensive internet filtering regime, the Chinese 'Great Firewall', which affects much internet commerce. This has provided cover for more aggressive 'online protectionism', benefiting local ISPs (such as the search engine, Baidu) over foreign competitors (such as Google). In 2009, a measure to force PC-makers to install a locally produced internet filter, ostensibly to block pornography, was 'delayed' after a barrage of opposition, mainly from US technology companies. Several measures targeting Google led to its unilateral withdrawal from China in 2010.[14]

Fifth, foreign-investment restrictions have been tightened. In November 2006, the National Development and Reform Commission announced a 5-year plan for foreign investment. It stressed a shift from 'quantity' to 'quality', tighter tax supervision and restricted foreign acquisition of 'dragon-head' enterprises. This was soon followed by a government 'guiding opinion' identifying an enlarged list of 'pillar' and 'backbone' sectors in which further foreign investment in SOEs was to be prevented. New provisions on mergers and acquisitions also contained vague language on 'national economic security' and 'critical industries', probably intended to block foreign acquisitions. The government is drawing up rules to scrutinize foreign acquisitions on national-security grounds. Foreign enterprises also fear that the new Antimonopoly Law, effective from August 2008, will be used to block mergers and acquisitions involving foreign-invested enterprises, and protect SOEs and other national champions. It contains vague language on the 'public interest', 'national economic security' and 'unreasonable prices', and no definition of market dominance. It has sweeping exemptions for SOEs. It may have stalled several deals involving MNEs; and it was used to block Coca Cola's acquisition of Huiyuan Juice (what would have been the biggest foreign takeover of a Chinese company).

The 2007 amendment to the foreign investment catalogue (SDRC–MOC 2007) suggests a more selective approach to foreign investment, targeting higher value-added sectors rather than basic manufacturing. It includes new restricted sectors such as biofuel production and soy crushing, and blanket prohibitions on foreign investment in movie production, news websites, audiovisual and internet services. Another government 'opinion' calls for expanded domestic market share in industrial-machinery manufacturing sectors, which could presage difficulties for foreign investors seeking control of leading domestic firms. Finally, the government promotes domestic services sectors through foreign-investment restrictions, notably in financial services and telecommunications.

Sixth, government procurement explicitly discriminates in favour of domestic enterprises. China has applied to join the WTO's Government Procurement Agreement, in line with its WTO-accession commitments but, predictably, negotiations have been glacial. It submitted a revised offer in 2010, much diluted by exempting local governments and SOEs. Overall, discriminatory government-procurement practices have become more pronounced. 'Buy China' measures, operating at national, provincial and municipal levels, were introduced as part of the fiscal-stimulus package in 2009.

More importantly, an 'indigenous innovation' policy, announced initially in 2006, is geared to promoting domestic technology companies at the expense of foreign competitors. In 2009, a government circular on 'national indigenous innovation product accreditation work' stipulated that, to qualify for accreditation for procurement preferences, intellectual property must be 'originally registered' in China, with 'Chinese intellectual property and proprietary brands', and that intellectual property must be 'totally independent of overseas organizations or industries'. The government then created a catalogue of 240 'indigenous innovation' products. In 2010, the authorities softened these rules following complaints from over 30 foreign-industry groups.

Other compulsory certification schemes restrict foreign access to government procurement. This applies to cars, car parts, information technology and telecom equipment, health-care equipment, and electro-technical and power-transmission equipment. Encryption-rich products such as firewalls, secure routers and smartcards must undergo compulsory certification according to Chinese standards if they are to qualify for government procurement. This can require handing over software source codes and other confidential information. Again, the government has agreed to delay implementation in response to complaints from foreign technology companies. Also, a new security classification scheme for technology products has been proposed. It contains vague language on 'critical infrastructure' and 'public security' that could bar FIEs from commercial projects in transport, telecoms, water, health care, energy and banking.[15]

The high-speed rail sector is a headline example of how government procurement has been used to build up national champions. Foreign suppliers have been restricted to joint ventures and forced to transfer sensitive technology in order to get contracts. In quick time, domestic firms, using foreign technology and with low-cost finance from state-owned banks, have got to the stage of competing with American, European and Japanese MNEs for contracts abroad.[16]

Seventh, energy sectors are largely insulated from global markets. Price controls apply to oil, natural gas, coal and electricity. Three giant SOEs dominate oil and gas, and the private sector is barred from production in oil, gas and coal. Export restrictions and imports controlled by state-trading enterprises protect SOEs in these sectors from international competition. That applies to nuclear and renewable energy as well. Foreign makers of electric cars, wind turbines and solar panels, for example, complain of being shut out of domestic projects. They are restricted to joint ventures and are subject to onerous local-content and technology-transfer requirements.

Eighth, China's 'investment nationalism' extends to its Go Out policy. SOEs benefit from cheap finance from state-owned banks. They enjoy strong political support to build infrastructure in, and secure long-term energy supplies from, resource-rich countries. Such capital-intensive outward investment contrasts with predominantly labour-intensive inward investment.

Ninth, China has become a prominent user of trade remedies. It had 102 AD measures in place by January 2010. It also launched three counter-vailing duty investigations in 2009.

And tenth, foreign business associations – especially from the USA and EU – continue to complain of opaque and unpredictable laws and regula-tions. This encompasses too short or no prior consultation before the release of laws and regulations (as was the case with the circular on indigenous innovation); and discretionary enforcement that leads to big differences in regulatory implementation in different parts of the country.[17]

Unilateral measures and the global economic crisis[18]

China's main response to the recent economic crisis was a supercharged fiscal and monetary stimulus amounting to almost a half of GDP in 2009. That comprised a direct fiscal-stimulus package of US$585 billion, and, far more important, state-directed bank lending of almost RMB10 tril-lion (US$1.5 trillion) in new loans. That ensured growth in 2009 of about 9 per cent, over 90 per cent of which was due to the stimulus. The latter went mostly into fixed-asset investment in physical infrastructure, though some of it inevitably seeped into financial and property markets. The stimulus's engine was ramped-up lending by state-owned banks to industrial SOEs.

Trade- and FDI-restricting measures have increased during the crisis. Some are directly crisis-related; others would probably have materialized with or without the crisis. VAT rebates on labour-intensive exports were increased, but this follows past practice, compensates for rebate reductions in 2006–07 and is not exactly clear-cut protectionism. There were 'Buy Chi-nese' government-procurement provisions, but China has longstanding dis-criminatory government procurement and is not yet a member of the WTO's Government Procurement Agreement. Tighter standards were used to ban a few European agricultural products. Subsidies and lower sales taxes have favoured the domestic car industry. A new Postal Law bans foreign compa-nies from providing certain domestic express-delivery services. There was stepped-up technology-related protectionism, e.g. indigenous-innovation measures and online-services restrictions. And more trade remedies were initiated. On the other hand, China reduced or eliminated some export duties, and opened up the domestic market to foreign travel agencies. It is also the most frequent target of other countries' crisis-related protectionism (Table 8.4), and has been on the receiving end of tariffs, import licensing, AD duties, and tighter standards on its exports of iron, steel, aluminium, footwear and toys.

Chinese protectionism has increased since the crisis broke, but not dra-matically or to the extent of reversing a 30-year liberalizing trend. Indeed, China does not figure in Global Trade Alert's (2010) list of top ten offenders on crisis-related trade-restrictive measures, whereas the EU-27, India, Russia and Brazil do (Table 8.5). Overall, the Beijing leadership has not rocked the

Table 8.4 Countries targeted by crisis-era trade-restrictive measures

Target	Number of discriminatory measures imposed on target		Number of pending measures which, if implemented, would harm target too	
	November 2010	Increase since June 2010	November 2010	Increase since June 2010
China	337	55	129	4
EU-27	322	56	88	8
USA	260	47	51	5
Germany	240	36	63	7
France	221	33	50	4
UK	214	33	48	4
Italy	211	36	53	3
Japan	192	24	50	4
Netherlands	191	21	45	3
Belgium	189	19	46	3

Source: Global Trade Alert (2010) *The 8th GTA Trade Report*, CEPR, London, at http://www.globaltradealert.org/sites/default/files/GTA8_0.pdf.

boat during or after the crisis: it has not resorted to aggressive mercantilism. Recent trade conflicts with the USA and EU over the measures mentioned above, as well as exchange-rate tensions, should not be exaggerated: they do not amount to a trade war. Protectionist responses have been heavily constrained by China's already deep integration into the world economy, particularly through processing trade and global manufacturing supply chains, and by its strong WTO commitments.

Preferential trade agreements (PTAs)

China is the driving force for PTAs in Asia. By 2010, it had 11 PTAs on the books, with 11 others under negotiation or proposed (Table 8.6). However, China's trade with its FTA partners is still a relatively small share of its overall trade, accounting for about a quarter of imports and less than a third of exports.

The China–ASEAN PTA, more than any other, is the one to watch in the region. It is the largest PTA ever negotiated, covering 11 diverse economies with a population of 1.7 billion. It came into force in January 2010.[19] There has been progress in eliminating tariffs on trade in goods. However, little progress has been made on NTBs in services and investment (both relatively weak agreements), and other issues. China has stronger 'WTO-plus' PTAs with Hong Kong and Macau (both admittedly special cases); a comprehensive PTA on goods with Chile; newly concluded PTAs with New Zealand, Singapore and Peru; and is negotiating PTAs with Australia, Iceland, the Gulf Cooperation Council and Norway. It has a partial-scope tariff agree-

Table 8.5 Crisis-era trade-restrictive measures by country

Rank	Ranked by number of measures	Ranked by the number of tariff lines affected by measures	Ranked by the number of sectors affected by measures	Ranked by the number of trading partners affected by measures
1	EU-27 (166)	Vietnam (926)	Algeria (67)	Argentina (174)
2	Russia (85)	Venezuela (785)	EU-27 (57)	EU-27 (168)
3	Argentina (52)	Kazakhstan (723)	Nigeria (45)	China (160)
4	India (47)	Nigeria (599)	Venezuela (38)	Indonesia (151)
5	Germany (35)	Algeria (476)	Vietnam (38)	Algeria (476)
6	Brazil (32)	EU-27 (467)	Germany (36)	India (145)
7	UK (31)	Russia (426)	Kazakhstan (36)	Russia (143)
8	Spain (25)	Argentina (396)	Russia (36)	Finland (132)
9	Indonesia (24)	India (365)	India (32)	Germany (132)
10	Italy (24)	Indonesia (347)	Ethiopia (32)	South Africa (132)

Source: Global Trade Alert (2010): *The 8th GTA Trade Report*, CEPR, London, at http://www.globaltradealert.org/sites/default/files/GTA8_0.pdf.

ment with Pakistan. Most recently, it signed an Economic Cooperation and Framework Agreement (ECFA) with Taiwan. This followed a series of bilateral agreements to liberalize highly restricted trade across the Taiwan Straits. But much remains to be done: ECFA is a 'framework agreement' with initially limited liberalization. China is also negotiating or thinking of negotiating rather weak PTAs elsewhere in the developing world, e.g. with Mercosur and the South African Customs Union. These are shallow, and are mostly preferential tariff reductions on a limited range of products.

China gives unilateral tariff preferences to 41 least-developed countries (LDCs). It has pledged to give duty-free access to 95 per cent of imports from LDCs, although no date has been specified for this.

China's approach to PTAs is pragmatic and eclectic (Antkiewicz and Whalley 2005), but is mostly 'trade light'. Even the China–ASEAN PTA is unlikely to create much extra trade and investment if it does not go substantially beyond tariff elimination in goods. China's PTAs are driven more by 'high politics' (competition with Japan to establish leadership credentials in East Asia; securing privileged influence in other regions) than by economic strategy. Foreign-policy 'soft power', i.e. diplomacy and relationship-building, is paramount.

This reflects the trade-light PTA pattern in Asia, and the established PTA pattern in other developing-country regions (Sally 2006). Politically sensitive sectors in goods and services are carved out, as are crucial areas where progress in the WTO is elusive (especially disciplines on AD duties and agricultural subsidies). Little progress is usually made in tackling domestic regulatory barriers (e.g. relating to investment, competition, government procurement, trade facilitation, cross-border labour movement, and food-

Table 8.6 China's RTAs

Partner country	Type	Status
ASEAN	Comprehensive Economic Cooperation Agreement	In effect
Asia Pacific	Preferential trade agreement (PTA)	In effect
ASEAN+6	ASEAN+6	Proposed/under consultation and study
ASEAN+3	Free trade agreement (FTA)	Proposed/under consultation and study
New Zealand	FTA	In effect
Australia	FTA	Framework agreement (FA) signed/FTA under negotiation
Chile	FTA	In effect
Costa Rica	FTA	Signed
Gulf Cooperation Council	FTA	Under negotiation
Hong Kong	Closer Economic Partnership Agreement (CEPA)	In effect
Iceland	FTA	FA signed/FTA under negotiation
India	FTA	Proposed/under consultation and study
Japan–Korea	FTA	Proposed/under consultation and study
Korea	FTA	Proposed/under consultation and study
Macao	CEPA	In effect
Norway	FTA	Under negotiation
Pakistan	FTA	In effect
Peru	FTA	In effect
Singapore	FTA	In effect
South Africa	FTA	Proposed/under consultation and study
Southern African Customs Union	FTA	Under negotiation
Switzerland	FTA	Proposed/under consultation and study
Taiwan	Economic Cooperation Framework Agreement	FA signed/FTA under negotiation
Thailand	FTA	In effect
Shanghai Cooperation Organization	FTA	Proposed/under consultation and study

Source: Asia Regional Integration Centre, at http://www.aric.adb.org/FTAbyCountryAll.php.

safety and technical standards). PTAs hardly go beyond WTO commitments, deliver little, if any, net liberalization and pro-competitive regulatory reform, and get tied up in knots of restrictive, overlapping rules of origin.

In addition to bilateral PTAs, China is at the heart of regional-economic-integration initiatives in East Asia (Kawai and Wignaraja 2008). An 'ASEAN Plus Three' PTA (the 'three' being Japan, South Korea and China) has been touted, as has a three-way Northeast Asia PTA (Japan, China and South Korea) and an 'ASEAN Plus Six' PTA that might include India, Australia and New Zealand. Visions of an East Asian Economic Community and even an Asian Economic Community have appeared on the horizon.

So far this talk is loose and without much substance. To begin with, regional trade integration is partial and skewed. It is restricted to East Asia; South Asia is the most malintegrated region in the world and has barely inserted itself into regional and global manufacturing supply chains. True, East Asian intra-regional trade and FDI have increased considerably. But they are a direct product of *global* economic integration, particularly in manufacturing. Their core is a dense network of production-sharing and trade in manufacturing parts and components, which are in turn linked to final markets in Europe and North America (Athukorala 2006; Baldwin 2006). Beyond these manufacturing niches, mainly in ICT products, East Asia remains highly malintegrated, beset by border and non-border barriers to intra-regional commerce.

Since the GEC, a newly fashionable argument holds that regional trade patterns are changing fast, and will favour regional production for regional consumption, i.e. a more comprehensive type of regional integration less reliant on the West. China is the hub of this new regionalism. Its booming domestic consumer market and still huge infrastructure requirements will attract greater exports of capital equipment and final goods – not just parts and components for assembly and re-export – from other East Asian countries. Indeed, there may have been an increase in this kind of East Asian trade in 2009–10, riding the wave of high Chinese growth while Western demand has shrunk. But these prognostications are highly premature and speculative. China has enjoyed a short-term consumption boost through massive government stimulus. That will inevitably wane. But it is highly questionable that it has had a *structural* shift to a more consumption- and less investment-orientated economy. And there is no serious empirical evidence to date that East Asian trade has become noticeably less reliant on extra-regional markets (Athukorala and Kohpaiboon 2010).

On the policy front, regional players are speeding ahead with bilateral PTAs. The existing pattern is of a patchwork of 'hub-and-spoke' PTAs, in a 'noodle bowl' of trade-restricting rules of origin. This does not seem to have done much harm so far but, if unchecked, it could slow down and distort the advance of regional and global production networks, as could region-wide PTAs that discriminate against extra-regional trade and FDI. Will bilateral PTAs be folded into simpler, more comprehensive region-wide

PTAs, especially in East Asia? Will a China–Japan–Korea PTA emerge? What about a China-centred ASEAN-Plus-Three PTA? Or even an ASEAN-Plus-Six PTA or an APEC PTA? Such initiatives may be spurred by the formation of a Trans-Pacific Partnership involving the USA, Japan, South Korea and others. But the odds are still stacked against region-wide PTAs, especially ones that will be more than trade-light. Countries are at widely different stages of development, with competing producer interests, significant barriers to trade with each other, and without a culture of deep cross-border cooperation. Moreover, bitter nationalist rivalries – especially between China, Japan and South Korea, and between China, India and Pakistan – will continue to stymie East Asian and pan-Asian regional-integration efforts for a long time to come.

Perhaps the best that can be expected is gradually stronger 'soft cooperation' in regional institutions such as the Asia Pacific Economic Cooperation (APEC) forum, the Association of South-East Asian Nations (ASEAN), ASEAN-Plus-Three and the East Asia Summit. They can be chat forums that gradually improve mutual surveillance and transparency, promote trade facilitation and 'best-practice' measures, and (at best) cement unilateral liberalization and help prevent its reversal in difficult times. Inevitably, China will be the most important player in these institutions; no stronger cooperation, hard or soft, will work without its lead.[20]

CHINA'S TRADE POLICY: CHALLENGES AHEAD

China's domestic climate for further trade-and-investment liberalization is clearly more inclement than it was before WTO accession, and there is greater industrial-policy interventionism. These tendencies are reinforced by a global climate of stalled liberalization, with a new wave of government 'crisis interventions' in the wake of the GEC.

From a market-liberal perspective, China should restrain its industrial-policy activism and its protectionist spillover. And it should go further in two respects: plug gaps in its implementation of WTO commitments; and proceed with WTO-plus reforms. But this is easier said than done, and it does not appear realistic in the current climate. Industrial-policy activists abound in Beijing and in provincial and municipal governments. In particular, sub-national officials enjoy considerable de-facto autonomy, which they often use to restrict competition and protect well-connected incumbents. And, for the time being, they have a fair wind in their sails.

On WTO implementation, China needs to improve its enforcement of the TRIPS, TRIMS, SPS, TBT and Subsidies and Countervailing Measures agreements, and improve WTO notification of its subsidies. Better enforcement of WTO agreements requires stronger restrictions on regulatory discretion at national and sub-national levels, especially on official 'encouragement' and 'guidance' of measures that are clearly incompatible with WTO obligations.

More transparency is also needed, e.g. freely and promptly circulating draft laws and regulations to interested foreign enterprises, and allowing them sufficient time for comment. That said, limits to regulatory discretion will prove very difficult in a country that still has not completed its journey from Plan to Market, and which has large, complex bureaucracies at national and sub-national levels.

What about WTO-plus reforms? China could further reduce applied import tariffs, especially on industrial goods. It should reverse export controls on raw materials and agricultural commodities. But its more substantial – and politically very tricky – challenge is to tackle high trade-related domestic regulatory barriers in goods, services, investment and public procurement.

Ideally, China would reduce measures to promote capital-intensive, SOE-dominated sectors at the expense of imports; align national standards with international standards, alongside a more active role in international standards-setting bodies; restart services liberalization (by easing capitalization requirements, equity restrictions, and licensing and operating procedures); lower foreign-investment restrictions (by pruning lists of sectors in which foreign investment is banned or discouraged, and not applying antitrust provisions to block foreign transactions in favour of national champions); limit online and high-tech protectionism; and gradually liberalize markets in government procurement and energy.

There are several tracks on which to pursue China's trade-related reforms: the unilateral (domestic) track; in the WTO; in PTAs; and in key bilateral and regional relationships, especially with the USA, EU and its East Asian neighbours. Each track is considered in turn below.

First, the primary thrust of trade-related reform must be unilateral, i.e. outside trade negotiations, and hitched firmly to domestic reforms to improve the business climate. Put another way, trade policy should be embedded in domestic economic policy and its institutional framework rather than being driven by external negotiations and international institutions. Trade-related regulatory reforms are bundled up with domestic politics and economics; initiating and implementing them is overwhelmingly a domestic affair; and the scope for productive international negotiations and agreements is restricted.

Chinese unilateral liberalization also has a vital external dimension. It is the biggest the world has ever seen, with its largest spillover effect in Asia. China's opening not only spurred Southeast Asian liberalization pre-Asian crisis; it probably helped prevent reversal of liberalization following the Asian crisis. It has also encouraged East Asian countries, post-Asian crisis, to further liberalize at the margin, for fear of losing trade and FDI to China. Not least, China has probably spurred Indian liberalization of import tariffs and FDI restrictions in some services sectors. Hence, much depends on this Chinese engine for future trade and FDI reforms, elsewhere in Asia and beyond. It is important that it re-energizes.

Second, China-induced unilateral liberalization is not a panacea. It does not lock-in liberalization against future backtracking. Nor does it provide fair, stable and predictable rules for international commerce. That leaves room for reciprocal negotiations and international agreements, particularly in the WTO.

The failure of the Doha Round (as of the time of writing) probably shows that future multilateral liberalization will be elusive and modest at best. Arguably, the best the WTO can hope for post-Doha is to lock in pre-existing unilateral liberalization through binding commitments, and gradually improve the functioning of multilateral rules. There should indeed be much stronger focus on safeguarding, updating and improving trade rules, in which China has such a substantial stake. This is more important for most WTO members than further multilateral liberalization. China should be active in plurilateral 'coalitions of the willing' to make key market-access and rule-making decisions and, correspondingly, take on stronger commitments than poorer, weaker and more recalcitrant developing countries. China, India and Brazil – the three developing-country 'big beasts' in the WTO – should exercise co-leadership alongside the USA, EU and perhaps Japan (if the last-named can get its act together). China's helping hand will be indispensable; arguably more important than those of India and Brazil. Given its trading weight, China is one of the 'big three' in the WTO, alongside the USA and EU. Without China's more active participation, it is doubtful that the Doha Round can be concluded. Post-Doha, it is vital that China move to the WTO foreground and play an active co-leadership role.[21]

Third, PTAs are generally trade-light; their noodle-bowl discriminatory patchwork causes complications for business and multilateral rules; and they are unlikely to spur regional and global integration. There should be much more caution with PTAs; and serious attempts made to minimize the damage from their discriminatory provisions. Again, China's lead will be important. It needs to signal its intention to avoid gimmicky initiatives, clean up existing weak and dirty PTAs, and make them more compatible with multilateral rules.

Fourth, China's key bilateral relationships, especially that with the USA, matter as much as what it does in the WTO and PTAs. These are, of course, two-way streets. The Beijing leadership is likely to arrest protectionist backsliding, and go farther with liberalization and structural reforms if it enjoys friendly, give-and-take relations with major trading powers. That also applies to its relations with its East Asian neighbours. This is probably necessary to overcome domestic opposition to change. Tub-thumping protectionism and belligerence by the USA about issues such as the Chinese exchange rate and current-account surplus, and imports of garments and other labour-intensive exports, as well as on security-related issues, invite a Chinese backlash and make its leadership more defensive. That is a recipe for reform stoppage and reversal.

It thus behoves the USA and other trading partners to strengthen 'constructive engagement' with China across a broad range of economic and foreign-policy issues, while containing foreign-policy belligerents and protectionist forces at home. This will, in turn, encourage Beijing to strengthen its key bilateral relationships and its participation in international institutions, contain aggressive nationalistic tendencies (especially directed at Taiwan and Japan) and, not least, step up economic reforms at home.[22]

Realism tells us that most of this wish list is not on Beijing's current agenda. It is not minded to curtail industrial policy, proceed with WTO-plus reforms, be proactive in WTO negotiations or restrain PTA permissiveness. But that same wish list is worth promoting so that it can be achieved, however partially and patchily, when political conditions are ripe.

Fifth, talk of constructive engagement in key bilateral relationships – especially with the USA – leads inevitably to consideration of global macroeconomic tensions. US complaints about an allegedly grossly undervalued renminbi and persistent Chinese current-account surpluses have become shriller – more so from Congress, perhaps less so from the Administration. China stands accused of protectionism via 'currency manipulation', which, it is said, constitutes an export subsidy. Via its current-account surplus, China is charged with adding to global imbalances at a time when demand in the West is depressed, and when the USA is attempting a shift from consumption to savings. Other countries succumb to the temptation of devaluing their currencies; a round of competitive devaluation ensues. This is the prelude to 'currency wars', which in turn threaten a new round of trade protectionism.

In September 2010, the US House of Representatives supported a bill to slap trade sanctions on China as retaliation for its currency manipulation. Fred Bergsten, Clive Crook, Martin Wolf and other luminaries have called for trade or capital-market sanctions if China does not fall in line. Ahead of the G20 summit in Seoul, the US proposed 'numerical targets' (of ± 4 per cent of GDP) to limit current-account imbalances.[23]

Large and persistent currency undervaluation and current-account surpluses, especially for a country as large and as important as China, can perhaps be a source of global instability, and indeed exacerbate protectionist pressures. One is reminded of the currency wars of the 1930s (some countries stayed on the gold standard while others left it), which triggered more trade protectionism than the Smoot-Hawley tariff.[24] But today the spectre of currency wars has not triggered a new round of protectionism – so far. And the negative consequences of currency undervaluation and current-account imbalances are probably, and perhaps vastly, exaggerated.

Much American reasoning on this set of issues has deep flaws, with dangerous policy inferences. The expert semi-consensus holds that the renminbi is undervalued, but no-one knows what the 'right' market exchange rate is or should be, and estimates of undervaluation range from 0–50 per cent. An obsession with nominal exchange rates is also misleading; various calculations of real exchange-rate undervaluation produce lower-range estimates. The assumption of a straightforward, mechanical translation from an undervalued currency to a current-account surplus is highly questionable, *especially* in China's case. Processing trade (imports of raw materials and components for assembly and export of finished goods all over the world) accounts for half of China's overall trade and nearly all its trade surplus. It blunts the effects of currency swings. It also vastly exaggerates China's bilateral and overall trade surpluses, for Chinese value-added in final processed exports is very modest (as is the case with Apple's iPods, iPads and iPhones) (Xing and Detert 2010). Also, a large and sudden renminbi revaluation could be very destabilizing for the Chinese export economy, without making a corresponding dent in the US current-account deficit (given that US production is highly unlikely to substitute for Chinese labour-intensive exports). American consumers and firms who use Chinese inputs would suffer through higher prices.

Underlying economic policies relating to savings, investment and consumption, notably underpricing of capital, land and energy, probably have a greater effect on external imbalances than exchange-rate valuations. So do other structural factors. China's 'double transition' – rural-to-urban migration and fast-paced industrialization, combined with a condensed demographic dividend (a large increase in the working-age ratio, speeded up by China's one-child policy) – gives it huge, long-lasting comparative advantage in labour-intensive exports. Since the 1990s, this has been accompanied by a reorientation of production and trade in global supply chains, as China has become the premier assembly hub for manufactured exports. Via processing trade, China runs deficits with other East Asian countries and surpluses with Europe and the USA. Correspondingly, other East Asian countries have seen their trade surpluses increase with China and decrease with the West. All this suggests that most of China's trade surplus – the biggest chunk of its current-account surplus – is not the result of 'unfair trade'; rather it results from modern, thoroughly 'normal', global integration. Which makes one wonder: is an obsession with national current-account imbalances warranted in a world of 21st-century globalization characterized by processing trade and vertically integrated global supply chains?[25]

That said, a Chinese move to *gradually* revalue the renminbi to a market-determined level, cautiously sequenced with domestic financial-sector reforms, is desirable. It is in China's domestic interest. It would help to allocate capital more efficiently and to control inflation. And it would probably ease global imbalances and protectionist pressures – although large imbalances will persist for the normal, structural reasons mentioned above. But the American obsession with a quick fix on the renminbi and the Chinese current-account surplus is both misguided and dangerous. Its analysis belongs to a world that pre-dates modern globalization, and its headline prescriptions (trade and/or capital-market sanctions) are crudely mercantilist.

An allied prescription – G20 coordination of exchange rates and global imbalances in a 'Plaza II accord' – is equally wrong. It presupposes knowledge of the 'right' exchange rates and external balances, which nobody has. Such a grand global design smacks of command-economy thinking and massive social engineering. It wilfully ignores what Hayek (1936) called a 'knowledge problem', inherent in complex market economies, and its policy nostrums are what Hayek also called a 'fatal conceit'. Also, deep-seated differences among G20 members on underlying economic policies have prevented and will prevent 'hard coordination' of *anything* – trade, macro-economic policy, financial regulation, structural reform or anything else for that matter. In that sense the G20 is no different from the G8. 'Soft' cooperation is the best that can be achieved; hard coordination is a will-o-the-wisp.

THE BROADER CONTEXT: CHINA'S HYBRID POLITICAL ECONOMY AND GEOPOLITICS

China's trade policies must be seen in the context of the domestic economy and its political arrangements, and also in the context of China's rising geopolitical power.

The uneasy coexistence of external openness and domestic industrial policy is but a reflection of hybrid conditions at home. Despite over three decades of market reforms, China's economy remains 'unbalanced'. Symptoms include over a third of the world's current-account surplus, foreign-exchange reserves amounting to half of domestic GDP, and household disposable income that is barely over a third of GDP. The private sector makes up about two-thirds of GDP, but the public sector retains some 'commanding heights'. The government and SOEs dominate banking, insurance, the bond market, telecoms, aviation, shipping, railroads, oil, coal, steel, natural gas, petrochemicals, power generation and distribution, and other sectors besides. Growth continues to rely on high rates of domestic saving and investment, but at the expense of repressed consumption. *Dirigiste* policies favour polluting, capital-intensive industrial and resource-based SOEs, state banks in a backward financial system and capital markets, and monopolistic services providers in other sectors. Externally, surplus savings plus an undervalued exchange rate contribute to global economic imbalances and generate extra trade tensions.

'Rebalancing growth' – making it more consumption- and less investment-driven – requires deep competition-enhancing reforms. Here the wish list is long: revaluation of the renminbi to something approaching market-determined levels; restructuring and privatization of SOEs and state-owned banks; financial-sector liberalization to liberate credit allocation, deepen equity and bond markets, and turn savings into more productive investments; secure private-property rights, including legal title to rural land; deregulation of internal trade to create a more integrated domestic market; liberalization of the household registration (*hukou*) system so that workers and their families can move more readily from the countryside to urban areas; market pricing for a range of inputs (land, water and other natural resources); and better provision of public services (health, education, pensions and social security).

Such reforms would lower transaction costs and improve the business climate, as would WTO-plus reforms on trade and FDI. They would also help reduce global macro-economic imbalances and lower trade tensions. But these are 'second-generation' reforms 'behind the border'. They concern factor markets (land, labour, capital and energy) as much as product markets. They lie at the heart of domestic economics and politics. They are much more difficult politically than 'first-generation' reforms, such as the earlier phase of trade and FDI liberalization 'at the border'. In China, needed reforms go to the core of the Communist Party–government–public sector nexus and its grip on power (Pei 2006; Huang 2008). It is unlikely to happen soon. Indeed, China's crisis response – essentially an investment binge – bolsters the public sector and state power at the expense of the far-less-subsidized private sector. It succeeded in arresting growth slowdown in 2009, but it exacerbates China's structural fault-line of over-investment and underconsumption. Its command-and-control mechanisms take market reform backwards. And there is the real risk of surplus manufacturing capacity flooding into anaemic export markets in Europe and North America, thereby inviting protectionist retaliation against China.

In essence, China's development trajectory follows that of other East Asian countries in massively overinvesting and misallocating capital, but its embedded political economy keeps it on the same treadmill. However, investment-driven growth is subject to diminishing returns (note the slowdown in total-factor-productivity growth since the late 1990s), and Chinese exports face a turbulent post-crisis external environment of depressed global demand and greater trade friction. Hence the need for structural reforms to deliver more sustainable, better quality growth.[26]

European and American business leaders also complain that they face a much more frustrating environment. Gone are the days when Western MNE executives were given the red-carpet treatment, showered with investment incentives, juicy contracts and ready access to senior officials. Now they face more regulatory obstacles, access to policy-makers is more restricted, and they are lectured to by party and government officials. To many it seems like Beijing intends to preserve, even enhance, its arbitrary power over foreign and domestic business, and to display its mercantilism more aggressively. US Chamber of Commerce and European Chamber of Commerce surveys of their members in China reveal a rising tide of discontent. Their treatment in China also makes them less keen to lobby on Beijing's behalf in Washington and in European capitals whenever China-bashing protectionist pressures arise.[27]

Such corporate sentiments are symptomatic of stalled reforms and even reform reversal – up to a point. It is easy to exaggerate and paint a black-and-white picture. The picture is much more mixed; it has many patches of light and shade. Contrary to sensationalist claims,[28] China is not about to disengage from the West, and especially the USA. It is not about to make a sudden switch from exports to reliance on domestic consumption. 'State capitalism' is not about to take over the economy. And China is not about to 'rule the world' – to become an aggressive leader in Asia and the wider world. For there are powerful countervailing forces. China's economic globalization, its embeddedness in multilateral rules and institutions (especially the WTO), its regional and bilateral trade relationships, all hem-in aggressive mercantilist tendencies. This has remained true during and after the recent crisis. Fundamental market reforms, including external liberalization, have not been reversed. FDI continues to increase. MNEs are still committed to staying in China and are making healthy profits there. Some of their discomfiture is inevitable since they are beginning to penetrate domestic markets, where regulatory protectionism is more entrenched and difficult to dislodge compared with less-regulated, more internationally exposed export-platform operations.

At bottom, the Beijing leadership remains pragmatic and internationally engaged. It does not want to rock the boat too much. But stalled trade and FDI liberalization, the absence of domestic structural reforms and creeping protectionism threaten to cause future trade tensions. They also diminish China's ability to look outward and exercise leadership in the regional and world economies.

On a final geopolitical note, it is clear that China has become more assertive in foreign policy since the GEC. Pragmatism, conciliation, charm offensives and other manifestations of 'soft power' seemed to characterize China's self-proclaimed 'peaceful rise' pre-crisis. Since then, China's growing self-confidence has shown a different face. China has said 'No' more often to the USA, e.g. on renminbi appreciation and numerical targets for current-account imbalances ahead of the G20 summit in Seoul. It said 'No' to the USA and EU on the climate-change agenda at the Copenhagen summit in late 2009. It has been more assertive in South Asia (cementing relations with India's neighbours and laying stronger claim to Arunachal Pradesh) and elsewhere in the developing world. It has also been more assertive in the East Asian neighbourhood; e.g. in the South China Sea and in a recent spat with Japan in the Senkaku Islands. Harsher rhetoric and occasional hectoring are more on display. To Robert Kaplan, these are manifestations of the expanding geography of a would-be hegemon of the Eastern Hemisphere. China is a rising 'über-realist' power, reaching across land and sea to secure energy supplies to fuel its economic growth – and rubbing up against the USA and other emerging powers such as India and Russia (Kaplan 2010). To Joseph Nye, China is dangerously miscalculating, displaying a combination of overconfidence in foreign policy and underconfidence in domestic affairs (Nye 2010).

China may be rising economically and geopolitically, but there remain binding constraints on its ability to lead externally, whether in its East Asian neighbourhood or on the global stage. It is still far behind the USA in terms of market size, living standards and military resources. Other countries, not least in East Asia, do not want to live under Chinese hegemony. Crucially, China lacks a tradition of external leadership, and its recent opening to the world economy is simply too new for it to exercise leadership assuredly. Rather the Chinese governing elite is too preoccupied with domestic political and economic issues to be willing and able to exercise external power strongly and responsibly. Its main concern is to keep its external environment safe for China's economic development, not to act as a regional or global policeman.

CONCLUSION

This chapter has covered broad Chinese trade-policy trends post-WTO accession: implementation of WTO obligations; dispute settlement; participation in the Doha Round; PTAs; and unilateral measures. In sum: China has a mixed record on WTO implementation; a flurry of litigation has followed several years of diplomatic reconciliation in dispute settlement; and China has been passive in the Doha Round. In contrast, it has been very active with PTAs, setting off a domino effect in East Asia. But its PTAs are trade light, driven more by foreign policy than commercial considerations. Finally, unilateral liberalization – the driving force of external opening in the 1990s – has stalled. There has been very little WTO-plus liberalization, while measures of selective protection, especially related to foreign investment and industrial-policy targeting, have increased. China's response to the GEC has reinforced these trends, but it does not represent a dramatic increase in protection or fundamentally reverse China's opening to the world economy.

Overall, China's policy terms of trade have shifted in the near-decade since it joined the WTO. It behaves more like a very large, complex economy and less like a small-to-medium-size open economy. It acts more often like a price-setter than a price-taker – witness its export restrictions on rare-earth metals. It is less comfortable as a willing rule-taker in the WTO. It inclines less to unilateral liberalization and more to hard-bargaining reciprocity. But it has yet to make the transition to proactive rule-setting and system-shaping – to co-leadership of the world trading system. That creates systemic tensions and a leadership vacuum, especially when the system's traditional leader, the USA, is down and diminished.

China's short-term challenge is to contain protection at home. That will send positive signals to contain protectionism worldwide. Beyond that, China's challenge is to stimulate further unilateral liberalization related to domestic structural reforms. That means tackling non-border, but still trade-related, regulatory barriers, especially in investment and services. Cleaning up PTAs and strengthening participation in the WTO are important auxiliary objectives. This should be seen in the context of further liberalizing the Chinese economy and 'rebalancing growth'. But this does not appear to be Beijing's agenda today. Not least, such second-generation reforms strike much closer than previous first-generation, product-market reforms to vested interests at the heart of the Party State. Nevertheless, pro-market reformers should work to make it tomorrow's, or the day-after-tomorrow's, agenda. This will succeed only when Chinese decision-makers perceive such an agenda to be in China's domestic interests. Finally, two-way constructive engagement in China's key bilateral and regional trade relationships is vital to contain protectionism and smooth China's further integration into the global economy. The US obsession with renminbi undervaluation and China's current-account surplus is not an exercise in constructive engagement. Indeed, it is quite the opposite.

NOTES

1 European Centre for International Political Economy and London School of Economics.
2 The central theme of Roach (2009).
3 Brazil, Russia, India and China.
4 I owe the insight that China is now one of the three big exporters of global order to a 2009 lecture given by Martin Wolf at the London School of Economics.
5 This section draws on Greene *et al.* (2006), Lardy (2002), Ianchovichina and Martin (2001), Mattoo (2003), Bhattasali *et al.* (2004), Athukorala and Hill (2010), and WTO (2010).
6 Brazil, India, Indonesia, Russia and China.
7 This section draws on WTO (2010) and USSTR (2010).
8 USSTR (2008): 1.
9 See http://www.wto.org/english/tratop_e/dispu_e/dispu_by_country_e.htm.
10 The issue in the first case was China's attempt to promote the domestic semiconductor industry through VAT rebates for locally manufactured integrated circuits (ICs). Imported ICs, however, faced the full VAT rate. The USA argued that this constituted a local-content measure in violation of the TRIMS agreement. China withdrew the measure after consultations. In the second case, the EU contested Chinese controls on coke exports, which limited the supply and raised the price of coke imports to the EU. China largely repealed the measure after consultations. In the last case, the USA argued that Chinese imposition of AD duties on kraft linerboards did not follow procedures in conformity with WTO AD rules. China repealed the duties after consultations.
11 See 'Proposal on flexible provisions for recently acceded members', WT/MIN(03) W/8, 4 September 2003, at http://www.wto.org.
12 The following draws on WTO (2010), USSTR (2010), European Chamber of Commerce in China (2010), Paulson (2008), Scissors (2009).
13 'Rare earths leverage', *Wall Street Journal,* 19 October 2010.
14 On Chinese online protectionism, see Hindley and Lee-Makiyama (2009).
15 'Foreign groups fear loss of contracts', *Financial Times,* 9 November 2010.
16 'A future on track', *Financial Times,* 24 September 2010.
17 The European Chamber of Commerce in China (2010) highlights these obstacles to foreign business above other barriers in its annual position paper.
18 This section draws on Sally (2009) and Erixon and Sally (2010).
19 The four new, less-developed ASEAN countries have until 2015 to implement their commitments.

20 On prospects for regional economic cooperation and integration, see Sally (2010).
21 Peter Sutherland, 'A future for the World Trade Organization?' *Jan Tumlir Policy Essay* 1, 2010, p. 9, European Centre for International Political Economy, available at http://www.ecipe.org/publications/jan-tumlir-policy-essays/a-future-for-the-world-trade-organisation/PDF.
22 This is the coda to Robert Zoellick's much-publicized speech on US–China relations (Zoellick 2005). It is also the underlying logic of the US–China Strategic Economic Dialogue, now renamed the Strategic and Economic Dialogue.
23 Martin Wolf, 'How to fight the currency wars with a stubborn China', *Financial Times,* 5 October 2010; Martin Wolf, 'Current-account targets are a way back to the future', *Financial Times,* 2 November 2010; Clive Crook, 'Time to get tough with China', *Financial Times,* 11 October 2010; Fred Bergsten, 'Obama has to tell Beijing some hard truths', *Financial Times,* 28 November 2010.
24 Douglas Irwin, 'Goodbye free trade?' *Wall Street Journal,* 15–17 October 2010.
25 Yang Yao (2012); Ikenson (2010); Yiping Huang, 'Fixing China's current-account surplus' *East Asia Forum,* 13 December 2009, at http://www.eastasiaforum.org/2009/12/13/fixing-chinas-current-account-surplus; Yiping Huang, 'Improving China's art in dealing with external pressures', *East Asia Forum,* 16 September 2010, at http://www.eastasiaforum.org/2010/09/16/improving-chinas-art-in-dealing-with-external-pressures; Yiping Huang and Bijun Wang, 'Rebalancing China's economic structure', *East Asia Forum,* 3 September 2010, at http://www.eastasiaforum.org/2010/09/03/rebalancing-chinas-economic-structure/.
26 Yu Yongding, 'China needs slower, better growth', *Financial Times,* 6 August 2010.
27 Alan Beattie, 'Trading blows', *Financial Times* 6 July 2010; 'China's frustrated "old friends"', *Wall Street Journal,* 9–11 July 2010; Joerg Wuttke, 'China is beginning to frustrate foreign business', *Financial Times*, 7 April 2010.
28 See Jacques (2009) and Bremmer (2010).

REFERENCES

Antkiewicz, A. and J. Whalley (2005) 'China's new regional trade agreements', *The World Economy,* 28(10): 1539–1557.
Athukorala, P. (2006) 'Product fragmentation and trade patterns in East Asia', *Asian Economic Papers,* 4(3): 1–27.
Athukorala, P. and H. Hill (2010) 'Asian trade: long-term patterns and key policy issues', *Asia–Pacific Economic Literature* 24(2): 52–82.
Athukorala, P. and A. Kohpaiboon (2010) 'China and East-Asian trade: the decoupling fallacy, crisis and policy challenges', in R. Garnaut, J. Golley and Ligang Song (eds) *China: the Next Twenty Years of Reform and Development*, pp. 193–220, Canberra: Australian National University E Press.
Baldwin, R. (2006) 'Multilateralising regionalism: spaghetti bowls as building blocs on the path to global free trade', *The World Economy,* 29(11): 1451–1518.
Beattie, A. and F. Williams (2008) 'Disputes sour Doha mood of optimism', *Financial Times*, 28 July.
Bhattasali, D., L. Shantong and W. Martin (2004) *China's Accession to the World Trade Organization, Policy Reform and Poverty Reduction,* Washington, DC: World Bank.

Bremmer, I. (2010) *The End of the Free Market: Who Wins the War Between States and Corporations?* New York: Penguin Books.

Erixon, F. and R. Sally (2010) 'Trade, globalisation and emerging protectionism since the crisis', *ECIPE Working Paper* No. 2, available at http://www.ecipe.org/trade-globalisation-and-emerging-protectionism-since-the-crisis/PDF.

European Chamber of Commerce in China (2010) 'European business in China', *Position Paper 2010/2011,* Beijing: ECCC, available at http://www.europeanchamber.com.cn/images/documents/marketing_department/beijing/publications/2010/executive_summary.pdf.

Gao, H. (2005) 'Aggressive legalism: the East Asian experience and lessons for China', in H. Gao and D. Lewis (eds) *China's Participation in the WTO,* pp. 315–351, London: Cameron May.

—— (2007a) 'China's participation in the WTO: a lawyer's perspective', *Singapore Yearbook of International Law*, 2007(11): 1–34.

—— (2007b) Taming the dragon: China's experience in the WTO dispute settlement system, *Legal Issues of Economic Integration*, 34(4): 369–392.

Global Trade Alert (2010) *The 8th GTA Trade Report*, CEPR, London, available at http://www.globaltradealert.org/sites/default/files/GTA8_0.pdf.

Greene, M., N. Dihel, P. Kowalski and D. Lippoldt (2006) 'China's trade and growth: impact on selected OECD countries', *OECD Trade Policy Working Paper* No. 44, 28 November, TD/TC/WP(2006)10/FINAL, available at http://www.oecd.org/trade.

Hayek, F.A. von (1937) 'Economics and knowledge', *Economica*, 4(13), 33–54.

Hindley, B. and H. Lee-Makiyama (2009) 'Protectionism online: internet censorship and international trade law', *ECIPE Working Paper* 12, available at http://www.ecipe.org/publications/ecipe-working-papers/protectionism-online-internet-censorship-and-international-trade-law/PDF.

Huang, Y. (2008) *Capitalism with Chinese Characteristics: Entrepreneurship and the State,* Cambridge: Cambridge University Press.

Ianchovichina, E. and W. Martin (2001) 'Trade liberalization in China's accession to the World Trade Organization', *World Bank Policy Research Working Paper*, No. 2623, Washington, DC: World Bank.

Ikenson, D. (2010) 'Manufacturing discord: growing tensions threaten the US–China economic relationship', *Trade Briefing Paper* No. 29, Washington, DC: Cato Centre for Trade Policy Studies.

Jacques, M. (2009) *When China Rules the World: The Rise of the Middle Kingdom and the End of the Western World,* London: Penguin Books.

Kaplan, R. (2010) 'The geography of Chinese power', *Foreign Affairs,* May/June: 22–41.

Kawai, M. and G. Wignaraja (2008) 'Regionalism as an engine of multilateralism: the case for a single East-Asian FTA', *ADB Working Paper on Regional Economic Integration* No.14, Tokyo: Asian Development Bank Institute.

Koyama, T. and S. Golub (2006) 'OECD'S FDI Regulatory Restrictiveness Index: revision and extension to more economies', *Economics Department Working Paper*, No. 525: 8–10, Paris: Organisation for Economic Co-operation and Development, available at http://www.oecd.org/dataoecd/4/36/37818075.pdf.

Lardy, N. (2002) *Integrating China into the Global Economy,* Washington, DC: Brookings Institute.

Mattoo, A. (2003) 'China's accession to the WTO: the services dimension', *Journal of International Economic Law*, 6(2): 299–339.

Nye, J. (2010) 'China's bad bet against America', *East Asia Forum*, 28 March, available at http://www.eastasiaforum.org/2010/03/28/chinas-bad-bet-against-america/.

Paulson, H.M. (2008) 'A strategic economic engagement: strengthening US–Chinese ties', *Foreign Affairs*, September/October, available at http://www.gmupolicy.net/china/readings/Paulson%20on%20engaging%20China.pdf.

Pei, M. (2006) *China's Trapped Transition*, Cambridge, MA: Harvard University Press.

Roach, S. (2009) *The Next Asia: Opportunities and Challenges for a New Globalisation*, London: Wiley.

Sally, R. (2006) 'FTAs and the prospects for regional integration in Asia', *ECIPE Working Paper* No. 1, available at http://www.ecipe.org/publications/2006/WPno1_06_Sally.pdf.

—— (2009) 'Trade policy in the BRIICS: a crisis stocktake and looking ahead', *ECIPE Policy Brief* No. 3, available at http://www.ecipe.org/publications/ecipe-policy-briefs/trade-policy-in-the-briics-a-crisis-stocktake-and-looking-ahead/PDF.

—— (2010) 'Regional economic integration in Asia: the track record and prospects', *ECIPE Occasional Paper* No. 2, available at http://www.ecipe.org/regional-economic-integration-in-asia-the-track-record-and-prospects/PDF.

Scissors, D. (2009) 'Deng undone: the costs of halting market reform in China', *Foreign Affairs*, May/June: 24–39.

SDRC–MOC (State Development and Reform Commission and Ministry of Commerce) (2007) Catalogue for the Guidance of Foreign Investment Industries (Amended in 2007), available at http://www.fdi.gov.cn/pub/FDI_EN/Laws/GeneralLawsand Regulations/MinisterialRulings/.

USSTR (United States Special Trade Representative) (2008) *National Trade Estimate Report on Foreign Trade Barriers: China*, available at http://www.ustr.gov.

—— (2010) *National Trade Estimate Report on Foreign Trade Barriers: China*, available at http://www.ustr.gov.

WTO (World Trade Organization) (2010) *Trade Policy Review: China*, available at http://www.wto.org.

Xing, Y. and N. Detert (2010) 'How iPhone widens the US trade deficits with PRC', *GRIPS Discussion Paper*, No. 10–21, available at http://www3.grips.ac.jp/%7Epinc/data/10-21.pdf.

Yang Yao (2012) 'Double transition and China's export-led growth', in Yiping Huang and Miaojie Yu (eds) *China's New Role in the World Economy*, pp. 45–67, London and New York: Routledge.

Zoellick, R. (2005) 'Whither China: from membership to responsibility?' Speech on US–China relations and remarks to the National Committee on US–China relations, New York, 21 September, available at http://www.state.gov/s/d/former/zoellick/rem/53682.htm.

9 Issues and options for social security reform in China

Li Shi[1]

INTRODUCTION

This chapter summarizes what is known and not known about the reform and reconstruction of China's social security system and the related social welfare programmes, the policy options debated in both official and academic circles, and recommendations for new options for social security system reform to be considered in the Twelfth Five-Year Plan. The term 'social security' here refers to social insurance and social welfare (relief) programmes such as free education and housing subsidies. Also discussed here are the strategic objectives of social security, why China currently needs a genuine social security system, the major problems of the current social security system and the policy debates concerning the establishment of the new system over the next 5–10 years.

It is widely realized that China is approaching a development stage where social security is playing a more important role than before in terms of stimulating economic growth, equalizing income distribution, alleviating poverty and maintaining social stability.[2] It is also recognized that the current social security system needs to be reformed in order to meet the challenges resulting from the transition of the system from one that protected the minority group of urban workers in the formal sector to one that protects all citizens (CRDF 2009). There is, however, considerable debate as to what kind of social security system can be applied in China, given the large differences between urban and rural areas in terms of income level, employment structure, fiscal capability of local governments and provision of social services (Zhao Renwei *et al.* 2006). The issues become more complicated when one takes into consideration what type of social protection is suitable for millions of rural migrant workers who have low incomes, high job and location mobility, and unstable employment (Zheng Gongcheng 2008).

Like many other developing countries, China has been striving to make its economy grow as fast as possible. From 1978 to 2008, gross domestic product (GDP) grew at nearly 10 per cent while household income in urban and rural areas grew at 8 per cent. By the end of 2008, GDP per capita reached US$3,100, raising China to the status of a low- to middle-income country. While China has made remarkable progress in economic growth, its progress in social development, particularly the reconstruction of a social security and welfare system, is still lagging. The transition of the social security system is still in progress and the present system contains many flaws. The private sector and self-employment have grown rapidly and become the largest employer of informal workers, most of whom are not covered by the system. In addition, rural migrant workers, mostly employed in the informal sector in urban areas, are also left out of the system.

Although China has significantly reduced poverty, the country has not been as successful in narrowing income inequality, which is now much wider than it was at the beginning of the economic reforms. The Gini coefficient for the whole country is currently estimated at around 0.47,[3] compared with 0.30 in the early 1980s (Adelman and Sunding 1987). The Gini coefficient in rural China rose from 0.26 in 1980 to 0.38 in 2007 (Figure 9.1), while the poverty rate declined from 30 per cent to 3 per cent. Since the mid 1990s, urban poverty has constituted a new phenomenon due to the increase in laid-off workers and consequently a widening income inequality as a result of the restructuring of state-owned enterprises (SOEs). The Gini coefficient in urban China surged from 0.16 in 1978 to 0.36 in 2007.

Though the poverty rate has declined over the past three decades, poverty remains a serious social problem. It is well known that 'official poverty' has been under-reported. The actual poverty incidence is certainly higher than the officially published figure (World Bank 2009a). While official statistics indicate that the poor numbered fewer than 15 million in rural areas in 2007, the number of individuals receiving income allowance from the *Di Bao* programme (the minimum living standard guarantee scheme) approached 43 million. According to a World Bank estimate, the rural poverty rate would rise to over 10 per cent if the two-dollars-a-day poverty line were applied (World Bank 2009a).

In addition, the large flow of rural migrant workers into cities exerts great pressure on employment for local urban workers. Unemployment is a huge challenge for the governments. The situation has been made worse by the

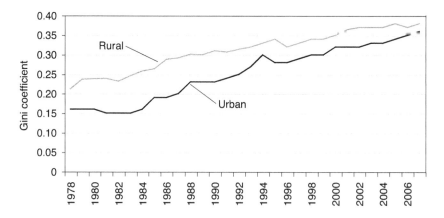

Figure 9.1 Changes in income inequality in urban and rural China, 1978–2007.
Source: Zhang Dongsheng *et al.* (2008).

global financial crisis, which retarded export growth and had consequent effects on employment.

Consumption as a proportion of GDP has decreased constantly since the mid 1990s, due partly to a decline in the share of labour income, and partly to a fall in the average propensity to consume, resulting from uncertainties relating to expenditures on health care, education and housing. This is especially true for those in the population not covered by the social security system. To negate the impact of the global financial crisis, local governments have tried hard to stimulate domestic demand since the second half of 2008. The measures taken are focused on increasing investment rather than stimulating consumption. It is believed that expanding the coverage of social security and raising the protection level will help stimulate household consumption.

Social instability has become a major concern for the Chinese Government since the number of social incidents and riots has escalated rapidly. According to the 2005 *Blue Book of China's Society*, the number of social conflicts increased from 10,000 in 1993 to 60,000 in 2003 (CAAS Institute of Sociology 2005). There are also reports that social conflicts have intensified in the past 4 years.

Building a comprehensive and fair social security system is one of the sensible options for the government in the Twelfth Five-Year Plan. There is a general consensus among Chinese scholars on this, although debates are rife concerning the different approaches to a new system.

SOCIAL AND ECONOMIC CHALLENGES FACING CHINA

Widening income inequality

China was an egalitarian society 30 years ago and has experienced a sharp increase in income inequality since the beginning of the 1980s. As a developing country, China has implemented separate and urban-biased economic and social policies for urban and rural areas, resulting in large differences between urban and rural households in terms of income level, accessibility of public services and human development (Riskin *et al.* 2001; Gustafsson *et al.* 2008). As indicated in Figure 9.2, the ratio of urban household income per capita to rural household income per capita rose from 2.5 in 1996 to 3.3 in 2007 in nominal terms.

Large-scale poverty

Whichever poverty measures are used, it is apparent that the number of poor has fallen by over 90 per cent since the end of the 1970s (Figure 9.3). However, when a different poverty line is adopted, a different figure is obtained. Poverty incidence is very sensitive to upward adjustment of the

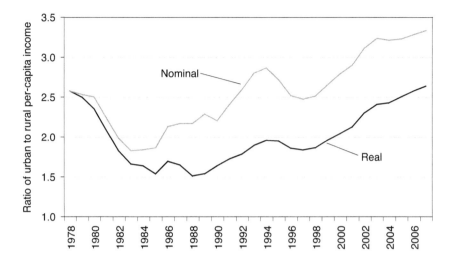

Figure 9.2 China's urban–rural income gap, 1978–2007. Source: CSP (2008: 101).

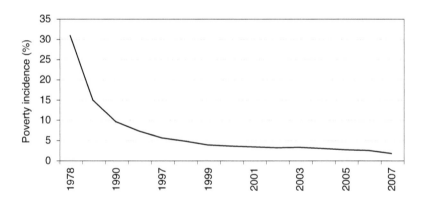

Figure 9.3 Rural population poverty incidence, 1978–2007, based on official sources.

poverty line, especially if it involves a large proportion of low-income people with income adjusted slightly higher than the official poverty line. The
official poverty as a percentage of rural average income has been declining
over time (Figure 9.4). Since 2008, the government began to adjust the official line upwards by 43 per cent for rural areas. As a result, the number of
people defined as 'poor' increased by over 200 per cent.[4]

However, the new official poverty line is still believed to underestimate
reality because it approximates to US$1 per person per day as suggested
by the World Bank. If the official line is raised to US$2 per person per day,
the poverty rate doubles, meaning that, in 2008, the rural poor population
would have been around 100 million (World Bank 2009a).

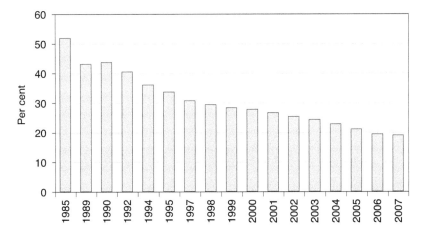

Figure 9.4 Rural official poverty line as a percentage of household per-capita income, 1985–2007.

High unemployment pressure

It is difficult to obtain an accurate estimate of the unemployment rate for a developing country like China, which has millions of rural surplus labourers, rural–urban migrant workers and informal sector workers. Even in urban areas, the government has never published unemployment rates comparable to the international benchmark. The government simply publishes an annual registered unemployment rate for urban areas (Figure 9.5). By definition, the unemployed are people who are registered in labour offices, covered by unemployment insurance and seeking employment services from governments. This implies that most rural–urban migrant workers and those in the informal sector are unlikely to be registered. Therefore, the official registered unemployment rate (Figure 9.6) is considerably underestimated. Some studies state that the underestimation is around 2–5 per cent, depending on the timing and whether or not rural migrant workers are included.

Increasing labour mobility

Like other developing countries, China is now still a labour-surplus economy with a large proportion of its labour force engaged in farming activities, although the urbanization process has accelerated since the mid 1990s. The latest statistics indicate there were 480 million labourers in rural areas in 2007, accounting for 62 per cent of the total number of labourers in China.[5] Nearly half were mobile, employed either in rural industry or in urban areas. The number of rural–urban migrant workers has been increasing and reached more than 130 million in 2006, as shown in Figure 9.7. Based on experience in developed countries, the process of rural–urban

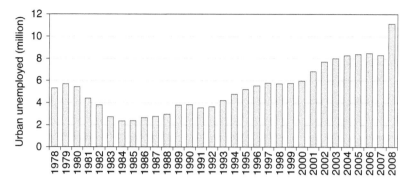

Figure 9.5 Number of urban unemployed in China (million), 1978–2008. Sources: CSP (2008: 46); NBS (2009).

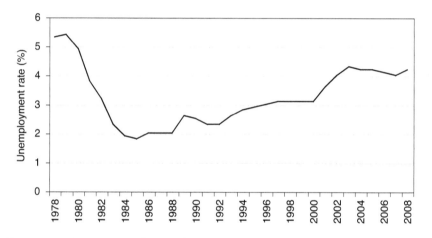

Figure 9.6 Urban registered unemployment rate in China, 1978–2008. Sources: CSP (2008: 46); NBS (2009).

migration in China will likely continue for the next two decades.[6] The majority of these workers are less-educated, unskilled, highly mobile, low-income earners not covered by social security (Li Shi 2008; Quheng Deng and Li Shi 2008). As migrant workers are registered in rural areas, they are generally at a disadvantage in the urban labour market in terms of employment opportunities, salary payment and accessibility to social security and public services.

Declining consumption propensity

Since the 1990s, China has experienced declining consumption as a percentage of GDP. As can be seen in Figure 9.8, total consumption as a percentage of GDP declined from 67 per cent in 1981 to 49 per cent in 2007. The decline was due largely to the fall in the share of household consumption. At the same time, the share of household consumption in GDP decreased by 17 per cent while the share of government consumption stayed in the 13–16 per cent range.

Data from the annual household survey conducted by the National Bureau of Statistics also indicate that household saving rates have been increasing since the early 1990s, in both urban and rural areas. Figure 9.9 shows that the household saving rate increased sharply from 10 per cent in the mid 1980s to 27 per cent in 2007 in urban China, while in rural China, a stunning rise occurred in the 1990s.

The decrease in the propensity to consume, and the increase in household savings, have had a negative impact on macro-economic growth, which is

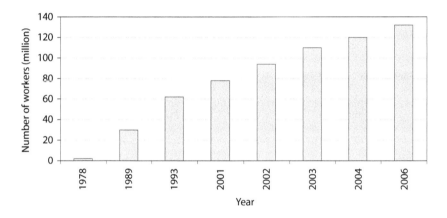

Figure 9.7 The number of rural–urban migrant workers in China, 1978–2006. Source: Li Shi (2008).

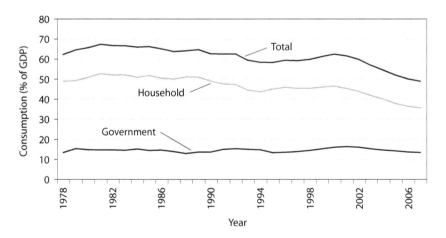

Figure 9.8 Changes in consumption as a percentage of GDP in China, 1978–2006. Data source: National Bureau of Statistics at http://www.stats.gov.cn.

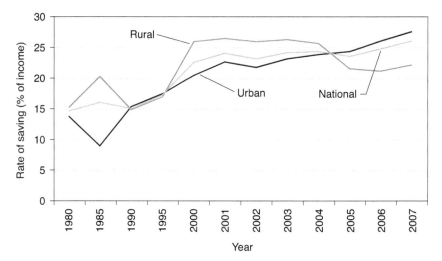

Figure 9.9 Rate of saving of households in urban and rural areas, and in China as a whole, 1980–2007. Note: The saving rate was calculated by using household income and consumption expenditure data from the household survey conducted annually by the National Bureau of Statistics.

increasingly dependent on export growth. Major reasons for the decline in consumption are the emerging economic uncertainties and the transition of the social security system. Households feel the impact of rising unemployment and higher payments for social security and public services such as medical care and education. To deal with these uncertainties, they have been increasing their savings.

Rising social conflicts

Social unrest is recognized as a major problem that can trigger social instability in China. According to diverse sources, incidences of social unrest have increased over the past decade. For example, citing Chinese Communist Party sources, Lum (2006) indicates that social unrest grew by nearly 50 per cent from 2004 to 2005 and that there were 87,000 cases of 'public order disturbances' including protests, demonstrations, picketing and group petitioning in 2005, compared with 74,000 in 2004. Although there are no reliable official statistics on the latest situation, it is expected that social unrest may now be even worse in some regions (Keidel 2005; Peng 2009).

STRATEGIC OBJECTIVES OF SOCIAL SECURITY

It is important for China – a developing country and a transition economy – to establish a desirable social security system to deal with its economic and social challenges. A well-functioning social security and welfare system is essential to achieve the overall objectives of providing insurance, poverty relief and income redistribution. Social security is expected to play an important role in stimulating domestic demand via reducing the saving rates of households, particularly for low- to middle-income groups, and in maintaining social stability.

THE SIX OBJECTIVES OF SOCIAL SECURITY

The objectives of social security, widely recognized by economists and sociologists, with applications particularly focused on China, can be summarized as follows (Barr 2001; Barr and Diamond 2008):

(a) *Insurance.* Social security has two major components – social insurance and social assistance – including social relief and financial support for specific population groups such as the aged and children. Social insurance is frequently referred to as social transfer programmes that deal with risks: the risk of unemployment, health-care expenses and inadequate income support during retirement (Feldstein 2005). For China, social security has a very important role in reducing risks, especially those resulting from uncertainties related to the transition process of an economy in terms of employment, income mobility and health care. The unemployment insurance, minimum income guarantee programme and medical insurance provide good examples of coverage in these aspects. Social insurance differs from private insurance in that it is mandatory and requires more intervention and obligation by governments, which may lead to disincentive effects on job-seeking and inefficient use of medical resources. It is crucial to design a desirable social security system to provide an optimal combination of insurance and incentives. Most countries, either developed or developing, are seeking solutions in line with their own specific conditions, and China is no exception (Feldstein 2005; Barr and Diamond 2008).

(b) *Poverty relief.* Without social security and social support, it is difficult for the poor to rise out of poverty. As modern poverty theory explains, poverty by nature easily generates even more poverty when low-income people fall into a poverty trap (Bowles *et al.* 2006). In circumstances where public services are lacking, poverty and illiteracy and/or illness form a vicious circle. Knight *et al.* (2010) provide strong evidence showing that children from low-income households in rural China have higher dropout rates in compulsory education than those from better-off households, and they have fewer opportunities to secure decent jobs and non-agricultural employment with higher compensation when they enter the labour market. The poverty structure has shown significant changes over the last decade. One is the increase in the proportion of the rural population falling into poverty due to illness and disability, reflecting inadequate access to medical insurance and services in rural China. The minimum living standard guarantee (MLSG) scheme has been quite successful in alleviating poverty in urban China since its widespread implementation in 2000, but it plays a limited role in narrowing income inequality (Li Shi and Sui Yang 2009). Drawing on experience from the MLSG scheme in urban areas, the government started to implement the same scheme in 2007 in rural areas, where the income level of households to be qualified as recipients is much lower than that in urban areas. Believed to be a more effective measure of poverty reduction in China, the MLSG scheme is also a supplementary measure to the traditional measure – through supporting economic development in the poor regions – of alleviating poverty.[7]

(c) *Income redistribution.* Social security has a function of income redistribution, but it is still debatable whether income redistribution should be a priority objective in designing a social security system (Feldstein 2005). Theoretically, social security has direct and indirect redistributive effects in society. The direct effects may not be so obvious and explicit, but the indirect effects cannot be ignored. A pension system such as pay-as-you-go (PAYG) has little effect on income redistribution in urban China since pensions are closely indexed to the previous wage of recipients, but there is no doubt that PAYG has an indirect effect on intergenerational distribution of income. The indirect effects become more significant in an ageing population. Medical insurance and compulsory education have even greater indirect effects on income distribution in the long term. Equal opportunities in access to education are crucial for narrowing income inequality within cohorts and generations. Over the past decade, rising returns to education have played an increasingly important role in widening wage inequality in urban China, but a significantly unequal educational attainment among urban employees also contributes to wage disparity (Li Shi 2008). Social security and welfare, such as an income allowance programme and free or subsidized education, have at the same time generally positive effects on income redistribution, from which low-income people will benefit more.

(d) *Consumption smoothing.* Social security in the form of a pension system has the obvious function of consumption smoothing – also called the piggy-bank function – for individuals in the long term. Chinese households, particularly low-income households in rural areas, frequently experience income fluctuations due to unemployment, volatility of product prices, disease outbreaks and natural disasters. Income fluctuation is one of the major causes of rural population falling into transient poverty (Whalley and Ximing Yue 2009). It is not surprising that income fluctuation inevitably leads to household consumption fluctuation. Therefore, social security, such as unemployment insurance, medical insurance and income-support programmes like the MLSG, has a strong impact on household consumption smoothing, especially in low-income households.

(e) *Consumption stimulation.* This objective is particularly important for countries like China with a continuing decline in the propensity to consume in the long term. The global financial crisis hit China's export sector seriously. Chinese economists and sociologists then appealed to the government to expand spending further on social security and public services in order to reduce consumers' risks and uncertainties and raise their propensity to consume.[8] Although there is no strong evidence showing that inadequate social security is a major cause of the decline in consumption in China, some attitudinal surveys indicate that saving for education, future medical needs and housing purchase are the primary reasons why people save.[9]

(f) *Social stabilizer.* In China's perspective, this is integral to social security. Many studies indicate that crime and social conflict are strongly correlated with unemployment, income inequality and poverty (Fajnzylber *et al.* 2002a,b) The correlation increases in countries that have no or inadequate social programmes to protect the poor and unemployed. To reduce social conflicts and create a more stable society, it is important for China to expand and strengthen the current system of social security. This will help build a harmonious economic and social environment for the implementation of Twelfth Five-Year Plan.

THE ROLE OF GOVERNMENT IN SOCIAL SECURITY

How governments in developed countries, and especially in welfare states, should contribute to social security has been an ongoing debate for a long time. There seems to be no single uniform rule applied to all countries (Feldstein 2005). In China's case, the government should play an increasingly important role in the provision of social security, although this does not mean that it should take full responsibility. There should be a clear division of labour between the government and the market in the provision of public services. Households and individuals are also major financial contributors to funding security programmes.

THREE BASIC PRINCIPLES

The strategic objectives of China's social security in the coming decades, and their relationship with overall development objectives, should be clarified. A desirable system should encapsulate the following three basic principles. First, there should be complete coverage for all groups – the young and the old, rural and urban residents, workers in the formal and informal sectors, and those employed and unemployed. Second, there should be portability of benefits, which means personal contribution to social security programmes; and qualifications should be portable with job mobility and migration across regions.

Third, there should be sustainability of coverage; that is, the standard of social security should not be maintained at a level beyond government fiscal capability, but should be raised incrementally with economic growth. It is widely accepted that expenditures on social protection in China are much lower than in other countries, and even most developing countries (CDRF 2009).

ELEMENTS OF THE SOCIAL SECURITY SYSTEM IN CHINA: PROBLEMS AND REFORM

Minimum living standard guarantee

Current situation and problems

The MLSG scheme was introduced in the late 1990s, and its implementation expanded rapidly in urban areas from 2001 and in rural areas since 2005.[10] The number of people supported by the MLSG since 2000 is shown in Table 9.1. In 2000, only 4 million of the urban population received support from the MLSG, but the number increased to almost 12 million in 2001 and 21 million in 2002. Since 2003, the number of urban residents receiving income allowance has been maintained at around 22–24 million. The big increase in the number of rural residents supported by MLSG occurred in 2005, the number rose by 70% compared to 2004. The increase accelerated over subsequent years, as indicated in Table 9.1.

In 2008, among the urban residents receiving income allowance, 3.5 per cent were formally employed, 16.3 per cent were informally employed, 13.6 per cent were aged people, 24.3 per cent were registered unemployed, 17.2 per cent were unregistered unemployed, 15.3 per cent were students and 9.8 per cent were other children. The average threshold level was 205 yuan and the average income received was 144 yuan per person per month in urban China in 2008, an increase of 13 per cent and 40 per cent, respectively, compared with 2007.

The programme currently covers all the population institutionally, but criteria for urban and rural residents are different and vary from one region to another. Although the number of rural residents supported by the MLSG

Table 9.1 Urban and rural population numbers (million) supported by the MLSG in China, 2000–08

	2000	2001	2002	2003	2004	2005	2006	2007	2008
Urban	4.0	11.7	20.6	22.5	22.1	22.3	22.4	22.7	23.3
Rural	3.0	3.0	4.1	3.7	4.9	8.3	15.9	35.7	43.1

Sources: China Ministry of Civil Affairs, *Statistical Report of China's Social Development in 2008*, available at http://cws.mca.gov.cn/article/tjbg/200906/20090600031762.shtml, accessed 22 May 2009.

now exceeds the number of urban residents, the threshold level for rural residents to be qualified as recipients and the average income received by rural residents are much lower than their urban counterparts. In 2008, the average threshold level for rural residents was 82 yuan and the average income each person received was 50 yuan per month.

Another problem is that the programme excludes certain population groups such as migrant households and college graduates. Since the programme is implemented by city or county governments, residents without local *hukou* (household registration) are not eligible for the programme.

Debates and policy options

Policy debates for the urban programme include whether rural–urban migrants should be covered and whether the differences in protection level across cities should be based on living costs rather than the financial ability of the government. Policy debates for the rural programme are concerned with the extremely low welfare standard and the wide differences in coverage and protection levels across regions. Some scholars believe that the programme should be more comprehensive, aiming at the most needy people, and should be implemented with employment-promotion measures that encourage the unemployed to return to the labour market quickly (Limei Jiang 2009; Yuebin Xu and Ziulan Zhang 2009).

One of the notable problems of the MLSG in urban areas and which is not widely discussed and not deemed as a problem by some scholars, is the exclusion of rural–urban migrant households from the scheme. The argument is that the programme is likely to generate a moral hazard for rural–urban migrants. Where the income of rural households is very much lower, the programme would induce rural people to move to urban areas if they are qualified as MLSG recipients. It is, however, more critical to provide employment services, such as job training, than to provide income allowance to rural migrants in urban areas (Xiaojie Lin 2006).

The aim of the MLSG is to reduce poverty in urban and rural areas, but households that are considered marginally less poor are more likely to be ignored by the programme in less-developed areas since the threshold level is set below the poverty line in these areas due to insufficient government revenue. Also hotly debated is whether college students should be covered by the MLSG. Given that scholarships and education loan coverage are limited, the programme should target students from poor households who can barely maintain their basic living standards (Xiaochun Liu *et al.* 2009).

How are the credentials of the programme maintained in the long term? It should be adjusted frequently with consideration of changes in consumer prices and economic growth. For example, the threshold level should be indexed to consumer prices and raised with household income growth. It should also be adjusted with changes in the minimum wage and unemployment benefits (Qichao Song and Xuejian Guo 2008).

It is critical for China to narrow the regional differences in terms of threshold level and coverage of the programme. The differences arise mainly from the varying financial capacity of local governments. To raise the threshold level and coverage in less-developed areas, it is crucial for the central government to take more financial responsibility by transferring more funds to less-developed areas (Huizhu Zhao (2008).

Given the fact that the threshold level in some areas is underestimated, even below the poverty line, not all the poor households are supported by the programme. To solve this problem, which happens in some cities and counties with financial difficulty, local governments should increase the threshold level in order to support and include households that were previously not qualified for the programme because their household income just scraped above the old threshold level. For instance, Anshan city in Liaoning Province started to provide special support to households with an income within 20 per cent above the threshold from 2009. The special support includes subsidies for employment, education, training, medical care, food, heating and so forth.

Basic medical care – financing and delivery

Current situation and problems

Since the mid 1990s, China has tried to work out a more efficient and economic medical care system. In 1998, the State Council issued 'The Resolution on Establishing the System of Basic Medical Insurance for Workers in Urban Areas', drawing on the experience of earlier local pilot reforms that indicated the need to introduce a national system of medical insurance. Currently, there are three types of medical insurance schemes. The first is the Worker Basic Medical Insurance (WBMI) scheme, which was transformed from public medical care implemented under the old planned system, covering urban workers and retirees. The second is the Urban Residents Basic Medical Insurance (URBMI) scheme for urban residents who are not covered by the first insurance type, including children, students and aged seniors without employment history. The third is the New Rural Cooperative Medical Insurance (NRCMI) scheme, covering only rural people.

The key challenges faced in the current medical care system are incomplete coverage of medical insurance, low funding from the government, high self-payment required from patients for medical services and unbalanced regional allocation of medical resources (CDRF 2009). By the end of 2008, nearly 150 million urban workers plus 50 million retired people had joined the WBMI scheme, and 118 million urban residents and 815 million rural residents had joined the URBMI and NRCMI schemes, respectively. The coverage of the WBMI, URBMI and NRCMI schemes was 99 per cent, 60 per cent and 85 per cent, respectively.

A more serious problem with the NRCMI scheme is its low reimbursement ratio, which is below 50 per cent in most rural areas. Given the rising medical costs in recent years, it is reported that most low-income rural families cannot afford medical services even though they are covered by the NRCMI.

Debates and policy options

The debates are centred on the following two interrelated issues. Who should be the financial contributors: the government, enterprises or individuals? And, should market mechanisms be introduced in medical service delivery? If the government finances health care by taxation, it is inevitable that the service options will be provided mainly by public hospitals. There would be a very limited role for market mechanisms to play (like the UK model). Another argument prevailing is that medical insurance, either public or commercial, should be a priority option and public hospitals should be privatized (similar to the American model).

For rural migrant workers, the question is: what kind of medical insurance will be beneficial to them? Zheng Gongcheng (2008) and Du Ping (2009) proposed a further classification of migrant workers: long-term migrant workers who settle down in a city to be covered by the WBMI; short-term or seasonal migrant workers to be covered by the NRCMI; and highly mobile migrant workers to be covered by special arrangements, for which an ideal solution is difficult to find because the current system is not transmissible across regions. You Chun (2009) suggested that coverage for migrant workers of high mobility be provided by commercial medical insurance that is subsidized by the government.

Encouraging migrant workers to join the WBMI scheme is a problem, as the high self-contribution required makes it unaffordable for low-income workers (Wei Luo 2008; Du Ping 2009). The WBMI requires that workers and their firms contribute 8 per cent of the total wage to it: 2 per cent coming from the worker and 6 per cent from the firm.

In Shenzhen, one of China's largest cities, most urban workers are rural migrants. To attract more migrant workers to participate in the medical insurance scheme, the city initiated new forms of medical insurance suitable for migrants. Meanwhile, the range of medical services covered and reimbursed by the insurance plan was expanded and the permissible reimbursement ratio was increased by more than 10 per cent.[11] As a result, over 70 per cent of the migrant workers participated in the medical insurance scheme by the end of 2008, a figure much higher than the national average.

National integrated medical care system

Most areas have adopted a medical care system that encompasses the three medical insurance scheme types, namely the WBMI, URBMI and NRCMI, but some cities have tried to create new systems. Yuhang in Zhejiang Province and Zhuhai in Guangdong Province, have merged the URBMI and NRCMI schemes into one system, whereas Dongguan in Guangdong Province merged the three types of medical insurance schemes into a single system.

How medical services should be delivered to the population is still hotly debated in China. Currently, public hospitals remain a dominant player in the medical service sector, accounting for over 90 per cent of all health-care institutions. Since the 1990s, the local governments have reduced the subsidies to public hospitals, which must earn a major part of their revenues from patients and the WBMI scheme. Some hospitals receive subsidies of as little as 10 per cent of their total revenue from governments. To sustain business and operations, the hospitals raise medical fees and coerce patients into paying for expensive medication and diagnostic tests that are unnecessary. As a result, medical costs have reached an unaffordable level for ordinary households. On one hand, high medical costs mean high contributions to medical insurance from workers and firms. On the other, it deprives households, particularly rural households that are not covered by insurance for medical services. These problems have led to heated debates on how best to deliver medical services to individuals, and whether public hospitals should be subsidized by governments directly or compete with each other for patients.

There are two camps of scholars on this issue. One camp is in favour of market mechanisms in the medical service industry. Hospitals, whether public or private, should create strong incentives to provide economic and efficient medical services to patients. The best way to achieve this is to tie and link the salaries of medical staff to their performance, and offer incentives to hospitals to operate more efficiently. This is just one side of the coin. The other side is to limit medical demand by cost sharing whereby a portion of the medical cost would be borne by patients themselves. For this, the framework of medical services would be consistent with demand and supply.[12] For employees, payment contributions come from three parties: government, firms and individuals. For non-employees (such as children and the unemployed etc.), payment contributions come from government and individuals. Individuals buy medical insurance from insurance companies, which pay hospitals for medical services rendered to individuals. As commercial agents, insurance companies have incentive to propose that hospitals lower medical costs and overcome the problem of abuse of medical services. Insurance companies can be state-owned, in which case the government can justifiably regulate their business behaviour. The other camp is in favour of free provision of medical services by the government. The government instead of the market should play a more important role in financing and delivering medical services (Ling Li 2006). The more extreme argument is that the government should give full financial support to public hospitals, which are required to provide free medical services to patients. In this system, government funding comes from taxation, and medical insurance is unnecessary since the government is a 'big medical insurance company'. There are two problems envisaged in this model. The first is how to make public hospitals operate more economically and efficiently. The second is to solve the 'free rider' problem associated with patients.

The government has not made any final decision on the future direction of medical care system reforms while pilot reforms are being conducted in several areas. However, all parties have reached a consensus that China needs a strong health-care system at the community level, and that this should be mainly the responsibility of the local governments. Therefore, at the beginning of 2009, the State Council issued two documents concerning further medical insurance reforms: 'Suggestions on Deepening Reform of Medical and Sanitation System', and 'Implementation Programs of Deepening Reform of Medical and Sanitation System in 2009–2011'. Three target goals for 2012 are: basic medical insurance coverage for all residents in both urban and rural areas; significant improvement in accessibility and quality of medical services; and substantial reduction in the financial burden for citizens receiving medical services.[13] To achieve the goals, five proposed measures, to be implemented in the next 3 years, are: coverage of basic medical insurance for urban and rural residents is to be raised to over 90 per cent; the contribution to the NRBMI (from both individuals and governments) is to be increased to 120 yuan per person, a considerable rise on the 30 yuan applicable in 2005; a medical system at the community level is to be established; and public hospitals are to be reformed.

Education development

Basic education

Current situation and problems

Over the past 10 years, China has implemented a 9-year compulsory education programme. By now, all children in rural and urban areas should receive at least 9 years of school education without paying any tuition fees. However, an acute problem with compulsory education is the significantly large disparity between urban and rural areas, and between regions, in the quality of education provided (CDRF 2009). Unlike children in cities, children in rural areas have little chance to get preschool education due to the shortage of kindergartens. Because of the lower quality of teachers and lack of teaching facilities, compulsory education in rural areas is of much lower quality than in urban areas. This contrast is even more striking between remote rural villages and megacities. The central government has recognized and mitigated the problem by increasing financial resources in rural areas and the western region to promote education quality. It will, however, take time to overcome the problem. Low–middle school graduates from rural areas, due to the low-quality education received, have no competitive advantage in labour markets when they move into cities. They typically become employed as unskilled workers by small firms with low pay and are more mobile across cities and jobs. They are also more likely to remain in the low-income category throughout their lives.

Debates and policy options

Now that the 9-year compulsory education programme has been realized, China should turn its focus to basic education. Perhaps it should either initiate a more ambitious programme, that is, a 12-year compulsory education programme as most developed countries did many years ago, or concentrate on improving the quality of the present compulsory education programme, especially in rural areas.

Debate on policy for basic education revolves around issues concerning whether or not compulsory education should be extended to 12 years and if more resources should be channelled to improve the quality of the current 9-year compulsory education. The bigger issue is how to improve the quality of compulsory education in rural areas, which is much lower than that in urban areas. The following policy options are proposed for the next 5 years. First, there is no doubt that rural primary and secondary education needs more financial support from the governments at all levels. In poor areas, financial support from the central government is crucial. Second, to improve the quality of rural education, it is crucial to attract more qualified teachers to teach in primary and secondary schools in poor and remote areas. Given the oversupply of college graduates resulting from the rapid expansion of higher education since 1999, the central government may consider initiating a special programme to encourage college graduates to teach in primary and secondary schools in rural areas.

Education of migrant children is another issue sparking policy debates. There are millions of rural-migrant children of school age living in cities, but most have difficulties gaining admission into public schools and have to go to private schools. The conditions in these schools are extremely unsatisfactory. Most teachers are unqualified, classrooms are unsafe and the quality of education is much lower than in urban public schools. Some of these schools are regarded as illegal by local governments, but they play an important role in providing education to migrant children. The current Chinese education system stipulates that local governments should take the main responsibility to finance compulsory education of local children in their communities, but the local governments find no incentive to do so for migrant children. As the central government has not implemented any nationwide policy concerning compulsory education for migrant children, local governments are concerned about more migrant children moving into their areas once the central government decides to implement a policy allowing migrant children to study in public schools. It is a significant quandary for city governments. The central government also faces the problem that any change in the education system in favour of migrant children in the cities would cause an influx of rural children into the cities.

The attitude that city governments adopt towards providing compulsory education for migrant children is understandable, but the consequences of their policy are unacceptable. Most migrant children will be disadvantaged and edged out in the urban labour market, thus generating intergenerational immobility among migrants in urban areas. To solve the problem, city governments must provide migrant children with the same public education that local urban children are entitled to. To coordinate policy implementation across cities, the central government should create a uniform nationwide curriculum. Meanwhile, the central government and provincial governments should increase and transfer funding to cities that face difficulties in expanding their educational capacity to migrant children.

In most parts of China, children enter primary school at 6 or 7 years of age and the enrolment rate is almost 100 per cent in urban and rural areas. However, not all have the chance to study in kindergarten. Some estimates indicate that about 30 per cent of 5-year-old children in urban areas do not attend kindergarten, and the percentage in rural areas is even higher. The Chinese Government should consider ensuring all children receive at least 1 year of preschool education. To encourage parents to send their children to kindergarten, local governments should therefore give subsidies, either to parents or to kindergartens. In more affluent areas, it is an option for governments to provide free preschool education for all children.

Junior–middle school graduates face difficulty in finding employment and are disadvantaged in terms of salary. What they learn in schools is often not what employers require and does not enhance their employability. A way to solve the problem is to provide skills training to these junior–middle school graduates which could last 6 months to a year, and should be free or highly subsidized. In 2008, about 5 million junior–middle school graduates stopped schooling and entered the labour market.

Higher education

Tertiary education in China has expanded rapidly over the past decade. College student enrolment has increased from 1.1 million in 1998 to 6.4 million in 2009, at an annual growth rate of 17.2 per cent.[14] The gross enrolment rate in tertiary education reached 23 per cent in 2009. The central and the local governments have at the same time increased their budgets for tertiary education. Spending by governments increased at 15.5 per cent annually from 1998 to 2006.[15]

However, with the rapid expansion of tertiary education, many problems have surfaced. The Chinese higher education system has maintained the typical features of the Soviet-style education system, mixed with the legacy of the Chinese economic planning system introduced in the 1950s. The problems in the higher education system have been widely criticized following Premier Wen Jiabao's query in 2006, 'Why can't our education system foster great academic masters?'[16] The criticisms can be summarized as follows:

(i)   Chinese universities lack creativity, motivation and mechanisms for innovation. Even though evidence shows that the publication of academic papers by Chinese scholars has increased considerably over the past decade with higher research funding, very few papers appear in top journals. The fundamental reason is that innovation and innovation-related research are not given enough attention by Chinese universities and governments (Lin Wang 2009).

(ii)   There is strong intervention from the government in the internal activities of universities. Due to the control and regulations in teaching and administrative activities, there is very limited room for universities to exercise their autonomy in student enrolment, faculty and staff recruitment, as well as setting the academic curriculum and disciplines (Liquan Ruan and Yuntong Hu 2009).

(iii)   There is a lack of good governance structure within universities (Fujia Yang 2009). The current administrative structure in Chinese universities is a system of 'president's responsibility under the Party Committee's leadership'. A serious flaw in this system is that there is no clear division between the tasks of the university's president and the Party secretary. In most cases, Party secretaries are more powerful than presidents, though presidents are also in the Party Committee. Presidents are appointed by the Ministry of Education or local governments instead of being appointed via recommendation and election by professors within universities. This puts presidents in an awkward position as they must report and be accountable to the higher level governments, and less accountable to their university colleagues. Although the 1995 Education Law stipulated that Chinese universities should draft a university charter specifying their responsibilities and accountability, none have actually taken the initiative towards better governance (Fujia Yang 2009, Qingshi Zhu 2009).

(iv)   Professors and teaching staff have little autonomy in administrative and academic matters within universities, even in choosing curriculum and textbooks. They have little role in decision-making processes. Some universities have a professorial committee, which is supposed to be a decision-making organization within colleges and universities but, in reality, the roles of the committee are very limited (Qingshi Zhu 2009). As a result, professors have little incentive to work hard and perform well.

(v)   There is no innovation-based evaluation system to gauge the performance of Chinese universities. The current evaluations are conducted by the Ministry of Education or local governments and they emphasize quantitative indicators such as the number of students, teaching staff, published papers, organized academic meetings, ongoing and completed research projects etc. The assessment pays little attention to activities and outcomes associated with innovation. Thus, allocation of financial and human resources is misleadingly channelled into activities and projects that have little or no breakthrough potential and innovativeness. In addition, the promotion benchmarks for teaching staff in most Chinese universities are based on seniority and publication quantity, whereas key criteria based on meritocracy such as creative research and new ideas are often ignored.

(vi)   There are many restrictions on the development of private universities. Most of the higher education institutions are public universities. There is therefore no socio-political environment for private universities to thrive. The governments impose too much red tape for private higher education institutions to obtain any form of approval.

(vii) The supply of university graduates cannot meet market demand due to the outdated curriculums, which are not orientated towards industry. As a result, the employment rate of college graduates within the first year of graduation has been declining (Mycos Research Institute 2009). The employment rate of college graduates within the first year of graduation was slightly above 85 per cent in 2008 due partly to the impact of the global financial crisis and partly to the demand–supply mismatch of college graduates in the labour market (Mycos Research Institute 2009). Thus, over 750,000, or nearly 15 per cent of new college graduates, were unemployed. Among college graduates who were employed within their first year of graduation in 2008, nearly one-third were in jobs that were unrelated to their field of study (Chunling Li and Boqing Wang 2009).

The Chinese economy has reached a stage where growth is increasingly dependent on the improvement of product quality and efficiency of enterprises. Innovation will play a critical role at this stage. Chinese universities should thus take responsibility for the promotion of innovation. To meet this challenge, the following reforms are needed for Chinese tertiary education:

(i)   Setting up effective mechanisms to encourage innovation and creative research. Financial resources from the governments or from other sources should be allocated to innovative research, especially projects that emphasize originality and cutting-edge ideas. Researchers should be provided with sufficient funds for their innovative work and be sufficiently rewarded for their contribution to academic and technology innovation.

(ii)   Reducing intervention from governments in internal affairs of universities. It is crucial for universities to be independent academically and administratively if they are expected to establish themselves as institutions known for innovativeness. The governments must understand that too much intervention in universities leads to inefficiency and low productivity.

(iii) Establishing an appropriate governance structure within universities, including reorganizing leadership of the Party in higher education. Under the current political system, the leadership of the Party in universities and education is de facto, and calling for withdrawal of Party leadership is absolutely unacceptable. However, there is still some room for redefining the role of the Party leadership in higher education by reorganizing the Party committees in universities (Fujia Yang 2009).

(iv) Giving more autonomy to professors by designing and reorganizing the professorial committee in universities and colleges. The committee should be one of the major decision-makers in the allocation of human and financial resources within universities. Committee members should be elected by professors and teaching staff, and take primary responsibility for their votes.

(v) Setting up an authorized and innovation-guided evaluation system for performance of universities. The system should be independent from government, political intervention and interest groups. The evaluation outcome should become one of the bases for governments to allocate research funds among universities.

(vi) Providing special and preferential policies for the development of private higher education institutions, apart from the implementation of a comprehensive set of regulations that would not discriminate against private providers of higher education. The policies should include simple legal registration and approval procedures for private universities, tax reductions or tax exemptions for donations and charitable contributions to private higher education institutions, and removal of barriers to obtain credit.

(vii) Giving greater autonomy to universities in terms of student enrolment. The current national college entrance exams can be considered one method – but not the only method – for universities to enrol new students. Universities should be given the freedom to determine the best admissions system and requirements, and to organize and determine the form of entrance examinations so that students with potential and creativity are identified and enrolled.

(viii) Reforming the academic curriculum in order to equip college graduates with the professional knowledge and skills to better meet employer expectations (Yanqing Ren 2009). A World Bank project on skills development in Guangdong Province stresses that a good balance has to be achieved between hardware, which includes facilities and equipment for education, and software, which encompasses curriculum, instructional materials and trained qualified teachers (World Bank 2009b). This emphasis can be applied to Chinese universities and colleges. Transforming the learning environment from one that is teacher-centred to one that is learner-centred is necessary. The learner-centred approach trains and equips students with skills such as problem solving, teamwork and communication that are much sought after by employers.

Housing security

Current situation and problems

Like all other countries in the world, China faces challenges in providing decent housing to low-income groups. Since the launch of housing reforms in the 1990s, most public housing has been privatized through apartment sales to tenants. Surveys have shown that, from 1988 to 2002, the percentage of urban households living in public housing fell from over 80 per cent to less than 20 per cent. Along with housing privatization, the commercial property market has also developed rapidly. In 2008, total revenues from the housing and real estate industry accounted for over 5 per cent of national GDP, becoming one of the major driving forces of the country's rapid economic growth. However, the growth of housing and real estate has resulted in unexpectedly high housing prices, especially in large cities. To stimulate housing market development, local governments stopped giving housing subsidies to urban households in the late 1990s. As a result, low-income households, together with millions of rural migrant households, cannot afford to buy their apartments. With skyrocketing housing prices, even middle-income households in cities face difficulties in affording larger and better apartments through the housing market. To some extent, the housing market has become a playground for speculation by the rich.

The problem is very clear: high housing prices drive low-income households out of the housing market and rule them out of any possibility of improving their housing situation. One solution is to reduce housing prices to an affordable level. Even though this solution is technically and economically feasible, it cannot be implemented politically: the local governments would strongly oppose this measure because their revenue from land sales would decline with falling housing prices. The second solution requires the governments to take responsibility for providing low-rent or low-price housing for low-income households, and even perhaps for middle-income households.

Debates and policy options

There are three possible solutions to the housing problem of low-income groups in urban China (CDRF 2009).

(a) Price-subsidized housing (*Jingji shiyong fang* or JSF) is restricted to low- and middle-income households. Housing is sold at prices lower than market prices to households that are qualified as the most needy and with an income below the threshold level set by local governments. The local governments' contribution is to provide free land to estate developers and to set housing prices. However, subsidized housing prices in large cities such as Beijing, Shanghai and Shenzhen have been rising with market prices to a level that is beyond the affordability of the low-income group.

(b) Rent-subsidized public housing (*Lianzu fang* or LZF) caters only to poor households, not migrant households. This programme has not attracted much attention from city governments because they need to spend more resources, both financial and in terms of land, to provide for LZF than for JSF, and the costs for managing and maintaining LZF are relatively higher.

(c) A housing cash-subsidy (*Zhufang xianjin butie* or ZXB) provides cash relief to households that have already bought housing or rented apartments in the market. This programme is not widely implemented and is in the pilot stage in developed areas.

Currently, most cities are implementing both JSF and LZF programmes at the same time, though the two are not 'balanced'. There are debates suggesting either JSF or LZF should become a priority housing policy for city governments. Some academics, on the other hand, strongly argue for the abolishment of JSF, based on the following rationales. First, the JSF programme is unfair. For example, one qualifying criterion for a JSF buyer is their current income rather than their permanent income. This is a possible scenario whereby some buyers are not really categorized as belonging to the low-income category if their past income records are taken into account. To qualify for and own a JSF apartment means a lifetime benefit. Second, the programme would encourage corruption. Due to the large profit gain involved from huge price differences between commercial housing and JSF, rent-seeking activities become common in the allocation of JSF. This argument augurs well for the LZF programme – whose merits are morally acceptable – to be considered a priority in urban housing policy in the future.

There is still a strong voice in favour of the JSF programme because it is, first, more acceptable to city governments and can be quickly implemented; and second, the programme helps meet the housing needs of middle-income households.

Another housing policy debate is how to provide housing for migrant households in cities. Currently, most rural migrants live in factory dormitories, temporary dormitories on construction sites, or basements of high-rise buildings in city communities or in suburban areas. Several case studies indicate that the housing conditions of rural migrants are worse than those of their urban counterparts, and even worse than those that rural people left behind in their hometowns (Li Shi 2008). Since rural migrants are low-income earners, they have no financial ability to buy apartments in the property market, and cannot even afford housing from the JSF. The only solution is to entitle them access to the LZF programme. Some cities recently initiated several pilot projects to provide LZF for rural migrant households.

The housing accumulation fund (*Zhufang Gongjijin*), a scheme that lacks fairness, should undergo reform. The current arrangement is that employees in the formal sector, such as civil servants and SOE workers, hold individual accounts for the housing accumulation fund. It is stipulated that employee and employer should each contribute 10 per cent of wages to the account, which is a similar approach to the housing subsidy. It means, however, that higher income earners obtain higher subsidies from this programme. There are two reform options for *Zhufang Gongjijin*. One is to completely abolish it, terminating payment of housing subsidies to these relatively higher wage earners. Alternatively, if the programme is to be maintained, it can be transformed into a scheme specifically for low- and middle-income employees who urgently need to improve their housing conditions.

Unemployment insurance and employment assistance

Current situation and problems

China is a developing country with a large surplus of labour in rural areas. As its dynamic economy undergoes transition, large numbers of workers are being laid-off from SOEs. Therefore, China must deal with the challenges of unemployment in urban areas and underemployment in rural areas. Ironically, the official unemployment rates are not as high as expected and are believed to be overestimated. Nevertheless, the government is certainly aware of the unemployment pressures. One of the major motivations for government desire to maintain high economic growth is to increase employment and alleviate unemployment pressures. After 10 years of rapid economic growth, the problems of unemployment and underemployment are not now as serious as they were in the late 1990s, when large numbers of workers were laid off from state-owned and urban collective enterprises. However, the recent global financial crisis no doubt intensified the problems as many export-orientated, labour-intensive enterprises closed down in the coastal areas.

Unemployment pressures cannot be significantly mitigated over the next 5 years. One reason is that about 25 million middle-school and college graduates are expected to enter the labour market each year from 2011 to 2015. This is due to a baby boom in the late 1990s. First, it is important to reform and improve the efficiency of the current unemployment insurance system and coverage. Second, it is imperative to encourage firms to create new employment opportunities and motivate graduates to actively search for new jobs. To deal with unemployment, it is widely recognized that state institutions, rather than private insurance, should play a more significant role. As Barr (2003) points out, even in developed countries, what seems more important is how to design an unemployment insurance plan that provides genuine protection and serves as an incentive for the unemployed to look for jobs. In China, the issue of protection is currently more important than the issue of incentive.

A major problem with China's unemployment insurance system is that only workers in the urban formal sector are covered. In 2008, the number of urban workers taking unemployment insurance reached 124 million, but that was only 41 per cent of the total number of urban employees. At the same time, the number of rural migrant workers covered by unemployment insurance was 15.5 million, accounting for less than 12 per cent of the total number of rural migrant workers in urban areas.[17] This implies that the majority of workers in informal sectors, such as rural migrant workers and workers in small private firms, are not covered by the current unemployment insurance system. Expanding the coverage of unemployment insurance should be a priority in the Twelfth Five-Year Plan.

Debates and policy options

Many of the policy debates generated in this area centre on the questions of whether migrant workers and workers in the informal sector should be covered by unemployment insurance, and whether they should be covered by the current system or an alternative scheme that is more suitable for them. All levels of Chinese government have reached a consensus that migrant workers should not be ignored in the unemployment insurance system.[18] However, there has been no agreement as yet on how to provide a system for them. Since migrant workers typically move frequently between jobs, employers and cities, it is obvious that the current insurance system is unsuitable for them. One option proposed in the 2009 Annual Development Report is that the unemployment insurance system for migrant workers be transportable between cities and provinces. Governments should be a major contributor to the system and the contribution required from migrant workers should be affordable and as low as possible.

College graduates are now more and more likely to become unemployed. It has become a social and even a political problem. Debates arise over whether unemployed graduates should be covered by unemployment insurance, who the main financial contributors to the insurance should be, and related issues.

Provision of various training programmes is part of the employment assistance targeting different population groups. An example is the Sunshine Project for migrant workers. However, there are questions about the effectiveness of training projects and the role that the government can play in assisting the unemployed and job seekers.

The current training programmes for rural migrant workers are generally short term, spanning 1–3 weeks. One such programme is the so-called urban life training guide, which helps migrant workers accommodate to urban life, but may not be very useful in helping them find a job because what they need most are skills or professional training. Governments should be providing migrant workers more skills or professional training opportunities.

Chinese governments may also consider setting up a national information network that provides and disseminates to migrant workers free and instant information on labour demand and supply, job opportunities, wages, and social security and labour protection.

CONCLUSION

China has made great achievements in economic growth, but has been lagging behind in terms of social protection and the provision of public services over the past three decades. As a result, the country is facing serious social and economic challenges, such as widening income inequality, large-scale poverty, high unemployment pressures, increasing labour mobility, declining consumption propensity and increasing incidence of social conflict and unrest. Research and experience in other countries indicate that an ideal social security system encompasses strategic objectives for both economic development and social stability.

Chinese governments at all levels have recognized the importance and necessity of a new social security system that incorporates wider coverage, higher efficiency and greater sustainability (CDRF 2009). Moreover, China is now financially capable of providing a system that benefits the entire population rather than focusing exclusively on urban workers in the formal sector. One of the challenges China faces is to quickly and impartially transform the current system into a new system acceptable to all parties.

It was a remarkable achievement for China to establish, over a period of less than 10 years, a nationwide poverty relief system, namely the minimum living standard guarantee scheme, which now supports nearly 70 million poor individuals in urban and rural areas. Now the system needs to be improved in terms of targeting accuracy, wider coverage and higher threshold levels (poverty lines), particularly in rural areas.

China is making a great effort to reform the current medical system, including financing mechanisms and the delivery of medical services. A consensus has been reached on some issues, while others are tabled for debate. It has been agreed that governments should assume greater responsibility for managing medical insurance systems and commit more financial contributions to them. Government medical relief should be given to the poorest people, especially those living in rural areas.

Compulsory education is a government responsibility. The problems associated with compulsory education are low educational quality in rural areas, unequal allocation of financial resources in favour of urban schools and scant attention to preschool education. To deal with these problems, it is imperative for the central government to control allocation of financial resources and increase fund transfers to rural education and education in less-developed areas. Moreover, governments should devise a plan to provide free preschool education to children in order to encourage early development of children's cognitive ability. In addition, it is proposed that governments look into the setting up of a free post-school professional training programme of 6–12 months duration for middle-school graduates, as they are currently having difficulties securing jobs in the competitive labour market.

Higher education reform is imperative in China. The main problem with higher education is insufficient incentive for professional staff to develop innovative breakthroughs and ideas. One explanation is the extensive government intervention in the internal affairs of universities (Lu Naihui and Yongping Zhang 2007). Therefore, a first step towards higher education reform would be to reduce this intervention and interference, and accord full autonomy to universities.

Housing problems have been on the rise since government withdrawal from provision of public housing to urban residents. Given the surging housing prices, a major problem is how to guarantee at least basic housing for low- and even middle-income households in urban areas. The city governments can tap three potential solutions, namely JSF, LZF and ZXB, to deal with this problem. In the long term, the JSF scheme should be gradually phased out and the LZF scheme should be expanded to solve the housing problems of poor urban households.

Unemployment insurance, with the coverage extended to workers in the informal sector and rural migrant workers, plays an integral role in maintaining social stability in China. The insurance offers income support to the unemployed on one hand, and helps them to find employment or self-employment opportunities on the other (Barr 2003). Employment assistance plays an important role in helping the jobless and protecting the employed from losing their jobs, especially in developing countries. The provision of a comprehensive information network offering employment information and a skills training programme would be very useful to the unemployed and to migrant workers with high job mobility.

ACKNOWLEDGEMENTS

This research was supported by the Cairncross Economic Research Foundation (Beijing). The author is very grateful for the constructive suggestions from Dr Edwin Lim, Dr Ian Porter and Professor Zhao Renwei, and comments from Professor Nicholas Barr, Professor Tony Atkinson and the participants in a project workshop held 27 July 2009 in Beijing, as well as from the participants in the China Social Policy workshop held on 9 November 2009 in Beijing. The author also acknowledges the research assistance provided by Ms Yang Sui and Ms Yang Xiuna. An earlier version of this chapter appeared in *China: an International Journal*, 9(1): 72–109 (2011).

NOTES

1 Li Shi (lishi@bnu.edu.cn) is Professor of Economics in the School of Economics and Business and Director of the Center for Income Distribution and Poverty Studies at Beijing Normal University.

2 It is important to note that social security has different coverage in different countries. For instance, the term is specifically related to the old-age, veterans and disability programmes in the USA, while in the UK, it is used to refer to all cash and tax transfers, both social insurance and social assistance. The Nordic countries, however, use the term in a broader sense, covering all measures to combat social insecurity. This chapter adopts the last of these concepts.

3 The China Household Income Inequality Project collected data in 2007 and made a preliminary estimation of national income inequality. The Gini coefficient was found to be 0.47.

4 While the previous official line was 836 yuan for rural households in 2008, the new line was adjusted upwards to 1,196 yuan, an increase of 43 per cent. At the same time, the rural poor population increased from less than 13 million to 40 million, or 207 per cent. The new line and the corresponding poor population figure can be found in the National Bureau of Statistics (NBS) of China (2009).

5 See CSP (2008: 43).

6 There were around 300 million rural labourers engaged in agriculture in 2007, accounting for 39 per cent of the number of total labourers in China as a whole. Assuming the number of rural labourers declines by 1 per cent each year, it will take 20 years for it to reach 10 per cent of the total labourers.

7 See detailed discussion about the supplemental role of the MLSG scheme in reducing poverty in rural Jiangxi Province in 'The rural MLSG and poverty alleviation: the same or supplemental role', available at <http://www.fupin.gansu. gov.cn/ zwzx/1181004710d3661.html>, accessed 5 June 2007.

8 Fang Cai and Yang Du, 'To achieve economic recovery with employment growth', blog article, 7 Feb. 2009 available at <http://blog.voc.com.cn/blog. php?do=showone&uid=337& type=blog&itemid=539446>, accessed 7 February 2009].

9 See discussion summary of 'Why Chinese love saving' on *Xinhuanet* available at <http://news. xinhuanet.com/fortune/2006-04/10/content_4405567.html>, accessed 10 April 2006.

10 A pilot programme to guarantee minimum living standards started in Shanghai in 1993. The central government issued the State Council's notice on establishing the minimum living standard guarantee system for urban residents in the whole of China in 1997 and, in 1999, decrees of urban minimum living standard guarantee, which then became a nationwide urban relief programme.

11 See *Xinhua Agency* report, 19 March 2009 available at <http://www.gov.cn/ jrzg/2009-03/19/ content_1263218.htm>, accessed 19 March 2009.

12 A detailed discussion of the argument can be found in Gordon Liu's seminar entitled 'Deepening reform of Medicare system, development as hard justification', delivered at the Unirule Institute of Economics, Beijing on 22 June 2009.

13 See a report in *China Labour and Social Security* (a Chinese newspaper) on 23 January 2006.

14 See CSP (2008: 415).

15 See CSP (2008: 430).

16 See speech by Premier Wen Jiabao given at a meeting held on 20 November 2006 with six university presidents, *People's Daily*, 28 November 2006.

17 Ministry of Human Resources and Social Security and National Bureau of Statistics (2009) 'Statistical report of human resources and social security development in China, 2008', available at <http://www.stats.gov.cn/tjgb/ndtjgb/qgndtjgb/t20090226_402540710.htm>, accessed 26 February 2009.
18 It was reported that the Ministry of Human Resources and Social Security decided to modify the 'Unemployment Insurance Decree' by adding specific clauses about unemployment insurance for migrant workers. See *Economic Observer*, 19 June 2009.

REFERENCES

Adelman, I. and David Sunding (1987) 'Economic policy and income distribution in China', *Journal of Comparative Economics*, 11(3): 444–461.
Barr, Nicholas (2001) *The Welfare State as Piggy Bank: Information, Risk, Uncertainty, and the Role of the State*, Oxford: Oxford University Press.
—— (2003) 'Preface' to the Chinese edition of *The Economics of the Welfare State*, Beijing: Press of Labour and Social Security.
Barr, Nicholas and Peter Diamond (2008) 'La réforme des pensions: principes, erreurs analytiques et orientations générales', *Revue Internationale de Sécurité Sociale*, 62(2): 5–33.
Bowles, Samuel, Steven N. Durlauf and Karla Hoff (eds) (2006) *Poverty Traps*, Princeton, NJ: Princeton University Press.
CAAS (Chinese Academy of Social Sciences) Institute of Sociology (2005) *Blue Book of China's Society 2005*, Beijing: Press of China Social Sciences Literature.
CDRF (China Development Research Foundation) (2009) *Reconstructing Welfare System in China,* Beijing: Press of China Development.
CSP (China Statistics Press) (2008) *China Statistical Abstract 2008*, Beijing: CSP.
Chunling Li and Boqing Wang (2009) 'Survey on current employment of Chinese college graduates', *Discussion Paper*, Institute of Sociology, Chinese Academy of Social Sciences.
Du Ping (2009) 'Exploration of the deficiency of China's medical insurance for migrant workers', *Population and Economics*, 2009 Supplement: 145–146.
Fajnzylber, Pablo, Daniel Lederman and Norman Loayza (2002a) 'What causes violent crime?', *European Economic Review*, 46(7): 1323–1357.
—— (2002b) 'Inequality and violent crime', *Journal of Law and Economics*, 45(1): 1–39.
Feldstein, Martin (2005) 'Rethinking social insurance', *NBER Working Paper*, No. 11250, Cambridge, MA: National Bureau of Economic Research.
Fujia Yang (2009) 'How to establish a modern system for Chinese universities', an interview report by Ma Guochuan, *Economic Observation*, 22 May.
Gustafsson, Bjorn, Li Shi and Terry Sicular (2008) *Income Inequality and Public Policy in China*, Cambridge: Cambridge University Press.
Huizhu Zhao (2008) 'The situation of rural lowest-level life security system and its problems', *Journal of Zhejiang Provincial Party School*, May: 54–59.
Keidel, Albert (2005) 'The economic basis for social unrest in China', paper presented at the Third European–American Dialogue on China, George Washington University, 26–27 May, available at <http://www. carnegieendowment.org/files/Keidel_Social_Unrest.pdf>.

Knight, John, Li Shi and Quheng Deng (2010) 'Education and the poverty trap in rural China: closing the trap', *Oxford Development Studies*, 38(1): 1–24.

Limei Jiang (2009) 'On secondary issue of minimum living standard guarantee system for urban residents in China', *Journal of Shandong Institute of Business and Technology*, 23(1): 19–25.

Lin Wang (2009) 'Studies on some issues in reform of high education', *Information of World Education*, October.

Ling Li (2006) 'Yiliao weisheng shiye fazhan ji yiliao tizhi gaige de shikao' ['Thoughts on development of medicare and medicare and sanitation and reform of medicare system'], *Nanfang wang* [Southcn.com], 20 December, available at <http://www.southcn.com/ nflr/zhongxinzu/fdbg/200612200398.htm>.

Liquan Ruan and Yuntong Hu, (2009) 'Reconstructing role of universities in higher education reform: defining relationship among government, market and university', *Heilongjiang Higher Education Study*, July.

Li Shi (2008) 'Rural migrant workers in China: scenario, challenges and public policy', International Labour Office (ILO), Policy Integration and Statistics Department, *Working Paper*, No. 89, Geneva: ILO.

Li Shi and Sui Yang (2009) 'Impact of *Di Bao* programme on inequality and poverty in urban China', *Population Science*, October.

Lu Naihui and Yongping Zhang (2007) 'Changes in the role of government in high education under globalization', *High Education Review of Beijing University*, January.

Lum, Thomas (2006) 'Social unrest in China', a report to Congress, 8 May, available at http://www.fas.org/sgp/crs/row/RL33416.pdf.

Mycos Research Institute (2009) *Report of Employment of College Graduates in China 2009*, Beijing: China Social Sciences Literature Press.

NBS (National Bureau of Statistics) (2009) *China Statistical Yearbook 2009*, Beijing: NBS.

Peng, James (2009) 'China may face social unrest as unemployment rises, report says', *Bloomberg*, 6 January 2009, available at <http://www.bloomberg.com/apps/news?pid=20601080&sid= aG8JAH3FwkmY&refer=asia>, accessed 6 January 2009.

Qichao Song and Xuejian Guo (2008) 'Improve the minimum subsistence guarantee system for urban residents', *China State Finance*, 15: 36–37.

Qingshi Zhu (2009) 'The soul of universities is to pursue excellence rather than power', an interview report by Ma Guochuan, *Economic Observation*, 29 December.

Quheng Deng and Li Shi (2008) 'Wage structures and inequality among local and migrant workers in urban China', paper presented at the workshop on rural–urban migration in China and Indonesia, Australian National University, Canberra, 10–12 December.

Riskin, Carl, Renwei Zhao and Li Shi (2001) *China's Retreat from Equality: Income Distribution and Economic Transition*, New York: M.E. Sharpe.

Wei Luo (2008) 'Preliminary exploration on the employment flexibility in urban area', *Health Economics Research*, 3: 31–33

Whalley, John and Ximing Yue (2009) 'Rural income volatility and inequality in China', *CESifo Economic Studies*, 55(3–4): 648–668, available at <DOI:10.1093/cesifo/ifp014>.

World Bank (2009a) 'China – from poor areas to poor people: China's evolving poverty reduction agenda – an assessment of poverty and inequality in China', *Report*, No. 48058, Washington, DC: World Bank.

—— (2009b) 'Skills development in Guangdong province, reducing inequality for shared growth in Guangdong Province, *Policy Note*, No. 8.

Xiaochun Liu, Baoyuan Liu and Xianming Liao (2009) 'Ponder over the establishment of minimum livelihood guarantee system for college students', *Education Research Monthly*, January: 88–89.

Xiaojie Lin (2006) 'Feasibility study on constructing the system of ensuring a minimum standard of living for rural labour migrants', *Population and Economics*, 2006(1): 75–79.

Yanqing Ren (2009) 'Education reform in "Great Education Revolution"', *High Education Study in Sciences and Technology*, August.

You Chun (2009) 'The solution and problems on migrant workers' medical insurance', *Shanghai Insurance*, January: 15–18.

Yuebin Xu and Xiulan Zhang (2009) 'Investigation on questions about social security system in rural and urban China', *Dong Yue Tribune*, 30(2): 32–37.

Zhang Dongsheng, Liu Hao and Wang Xiaozuo (eds) (2008) *Annual Report of Household Income Distribution in China, 2008*, Beijing: Economic Science Press.

Zhao Renwei, Desheng Lai and Zhong Wei (eds) (2006) *Economic Transition and Reform of Social Security in China,* Beijing: Beijing Normal University Press.

Zheng Gongcheng (2008) *Zhongguo Shehui Baozhang 30 Nian* [*Social Security in China in the Last Three Decades*], Beijing: The People's Press.

10 Chinese outward direct investment

Is there a China model?[1]

Yiping Huang and Bijun Wang[2]

INTRODUCTION

Outward direct investment (ODI) has been mainly a phenomenon of advanced economies. Developing countries tend to be on the recipient side of such investment. This traditional pattern started to shift gradually when China commenced economic reform in the late 1970s. Korea, Chinese Hong Kong and Taiwan, still developing economies at that time, began to gradually relocate their labour-intensive manufacturing factories to the Chinese mainland.

China is now an important player in the global ODI scene. Of course, this is a relatively recent phenomenon. Before 2004, the size of China's ODI was trivial. From 2004, China's ODI grew significantly, coinciding with the dramatic expansion of China's current account surplus. Total ODI increased from US$2.85 billion in 2003 to US$56.53 billion in 2009, which equates to an average annual growth rate of 55 per cent. China's share in global ODI rose from 0.45 to 5.1 per cent during the same period. In 2009, China was not only the largest developing-country investor but also the fifth-largest investor in the world, following the USA, France, Japan and Germany.

The Chinese case poses an interesting question regarding the conventional perception that ODI is dominated by developed countries after they accumulate enough capital, technology and management skills. China does enjoy comparative advantages in certain manufacturing industries, evidenced by its export competitiveness. Surprisingly, however, these are not the areas in which Chinese ODI is concentrated. According to the official statistics, most Chinese ODI is in the service industry, including commercial services, finance, retail and wholesale. However, the service industry tends to lag well behind many other industries, even within the Chinese economy.

Study of Chinese ODI is a relatively new but rapidly growing field. Most studies in this area are descriptive, reviewing historical trends, the changing composition of industry and/or destination, and the evolution of government policies (e.g. Wu and Chen 2001; Deng 2003, 2004). Some studies focus on very useful in-depth case studies, especially high-profile ODI cases (e.g. Liu and Li 2002). A number of recent studies empirically examine determinants of Chinese ODI (Buckley *et al.* 2007). All these analyses provide valuable insights for understanding the pattern and characteristics of Chinese investment.

However, the big question remains: why are Chinese enterprises investing so much overseas at such an early stage in China's economic development? There are a number of potential explanations for China's prominent role in global ODI. For instance, it could simply be a result of the size effect. Because China is a large country, even a relatively low propensity to invest overseas could add up to a large amount. It might be the consequence of financial repression at home. Repressive financial policies reduce the cost of capital and make abundant capital available to the state-owned enterprises (SOEs). Finally, it could also be motivated by the desire to strengthen domestic production, made possible through the acquisition of advanced technologies, brand names, better management skills and stable supplies of raw materials, for example. These potential explanations may not be mutually exclusive.

The central research question of this chapter is whether Chinese ODI follows a unique model, different from the ODI by developed countries. We try to answer this question in several steps. We first examine the industry composition of Chinese ODI to see if overseas investment is concentrated in areas where China does well in either domestic or export markets. We then apply statistical analyses to explore which characteristics of host countries attract Chinese ODI, such as market size, income level and legal environment.

This study arrives at a preliminary but clear conclusion. Chinese ODI is indeed very different from ODI by developed economies. The main motivation for Chinese ODI is not necessarily to seek high profits from these investment projects. Traditional factors determining foreign direct investment (FDI) flows, such as market size, labour cost and legal environment, generally do not matter. Instead, the international competitiveness of advanced economies and the resource endowment of developing economies are important features attracting Chinese ODI.

We conclude that the direct objective of Chinese overseas investment is to strengthen the competitiveness and sustainability of domestic production. The channels for realizing such an objective could include acquiring advanced technology, securing commodity supply or even facilitating exports.

This is only a first-step analysis and the conclusion should be treated as a tentative hypothesis that needs to be validated by further research. It would be helpful if we could test this hypothesis using firm-level data. Meanwhile, this China model of ODI might also be a transitional phenomenon. As the Chinese economy develops further, its ODI behaviour might converge with that of developed countries. Nevertheless, China's experiences should provide useful reference for the understanding of ODI for other developing countries.

This chapter is organized as follows. The next section reviews the published literature. The third section describes the ownership composition of investors and the industry distribution of Chinese ODI, while the fourth explores the question of whether Chinese ODI is concentrated in industries that perform relatively better in either the export market or the domestic economy. The fifth section conducts an analysis of the determinants of location choices, and the last section provides some concluding remarks.

LITERATURE REVIEW

The majority of studies on the determinants of ODI attempt to answer three important questions. First, which firms are qualified to invest abroad? Second, what are firms' motives for ODI and what determines their investment location choices? Third, why do countries or enterprises choose FDI over exporting or licensing?[3] In this chapter, our discussion focuses on the first two questions.

What sorts of companies are able to invest overseas? According to Bain (1956) and Hymer (1960), firms engaging in ODI should possess and exploit some monopoly power. Dunning (1958) and Safarian (1966) point out that investing firms usually possess scarce, unique and sustainable resources and capabilities, such as patents, brands or production process capabilities. These aspects of competitiveness are firm-specific or ownership-specific advantages. By making use of any or a combination of these advantages, assets can be exploited to drive revenue growth. The ultimate intended result is an improvement in the efficiency of a firm's operation.

Since the early 1990s, developing countries, especially the Asian developing countries, have seen very rapid growth in ODI (UNCTAD 2006). According to Dunning (2000), the competitive advantages of transnational corporations (TNC) from developing countries, which might be country specific as well as firm specific, are probably different from those that the prevailing theory usually considers, such as firm-specific or ownership-specific advantages. A 2006 *World Investment Report* summarizes three segments of the competitiveness of the TNC from developing countries (UNCTAD 2006): expertise and technology-based ownership advantages in a number of industries; advantages gained from access to home-country resources and activities where the government could exert great influence; and advantages achieved through specialization in part of the production value chain.

With these advantages, some of the TNC from developing countries might be able to compete with TNC from developed countries and engage in asset-exploiting ODI. Some firms engaging in ODI do not have firm-specific or ownership-specific competitive advantages. Firm-specific competitive advantages are particularly lacking. Instead, they seek to acquire firm-specific strategic assets, such as research and development facilities, particular technologies or brands, distribution networks and managerial competencies. This type of ODI is often identified as 'asset augmenting'.

Dunning (2000) argues that even for 'asset augmenting' ODI, firms, especially TNC from developing countries, also have to possess some unique, sustainable resources and capabilities. He points out that China's ODI is both asset exploiting and asset augmenting (Dunning 2006). For asset augmenting, the advantages lie in China's ability to generate funds and its superior access to large markets across Chinese economic space.

What are the determinants of ODI locations? The published literature often identifies market size or market potential of the host country as important determinants. However, such factors might change over time. Some studies examine the relationship between ODI and trade. In theory, exporting and ODI are two alternative means of penetrating foreign markets: exporting goods to satisfy external demand or exporting capital and producing locally. Empirical analyses, however, do not always support this hypothesis. For instance, Blonigen (2001, 2005) believes that the existing trade relationship between the investing economy and the host country could facilitate ODI because of the experience gained in trade.

In seeking resources, relative abundance of natural resources and labour significantly influence the choice of investment location (Buckley and Casson 1976). In the 1970s, the main motivation for Japan's ODI was to acquire resources and raw materials to support domestic economic growth. Similar considerations might apply to today's China and India (Duanmu and Guney 2009).

Researchers have begun to pay attention to the impacts of basic macro-economic conditions on ODI decisions, including changes in exchange, inflation and tax rates, and in the legal environment. Dunning and Lundan (2006) assert that the institutional capabilities of firms, and the incentive structure and the enforcement mechanisms of home and host countries, are increasingly affecting the clustering, leveraging and learning aspects of TNC activity, particularly of third-world TNC.

Johanson and Vahlne (1977) and Sharma and Blomstermo (2003) argue that the pattern of internationalization has been largely determined by dynamic interaction between increasing foreign market commitments and the knowledge and experience gained from other countries. For example, enterprises, especially those inexperienced ones from developing countries, tend to engage in ODI in economies that are geographically proximate, with similar cultures and languages (Davidson 1980; Culpan and Akcaoglu 2003).

Poor institutional factors and associated risks usually deter ODI (Wheeler and Mody 1992; Lepsey 1999). Baniak *et al.* (2003) find that macro-economic as well as institutional inefficiency of host countries deter ODI from enterprises that are aiming for long-term development in host countries. However, these same factors promote those enterprises seeking short-term rents.

WHO INVESTS OVERSEAS AND WHERE?

In 2008–09, SOEs dominated in terms of number of shares in China's ODI, whereas limited liability companies (LLCs) held the largest stake in the total number of investment projects (Table 10.1).

Table 10.1 Investor structure by industrial and commercial registration, 2008–09

	Share in number (%)	Share in China's ODI stock (%)
State-owned enterprises	14.8	69.40
Limited liability companies	54.0	21.05
Private enterprises	8.4	1.00
Stock limited corporations	8.0	6.10
Cooperative enterprises	5.7	1.10
Foreign investment enterprises	3.3	0.65
Collective-owned enterprises	1.4	0.35
Hong Kong, Macao and Taiwan-invested firms	1.8	0.10
Others	2.7	0.25

Sources: *Statistical Bulletin of China's Outward Foreign Direct Investment*, published by Ministry of Commerce (MOFCOM), and authors' calculation.

This has not always been the case. Before 2005, SOEs had a larger share than LLCs in terms of both stock value and number of projects. The share of SOEs declined steadily from 43 per cent in 2003 to 13.4 per cent in 2009.

However, this does not mean that the importance of SOEs in Chinese ODI declined. SOEs possessed 69.4 per cent of China's total ODI stocks in 2008–09, whereas LLCs held only 21.05 per cent.

The fact that SOEs dominate Chinese ODI is interesting, and deserves further investigation. Without proper firm-level data, we cannot explore this issue statistically. Nevertheless, we might still be able to speculate on SOEs' prominent role in Chinese ODI. It is possible that SOEs are able to invest overseas because they have greater access to finance and pay less attention to profitability than do LLCs. SOEs normally receive stronger support from the government but, at the same time, are often tasked to achieve the country's strategic goals (Dunning and Lundan 2006). If this is the case, then these SOE investors would not necessarily invest in areas where China does well.

The industry distribution of China's ODI differs markedly from that of other countries. The primary sector accounted for 18.72 per cent of total China's ODI between 2006 and 2008. In comparison, for developed countries and for developing economies in general, the primary sector accounted for only 7.84 and 8.38 per cent of total ODI, respectively. The primary sector makes up a larger share of China's ODI in comparison with that of developed countries and developing economies. Investments in mining, quarrying and the petroleum industry make up 97 per cent of China's ODI in the primary sector (Table 10.2). This might reflect the strategy of Chinese ODI being made to secure long-term supplies of resources (Buckley and Casson 1976).

More surprising was the distribution of Chinese ODI between manufacturing and service industries. The manufacturing sector accounted for an extremely low share, only 4.72 per cent of the total (Table 10.2). Services

Table 10.2 Industry distribution of outward direct investment flows, 2006–08

Sector/industry	Developed country (%)	Developing economy (%)	World (%)	China (%)
Primary	7.84	8.38	7.95	18.72
Agriculture, hunting, forestry and fishing	0.04	0.29	0.07	0.62
Mining, quarrying and petroleum	7.80	8.09	7.89	18.10
Manufacturing	24.12	15.02	23.21	4.72
Services	60.01	69.25	60.93	76.57
Electricity, gas and water	0.51	0.93	0.55	1.55
Construction	0.42	1.36	0.53	1.08
Trade	5.61	8.17	5.88	13.98
Hotels and restaurants	0.20	0.15	0.19	0.04
Transport, storage and communications	3.23	3.77	3.29	7.95
Finance	24.38	18.10	23.74	18.91
Business activities	23.46	33.37	24.42	31.28
Public administration and defence	0.06	0.00	0.05	0.00
Education	0.03	0.00	0.02	0.01
Health and social services	0.01	0.00	0.01	0.00
Community, social and personal service activities	0.33	0.16	0.31	0.15
Other services	0.87	0.54	0.84	1.60
Unspecified tertiary	0.92	2.67	1.09	–
Private buying and selling of property	0.17	0.00	0.16	–
Unspecified	7.85	7.35	7.80	–

Sources: UNCTAD and authors' calculation.

accounted for 76.57 per cent of China's total ODI. The proportion of service industries in total ODI was often 60.01 per cent for developed countries and 69.25 per cent for developing economies (Table 10.2).

DO CHINESE ENTERPRISES INVEST IN AREAS WHERE THEY DO WELL?

To determine whether Chinese ODI occurs in areas where China does well, we provide a comparison of industry composition of ODI using two sets of indicators: (i) revealed comparative advantage (RCA); and (ii) relative strength of domestic production. The first measures Chinese industry's competitiveness in international markets. The second reveals the importance of individual industries in the Chinese economy. We brought in the second set of indicators because not all service activities are exportable.

The 'revealed' comparative advantage index was originally proposed by Balassa (1965). He suggested that the comparative advantage of a country's industry could be revealed by the ratio of the share of an individual sector's exports in total exports to that share for the world. Generally speaking, an index value less than 1 implies relative disadvantage, whereas a value greater than 1 indicates relative advantage.

We follow the definition of Balassa (1965):

$$RCA_{c,i,t} = \frac{\dfrac{EX_{c,i,t}}{\sum_c EX_{c,i,t}}}{\dfrac{\sum_i EX_{c,i,t}}{\sum_i \sum_c EX_{c,i,t}}} \tag{1}$$

where $EX_{c,i,t}$ denotes exports of industry i of country c in year t. $RCA_{c,i,t}$ denotes the RCA of industry i of country c in year t. We calculated each $RCA_{c,i,t}$, and then obtained the average value (Table 10.3). Unfortunately, the data in the Chinese industry classification are quite aggregated. However, they still offer some useful insights.

Three industries had RCA values greater than 1: goods, construction and commercial services.

Comparing China's RCA with the RCAs of major host economies of Chinese ODI, we found that China did not have comparative advantage in communications and financial services, relative to the host economies. In addition, 79 per cent of major host economies had higher RCA than China in the services sector, and 50 per cent in the transportation sector.

Although China's RCA in commercial services was 1.04, it was still lower than the RCA values of major host economies of Chinese ODI. In fact, approximately 65 per cent of major host economies had higher RCA than China in commercial services. Similarly, despite China's RCA for computers and information technology (0.65) being less than 1, only 37 per cent of major host economies performed better than it.

We conclude that China enjoys the strongest RCA, relative to its host economies, in construction, followed by goods, then computers and IT. It has the weakest comparative advantage in communications, financial services and the services sector in general.

To validate these findings, we also compare China's RCA with the RCAs of all host economies of Chinese ODI. It is found that China's RCA is more significant for goods, computers and IT, whereas the revealed comparative disadvantages are less obvious for communications, financial services and commercial services.

Does China make more ODI in industries with stronger RCAs, or does it make less ODI in industries with weaker RCAs? The answer is clearly 'no'. In industries in which China revealed the highest comparative advantages

Table 10.3 Calculated average revealed comparative advantage, 2003–09

	Goods	Services						
		Total	Transportation	Communication	Construction	Financial services	Computers and IT	Communication services
Home country								
China	1.13	0.46	0.98	0.41	1.78	0.03	0.65	1.04
Major host economies								
Algeria	1.19	0.26	–	–	–	–	–	–
Australia	0.97	1.12	0.84	0.88	0.12	0.34	0.68	1.02
Bahamas	0.26	3.95	0.12	–	–	–	–	1.06
Canada	1.08	0.70	0.77	1.64	0.17	0.51	1.48	1.05
Germany	1.06	0.75	1.09	0.96	2.79	0.61	1.22	1.04
Hong Kong	1.01	0.95	1.43	0.57	0.27	1.52	0.10	1.04
Indonesia	1.12	0.53	0.86	3.47	1.87	0.29	0.23	1.04
Kazakhstan	1.15	0.40	2.20	1.31	0.16	0.18	0.02	1.04
Korea	1.07	0.71	2.46	0.47	0.11	0.56	0.06	0.97
Luxembourg	0.37	3.54	0.28	1.53	0.35	8.63	0.88	1.05
Macao	0.23	4.06	0.18	0.28	–	0.06	–	1.07
Malaysia	1.09	0.65	0.94	0.99	1.73	0.06	0.51	1.04
Mongolia	0.93	1.30	1.64	1.20	0.07	0.14	0.09	1.03
Myanmar	1.17	0.32	1.75	–	–	–	–	0.96
Nigeria	1.18	0.29	2.31	0.63	–	0.10	–	0.88
Pakistan	–	–	1.37	2.41	0.40	0.18	0.49	0.61
Russia	1.12	0.51	1.55	1.26	3.99	0.27	0.47	1.07
Saudi Arabia	1.18	0.26	0.83	0.85	–	0.98	–	1.07

Table 10.3 (continued)

	Goods	Services						
		Total	Transportation	Communication	Construction	Financial services	Computers and IT	Communication services
Singapore	1.00	1.00	1.65	0.53	0.52	0.89	0.30	1.04
South Africa	1.05	0.79	0.61	0.80	0.16	0.73	0.28	1.05
Sudan	1.21	0.17	0.48	1.86	0.57	0.86	0.03	0.91
Turkey	0.94	1.22	0.88	0.75	1.68	0.21	0.01	1.07
UK	0.79	1.85	0.65	1.38	0.27	3.01	1.13	1.06
USA	0.87	1.51	0.73	0.72	0.55	1.34	0.49	1.02
Zambia	1.13	0.48	1.38	2.01	1.38	0.40	0.66	0.79
% China ODI	0.33	0.79	0.50	1.00	0.17	1.00	0.37	0.65
All host economies								
Max	1.23	5.04	2.70	5.56	16.91	8.63	9.60	1.18
Min	0.07	0.05	0.05	0.22	0.01	0.00	0.00	0.43
Average	0.93	1.3	1.18	2.06	1.29	0.5	0.65	0.99
% China ODI	0.18	0.79	0.49	0.96	0.17	0.95	0.26	0.44
Num Econ	130	130	122	111	81	94	93	112
% China ODI	0.06	0.71	0.06	0.01	0.01	0.15	0.01	0.32

Sources: UNCTAD, and authors' calculation.
Note: 'Major host economies' refers to those economies which have been the top 10 destinations of China's ODI in any year from 2003 to 2008. 'All host economies' refers to those economies that are to be analysed empirically later. In fact, compared with the full destinations of China's ODI, 17 economies are dropped because of the unavailability of key variables.

(construction, goods, and computers and IT), ODI accounted for only 8 per cent of China's total ODI. In comparison, in industries where China enjoyed the weakest comparative advantages (communications, financial services and services), ODI accounted for 1, 15 and 71 per cent, respectively, of China's total ODI.

However, RCA might not accurately reflect Chinese industry's strength, especially in the case of non-tradable sectors. To overcome this problem, we construct a relative industry concentration index (ICI). Following RCA, ICI is defined as the proportion of an industry's share in the economy relative to its average share in the world (or a group of countries). Again, an ICI value greater than 1 implies more-advanced activity development of the industry, whereas an ICI value less than 1 suggests less-advanced activity development of the industry.

We first calculate the share of selected industries/sectors in GDP for each economy from 2003 to 2008. We then obtain the average value (denoted by 'S'). Like the calculation of RCA above, we divide the share of those industries/sectors in GDP of each economy by that of the world average, and obtain the relative share (denoted by R_S). Again, the results (Table 10.4) provide some interesting findings.

Looking at China's R_S, 'manufacturing', 'construction' and 'agriculture, hunting, forestry and fishing' are well developed in relative terms in China. However, 'wholesale, retail trade, restaurants and hotels' and 'transport, storage and communications' are underdeveloped industries in China.

Comparing the investing industries' shares in China's GDP with those of major host economies, the notable features include an extremely high share for manufacturing (41 per cent in China versus 13 per cent for the world as a whole) and a surprisingly low share for the tertiary sector (39 versus 55 per cent).

Industries like 'manufacturing', 'agriculture, hunting, forestry and fishing' and 'construction' are relatively more advanced in China. In contrast, tertiary sector industries, especially 'wholesale, retail trade, restaurants and hotels' and 'transport, storage and communications', are underdeveloped in China.

Again, Chinese ODI is not concentrated in industries that are more advanced domestically. Hence, Chinese ODI is not concentrated in industries where China is stronger, whether measured by export market performance or domestic activity strength.

WHAT DETERMINES CHINA'S OUTWARD DIRECT INVESTMENT DESTINATION?

We now turn to explore determinants of Chinese ODI location choices, to further our understanding of the pattern of Chinese overseas investment. We conduct this analysis by applying the well-established gravity model approach. The basic specification of the gravity model for Chinese ODI is as follows:

$$In(odif_{i,t}) = \alpha + \beta_1 In(r\_service_{i,t}) + \beta_2 In(exportotal_{i,t}) + \beta_3 In(importotal_{i,t})$$
$$+ \beta_4 In(gdp_{i,t}) + \beta_5 In(pgdp_{i,t}) + \beta_6 raw_{i,t} + \beta_7 law_{i,t} + \beta_8 contig_i + \beta_9 comlang_i \qquad (2)$$
$$+ \beta_{10} In(dis_i) + \varepsilon_{i,t}$$

$$In(odif_{i,t}) = \alpha + \beta_1 In(serviceingdp_{i,t}) + \beta_2 In(exportotal_{i,t}) + \beta_3 In(importotal_{i,t})$$
$$+ \beta_4 In(gdp_{i,t}) + \beta_5 In(pgdp_{i,t}) + \beta_6 raw_{i,t} + \beta_7 law_{i,t} + \beta_8 contig_i + \beta_9 comlang_i \qquad (3)$$
$$+ \beta_{10} In(dis_i) + \varepsilon_{i,t}$$

where i denotes host country of China's ODI (in our sample, there are 130 host countries) and t denotes time (the time period of our sample is from 2003 to 2009). During this period, the Ministry of Commerce (MOF-COM 2003–09) published the *Statistical Bulletin of China's Outward Foreign Direct Investment* every year (Table 10.5 lists the descriptive statistics and their sources). The correlation matrix also indicates that there is generally no multicollinearity problem.

The key variables are '*r_service*' and '*serviceingdp*,' which are relative RCAs in the service sector and the share of the service sector in GDP, respectively. These two variables are related to the discussions about performance of the Chinese service sector in both export and domestic markets.

'*Exportotal*' and '*importotal*' reflect impacts of trade. The variables '*gdp*' and '*pgdp*' are proxies for market size and labour cost. '*Raw*' represents the resource-seeking motivation and '*law*' is used to describe the institutional environment. '*Contig*' and '*dis*' show the effects of geographical proximity on China's ODI. '*Contig*' and '*comlang*' represent the influence of a similar culture or language.

To capture the interaction between institutional factors and industry development/RCAs of the service sector, we also include the following interaction terms: the product of law and relative RCAs in services, which is expressed by '*lawr_service*', and the product of law and the share of the service sector in total GDP, which is expressed by '*lawserviceingdp*'.

We use both the pooled ordinary least squares (POLS) and the random effects (RE) generalized least squares methods to estimate Equations (2) and (3). We do not use a fixed effects (FE) model for two reasons. First, we want to investigate the effects of time-invariant variables, such as '*contig*', '*comlang*' and '*dis*', to obtain a better understanding of China's ODI. However, if FE is used, they will all be eliminated. Second, in our sample, the time span is short, from only 2003 to 2009, while the number of countries is large, reaching 130. Therefore, the within effects are limited, and it is acceptable not to use FE.

We conduct a Lagrangian multiplier (LM) test to determine whether POLS or RE better fits the data. The significant value for the LM test means that RE estimation is preferable to that of POLS. We then estimate Equations (2)

Table 10.4 Share (S) and relative share (R_S) of industry sectors in GDP, 2003–08

| | Primary | | Secondary | | | | | | Tertiary | | | |
| | Agriculture, hunting, forestry and fishing | | Manufacturing | | Construction | | Total | | Wholesale, retail trade, restaurants and hotels | | Transport, storage and communications | |
	S	R_S	S	R_S	S	R_S	S	R_S	S	R_S	S	R_S
Home country												
China	0.12	0.98	0.41	3.15	0.05	1.08	0.39	0.77	0.09	0.61	0.06	0.71
Major host economies												
Algeria	0.08	0.70	0.05	0.36	0.08	1.56	0.30	0.59	0.10	0.72	0.07	0.83
Australia	0.03	0.22	0.10	0.79	0.07	1.34	0.63	1.24	0.12	0.88	0.07	0.88
Bahamas	0.02	0.14	0.04	0.33	0.09	1.84	0.78	1.54	0.22	1.55	0.09	1.12
Canada	0.02	0.16	0.14	1.11	0.06	1.10	0.62	1.22	0.13	0.95	0.07	0.83
Germany	0.01	0.07	0.21	1.60	0.04	0.74	0.63	1.23	0.11	0.77	0.05	0.65
Hong Kong	0.00	0.01	0.03	0.24	0.03	0.58	0.87	1.71	0.27	1.90	0.09	1.17
Indonesia	0.14	1.15	0.28	2.12	0.07	1.42	0.40	0.79	0.16	1.11	0.06	0.81
Kazakhstan	0.06	0.52	0.12	0.96	0.08	1.58	0.52	1.03	0.13	0.92	0.12	1.44
Korea	0.03	0.25	0.25	1.89	0.07	1.37	0.53	1.04	0.10	0.71	0.06	0.78
Luxembourg	0.00	0.04	0.08	0.62	0.06	1.10	0.75	1.46	0.10	0.74	0.08	1.06
Macao	–	–	0.03	0.26	0.07	1.45	0.69	1.34	0.09	0.66	0.04	0.44
Malaysia	0.09	0.78	0.29	2.23	0.03	0.60	0.44	0.87	0.13	0.92	0.07	0.85
Mongolia	0.21	1.74	0.04	0.29	0.02	0.43	0.39	0.77	0.09	0.65	0.11	1.31
Myanmar	0.50	4.17	0.11	0.81	0.04	0.77	0.35	0.68	0.23	1.61	0.10	1.21
Nigeria	0.33	2.78	0.03	0.21	0.01	0.24	0.24	0.47	0.13	0.96	0.03	0.39
Pakistan	0.20	1.64	0.18	1.35	0.02	0.48	0.49	0.97	0.17	1.18	0.12	1.46
Russia	0.05	0.40	0.16	1.21	0.05	1.02	0.51	1.01	0.19	1.34	0.09	1.11
Saudi Arabia	0.03	0.28	0.10	0.73	0.05	0.97	0.35	0.68	0.06	0.39	0.03	0.42

Table 10.4 (continued)

	Primary		Secondary				Total		Tertiary			
	Agriculture, hunting, forestry and fishing		Manufacturing		Construction				Wholesale, retail trade, restaurants and hotels		Transport, storage and communications	
	S	R_S	S	R_S	S	R_S	S	R_S	S	R_S	S	R_S
Singapore	0.00	0.00	0.24	1.84	0.04	0.79	0.70	1.36	0.18	1.30	0.13	1.67
South Africa	0.03	0.23	0.17	1.29	0.02	0.47	0.58	1.14	0.12	0.87	0.08	1.03
Sudan	0.33	2.78	0.09	0.67	0.04	0.81	0.43	0.85	0.16	1.14	0.12	1.45
Turkey	0.09	0.73	0.17	1.31	0.05	0.91	0.55	1.08	0.15	1.04	0.14	1.71
UK	0.01	0.07	0.12	0.92	0.05	1.05	0.68	1.33	0.13	0.91	0.06	0.79
USA	0.01	0.09	0.13	1.03	0.05	0.94	0.77	1.51	0.15	1.09	0.06	0.75
Zambia	0.20	1.71	0.10	0.80	0.12	2.38	0.48	0.94	0.20	1.45	0.04	0.56
Average	0.10	0.86	0.13	1.00	0.05	1.04	0.55	1.07	0.14	1.03	0.08	0.99
% of China's ODI	0.28	–	0.00	–	0.35	–	0.81	–	0.92	–	0.77	–
All host economies												
Maximum	0.63	5.25	0.41	3.15	0.12	2.40	0.87	1.71	0.27	1.93	0.21	2.63
Minimum	0.00	0.00	0.00	0.00	0.01	0.20	0.04	0.08	0.01	0.07	0.00	0.00
Average	0.12	1.00	0.13	1.00	0.05	1.00	0.51	1.00	0.14	1.00	0.08	1.00
% China ODI	0.36	–	0.00	–	0.38	–	0.80	–	0.90	–	0.78	–
No. of economies	129		130		130		130		130		130	
% of China's ODI	0.01		0.07		0.01		0.73		0.14		0.08	

Sources: UNCTAD, and authors' calculation.

Note: 'Major host economies' refers to those economies which have been the top 10 destinations of China's ODI in any year from 2003 to 2008. 'All host economies' refers to those economies that are to be analysed empirically later. In fact, compared with the full destinations of China's ODI, 17 economies are dropped because of the unavailability of key variables.

Table 10.5 Descriptive statistics

Variable	Label	Mean	Standard deviation	Source
Annual outflow of Chinese outward direct investment, US$0'000	odif	182.7301	1965.90	MOFCOM, PRC
Relative revealed comparative advantage in services	r_service	2.71	2.20	UNCTAD and authors' calculations
Share of tertiary sector in GDP	serviceingdp	0.54	0.16	UNCTAD
China's exports to the host country, US$ million	exportotal	7,162.46	23,372.52	UNCTAD
China's imports to the host country, US$ million	importotal	5,564.80	16,319.10	UNCTAD
GDP, US$ million	gdp	352,101	1,272,091	UNCTAD
GDP per capita, US$	pgdp	12,484.99	18,009.35	UNCTAD
Host country's ratio of raw material exports to its total merchandise exports (including fuels, ores and metals) to its total merchandise exports and a proxy for the abundance of natural resources	raw	28.03	30.84	World Bank world development indicators
Rule of Law, [−2.5 to 2.5], the higher the better	law	−0.02	1.02	World Bank Institute governance indicators
Whether the two countries are contiguous; '1' denotes contiguous	contig	0.09	0.29	CEPII
Whether the two countries share a common official language; '1' denotes share a common language	comlang	0.04	0.19	CEPII
Distance (kilometres) between capital of host country and Beijing	dis	8915.19	4067.27	CEPII

Source: Authors' calculation using stata 10.

and (3) using three different country samples: the entire sample, OECD countries and non-OECD economies (see Tables 10.6–10.8).

For the full sample, neither the host countries' relative RCAs in the service sector nor their development of the service sector is significant in attracting China's ODI. Trade, especially China's exports to the host economies, has a positive impact on China's ODI. However, this is not the case for China's imports from the host economies.

Market seeking is not a driving force for ODI. All coefficients for GDP are not significant. This indicates that Chinese investors do not care about the market sizes of the host countries.

Most coefficients for GDP per capita are also insignificant. In fact, some of the coefficients for GDP per capita are significantly negative, which means the richer the host economies, the smaller China's ODI. GDP per capita might indicate an economy's market potential. For this study, however, this is probably a more important indicator for the cost level because, in most countries, positive correlations between wage rates and GDP per capita exist. Chinese investors do not care about institutional risks in host economies. The coefficient of '*law*' is not significant, although it is positive. However, inexperienced Chinese TNCs prefer to make direct investments in host economies with which they are more familiar. An alternative explanation, however, is that economies with better legal environments are more restrictive in terms of Chinese ODI. Seeking raw materials is an important motivation for Chinese ODI. All the coefficients of '*raw*' are significantly positive. Having a common language (*comlang*) and a border connection (*contig*) play positively significant roles in China's ODI. This is consistent with the conventional FDI literature. However, distance is not a consideration for China's ODI, as evidenced by the insignificant coefficient of '*dis*'.

OECD countries and non-OECD economies demonstrate rather different characteristics in our empirical results. First, for OECD countries, both their relative RCAs in the service sector and their service shares in GDP have positive effects in terms of attracting Chinese ODI. This means that the more comparative advantages possessed by, and the better the development of the service sector in OECD countries, the greater the ODI from China. However, for non-OECD economies, it is just the opposite: the more comparative advantages held by and the better the development of the service sector in non-OECD countries, the smaller the amount of ODI from China.

Our speculation is that Chinese firms intend to learn from the experiences of, and to acquire new technologies from, the service sectors of OECD countries. Through this learning process and from spillover effects, it is hoped that the development of China's own service sector will be advanced. China also invests large amounts of money in the service industries of non-OECD economies. However, this is not because the non-OECD economies enjoy better service sector development. On the contrary, the more developed the service sector of non-OECD economies, the less direct investment will be placed there.

Table 10.6 Results for the determinants of China's outward direct investment, full sample

	(1)POLS	(2)REs	(3)POLS	(4)REs
r_service	-0.0231	-0.0256		
	(0.0553)	(0.0879)		
lawr_service			0.0691*	0.0484
			(0.0383)	(0.0563)
lnexportotal	0.512***	0.387**	0.511***	0.385**
	(0.1120)	(0.1690)	(0.1110)	(0.1680)
lnimportotal	0.0539	0.0472	0.0714	0.056
	(0.0534)	(0.0655)	(0.0512)	(0.0633)
lngdp	-0.0399	0.058	-0.0282	0.0829
	(0.1130)	(0.1810)	(0.1120)	(0.1800)
lnpgdp	-0.255**	-0.198	-0.283***	-0.265*
	(0.1040)	(0.1750)	(0.0921)	(0.1530)
raw	0.0151***	0.0112**	0.0149***	0.0121***
	(0.0034)	(0.0055)	(0.0029)	(0.0047)
law	0.189	0.0558		
	(0.1560)	(0.2500)		
contig	1.076***	1.133*	0.997***	1.086*
	(0.3410)	(0.6660)	(0.3330)	(0.6490)
comlang	3.146***	3.386***	3.131***	3.379***
	(0.5500)	(1.0600)	(0.5480)	(1.0490)
lndis	0.108	0.0844	0.0922	0.0749
	(0.1860)	(0.3440)	(0.1840)	(0.3380)
Observations	559	559	559	559
R-squared	0.459	0.4558	0.461	0.4578
LM test	chi2(1)=207.53***		chi2(1)=208.02***	

	(5)POLS	(6)REs	(7)POLS	(8)REs
serviceingdp	-0.769	-1.78		
	(1.1790)	(1.5360)		
lawserviceingdp			0.557**	0.373
			(0.2720)	(0.4480)
lnexportotal	0.475***	0.444***	0.463***	0.438**
	(0.1180)	(0.1840)	(0.1180)	(0.1840)
lnimportotal	0.142**	0.0587	0.153***	0.0723
	(0.0581)	(0.0709)	(0.0566)	(0.0698)
lngdp	-0.171	-0.0464	-0.166	-0.0467
	(0.1230)	(0.1990)	(0.1220)	(0.1980)
lnpgdp	-0.129	-0.0551	-0.269**	-0.222
	(0.1300)	(0.2110)	(0.1120)	(0.1950)
raw	0.0146***	0.0116*	0.0171***	0.0160***
	(0.0042)	(0.0066)	(0.0034)	(0.0058)
law	0.135	0.0724		
	(0.1760)	(0.2890)		
contig	0.916**	1.109	0.908***	1.013
	(0.3580)	(0.6980)	(0.3430)	(0.6840)
comlang	2.711***	3.126***	2.444***	2.761**
	(0.6280)	(1.1500)	(0.6040)	(1.1260)
lndis	0.0188	0.0829	0.0113	0.0286
	(0.2020)	(0.3750)	(0.1940)	(0.3660)
Observations	476	476	476	476
R-squared	0.439	0.4343	0.443	0.4382
LM test	chi2(1)=160.42***		chi2(1)=152.39***	

Notes: Standard errors in parentheses. ***, **, * indicate that the coefficient is significant at the 1%, 5% or 10% level, respectively.

Table 10.7 Results for determinants of China's outward direct investment, OECD countries

	(1)POLS	(2)REs	(3)POLS	(4)REs		(5)POLS	(6)REs	(7)POLS	(8)Res
r_service	0.396**	0.367			serviceingdp	10.48**	10.39*		
	(0.1660)	(0.2460)				(4.6430)	(6.2260)		
lawr_service			0.338***	0.321**	lawserviceingdp			1.795**	1.487
			(0.0993)	(0.1430)				(0.8000)	(1.1600)
lnexportotal	1.404***	1.446***	1.336***	1.361***	lnexportotal	0.809**	0.911	0.952**	1.106**
	(0.3290)	(0.5130)	(0.3230)	(0.4940)		(0.3770)	(0.5690)	(0.3650)	(0.5440)
lnimportotal	0.593**	0.617	0.510**	0.517*	lnimportotal	0.561**	0.627*	0.331	0.358
	(0.2500)	(0.3860)	(0.1980)	(0.2940)		(0.2450)	(0.3630)	(0.2240)	(0.3260)
lngdp	-0.641*	-0.72	-0.423	-0.45	lngdp	-0.185	-0.4	0.022	-0.204
	(0.3290)	(0.4940)	(0.3000)	(0.4560)		(0.3570)	(0.5190)	(0.3580)	(0.5200)
lnpgdp	-0.245	-0.0292	-0.654*	-0.555	lnpgdp	-0.83	-0.521	-0.781	-0.539
	(0.4630)	(0.6760)	(0.3840)	(0.5700)		(0.5390)	(0.7470)	(0.5170)	(0.7250)
raw	0.0109	0.00841	0.0127	0.0103	raw	0.0247	0.0227	0.0104	0.00625
	(0.0107)	(0.0163)	(0.0104)	(0.0156)		(0.0149)	(0.0214)	(0.0125)	(0.0176)
law	0.278	0.109			law	0.568	0.265		
	(0.5060)	(0.7590)				(0.5670)	(0.8300)		
lndis	0.391	0.506	0.193	0.276	lndis	-0.279	-0.0551	-0.155	0.0718
	(0.3710)	(0.5940)	(0.3470)	(0.5460)		(0.4080)	(0.6250)	(0.3980)	(0.6100)
Observations	150	150	150	150	Observations	120	120	120	120
R-squared	0.529	0.5265	0.545	0.5434	R-squared	0.517	0.5122	0.509	0.5042
LMtest	chi2(1)=15.16***		chi2(1)=14.26***		LMtest	chi2(1)=6.95***		chi2(1)=7.06***	

Notes: Standard errors in parentheses. ***, **, * indicate that the coefficient is significant at the 1%, 5% or 10% level, respectively.

Table 10.8 Results for the determinants of China's outward direct investment, non-OECD countries

	(1)POLS	(2)REs		(3)POLS	(4)REs
r_service	−0.0928*	−0.0674	serviceingdp	−2.207*	−2.435*
	(0.0549)	(0.0880)		(1.1360)	(1.4720)
lawr_service	0.0312	0.0363	lawserviceingdp		
	(0.0498)	(0.0769)			
lnexportotal	0.362***	0.232	lnexportotal	0.374***	0.317*
	(0.1100)	(0.1650)		(0.1160)	(0.1780)
lnimportotal	0.0383	0.0416	lnimportotal	0.119**	0.0598
	(0.0510)	(0.0614)		(0.0552)	(0.0668)
lngdp	0.0493	0.183	lngdp	−0.111	0.0244
	(0.1170)	(0.1900)		(0.1250)	(0.2000)
lnpgdp	−0.203*	−0.182	lnpgdp	0.00851	0.0386
	(0.1040)	(0.1740)		(0.1260)	(0.2060)
raw	0.0122***	0.00922*	raw	0.0139***	0.0128**
	(0.0036)	(0.0056)		(0.0042)	(0.0065)
law	0.188	0.0525	law	0.364*	0.371
	(0.2210)	(0.3550)		(0.2080)	(0.3200)
contig	1.432***	1.404**	contig	1.339***	1.387**
	(0.3370)	(0.6630)		(0.3550)	(0.6790)
comlang	3.253***	3.484***	comlang	2.668***	2.807**
	(0.5390)	(1.0410)		(0.6430)	(1.1390)
lndis	0.278	0.199	lndis	0.27	0.214
	(0.2190)	(0.3970)		(0.2360)	(0.4240)
Observations	409	409	Observations	356	356
R-squared	0.541	0.5371	R-squared	0.534	0.5303
LMtest	chi2(1)=131.79***		LMtest	chi2(1)=104.90***	

Notes: Standard errors in parentheses. ***, **, * indicate that the coefficient is significant at the 1%, 5% or 10% level, respectively.

Second, although both China's exports to OECD countries and to non OECD economies display a positive indicator for China's ODI, the situation for imports is different. For OECD countries, the more China imports from the host economy, the more China invests. However, even if China has imported a great deal from non-OECD economies, China's ODI is not affected by this factor.

Third, China's ODI in non-OECD economies is driven by resource seeking. This, however, does not hold, at least not statistically, for OECD economies. Such a pattern is evident for the coefficient of 'raw'. Of all eight specifications' coefficients of 'raw', none is statistically significant for OECD countries. In contrast, the coefficients of 'raw' for non-OECD economies are all significantly positive.

OECD countries and non-OECD economies also share some common characteristics with regard to attracting Chinese ODI. For instance, both

OECD and non-OECD economies' GDP and GDP per capita have no effect in terms of attracting China's direct investment; both OECD and non-OECD economies' rule of law (*'law'*) and their distance to China are insignificant in terms of influencing Chinese ODI.

CONCLUDING REMARKS

The existing literature on China's ODI tends to directly address firms' motivations and location choices for ODI, avoiding the discussion of what qualifies firms to invest abroad. One important reason for this is the lack of firm-level data. After all, China's TNCs are still new players in the international market.

By analyzing the distribution of industries that have been invested in and their RCAs, as well as their development in terms of share in GDP, we find that China's ODI is neither based on RCAs nor on choosing the industries with higher levels of development. Admittedly, such findings derive from a very approximate analysis, based on rough industry data rather than complete firm data. However, the present study will help to fill a gap in the existing published literature and more detailed work could follow.

We incorporate the 'revealed' comparative advantages of the selected industries and their share in GDP in China and its host economies into the standard model of ODI determinants. We find that China's ODI has its own Chinese characteristics.

First, although the majority of China's ODI is focused on the service sector, its investment behaviour in terms of the development/RCAs of the service sector in host economies differs between OECD countries and non-OECD economies. For OECD countries, the more comparative advantages held by, and the more advanced the development of the service sector, the greater the ODI from China. It could be inferred that Chinese firms intend to learn from the experience and technologies of the service sectors in OECD countries. In contrast, for non-OECD economies, the more comparative advantages and the more advanced the development of service sectors, the smaller the amount of ODI from China. It seems that Chinese firms intend to compete in non-OECD countries.

Second, the level of China's exports to host economies is a significantly positive indicator for China's ODI. The more China exports to a nation, the more China invests in that nation. There are two interpretations for this pattern. On the one hand, the more China exports to the market, the better the knowledge and experience China can gain. For a newcomer to outward investment, such knowledge and experience could facilitate direct investment, as is the case with a common language or when sharing a common border. On the other hand, China's ODI may be used to service exports.

Third, market seeking is not a driving force of China's ODI. Both host economies' GDP and GDP per capita appear to have no influence on

China's ODI decisions. Instead, seeking raw materials – more specifically, fuel, ores and metals – is a considerable motivator for China's ODI. However, this statement holds only for non-OECD countries.

Findings from the present study prompt us to suggest that there is probably a 'China model' for ODI, in which, for China, the motivation for and determinants of ODI differ significantly from those of developed countries. For instance, empirical estimation in this study confirms that Chinese investors do not pay close attention to either the market size or the cost advantages of host economies. In fact, they do not invest in industries where they do well in either domestic or international markets. Rather, they are attracted by advanced development in OECD countries and by resources in non-OECD countries.

The motivation for the 'China model' is strengthening domestic industry (or production) through ODI. ODI does this through the acquisition of management skills, technology, brands or raw material supply. Clearly, the purpose here is not to directly expand overseas markets, certainly not for the invested projects. A similar ODI path was followed by Japan in the 1970s. However, Japanese ODI was not as prominent in the world economy then as Chinese ODI is today. Such investment is probably based on strategic decisions. However, it is also made possible by some special institutional features, such as the dominance of SOEs in certain Chinese industries and the existence of financial repression, which not only represses the costs of capital but also makes large amounts of capital available to SOEs. Therefore, SOEs are still a dominant player in Chinese ODI.

The 'China model' may be a transitional phenomenon. If wages continue to rise rapidly, China might eventually move its textile and clothing, toys and travel goods factories to lower cost countries. Such investment would be more consistent with the market- or low-cost-seeking motivations in traditional FDI theory. If further liberalization of the financial industry leads to rising costs of capital, and to a weakening of the state sector, the importance of the China model may also decline. In any case, the hypothesis of the China model proposed in this study is no more than a preliminary one. Further study is required to establish its validity.

NOTES

1 This paper is a part of a joint research project of the Australian National University, the Development Research Center of the State Council and Peking University. Research for this paper was partially funded by the Ford Foundation. The authors are grateful to Peter Drysdale, Yongsheng Zhang, Ligang Song, Yan Shen, Miaojie Yu and many graduate students at the National School of Development of Peking University for valuable comments and suggestions. An earlier version of the chapter appeared in *China & World Economy*, 19(4): 1–21 (2011).
2 Yiping Huang, Professor of Economics, China Macroeconomic Research Center, National School of Development, Peking University, Beijing, China. Email:

yhuang@ccer.edu.cn. Bijun Wang, PhD candidate, China Center for Economic Research, Peking University, Beijing, China. Email: wangbijunccer@yahoo.cn..
3 The third question is mainly related to the field of industry organization theory, which is beyond the scope of the present study. Therefore, here we discuss issues related to only the first two questions.

REFERENCES

Bain, Joe Staten (1956) *Barriers to New Competition*, Cambridge, MA: Harvard University Press.

Balassa, Bela (1965) 'Trade liberalization and revealed comparative advantage', *Manchester School of Economic and Social Studies, Bulletin*, 33(2): 99–117.

Baniak, Andrzek, Jacek Cukrowski and Jan Herczynski (2003) 'On the determinants of foreign direct investment in transition economics', *Problems of Economic Transition*, 48(2): 6–28.

Blonigen, Bruce (2001) 'In search of substitution between foreign production and exports', *Journal of International Economics*, 53(1): 81–104.

—— (2005) 'A review of the empirical literature on FDI determinants', *NBER Working Paper* No. 11299, Cambridge, MA: National Bureau of Economic Research.

Buckley, Peter and Mark Casson (1976) *The Future of the Multinational Enterprise*, London: Macmillan.

Buckley, Peter, Jeremy Clegg, Adam Cross, Xin Liu, Hinrich Voss and Ping Zheng (2007) 'The determinants of Chinese outward foreign direct investment', *Journal of International Business Studies*, 38(4): 499–518.

Culpan, Reflk and Emin Akcaoglu (2003) 'An examination of Turkish direct investments in Central and Eastern Europe and the Commonwealth of Independent States', in Svetla Trifonova Marinova and Marin Alexandrov Marinov (eds) *Foreign Direct Investment in Central and Eastern Europe*, pp. 181–197, Farnham: Ashgate.

Davidson, William H. (1980) 'The location of foreign direct investment activity: country characteristics and experience effects', *Journal of International Business Studies*, 11(2): 9–22.

Deng, Ping (2003) 'Foreign direct investment by transnationals from emerging countries: the case of China', *Journal of Leadership and Organizational Studies*, 10(2): 113–124.

—— (2004) 'Outward investment by Chinese MNCs: motivations and implications', *Business Horizons*, 47(3): 8–16.

Duanmu, Jing-Lin and Yilmaz Guney (2009) 'A panel data analysis of locational determinants of Chinese and Indian outward foreign direct investment', *Journal of Asia Business Studies*, 3(2): 1–15.

Dunning, John H. (1958) *American Investment in British Manufacturing Industry*, London: Allen and Unwin, reprinted by Arno Press, New York.

—— (2000) 'The eclectic paradigm as an envelope for economic and business theories of MNE activity', *International Business Review*, 9(1): 163–190.

—— (2006) 'Comment on Dragon multinationals: new players in 21st century globalization', *Asia Pacific Journal of Management*, 23(2): 139–141.

Dunning, John H. and Sarianna M. Lundan (2006) *The MNE as a Creator, Fashioner and Respondent to Institutional Change*, Universities of Reading, Rutgers and Maastricht (mimeo).

Hymer, Stephen (1960) 'The international operations of national firms: a study of direct foreign investment', PhD thesis, Department of Economics, Massachusetts Institute of Technology, MA.

Johanson, Jan and Jan-Erik Vahlne (1977) 'The internationalization process of the firm – a model of knowledge development and increasing foreign market commitments', *Journal of International Business Studies*, 8(1): 23–32.

Lepsey, Robert E. (1999) 'The location and characteristics of US affiliates in Asia', *NBER Working Paper* No. 6876, Cambridge, MA: National Bureau of Economic Research.

Liu, Hong and Li Kequan (2002) 'Strategic implications of emerging Chinese multinationals: the Haier case study', *European Management Journal*, 20(6): 699–706.

MOFCOM (Ministry of Commerce of the People's Republic of China) (2003–09) *Statistical Bulletin of China's Outward Foreign Direct Investment,* available at http://www. mofcom.gov.cn/tongjiziliao/tongjiziliao.html, accessed August 2010.

Safarian, A. Edward (1966) *Foreign Ownership of Canadian Industry*, Toronto: McGraw Hill.

Sharma, Deo and Anders Blomstermo (2003) 'The internationalization process of born globals: a network view', *International Business Review*, 12(6): 739–753.

UNCTAD (United Nations Conference on Trade and Development) (2006) *World Investment Report 2006: FDI from Developing and Transition Economies: Implications for Development*, New York and Geneva: United Nations.

Wheeler, David and Ashoka Mody (1992) 'International investment location decisions: the case of U.S. firms', *Journal of International Economics*, 33(1–2): 57–76.

Wu, Hsiu and Chien-Hsun Chen (2001) 'An assessment of outward foreign direct investment from China's transitional economy', *Europe–Asia Studies*, 53(8): 1235–1254.

11 History matters
China and global governance

Wendy Dobson[1]

INTRODUCTION

The profound transformation underway in the world economy passed another milestone in August 2010 when the Japanese government released its second-quarter GDP numbers. These indicated that China's economy had overtaken Japan's in size, to become the world's second-largest economy after the USA. China and India, the two most populous countries on the planet, are successfully integrating into the world economy while the large, advanced economies struggle with what is likely to be years of below-potential growth following the global financial crisis. So far, this shift in the centre of economic gravity is remarkable in that, while not without bilateral tensions, relationships among the world's major states are both peaceful and collaborative in promoting common interests and collective action.

China's sheer size and dynamism are moving it to the top of many rankings (Box 11.1). It is the world's largest creditor and accumulator of foreign-exchange reserves, the largest goods exporter and the largest importer of iron ore, copper, potash, timber products and Saudi crude oil. Some Chinese companies are now the world's largest by market capitalization. For 30 years it has been the world's fastest-growing economy, advancing more rapidly than anyone anticipated to parity with the USA. It is at the heart of the globalization of production with all major manufacturers of consumer goods and durables located there. Significantly, Chinese see themselves as returning to the centre of the world economy, a position China held for centuries between 1300 and 1820 (Maddison 2006).

China's size creates external expectations of its global leadership role that are frustrated by factors that every Chinese economist knows well (Box 11.2). China is still poor, measured by per-capita income; its population is ageing and the number of new labour market entrants is already shrinking. Thirty years of rapid growth has generated serious income and regional inequalities, and environmental degradation is a rising public concern. The dash for jobs generated by industrial growth cannot be sustained. Correcting the imbalances is not an easy task since powerful interests that have relied on underpriced factor inputs (energy, land, capital and the environment) will have to be compensated.

Underlying these challenges is a unique mix of state and market institutions. The 120 central-state-owned enterprises, for example, are huge conglomerates with complex ownership structures interlinked with state power. And the financial sector is bank-dominated and government-owned, while its monetary system is shaped by a strong political commitment to exchange-rate stability.

We have, therefore, a complex tapestry to apply to consideration of the subject of China and global governance. The relationship is very much two way. Looking back, China's remarkable development was inextricably tied up with decisions to rely on the norms and rules of, as well as the advice of and technical assistance from the established institutions. China's embrace of the global institutions and their rules helped guide its economic success in pulling millions of people out of poverty, creating millions of modern sector jobs and deepening its integration into the world economy. Tackling its relative poverty is a key driver in the story of China's economic ascent. Located in the neighbourhood of the 'Asian miracle' and facing a Malthusian crisis in the 1970s following the upheavals of Mao's class struggles, the Communist Party leadership moved pragmatically to restore balance between population and economic production. Jobs became a central objective. As local experiments with decentralized rural production showed success, governments moved to reform incentives throughout the country to draw in potential opponents who benefited from the status quo. Domestic institutions were then changed in ad-hoc fashion that continues to this day. Industrial production benefited from foreign know-how and capital, particularly from China's diaspora and East Asian neighbours. In the late 1990s the radical restructuring of the state production sector opened the way for non-state firms, which now account for more than 80 per cent of

---

Box 11.1 China in the world economy

1. Real GDP growth (%)

	1990	2000	2007	2015
China	3.8	8.4	13	7.9
Japan	5.2	2.9	2.4	1.7
USA	1.9	3.7	2.1	2.3

2. GDP relative to USA (2009 US$ million)

	1990	2005	2020
China as percentage of US	6.4	30	66–82

3. Share of world merchandise exports (%)

	1990	2009	2014
China	3	9.6	12
Japan	8.3	5	
USA	11.4	8.5	
Germany	12.2	9	

4. Gross capital formation (% of GDP)

2000	35
2007	43

5. China is the world's largest importer of iron ore, potash, Saudi crude oil, copper, timber products.

6. By market capitalization reported in *Forbes Magazine* (7 May 2010) the following Chinese companies rank in the top 20 globally: ICBC (#5), PetroChina (#13), CCB (#17).

Sources: Kuijs 2009; http://data.worldbank.org/indicator/NY.GDP.MKTP.KD.ZG; http://stats.wto.org/StatsticalProgram/WSDBViewData.aspx?Language=E; WTO State of Trade 2009

industrial production. The World Bank became involved following Deng Xiaoping's meeting with Robert McNamara around 1980 (Kent 2007; Zoellick 2010). The 15-year negotiation to join the World Trade Organization was instrumental in China's acceptance of the global rules of the road and a major driver of domestic policy reforms to change the planned economy, its institutions and its managers into more market-orientated ones. The strategy has had a spectacular pay-off.

Looking forward, China's impact on the global economic order is still an open question. Its economic size and dynamism make it both 'systemically significant' and increasingly a political force to be reckoned with. Will that reckoning be peaceful? The Chinese people are strongly supportive of China once again taking its rightful place in the world and reversing 200 years of conflict and humiliation by foreign powers. How will China participate in the world's economic and political institutions as it integrates into world markets? As its size and confidence grow, will its behaviour influence their goals and operations, for worse or better?

We are reminded by historians that earlier economic transitions caused upheavals. Although peaceful, in the transition from British to US hegemony after the First World War, US economic policies took advantage of liberal UK trade policies. Japan's rapid investment- and export-led growth after the Second World War caused major economic imbalances in the 1980s as the economy achieved greater systemic significance. The way these imbalances were dealt with by Japan and its major economic partners echoes in the

---

Box 11.2 China's challenges

1. Per-capita income (end-2007, US$)

China	2,430
Japan	34,310
USA	39,932

2. Median age

	2010	2020	2030
China	34.2	37.1	41.1
Japan	44.7	48.6	52.2
USA	36.6	37.9	39.5

3. Number of 15–24-year-olds

2000	197 million
2010	229 million
2020	180 million
2030	178 million

4. Income inequality (Gini index)

	2007
China	41.5
India	36.8
Canada	32.6
USA	40.8

5A. CO_2 emissions (total kilotonnes)

	2005	2007
China	5,609,477.7	6,533,018.3
USA	5,836.473.5	5,832,194.0
World	29,205,744.0	30,649,360.0

5B. CO_2 emissions (tonnes per capita)

	2005	2007
China	4.3	5.0
USA	19.7	19.3
World	4.5	4.6

Sources: http://hrdrstats.undp.org/en/indicators/lbl.html; http://esa.un.org/unpp
http://data.worldbank.org/indicator/EN.ATM.CO2E.PC/countries/CN-4E-XN; United Nations: World Population Prospects; The 2008 Revision Population Database.

minds of policy-makers in tackling the international imbalances underlying the global financial crisis. The tendency to blame yen appreciation as the cause of Japan's decades-long stagnation is to misread history. The real culprits were mistakes in monetary policy, weak regulatory institutions (Corbett and Ito 2010; Posen 2010) and failure to implement the 1986 Maekawa report on economic restructuring.

China's economic and security relationships with the United States, still the pre-eminent power in both hard- and soft-power terms, and the architect of the postwar global order, is central to China's conduct in the global order. The hard-power relationship both drives and is constrained by the realities of economic interdependence. Even as they cooperate they mistrust each other. As we see in a later section, the USA accommodates China's rise but what will happen if China does not support the rules and norms of the system of which the USA is the architect?

The next section explores the prevailing framework of global economic governance, how it might change to accommodate China and how these ideas accord with those expressed in Chinese discourse and analysis. The third section examines China's approach to the provision of key public goods in the G20, the World Trade Organization (WTO), International Monetary Fund (IMF) and the World Bank, and the Financial Stability Board (FSB), as well as related regional institutions and the climate-change framework negotiations. China's behaviour towards its Asian neighbours, which until 200 years ago it dominated peacefully through political and commercial relationships, will be a factor shaping the global order. The final section draws conclusions based on the evidence, and examines both the reasons for, and future implications of, China's growing assertion of its own interests.

PERSPECTIVES ON GLOBAL GOVERNANCE

What is the meaning of global governance, as established by the Western countries? What changes are contemplated to accommodate China? What are Chinese perspectives on these issues? At its most abstract, global governance is the rule making and exercise of power on a global scale by entities working within organizations functioning on democratic principles and accountability (Keohane 2002). These entities include governments, corporations, individuals, civil society organizations and other non-state actors. Joint action in these institutions is based on common interests and values; members agree to abide by common rules and share the work of the institutions. The institutions in turn are accountable to their members.

Global *economic* governance, the main focus of this paper, was established in the postwar period through the Bretton Woods institutions (the IMF and World Bank), the World Trade Organization (WTO), the Basel financial institutions centred at the Bank for International Settlements and the G7 leaders' summits established by French and German leaders in 1975.

Governments cooperate in these institutions to produce non-rivalrous 'international' public goods from which no-one can be excluded and which no government can produce by acting on its own. More broadly these public goods include peace, law and order, open and efficient markets, economic and financial stability, freedom from poverty and communicable disease, and a clean environment.

As economies have become more interdependent, governments have cooperated in promoting and maintaining economic and financial stability – even coordinating economic decision-making – in theory to modify national policies in recognition of international economic interdependence. This definition of economic policy coordination can be used as a benchmark to evaluate the extent to which governments alter policies either in response to peer pressures or in recognition of the consequences of spillovers. This does not mean governments give precedence to international goals over domestic ones. But coordination or cooperation is a way of expanding choices available to national policy-makers because it gives them influence over policy choices of other cooperating governments. Further, while collective action involves ceding some national sovereignty, governments, in deciding to cooperate, exercise sovereignty (Dobson 1991).

Relations among national governments can be seen as ranging along a spectrum from conflict to supranational integration where governments set common policy in a forum to which they have ceded significant authority (Box 11.3). In between, independent policy-setting reflects purely national objectives, while cooperating governments act on enlightened self-interest, taking potential spillovers beyond national borders into account – even engaging in policy bargaining with their peers and coordinating policies. In its broad sense, economic cooperation characterizes the Bretton Woods institutions created by the Western alliance after the Second World War, which observe principles of governance common to the founding democracies: market competition, transparency, and the rule of law and respect for human rights. Since the end of the Cold War in the early 1990s, however, these institutions have come to be regarded as exclusive clubs suffering from democratic deficits; representing a shrinking share of economic activity and slow to respond to the growing systemic significance of China, India, Russia and Brazil, whose policies and performance increasingly spill over onto their neighbours and trading partners.

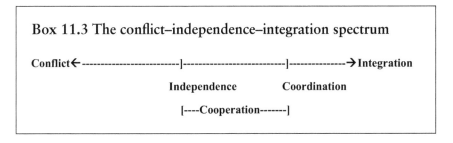

Box 11.3 The conflict–independence–integration spectrum

Nevertheless, these principles are still the reference point in external views of China's participation in the international order. Some optimists who are persuaded by China's historical role and the size of its economy predict a powerful China acting independently and reshaping the order. China asserts its own values, returning to the tributary system in East Asia, inevitably challenging the USA for global pre-eminence (Jacques 2009). Others see China's future transformation into an urban, green and innovative society as having a similar impact: an assertive China securing natural resources, building soft power, taking a higher profile in international organizations and changing the rules of the game (Economy 2010).

Pessimists discount China's future influence because of the exigencies of rising economic inequality, environmental degradation and the weak financial system, circumstances that will preoccupy it at home for the foreseeable future, just as domestic preoccupations have caused it to turn inward in the past (Bardhan 2005; Friedman 2009; Pei 2009). Intermediate positions argue that most modern societies now accept that a stable world order is based on key Western principles of democracy, the rule of law and social justice. The challenge in the post-unipolar world is to apply these principles in pragmatic ways through partnerships with emerging powers that recognize cultural differences (Mahbubani 2008). China accepts and participates in this world order, seeing itself more as a counterbalance to other major powers and primarily focused on its huge domestic economic challenges (Dobson 2009).

Too often, the popular debate is framed in zero-sum terms. Political and security analysts tend to conflate economic with hard power and assume relationships among great powers are zero-sum. Yet economic power is not simply the absolute size of an economy but the ability to get others to change their positions through persuasion and economic threats such as freezing bank accounts, distributing bribes and exerting other forms of influence that others emulate (Nye 2004). Political analysts also think in Eurocentric historical concepts of empire, primacy and imperialism and predict conflicts with zero-sum outcomes in which China 'wins' and the USA 'loses' (as do China's two huge Asian neighbours Japan and India, which are also assumed to compete for domination). China's search for new sources of natural resources adds to these perceptions (China's rising foreign direct investment (FDI) and government aid to producing countries in Africa and Central Asia, for example). Calls from nationalists within China advocate more assertive behaviour in the region and the greater exercise of power in the world, commensurate with China's growing size. Some Americans predict inevitable bilateral conflict (Kagan 2008).

The official American view is both pragmatic and positive-sum as expressed by President Obama in his November 2009 Tokyo speech:

> … in an interconnected world, power does not need to be a zero-sum game, and nations need not fear the success of another. Cultivating spheres of cooperation – not competing spheres of influence will lead to progress in the Asia Pacific.

… America will approach China with a focus on our interests … important to pursue pragmatic cooperation with China on issues of mutual concern, because no one nation can meet the challenges of the twenty-first century alone, and the United States and China will both be better off when we are able to meet them together. That's why we welcome China's effort to play a greater role on the world stage – a role in which their growing economy is joined by growing responsibility. China's partnership has proved critical in our effort to jumpstart economic recovery. China has promoted security and stability in Afghanistan and Pakistan. And it is now committed to the global nonproliferation regime, and supporting the pursuit of denuclearization of the Korean Peninsula. So the United States does not seek to contain China, nor does a deeper relationship with China mean a weakening of our bilateral alliances. On the contrary, the rise of a strong, prosperous China can be a source of strength for the community of nations.

(US White House 2009)

Secretary of State Hillary Clinton in her September 2010 'New American moment' speech (Clinton 2010a) and elsewhere has elaborated this view, emphasizing that US leadership will rely on partnerships based on principles of shared responsibility.

Reforming the global institutions

While there is consensus on the need to reform the international institutions, there is no consensus on what to do. The WTO and IMF are seen as flawed in their mandates and operation. The WTO's single-undertaking approach to multilateral negotiations makes the rounds increasingly difficult to manage with such a large and diverse membership. The Asian economies' trust in the IMF as manager of balance-of-payments crises was shredded during the Asian financial crisis and countries have since moved to self-insure by building their foreign-exchange reserves. Views on what to do include improving the status quo, creating new centralized institutions suggestive of global government and decentralizing the existing institutions.

A number of transformations in the world economy are putting pressures on the existing institutions. The nation state is the central player but diverse interests and players (corporations, individuals, civil society and social organizations, criminal networks and terrorists, and cross-border coalitions) are now interconnected by information technologies, and project voices they expect to be heard. At the same time the sources of rivalry and instability are changing. Armed conflicts of the nineteenth century over military rivalries and territorial ambitions have been replaced by globalization, by aspirations to higher living standards, pressures on the global commons, migration pressures and concerns such as market access, treatment of foreign investors, access to technology and industrial espionage.

The traditional top-down approach is declining in effectiveness and legitimacy in this more diverse world of changing threats. The Bretton Woods institutions are being pressed towards universal membership and consensus decision-making, similar to the United Nations (UN), to increase their legitimacy. But the fallouts of consensus decision-making are reduced ability to undertake internal reforms, let alone take effective and timely action.

As well, global leadership is in flux. American leaders' commitments to continued global and regional leadership notwithstanding, the USA must become a 'frugal' superpower as it tackles its huge, long-term fiscal imbalance. On climate change, the most important collective issue of our time, it is 'missing in action', as its response is driven more by domestic than global interests. With no other power moving to fill the leadership vacuum other nations must grapple with a power 'disequilibrium': the need for strong leadership to deal with rising pressures on the global commons is widely recognized but there is no single dominant state willing or able to deliver. As Secretary Clinton argues, partnerships, networks and mini-lateral agreements are parts of the way forward. The US role in the outcome will be crucial, but not decisive.

There have been calls for reform of the global financial institutions in the wake of the global financial crisis. The UN Commission of Experts on Reforms of the Monetary and Financial System (UN 2009) proposed new organizations based on the universal membership of the UN. French President Sarkozy advocated more centralized financial regulatory institutions. But most governments, in the belief that good regulation begins at the national level by strengthening the prudential oversight of financial institutions to ensure their safety and soundness, are unwilling to cede sovereignty to a global super-regulator. The size and reach of global regulators cannot make up for the local knowledge and judgement of national regulators who must be very knowledgeable about the institutions they oversee.

The other reform option is to decentralize the institutions, either by making them into global hubs for more decentralized networks of member countries with common interests, or by creating regional sub-entities.

Robert Lawrence argues that a more decentralized WTO would better accommodate the diverse membership, better achieve the central mission of deeper economic integration and alleviate its growing institutional problems (Lawrence 2006). His club-of-clubs proposal sees the entire membership involved in rule making but members would not have to join agreements that groups of members with similar interests might negotiate. All members would still use the dispute settlement mechanism, but any penalties would apply only to the 'club' agreement that was violated. Eichengreen (2009) suggests a 'World Financial Organization' analogous to the WTO, but with a decentralized structure with obligatory membership by countries whose financial institutions wish to engage in cross-border activities. The organization would set standards and rules for supervision and regulation, with each member having room to tailor regulation to the structure of their financial markets. An independent body of experts analogous to WTO dispute-settlement panels would monitor whether countries have met their obligations and impose penalties for poor performance.

Kawai and Petri (2010) argue that while provision of the public goods supplied by the WTO, IMF, World Bank and Financial Stability Board would still be global, these institutions would coordinate the supply of related services by regional institutions in those countries in the region that are the decision-makers. This innovation implies the principle of subsidiarity, by which activities are carried out at the level at which they are most effectively produced, but accountability is to the global rules. It also supports the concept of competitive supply and evolving membership in arrangements according to common interests.

Little movement is discernible in either direction, although in regional finance the multilateralized Chiang Mai Initiative (CMIM) is a step towards an Asian Monetary Fund, and the European Central Bank has created the European Financial Stabilization Fund to mitigate sovereign debt crises. The central issue is that, while these mechanisms meet the democratic deficit, questions of effectiveness remain. Regional decentralization is particularly interesting in Asia where, as home to three of the world's largest economies who mistrust each other, members have hedged against Chinese domination by retaining US engagement in the region, but where the production of well-defined regional public goods could provide a foundation for cooperation and trust building.

In sum, there is a willingness to accommodate China in the global institutions, and a few ideas for further reform – all of which come from the West. What are the Chinese perspectives on these matters?

Chinese perspectives on the global order and China's role

There is no single 'China Inc.' voice on China's role; rather, many voices in both the security and economic spheres. There are many fewer voices on global governance. One evident cleavage in Chinese debates is between the military, intelligence and security communities and the economic managers and internationalists. The former are increasingly vocal about China's growing clout and favour more assertiveness, particularly at home and in the region. There is also public support for the proposition that the Chinese economy is sufficiently robust, demonstrated by its successful navigation of the global crisis, that China should be more assertive in pursuing its own interests and reversing its history of humiliation in the region. Economic managers and internationalists are much more cautious. Yes, China's size and rise imply that it should take more global responsibility. But it does not yet have the capabilities to do so. It is still a developing nation with major modernization challenges and economic institutions that are still evolving.

In the early years after the founding of the People's Republic in 1949, China was hostile to global institutions and governance. Although a founding member of the UN, the existence of both Beijing and Taipei administrations caused a UN debate lasting until 1971 over who should take the seat. Membership in the scientific, technical and financial organizations followed, including in the World Bank and the IMF. In all these difficult negotiations,

China's self-interest and considerations of sovereignty (particularly with respect to Taiwan's membership) were front and centre (Kent 2007). By 1978, when its economic transformation began, the Chinese leadership recognized that in the age of globalization there was little choice but to integrate into the international economy – and its institutions – in order to modernize itself.

China is a member of the Security Council but its role in the UN reflects its multifaceted view of itself: 'back' as a major power, still-poor but pursuing its own interests, which may include counterbalancing the USA on security issues such as Iran and North Korea.

This focus was not arrived at lightly. From the 1990s, the party leadership studied the benefits and costs of economic globalization before deciding to open up in ways that preserve Chinese autonomy. Joining the WTO in 2001 required China to conform to international rules and norms; accordingly, major changes were made in China's domestic regimes.[2] At the same time, changes were made to manage the perceived risks of greater openness to domestic economic security, national sovereignty and domestic political and cultural values that could weaken national governance. Foreign investors were denied access to the pillar industries (energy, transportation, communications, finance, education and the mass media) and the speed of change in key prices such as the exchange rate was to be gradual and controlled; China would also more actively promote its own cultural values (Yu Keping 2009). Expressing its sovereignty, the government signed more than a thousand bilateral and multilateral treaties between 1998 and 2002, participated in anti-terrorist actions, pushed negotiations along with North Korea, founded the Shanghai Cooperation Organization and proposed the strategy of harmonious development (Yu Keping 2009).

Chinese scholars also describe China as a regional power with limited global interests; one that will take on a greater cooperative profile in East Asia. There is an explicit acceptance in China of a central precept of East Asian development – that regional political stability has made it possible to focus exclusively on economic development. Wealth, not bullets, is the route to power and influence. As a growing regional economic power it will exert its political influence there and open its markets to serve as the regional locomotive by making opportunities for its neighbours (Zhang and Tang 2005).

In 2006 President Hu Jintao set forth China's principles for scientific development in a 'harmonious world' (*hexie shijie*) that include independence, self-reliance and peaceful coexistence in which differences are respected and security is based on mutual trust, benefits, equality and cooperation. These principles were proposed as an alternative vision of global governance and imply several criticisms of Western principles (Wang and Rosenau 2009):

- The status quo order is 'undemocratic'; the democratic deficit in international institutions, dominated by Western nations and serving their own interests (and tolerating US unilateralism) should be reduced.
- North–South economic disparities are growing; wealthy advanced nations practise double standards in which they expect, from developing

nations, concessions that are not reciprocated. These disparities should be reduced through 'shared development and common prosperity'.
- Countries have differing histories and cultures and therefore differing political systems and economic models. The international system should observe diversity and tolerance and countries should not interfere in each other's affairs but seek 'reconciliation amid differences'.
- Cross-border crises and conflicts should be resolved through cooperation rather than the use of force.

The subtext of these principles is that the USA should become a normal country, abide by international law itself, be more 'democratic' in treating China as an equal and, along with other large Western economies, open its markets more to developing countries and rely more on the UN system in multilateral diplomacy. There is much in common with Western reliance on international rules and understandings and respect for universal values of justice, fairness and mutual assistance. Yet China's own perspective persists of itself as a developing country, lacking in the capabilities to lead in the world order (some call this a 'small country mentality'), which frustrates expectations that, as a major power, it will observe, even enforce, global rules and norms and modify national policies in recognition of interdependence.

GLOBAL ECONOMIC GOVERNANCE AND CHINA'S ROLE

The 2008–09 financial crisis highlighted this interdependence. When demand dried up in the OECD countries as households and businesses repaired their balance sheets, the effects of the recessions cascaded through global supply chains to the export-led Asian economies. Asia's financial institutions, having reformed since the 1997–98 crises, escaped the worst of the financial crisis but Asian producers suffered heavily from the disappearance of final demand in US, European and Japanese markets.

The severity and global spread of the crisis opened a window for a long overdue and pragmatic overhaul of global summitry. A meeting of G7 leaders in the depths of the crisis in November 2008 would have been irrelevant – and unthinkable. With G20 finance ministers and central bank governors having formed a G20 forum after the Asian crisis, elevating G20 meetings to the leaders' level was an obvious choice, and one supported by China. Significantly it was leaders who managed the crisis, using the international institutions to implement their decisions. At the Pittsburgh summit in 2009, leaders formalized their agenda around a macro-economic framework for balanced and inclusive growth, financial regulatory reforms, resuscitating the global trade negotiations and extending inclusive growth to smaller developing countries.

At their initial meetings, G20 leaders tasked the IMF with providing appropriate liquidity to requesting countries and reforming its governance to better reflect the changing shape of the global economy; the WTO was contracted to conclude the Doha Round, while the World Bank was tasked with addressing poverty in developing countries. The Financial Stability Forum's membership was expanded and upgraded to a Board.

THE G20

With the G20 largely being created to include China as an equal partner, what has been China's role? As one of the world's largest trading nations and the largest creditor it has been in the hot seat over its managed exchange rate and foreign-exchange reserves accumulation far beyond prudent levels to cover import requirements (Figure 11.1; Table 11.1). Since 2008, China's role has been constructive. It has advanced a proposal for the Special Drawing Right (SDR) to become the world's super-sovereign reserve currency, a reform that would serve its own as well as the global interest. Exchange-rate policy, which re-pegged the currency to the US dollar in the depths of the 2008 crisis, moved modestly in 2010 towards greater nominal flexibility in the face of intense external pressure that continued through to the November summit in Seoul.[3] China's response to the pressure was, in effect, 'no, now would not be in our interests'. But China remained engaged in the rebalancing issue, participating in the 'enhanced' Mutual Assessment Process to promote external sustainability, a process with a collective goal but which gives discretion to each government in how it contributes to that goal.

At the Toronto summit, President Hu Jintao outlined his views of G20 priorities in words that imply support for the existing global institutions and a desire to see them work better:

- a 'guiding role in shifting international economic cooperation towards … long-term perspective … from coordinating stimulus measures … to promoting long-term governance and from passive response to proactive planning.'
- '… accelerate(s) the establishment of a new international financial order that is fair, equitable, inclusive and well-managed….' and '… that is good for the growth of the real economy'; and
- Builds '… an open and free global trading regime … reject all forms of protectionism and unequivocally advocate and support free trade.' (*Xinhua* 2010a)

China has also pursued its main interest in gaining greater voice in the international institutions by joining dialogues organized by other large economies – Russia and Brazil – that called for 'democratic and balanced global governance' giving developing countries an active voice in defining their own futures; dialogues that trumped any regional initiatives.[4]

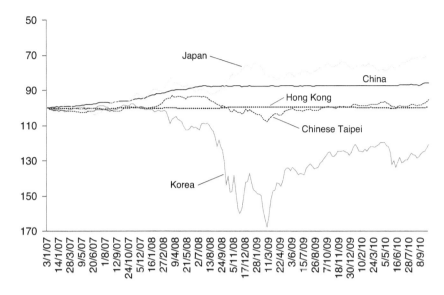

Figure 11.1 Currency movements, US dollar to local currency (base = January 2007). Source: PECC (2010).

Table 11.1 Foreign-exchange reserves (US$ billion), minus gold, various countries

	May 2010	*Percentage of nominal GDP*	*Months of imports*
Australia	33.21	3.3	2.1
China	2,456.19	49.3	28.6
Hong Kong	256.10	121.6	8.3
Indonesia	71.75	13.3	8.1
Japan	1,011.61	20.0	18.8
Korea	270.14	32.4	8.5
Malaysia	94.11	48.8	7.7
Singapore	198.36	108.8	8.6
Thailand	140.22	53.1	11.1
United States	113.13	0.8	0.7

Source: IMF.

THE WTO, TRADE AND INVESTMENT LIBERALIZATION AND DISPUTE SETTLEMENT

While the G20 was founded to include it as an equal player, China had to work long and hard to join the WTO in 2001. It had to accept designation as a non-market economy in anti-dumping and safeguard cases, and agree to annual compliance reviews. Yet China has been a huge beneficiary of the rule-based international trading regime. Almost 80 per cent of industrial production now originates in non-state firms; trade accounts for nearly 40 per cent of GDP; it is the world's largest merchandise exporter, a major importer, the leading emerging market destination for foreign direct investment (FDI) and an increasingly important source of outward FDI. It is an active participant in the WTO dispute-settlement mechanism, where it is complainant in seven cases, respondent in 18 cases and participant as third party in 69.[5]

The role of the WTO in China's emergence as an economic titan is indisputable, yet China is a relatively passive player in WTO governance. The Doha Development Round has languished far beyond its targeted 2005 completion date because its centrepiece is difficult issues left over from previous rounds while new concerns like green protectionism, rising commodity prices and financial instability have marginalized its agenda. The single undertaking adds to the difficulties of concluding an agreement among the large and diverse membership. Business interest in the round is difficult to find. Powerful farm lobbies in the USA and India played roles in the breakdown in July 2008. Instead of using its superstar status to push back at such foot dragging and its potential impact on the Doha Round and the institution, China sided with India's demands, based on its own interest groups.

At the outset of the Doha Round, China argued that it had 'already given' in the accession talks; this was a reasonable position at the time but now a decade has passed. As a major beneficiary of the regime it is reasonable to expect China to provide a new offer such as its 2010 proposal to join the government procurement agreement, 9 years after it promised to do so.

Instead China has focused on regional trade agreements (RTAs). Most of China's regional trade is in goods, and much of the liberalization is tariff reductions; difficult non-tariff barriers receive less attention, yet they matter to services trade.[6] Studies also show that sub-regional agreements produce outcomes that are inferior to region-wide RTAs or to agreements among the large countries (Park and Cheong 2008). Quantitative studies have shown that the liberalizing gains increase with the size of the agreement (Kawai and Wignaraja 2009).

With the exception of its bilateral free-trade agreement (FTA) with New Zealand, China's RTAs reveal more of an interest in foreign policy objectives than economic liberalization (Table 11.2). The China–ASEAN agreement (CAFTA) was a friendly initiative aimed at increasing bilateral market access with East Asia's 'core' economies. It took effect on 1 January 2010 and covers an estimated US$4.5 trillion in trade volume, with 90 per cent of goods to be traded tariff-free. Problems lie ahead, however. Usually the gains from trade are realized through specialization, differentiation and increases in intra-industry trade. But the structure of China's two-way trade, particularly with Indonesia and the Philippines, is very similar, and therefore competitive rather than complementary. In contrast, these countries gain through complementary trade with Japan, South Korea and the USA.

Table 11.2 China's bilateral trade agreements

Implemented	Under negotiation	Feasibility study
China–ASEAN	China–Australia	China–India
China–Chile	China–Gulf Cooperation Council (GCC)	China–Japan–Korea
China–Costa Rica	China–Iceland	China–Korea
CEPA–Hong Kong	China–Norway	China–Switzerland
China–New Zealand		
China–Pakistan		
China–Peru		
China–Singapore		

Sources: China Ministry of Commerce; Schott (2010).

The plethora of regional and trans-Pacific agreements on the drawing boards was acknowledged by APEC leaders in their 2010 Yokohama summit communiqué. They committed to 'take concrete steps toward FTAAP' which should be 'pursued as a comprehensive free trade agreement …' APEC will act as an 'incubator of FTAAP' and play a 'critical role in defining, shaping and addressing the next generation trade and investment issues FTAAP should contain' (APEC 2010). Proposals for ASEAN plus 3 and 6 agreements were already on the table and the USA (with Australia, Malaysia, Peru and Vietnam) is now negotiating to join the Trans-Pacific Partnership (TPP), a comprehensive high-quality FTA spearheaded by New Zealand, Chile, Singapore and Brunei Darussalam and open to any country wishing to join. The resulting nine-country negotiation figured prominently in the lead up to the US-hosted APEC leaders' meeting in 2011 in Honolulu when President Obama committed to complete the negotiation. This negotiation is also envisaged to create a baseline in its standards and comprehensiveness with which other applicants will be expected to comply. The ultimate benefits of the TPP will depend on other large Asian economies joining (USTR 2009) and it remains unclear how the TPP or the other proposals for a regional FTA will play out.

China is thus a major beneficiary of the open world trading regime but is doing little to maintain the system. It could re-energize the Doha Round by joining the government procurement agreement, engaging in sectoral liberalization agreements and pushing the services liberalization talks (services now account for 40 per cent of GDP). In return, the USA and the advanced economies should respond to China's desire to be recognized as a market economy and end the humiliating annual compliance reviews (Hufbauer and Lawrence 2010). Within the region, China also faces contradictions between its economic size and dynamism and its domestic preoccupations. Developing countries feel the competitive pressures of its managed currency; it is a foot dragger on region-wide liberalization, which all studies show provides the largest overall benefits. This issue is made more complex because the smaller economies benefit from access to the US market and see its presence as a hedge against Chinese dominance.

INVESTMENT LIBERALIZATION

Compared with the trade regime, China is asserting its interests more strongly with respect to direct investment and the treatment of foreign nationals in China, raising questions about whether domestic interests will trump international rules. In the absence of an international investment regime, countries negotiate their own agreements for non-discriminatory treatment of foreign investors and the treatment of foreign citizens. China's policies have explicitly encouraged FDI inflows since the special economic zones were set up in the 1980s. China pre-committed in the WTO accession talks to open its service industries, particularly financial services, to foreign entrants after a designated phase-in period. Since the 'Going Out' strategy was introduced, large enterprises and the main sovereign wealth fund, the China Investment Corporation, have become active international investors both as acquirers of real and financial assets and investors in greenfield projects. The shock of the global crisis, which saw many foreign investors lay off millions of Chinese workers or even abandon their investments, strengthened the Party's resolve to reduce reliance on foreign technology and diversify sources of commodity supply. The 2015 science and technology strategy encourages innovation and patenting and imposes new requirements on foreign multinationals, weakens protection of intellectual property and relies on discriminatory government procurement policies, all of which have fanned fears of a new nationalism in Chinese policies.

The conviction and imprisonment of two foreign nationals, one Australian and the other American, on charges of bribery (the first case) and violating laws on state secrets (in both cases), have raised questions about the interrelationships among business, politics and the Chinese legal system. In both cases, foreign governments have argued that the lack of transparency in the legal process violated China's own bilateral consular agreements and laws about consular rights (Cohen 2010). China's frustration with the international iron-ore cartel helps to explain the first case, because the cartel has shown little price flexibility in recent negotiations with China, its largest customer. Two other factors are also at issue: frustration with the lack of success of the Chinese Aluminum Company (Chinalco) in acquiring certain assets of Rio Tinto, an Australian cartel member, and frustration with alleged activities in China by Rio Tinto employees, the latter undermining the authorities' attempts to consolidate the fragmented steel industry's position in the negotiations. Chinese actions were a pointed warning.

What does this new assertiveness imply about China's observation of global rules? In the natural resources industries, China's behaviour needs to be viewed in the wider context of its interests in, on the one hand, attracting foreign know-how through FDI and, on the other, extending national champions' business strategies abroad – and how these firms are treated abroad. Given China's state-led business model, are Chinese state-owned enterprises driven by strategic rather than market factors in their decision-making?

The evidence is mixed. Resource-seeking FDI is one of the least-sophisticated forms of FDI; resource companies invest upstream in exploration activities to expand available supplies, or they make acquisitions to access existing sources of supply for their own uses. A recent study of 16 cases of the outward FDI in natural resources industries concludes that less than 20 per cent of the FDI cases (in Angola, Nigeria and Russia) were intended to tie up sources of supply for Chinese use (Moran 2010). Another study (Steinfeld 2010), of the 2005 China National Offshore Oil Corporation (CNOOC) bid for Unocal, asserts that CNOOC's main objective was commercial; the negotiations were carried out along commercial lines and the involvement of bureaucrats was minimal. China did not even have an energy ministry at the time. The fragmented bureaucratic structure does not suggest China Inc. Rather, company behaviour suggests intense competition within a domestic oligopoly; one that is struggling to master the international regulations of the mergers and acquisitions game whose rules are set by international stock exchanges.

But the record in the telecommunications industry is less clear. China's national innovation strategy provides fiscal and other incentives for high-tech products, encourages a patenting drive, requires foreign suppliers of information-technology security products to reveal source codes and other proprietary information, and uses government procurement to favour Chinese products. Despite charges that such policies are mercantilist and encourage technology theft, the impacts on indigenous innovation are mixed: the authorities have backtracked on some measures and have actually improved their offer to the WTO's government procurement agreement. Foreign producers have gained from new spending on the shift to third-generation mobile technology while losing market share in wind power and second-generation telecoms equipment (Kennedy 2010).

This evidence suggests a lack of coordination *within* Beijing among economic policy-makers, industry ministries and other political interests. Such a lack of coordination has unintended consequences. First, missteps and misjudgements at home required the government to backtrack on some aspects of the techno-nationalist innovation strategy and to improve its WTO offer on government procurement. Second, it encourages suspicion abroad, with other states moving to block Chinese producers. For example, Huawei, now a leading global telecom equipment supplier, faces suspicions that Chinese-made equipment will be used to compromise national security. Such suspicions have prompted authorities to block both trade and FDI in some countries. The Indian Government temporarily blocked imports of Chinese equipment, causing procurement problems for its rapidly expanding mobile phone network. Huawei resolved the issue by agreeing to demands to deposit source code in escrow. US politicians have also claimed that Huawei is a company under the direction of the Chinese military and should be blocked from entering the supply chains for the US military, law enforcement and the private sector.[7]

INTERNATIONAL MONETARY COOPERATION, EXCHANGE-RATE REGIMES AND THE IMF

China's role in the international monetary system is clearly internationalist; so far it has worked within the system to advance its interest in a voice consistent with its economic size. Conceived by Bretton Woods architects as the next best thing to a world central bank, the IMF mandate was initially based on a system of fixed exchange rates, which collapsed when major reserve currency countries were unwilling to change policies to maintain exchange-rate equilibrium. Fixed and flexible exchange-rate regimes proliferated and the IMF's role evolved to promote international monetary cooperation necessary to maintain orderly exchange-rate arrangements and expand world trade. It conducts regular surveillance of members' macro-economic policies and provides technical support and short-term liquidity to members with balance-of-payments difficulties. Yet, when official capital flows were overtaken by private flows by the mid 1990s, the IMF's resources shrank in relative terms and the nature of its borrowers changed. The advanced countries continued to dominate its decision-making and determination of conditions on borrowers (who were, increasingly, smaller developing countries with little say in how the Fund was run).[8]

These issues came to a head during the 1997–98 Asian financial crisis when, rightly or wrongly, the IMF was perceived to have deepened the crisis by treating Asian borrowers with liquidity problems as if they were insolvent with structural problems (Ito 2007). Resentful borrowers repaid their loans early and began self-insuring by accumulating foreign reserves larger than those needed to cover imports and short-term liabilities.

By the time of the 2008–09 crisis, the IMF's reduced resources and credibility problems were such that it was not a significant player. Its resources, at around US$250 billion, paled in comparison to Asia's central banks, whose foreign-exchange reserves totalled nearly US$5 trillion in 2010 (Table 11.1) and sovereign wealth funds that managed more than US$2 trillion in 2006 (Truman 2007). Central banks, led by the US Federal Reserve Board, were also active in bilateral swap arrangements to address short-term liquidity problems.

G20 leaders resuscitated the Fund by restoring its resources to US$1 trillion and encouraging it to set up new facilities to help countries solve credit problems.[9] The IMF streamlined its lending framework and conditionality, providing adjustment support through short-term lending facilities by which countries qualifying on an ex ante basis can access loans immediately, as well as other credit lines on precautionary bases without conditions.[10]

IMF governance reform agreed at the Seoul G20 summit in November 2010 will make China the third-largest shareholder. How will China use this increased clout? As it assumes more power in governance, will it support enhanced IMF staff objectivity in surveillance of members' economic performance? Will the USA and China be willing to move discussions of their macroeconomic interdependence into the IMF? Or will China favour a regional institution, possibly with different rules, where it has even more clout?

China has both dragged its feet and proposed reform. The slow adjustment of its nominal exchange rate (Figure 11.1) has drawn strong US criticism with some arguing that 'rejection of a flexible exchange rate' is a direct challenge to the international monetary order (Bergsten *et al.* 2008: 17). China was also one of the last (along with the USA) to agree to an IMF evaluation of its financial system through the Financial Sector Assessment Program. In contrast, China actively pursued governance reforms to raise its voting strength and adopt the SDR as a super-sovereign reserve currency to provide an alternative way to reallocate its foreign-exchange reserves. Central bank governor Zhou Xiaochuan (2009) argued that current arrangements relying on a single national currency are flawed, because of the potential for conflicts between domestic goals and international responsibilities. As the dollar-based system has become more volatile, developing and emerging market economies have diverted foreign-exchange reserves from more productive uses to self-insure. Using the SDR in this way would allow large holders of US government securities to diversify their holdings within the IMF, thereby avoiding exchange market volatility (Bergsten 2009). But the proposal has gained little traction because of the entrenched position and convenience of use of the US dollar for both market participants and governments.

Regionally, China has been active in multilateralizing the Chiang Mai Initiative (CMIM), the regional emergency financing mechanism set up in 2000 as bilateral currency swap agreements among the members of ASEAN+3. The 1997–98 crisis crystallized awareness that much of East Asia's high savings were intermediated in the world's financial centres rather than in the region. Initiatives to deal with this include regional bond markets for local currency issues, and pooling foreign-exchange reserves by central banks to increase liquidity. In 2010, the CMI swaps, which then totalled US$120 billion, with 80 per cent contributed by China, Japan and South Korea, were pooled into the CMIM common fund, supported by governance and voting structures to make it accountable to its members. Like the IMF, CMIM will provide short-term emergency financing to its members. An important aspect of its structure is the surveillance unit whose first director is a Chinese national appointed in 2011. Whether its methodology will be consistent with that of the IMF remains to be seen. If it is, governments will share information about their economic policies and performance with the surveillance unit and agree to an early-warning system to prevent future crises.

Within China, changes that are in progress for domestic reasons will bring about some alignment with the global rebalancing objective. China's investment-driven, export-led growth is unsustainable. The economy needs to rebalance towards greater reliance on domestic demand. The heavy emphasis on investment is supported by underpriced inputs for energy, land, capital and the environment (Kuijs 2009; Huang and Wang 2010). Capital is priced by the central bank, which manages interest rates to support exchange-rate stability for exporters and provides the government-owned banking system with generous and riskless spreads (Dobson and Kashyap 2006; Dobson 2009a; Prasad 2009). At the same time, the 'disinterested authoritarian capitalism' that has delivered China's material prosperity has entrenched interest groups that could block reforms to transfer wealth, undermine the impartiality and block reforms to respond to popular demands for greater political pluralism (Yao 2010).

The 12th Five Year Plan proposed in October 2010 signalled the Party's collective awareness of the need to restructure the economy. Changes in domestic policy are expected to increase imports and the weight of consumption relative to investment and exports in total GDP. This will be done through policies to boost employment and household incomes through higher wages, more labour mobility, higher public spending on rural infrastructure, health, education and pensions, better access to market finance for employment-creating SMEs and deregulation of service sectors currently dominated by large state monopolies.

There is recognition that such key prices as the exchange rate and interest rates cannot be managed indefinitely and that more flexibility is required. The central bank characterizes abandoning the US dollar peg as a continuation of the managed exchange-rate regime adopted in 1994 (Hu 2010). A more flexible exchange rate (assuming it would appreciate) would facilitate domestic economic rebalancing. Rebalancing is also necessary to ensure the safety of China's accumulated reserves, which will lose value as the US dollar depreciates or if US inflation picks up and US bond prices decline (Yu Yongding 2009). In real terms, the exchange rate has strengthened against the US dollar by almost 50 per cent since 2005 (*The Economist* 2010a) as Chinese prices have risen much faster than those in North America. Change in the nominal rate, however, will be gradual and controlled, according to China's needs. Gradual internationalization of the yuan by liberalizing instruments available through Hong Kong, swap agreements with other central banks, increased foreign access to the interbank bond market, and greater use of the yuan in trade finance will facilitate more renminbi (RMB)-based international transactions. Eventually the RMB could become an international reserve currency. For this to happen, however, the capital account must be fully convertible, which will open China to global capital flows from which it is now protected, and loosen control over monetary policy (Dobson and Masson 2009).

In summary, China is not only engaged in IMF governance but also has proposed a fundamental reform. It has said 'no' to outside pressures for exchange-rate appreciation but has participated in the G20's enhanced surveillance process, which relies on IMF analysis. There are two tests of China's recognition of the external impacts of its domestic policy choices: one is its willingness to be transparent in the regional surveillance within the CMIM where it is a major shareholder; the other is political – will the Twelfth Plan focus on structural reforms survive the onslaught of vested interests? Greater exchange-rate flexibility would facilitate the structural shift towards consumption. A market-determined exchange rate is also essential to the development of the deep and liquid market-based financial system and the more efficient use of capital that are necessary if China is to become an economic power with international influence commensurate with its modern and complex economy.

DEVELOPMENT FINANCE AND THE WORLD BANK

The World Bank and the regional multilateral development banks provide development finance through loans, grants and technical assistance to developing countries, to promote poverty reduction and economic development. The network of banks is more decentralized than the IMF system and the regional banks are largely run by countries in the regions. The World Bank is governed by its shareholders but developing countries criticize it for reflecting the development priorities imposed by the advanced countries rather than those of the developing countries themselves. Since 1980, China's relationship with the World Bank has been harmonious. China continues to borrow for projects ranging from energy efficiency and environmental protection to urban and rural development. In 2007, China became a net contributor to the World Bank's International Development Assistance mechanism and, in 2010, its third-largest shareholder. A Chinese national is the World Bank's chief economist.

FINANCIAL MARKET OVERSIGHT AND STABILITY

The global financial crisis highlighted the paradox between the national scope of financial supervision and the global reach of capital markets and institutions. While strong and modern national financial systems are essential to stable markets, national regulators cannot prevent cross-border financial crises by acting on their own. They must coordinate and communicate among themselves. The Financial Stability Forum set up by G7 governments to facilitate such cooperation after the Asian crisis was based at the Bank for International Settlements and closely related to the Basel Committee. But the institution lacked legitimacy and relied on voluntary implementation of its guidelines and recommendations. G20 leaders expanded its membership and changed its name to the Financial Stability Board (FSB), charging it to work closely with the IMF in implementing its recommendations and guidelines through the Fund's surveillance and its Financial Sector Assessment Program (FSAP), which focuses on national financial systems and their prudential supervision.

China has been relatively passive in the financial supervisory debates and inactive in the region, although a group of East Asian economists has recommended intensified supervision of financial institutions engaging in cross-border business and an Asian Financial Stability Dialogue to deepen regional financial integration (ADBI 2009). It has yet to gain any traction, however.

CLIMATE CHANGE

In 2009, China surpassed the United States to become the world's largest absolute emitter of greenhouse gases while ranking far down the list in per-capita terms (Box 11.1). China is a charter member of the UN Framework Convention on Climate Change and participated in the December 2009 Copenhagen talks that ended with a last minute non-binding accord. It sees itself as part of the developing world in the divisions over negotiating the measurement and verification of emissions reductions; it is an advocate of the rich countries funding clean energy technology in developing countries and the Clean Development Mechanism and the establishment of offset markets.

Yet, pushed by domestic pressures, China is in important ways becoming a climate change poster child. It has unilaterally committed to a 40–45 per cent reduction in energy intensity by 2020. The Twelfth Plan contains obligatory targets to increase renewable energy supplies to 15 per cent of the primary energy mix. Industrial policies will encourage green production (such as hybrid and electric autos) and, on the supply side, there are reports of an investment package of much as US$740 billion in an energy development plan over the next decade.

China claims and receives little credit for such initiatives. It also hesitates to lead, because of its commitment to the developing-country coalition. Its detractors decry the reliance on industrial policies and criticize its profile among developing countries as detracting from a global regime. Yet, in many ways China's behaviour is reminiscent of the sometimes eccentric views of French leaders that push a 'French' perspective and position on international issues. In China's case such a stance puts the advanced industrial countries on notice that they cannot always expect to have things their way.

ASIAN REGIONALISM

Within the Asian region China's charm offensive saw it play a relatively passive role in regional institutions while competing with Japan, India and the USA outside. It faces determined efforts by the ASEAN 'core' economies to divert this competition into regional cooperation in the nascent regional financial and trade institutions. But progress on the 2015 target for an East Asian community proposed by the 2001 Vision Group is slow; decisions rely on consensus, and activity is focused more on members' interests than on advancing common rules or standards. Trading patterns are lopsided in regional production networks, with China a major importer from its neighbours but competing directly with some of them in final goods markets. The 2004 expansion of ASEAN+3, over China's objections, to include India, Australia and New Zealand to form the East Asian Summit (EAS) cuts two ways in that this and other cooperative institutions serve its objective of developing closer friendly relationships in the neighbourhood but US and Indian inclusion provide a counterbalance.

Good relationships with the neighbourhood allow China to concentrate on its many domestic challenges. When government representatives talk about China's 'peaceful development' they are at pains to elaborate that this means no expansion, no hegemony and no alliances. The message has the implicit subtext that if China gets its domestic development right its influence will automatically expand with its growing economic and political clout. The cooperative networks also help to overcome the ambivalence that many feel about China, summed up by the observations of some Asian neighbours who say, 'Don't call China a threat', while others admonish, 'Don't forget China is a threat'.

China's recent more assertive behaviour on resource and boundary issues has alarmed its neighbours. The tone and behaviour toward regional partners appears to be motivated by growing confidence and a desire to reverse historical humiliation. The territorial dispute with Japan over the Diaoyu/Senkaku Islands suggests the two governments apply different frameworks; China uses historical evidence while Japan takes a more legalistic approach. The clash, characterized as 'shock and awe' and a test of China's peaceful rise doctrine (Funabashi 2010), raised questions whether such disputes can be resolved. What does this mean? Is the long-held conviction weakening that political stability is necessary for wealth and development as stepping stones to power and influence? Are we seeing jostling in the run-up to the 2012 leadership transition? China's next top leaders will be largely from civilian ranks of new entrepreneurs and the communist youth league rather than the People's Liberation Army or the foreign policy establishment. The resulting credibility vacuum on national security may encourage them to appear to be tough-minded; figures in defence and foreign affairs are also moving to fill the vacuum (Page 2010).

What will happen when the leadership transition is complete? Will there be a return to a harmonious equilibrium, or more external tensions? The current uncertainty is potentially counterproductive for China in that its neighbours react by moving closer to the USA for reassurance. While China is driving East Asia's economic integration, and its diplomatic influence is spreading, it is unlikely that China will replace the USA as the region's guarantor of peace and stability. In an October 2010 speech (Clinton 2010b) US Secretary of State Hillary Clinton made clear that the USA is increasing its participation in the region's institutions. Most likely we are seeing a new regional dynamic in which the USA must accommodate a more assertive and powerful China. Whether this will be a positive-sum relationship depends on both governments and will presage their roles in the global institutions.

CONCLUSIONS AND LOOKING TO THE FUTURE

Is China willing to change its policies in recognition of international interdependence? The evaluation in this chapter indicates that the answer varies with the forum:

- 'Yes' in the G20, where President Hu Jintao has played a constructive role. Even on the imbalance issue, whose formulation China does not accept, China has helped shape a broader cooperative process aimed at the collective goal while according flexibility to governments as to their contributions.
- 'No' in the WTO where, despite the benefits of accession and now one of the world's largest trading nations, China has not offered leadership necessary to conclude the Doha Round; nor does it observe WTO principles of non-discrimination toward foreign investors and producers.
- 'Yes' in the IMF where China has pushed on governance issues and participated in the broad goals and approach to imbalances, but said 'No' on exchange-rate adjustment pressures from peers.
- 'Yes' to the World Bank, as a supporter of the regime but increasingly competing for influence through parallel but bilateral aid programmes in developing nations, particularly those with abundant natural resources.
- 'Yes' and 'No' in the United Nations Framework Convention on Climate Change, whereas China has, at home, taken major unilateral initiatives to define energy intensity reduction targets, develop renewable energy sources and push as a first-mover into green technologies and processes. Yet it receives little credit, in part because it has not leveraged these initiatives in the global forum where a vacuum has been created by the inaction of the US Congress. To provide such leadership at the global level, however, is seen as breaking solidarity with the developing-country position in the talks.
- 'Yes' in regional organizations where China has led the expansion of regional FTAs and cooperated in trade and financial forums but is offended by the hedging strategies of its neighbours in both the economic and security forums; recent assertiveness on border issues has also been counterproductive as noted earlier.

In this summary the pattern is 'Yes, but …' Yes, there is little evidence that China undermines or reshapes the global order where its behaviour now has consequences – footdragging in the Doha Round, blocking (along with others) OECD country positions in the climate change talks and aggressively trying to frustrate price setting of key commodities in international markets. It has largely played by the existing rules of multilateralism and its role is largely constructive. In the Asian region China has been receptive to its neighbours' economic initiatives.

But ... there is a significant contradiction between China's continuing ambivalence about assuming a role commensurate with the world's second-largest economy and leveraging its economic strength, as powerful internal interests are pushing to do.

Why the more assertive and shrill behaviour in the past 2 years? What has changed? First, China successfully escaped the global economic crisis; its economy boomed while the largest market economies struggled. The rise of its economic weight in the world is considered by some to coincide with the relative (and long-term) decline of the USA. They see the crisis as proof of the weaknesses of the market-based system and commendation of China's unique mix of state and market institutions (overlooking the fact that the Canadian and Australian economies also avoided the crisis because of strong, deep and liquid market-based financial systems, prudent regulation and flexible exchange rates). Second, there are difficulties in coordinating policies within Beijing itself, particularly industrial policies – a problem familiar to officials in other large economies. Third, China is undergoing a major leadership transition in which competition for influence among multiple factions makes it difficult to take strong and well-defined positions.

Should we conclude that things will go back to 'harmonious development' in 2012 when the leadership issue is settled? The answer is 'No'. A more assertive China is likely to be the new normal, just as it is reasonable to see it develop new capabilities in international bargaining.

What might be the consequences of the new normal for the global economic order?

History matters. China has little historical experience of cooperating with peers. China is accustomed to pursuing its goals independently and is highly sensitive to direct external pressures and to milder forms of surveillance and peer pressure. Even so, examples of China's willingness to modify its own economic policies in recognition of international interdependence include resisting nominal exchange-rate appreciation in the 1997–98 Asian crisis which reaped much goodwill; undertaking the large stimulus package in 2008 which was good for China and good for the world; and helping to connect the poorer ASEAN economies with large infrastructure and other investments in region. In each example there is a clear congruence of domestic and collective interests. The test of China's willingness to engage in closer economic cooperation with its regional neighbours will come in the next few years as the ASEAN+3 Macroeconomic Research Office (AMRO) develops its surveillance role in CMIM.

Chinese economists argue that China still lacks the capabilities to take more responsibility for the system from which it has drawn such benefit. China is uncomfortable with multilateralism and prefers bilateral diplomacy or small groups, where it is quite active. Thus, one possible outcome of the new confidence may be less attachment to the multilateral institutions. Will they be seen as having served their purpose in providing frameworks useful to China's growth and modernization but of limited relevance to a booming state-led Chinese economy?

There are several risks in such a scenario. One is that China might over-play its hand. This is not the first time the USA has been in apparent decline before rebounding because of its economic flexibility and political resilience. This time may be different but it is too soon to count out the USA. At the same time, China should not underestimate its domestic economic chal-lenges. Continued reliance on the Plan could be its Achilles heel. So far, the outlines of the Twelfth Plan seem to rely heavily on the proven interven-tionist capabilities of the Chinese state to bring about structural change, rather than on market forces. Will intervention work in encouraging people to consume more? The answer is far from clear. Further, China's goals for international financial influence and economic power will depend on open-ing the capital account and greater exchange-rate flexibility. Before either can happen, China needs a modern financial sector and an independent central bank, neither of which seems to be in the cards. Still, for different reasons China, too, could surprise us.

These questions spill over to the second risk – for the global economic order. Politics matter, too. It has been argued that the recipe for a peaceful transition in the global power structure is for the incumbent to accommo-date the newcomer and for the newcomer to adhere to the existing rules. Mutual trust is necessary for this proposition to be realized. The Chinese fear that a declining USA will block China's rise. US interests mistrust China's intentions. Will a more confident China change the rules by push-ing its state-led economic model in the global institutions? Will it tip the balance towards more government intervention in price setting and owner-ship? Will it put more emphasis on relationships than on transparency? Yet, each country has a strong common interest in globalization, open markets and a stable political world. The suspicions on both sides must be dealt with through communication, confidence building and cooperation. One menu includes greater openness in the bilateral security relationship, less competition and more cooperation in maintaining Asian security, greater collaboration on human security in the region and greater emphasis on people-to-people contacts (*The Economist* 2010b). If this mutual mistrust is not removed there is the danger a deep antagonism will develop. It would help if the USA were to allow itself to be constrained by observing the glo-bal rules in order to constrain China.

In conclusion, it should be no surprise that the spectacular speed and magnitude of China's rise disturbs the global status quo in unexpected ways and creates external expectations of China that it is not yet prepared for or has the capacity to satisfy. Nevertheless, a more assertive China creates a new, more complicated, normal that replaces the relative simplicity of America's 'unipolar moment'. The established global framework has much to commend it to China's leaders but their adherence or contributions to strengthen the global order will for the foreseeable future depend heavily on US behaviour and, more importantly, on US investment in confidence-building that is essential to a stable long-term relationship with an ancient civilization that has returned to global pre-eminence.

NOTES

1 Co-Director, Institute for International Business, Rotman School of Management, University of Toronto, Canada (Dobson@rotman.utoronto.ca). This chapter has benefited from valuable comments by my discussants Peter Petri and Zhang Yuyan, PAFTAD conference participants, and Joseph Caron and Peter Harder. The responsibility for the final version is, of course, mine alone.

2 To join the WTO 30 central ministries and departments were directed in 2002 to change 2,300 laws and regulations (eliminating many of them) and 100,000 local laws a,nd regulations at the provincial and autonomous region levels (Yu Keping 2009).

3 While accelerating the pace of nominal appreciation just before the summit.

4 China participated in BRIC meetings and the BASIC talks consisting of Brazil, South Africa, India, China, and in dialogues including India, Brazil, South Africa and Mexico (*Xinhua* 2010b).

5 Details can be found at http://www.wto.org/english/tratop_e/dispu_e/dispu_by_country_e.htm accessed July 16 2010.

6 More than half of Asia's merchandise exports are now shipped within the region. But it remains heavily dependent on external markets for final demand. Analysis of Asia's intraregional exports in 2006 shows that, while 48.2 per cent of Asia's exports were shipped to Europe and North America, when parts and components were taken into account the share rose to 67.5 per cent (ADB 2008).

7 Since 2008 three Huawei bids have failed (for 2Wire, a Motorola unit and 3Com) due to fears the bids would not secure regulatory approval. A supply contract with Sprint Nextel is also being challenged. Huawei is now trying a route used in the past by the Japanese: divert FDI to Canada and invest in research and development in Canadian telecoms to create acceptable bona fides in the US market (Sturgeon 2010).

8 Even so, small countries have repeatedly indicated they find Fund surveillance and advice helpful even though large countries have tended to ignore it.

9 In April 2009, leaders authorized a one-time SDR allocation of US$250 billion and US$500 billion in new borrowing from Fund shareholders under the New Arrangements to Borrow (NAB). Japan and the European Union each agreed to lend US$100 billion and China indicated its willingness to provide US$40 billion in other ways.

10 Including the short-term liquidity facility, or SLF, and the flexible credit line facility, or FCL, and the Precautionary Credit Line, or PCL.

REFERENCES

ADB (Asian Development Bank) (2008) *Emerging Asian Regionalism*, Manila: ADB.

ADBI (Asian Development Bank Institute) (2009) 'Recommendations of policy responses to the global financial and economic crisis for East Asian leaders', available at <http://www.adbi.org/key-docs/2009/.policy.global.financial.crisis.east.asian.leaders/>.

APEC (Asia Pacific Economic Cooperation) (2010) 'APEC Leaders' Declaration (The Yokohama Declaration)', Yokohama, Japan, 14 November, available at <http://www.apec.org/Meeting-Papers/Leaders-Declarations/2010/2010_aelm.aspx>.

Bardhan, Pranab (2005) 'China, India superpower? Not so fast!', *YaleGlobal Online*, 25 October, at <yaleglobal.yale.edu>.

Bergsten, C.F. (2009) 'We should listen to Beijing's currency idea', *Financial Times*, 9 April.

Bergsten, C.F., C. Freeman, N.R. Lardy and D.J. Mitchell (2008) *China's Rise: Challenges and Opportunities,* Washington, DC: Peterson Institute for International Economics and Center for Strategic and International Studies.

Clinton, Hillary Rodham (2010a) 'Remarks on United States foreign policy', speech at the Council on Foreign Relations, Washington, DC, 8 September.

—— (2010b) 'America's engagement in Asia–Pacific', speech at Kahala Hotel, Honolulu, HI, 28 October.

Cohen, Jerome A (2010) 'How China handles "State secrets" prosecutions: Xue Feng's Case', *South China Morning Post,* 21 July.

Corbett, Jenny and Takatoshi Ito (2010) 'What China should learn from Japan', *Vox–EU,* 30 April.

Dobson, Wendy (1991) *Economic Policy Coordination: Requiem or Prologue?,* Washington, DC: Institute for International Economics.

—— (2009) *Gravity Shift: How Asia's New Economic Powerhouses Will Shape the 21st Century,* Toronto: Rotman – University of Toronto Press.

Dobson, Wendy and Anil Kashyap (2006) 'The contradictions in China's gradualist banking reforms', *Brookings Papers on Economic Activity*, No. 2, Washington, DC: Brookings Institution.

Dobson, Wendy and Paul Masson (2009) 'Will the renminbi become a world currency?', *China Economic Review,* 20(1): 124–135.

Economist, The (2010a) 'Nominally cheap or really dear?', 6 November.

—— (2010b) 'Friend or foe? A special report on China's place in the world', 4 December.

Economy, Elizabeth (2010) 'The game changer', *Foreign Affairs*, November/December: 142–152.

Eichengreen Barry (2009) 'The G20 and the crisis', available at <http://www.voxeu.org/index.php?q=node/3160>, accessed 15 March 2009.

Friedman, George (2009) *The Next 100 Years: A Forecast for the 21st Century,* New York: Anchor Books.

Funabashi, Yoichi (2010) 'Japan–China relations stand at ground zero', *The Asahi Shimbun*, 9 October.

Hufbauer, Gary and Robert Z. Lawrence (2010) 'Let's do a Doha deal', *East Asia Forum,* 22 July, available at <http://www.eastasiaforum.org/2010/07/22/lets-do-a-doha-deal/>.

Hu, Xiaolian (2010) 'A managed floating exchange rate regime is an established policy', People's Bank of China, 15 July, available at pbc.gov.cn/publish/English/956/2010.

Huang, Yiping and Bijun Wang (2010) 'Rebalancing China's economic structure', *East Asia Forum,* available at <http://www.eastasiaforum.org/2010/09/03/rebalancing-chinas-economic-structure/>.

Ito, Takatoshi (2007) 'The Asian currency crisis and the International Monetary Fund, 10 Years later: an overview', *Asian Economic Policy Review*, 2(1): 16–49.

Jacques, Martin (2009) *When China Rules the World,* London: Penguin Group.

Kagan, Robert (2008) *The Return of History and the End of Dreams,* New York: Knopf.

Kawai, Masahiro and Peter A. Petri (2010) 'Asia's role in the global economic architecture', *ADBI Working Paper Series*, No. 235, Tokyo: Asian Development Bank Institute.

Kawai, Masahiro and Ganeshan Wignaraja (2009) 'Asian FTAs: trends and challenges', Asian Development Bank paper, 12 March, Manila: ADB.

Kennedy, Scott (2010) 'Indigenous innovation: not as scary as it sounds', *China Economic Quarterly*, 14(3): 15–20.

Kent, Ann (2007) *Beyond Compliance: China, International Organizations and Global Security,* Stanford, CA: Stanford University Press.

Keohane, Robert O. (2002) 'Global governance and democratic accountability', unpublished manuscript.

Kuijs, Louis (2009) 'China through 2020 – a macroeconomic scenario', *Research Working Paper* No. 9, Washington, DC: World Bank China Office, available at <http://www.worldbank.org.cn/english>.

Lawrence, Robert (2006) 'Rulemaking amidst growing diversity: a club-of-clubs approach to WTO reform and new issue selection', *Journal of International Economic Law*, (9)4, 823–835.

Maddison, Angus (2006) 'Asia in the world economy 1500–2030 AD', *Asian Pacific Economic Literature*, 20(2): 1–37.

Mahbubani, Kishore (2008) *The New Asian Hemisphere: the Irresistible Shift of the Global Power to the East*, New York: Public Affairs.

Moran, Theodore H. (2010) *China's Strategy to Secure Natural Resources: Risks, Dangers, and Opportunities*, Policy Analyses in International Economics Series No. 92, Washington, DC: Peterson Institute for International Economics.

Nye, Joseph (2004) *Soft Power*, New York: Public Affairs.

PECC (Pacific Economic Cooperation Council) (2010) *State of the Region 2010–2011*, Singapore: PECC.

Page, Jeremy (2010) 'PLA gains political clout', *Wall Street Journal*, 5 October.

Park Yung Chul and Inkyo Cheong (2008) 'The proliferation of FTAs and prospects for trade liberalization in East Asia', in Barry Eichengreen, Charles Wyplosz and Park Yung Chul (eds) *China, Asia, and the New World Economy*, pp. 87–112, Oxford: Oxford University Press.

Pei, Minxin (2009) 'Think again: Asia's rise', *Foreign Policy*, July/August, available at <http://www.foreignpolicy.com/articles/2009/06/22/think_again_asias_rise?page=full>.

Prasad, Eswar (2009) 'Is the Chinese growth miracle built to last?', *China Economic Review*, 20(1): 103–123.

Posen, Adam (2010) 'The realities and relevance of Japan's great recession', *Working Paper* No. 10–7, Washington DC: Peterson Institute for International Economics.

Schott, Jeffrey J. (2010) 'Getting to the FTAAP via the TPP Turnpike', presentation to the Peterson Institute for International Economics – Japan Economic Foundation Conference, *A Trans-Pacific Partnership and the Future of the Asian Region*, 25 October.

Steinfeld, Edward S. (2010) *Playing Our Game: Why China's Rise Doesn't Threaten the West,* Oxford: Oxford University Press.

Sturgeon, Jamie (2010) 'Huawei joins Canadian tech incubator', *Financial Post,* 26 August, available at <http://www.canada.com/Huawei+joins+Canadian+tech+incubator/3445704>.

Truman E.M. (2007) 'Sovereign wealth funds: the need for greater transparency and accountability', *Policy Briefs in International Economics,* PB07-06, Washington, DC: Peterson Institute for International Economics, available at <http://www.petersoninstitute.org>.

UN (United Nations) (2009) 'The Commission of Experts on Reforms of the International Monetary and Financial System: Recommendations', available at <http://www.un.org/ga/president/63/commission/financial_commission.shtml>.

USTR (United States Trade Representative) (2009) Letters to Hon. Nancy Pelosi and Sen. Richard Byrd notifying of the President's intention to enter into negotiations of Trans-Pacific Partnership Agreement, 12 December, available at <http://www.ustr.gov/tpp>.

US White House (2009) 'Remarks by President Barack Obama at Suntory Hall', 14 November, available at <http://www.whitehouse.gov/briefing>.

Wang, Hongying and James N. Rosenau (2009) 'China and global governance', *Asian Perspective*, 33(3): 5–39.

Yao, Yang (2010) 'The end of the Beijing consensus', *Foreign Affairs Snapshot*, 2 February, available at <http://www.foreignaffairs.org>.

Yu, Keping (2009) *Democracy is a Good Thing,* Washington, DC: Brookings Institution Press.

Yu, Yongding (2009) 'China's policy responses to the global financial crisis', Snape Lecture, Melbourne, 25 November, available at <http://www.pc.gov.au/lectures/snape/yongding>.

Xinhua (2010a) 'Hu calls for balanced global economic growth', 28 June.

—— (2010b) 'Commentary: BRICs dialogue conducive to global economic governance', 16 April.

Zhang, Yunling and Shiping Tang (2005) 'China's regional strategy', in David Shambaugh (ed.) *Power Shift: China and Asia's New Dynamics,* pp. 48–68, Los Angeles, CA: University of California Press.

Zhou Xiaochuan (2009) 'Reform the International Monetary System', People's Bank of China, available at <http://www.pbc.gov.cn/english>.

Zoellick, Robert B. (2010) 'Remarks for celebration of the 30th anniversary of China – World Bank partnership', Beijing: World Bank Group, 13 September.

Index

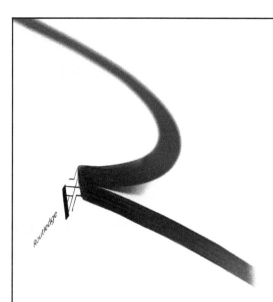

New eBook Library Collection

Taylor & Francis **eBooks**
Taylor & Francis Group

eFocus on Routledge/ECPR Studies in European Political Science

30 day free trials available!

The Routledge/ECPR Studies in European Political Science series is published in association with the European Consortium for Political Research - the leading organisation concerned with the growth and development of political science in Europe.

The series presents high-quality edited volumes on topics at the leading edge of current interest in political science and related fields, with contributions from leading European scholars.

The Series Editor is **Thomas Poguntke**, Ruhr-Universität Bochum, Germany.

Now for the first time, this series is available as a comprehensive eCollection comprising 69 eBooks.

Key titles in the collection include:

- *Social Capital and European Democracy*, edited by **Marco Maraffi**, University of Milano, Italy; **Kenneth Newton**, University of Southampton, UK; **Jan Van Deth**, University of Mannheim, Germany; and **Paul Whitely**, University of Essex, UK.

- *Politicians, Bureaucrats and Administrative Reform*, edited by **B. Guy Peters**, University of Pittsburgh, USA; and **Jon Pierre**, Gothenburg University, Sweden.

- *The Territorial Politics of Welfare*, edited by **Nicola McEwen**, University of Edinburgh, UK; and **Luis Moreno**, Spanish National Research Council (CSIC), Madrid, Spain.

The **European Consortium for Political Research** (**ECPR**) is an independent scholarly association of 350 institutional members, supporting and encouraging training, research and cross-national co-operation of many thousands of academics and graduate students specializing in political science and all its sub-disciplines.

eFocus on ECPR is available as a subscription package of 69 titles with 5 new eBooks per annum.

Recommend this package to your librarian today!

Order now for guaranteed capped price increase.

For a complete list of titles, visit:
www.ebooksubscriptions.com/eFocusECPR
www.ebooksubscriptions.com

For more information, pricing enquiries or to order a free trial, please contact your local online sales team:

UK and Rest of the world

Tel: +44 (0) 20 7017 6062
Email: online.sales@tandf.co.uk

United States, Canada and South America

Tel: 1-888-318-2367
Email: e-reference@taylorandfrancis.com

For Product Safety Concerns and Information please contact our EU
representative GPSR@taylorandfrancis.com
Taylor & Francis Verlag GmbH, Kaufingerstraße 24, 80331 München, Germany

www.ingramcontent.com/pod-product-compliance
Ingram Content Group UK Ltd.
Pitfield, Milton Keynes, MK11 3LW, UK
UKHW021834240425
457818UK00006B/188